Out of Control

SUNY series in Contemporary Jewish Thought

Richard A. Cohen, editor

Out of Control
Confrontations between Spinoza and Levinas

Richard A. Cohen

Cover photograph, "Stairs on Pylimo Street in the Year 2015," by Jolanta Saldukaityte, Vilnius, Lithuania, 2015

Published by State University of New York Press, Albany

© 2016 State University of New York

All rights reserved

Printed in the United States of America

No part of this book may be used or reproduced in any manner whatsoever without written permission. No part of this book may be stored in a retrieval system or transmitted in any form or by any means including electronic, electrostatic, magnetic tape, mechanical, photocopying, recording, or otherwise without the prior permission in writing of the publisher.

For information, contact State University of New York Press, Albany, NY
www.sunypress.edu

Production, Eileen Nizer
Marketing, Anne M. Valentine

Library of Congress Cataloging-in-Publication Data

Cohen, Richard A., 1950– author.
  Out of control : confrontations between Spinoza and Levinas / Richard A. Cohen.
    pages cm. — (SUNY series in contemporary Jewish thought)
  Includes bibliographical references and index.
  ISBN 978-1-4384-6109-0 (hc : alk. paper)—978-1-4384-6110-6 (pb : alk. paper)
  ISBN 978-1-4384-6111-3 (e-book)
  1. Jewish philosophy. 2. Philosophy, Modern. 3. Spinoza, Benedictus de, 1632–1677. 4. Lévinas, Emmanuel. I. Title.

B5800.C65 2015
199'.492—dc23   2015030785

10 9 8 7 6 5 4 3 2 1

If anyone were to say that I could not have done what I thought proper if I had not bones and sinews and other things that I have, he would be right. But to say that those things are the cause of my doing what I do, and that I act with intelligence but not from the choice of what is best, would be an extremely careless way of talking. Whoever talks in that way is unable to make a distinction and to see that in reality a cause is one thing, and the thing without which the cause could never be a cause is quite another thing.

—Socrates, in Plato's *Phaedo* (99a–b)

Not the man who denies the gods worshipped by the multitude, but he who affirms of the gods what the multitude believes about them, is truly impious.

—Epicurus, Letter to Menoeceus

Comprehending God as the one substance outraged the age in which this definition was proclaimed. . . . this was due to the instinctive recognition that self-consciousness was only drowned in it and not preserved.

—Hegel, preface to *Phenomenology of Spirit*

To love a person is to help that person. . . . If he becomes so wise that he overcomes his nature and neither loves nor hates, he is no longer a man but a flint-stone.

—Samuel David Luzzatto

Contents

Preface and Acknowledgments ... ix

List of Abbreviations ... xxi

Introduction ... 1

Chapter One
Levinas, Spinozism, Nietzsche, and the Body ... 31

Chapter Two
Prophetic Speech in Levinas and Spinoza (and Maimonides) ... 57

Chapter Three
Levinas and Spinoza: To Love God for Nothing ... 83

Chapter Four
Levinas and Spinoza: Justice and the State ... 103

Chapter Five
Spinoza's Prince: For Whom Is the *Theological-Political Treatise* Written? ... 119

Chapter Six
Levinas on Spinoza's Misunderstanding of Judaism ... 189

Chapter Seven
Thinking Least about Death: Mortality and Morality in Spinoza, Heidegger, and Levinas ... 237

Chapter Eight
Spinoza's Spleen: "Babies, Fools, and Madmen" 279

Works Cited 317

Index 323

Preface and Acknowledgments

What are the origins of this book? Can they be traced, disentangled, or even identified? Surely, it has little to do with the Latin I barely studied in junior high! Or the French I later did learn. But who knows? Beyond the unilluminating truism that one's entire life stands behind the present moment, I can say that the volume at hand is the labor of several decades. Not the exclusive labor but an ever-present one. A long germination, a long growth, with fruits from several seasons. Let me start its story with my encounter with philosophy proper.

My initiation and apprenticeship in philosophy began in the long 1960s, when I was an undergraduate. Three initiations. One, a first book—to discover novel thoughts, novel arguments, the work of reason, the discovery of this strange unexpected discipline "philosophy" in a philosophy book, a philosopher's book. For me it was Bergson's *Time and Free Will*. What a propitious beginning! I remain convinced of Bergson's genius to this day. Two, the happy chance of tutelage in a university department of philosophy not only bearing the name "philosophy," as if a label could guarantee anything in this regard, but comprised of the real thing, vigilant and intelligent souls, seekers in the heights and depths, lovers of wisdom, professors dedicated in all seriousness to the grand tradition of philosophy, from the Argonauts of old to the most contemporary French and German explorers. Penn State, what a happy chance for me that its philosophy department—assembled by John Anderson—was just at that time one of the very best in America, faithful still to the Western heritage of perennial questions, questionable and fundamental questions with no answers, or too many. Three, and no less fortuitous, a teacher—noble calling—and not only a scholar, someone whose wide erudition and high intelligence nourished a philosophical life, ideas tested beyond the web of mere logic, faced deeply, intensely, experimentally, personally, with the whole of his being. Alphonso Lingis—whatever his ideas, here came inspiration. Here I learned of the philosopher not a profession or career, but the more dangerous and rewarding calling of a vocation, the philosopher as free variable. Of course, too, it was also because of Lingis that I encountered so early the thought of Emmanuel Levinas. It changed my life to this day. Perhaps only then did my true apprenticeship begin. For these initiations, and for so much else that came from "the sixties," I remain always grateful. Through them I awakened to the challenges of philosophy, seduced into its love of wisdom.

One concrete result: In 1980 I received my PhD in philosophy, my dissertation written on Levinas's social theory of time. In those days Levinas was barely known outside of Paris and the Low Countries, and his theory of time was even less known, if known at all. This even though his theory of time offered—and still offers—the only radical alternative to then-dominant "ecstatic" theories of temporality of Bergson, Husserl, and Heidegger. The latter, to be sure, had only recently toppled the previous long-standing theory of discrete time, "clock time," the time of the specious present, of instants somehow succeeding and separated from one another by non-being—the time Zeno's paradoxes incisively deconstructed, setting the longest-standing unsolved problem for philosophy in its millennial history. Levinas's "diachronic" conception of time, as I tried to show, had not only grasped time more deeply than discrete time but also went beyond and exposed the limitations of its critics' then current—and still current—ecstatic theories of time. What a sharp contrast to Spinoza, adherent of discrete time, who prolongs the classic tradition of philosophy and theology—silencing but not answering Zeno—by subordinating time to eternity. It is no exaggeration to say that all of contemporary philosophy begins by taking time seriously.

In my studies I had read Spinoza along with the other "great philosophers." In 1978 I translated the central chapter, "La philosophie," of Gilles Deleuze's slim 1970 volume entitled *Spinoza* (not his larger 1968 book, *Expressionism in Philosophy: Spinoza*). Deleuze, for all else that he became, began as a great expository and interpretive scholar. Because this chapter was short, I sent my translation as an article to two journals, both of which rejected it (though the editor of one, Marx Wartofsky of *The Philosophical Forum*, praised the translation, much to my pleasure). This small effort has gathered dust on my bookshelves ever since; clearly, I had jumped the Deleuze gun, for the entire little

Spinoza book was later published in a translation by Robert Hurley in 1988 under the title *Spinoza: Practical Philosophy*.

My non-publication translator's relation to Spinoza actually began earlier, and in relation to Levinas. I attended Levinas's classes at the Sorbonne during the 1974–1975 academic year, his penultimate there. At that time I proposed and obtained his permission to translate into English all of his separate pieces on Spinoza (three articles and a book review of Harry Austryn Wolfson's Spinoza book). This, I thought and apparently Levinas thought so too, would make a small but interesting volume in English by Levinas exclusively devoted to Spinoza. I can no longer remember why this nice book proposal did not come to fruition, but it did not.

In any event, I began teaching Spinoza's *Ethics* and *Theological-Political Treatise* in the 1980s after I began my academic "career." I ended up teaching the *Theological-Political Treatise* on a regular basis—almost once every year—starting in the fall of 1994. I would on occasion teach Spinoza's *Ethics*, but less often, since my classes—with the exception of those at the University at Buffalo—were offered in undergraduate programs.

My work on Levinas—Levinas's work on me!—continued unabated. Besides translating collections of essays and books by Levinas, and editing some volumes on his work, over the past two decades I have published three of my own books on Levinas, in 1994, 2001, and 2010, collecting together my own essays. Call it "secondary," and it is, but to this day I do not believe Levinas's thought has been sufficiently appreciated and needs to be read more and more deeply, despite the many alleged and ambitious "criticisms" that have appeared—with increasing frequency keeping pace with Levinas's increasing "fame"—and that to my mind have missed the mark.[1]

During the past two decades, I have also published essays and articles on Spinoza and Levinas. In anticipation of the present volume, however, I did not include these pieces in my own three Levinas books.

---

1. Derrida, for instance, in *Adieu to Emmanuel Levinas*, writes of "the *oeuvre* of Emmanuel Levinas. It is so large that one can no longer glimpse its edges. And one would have to begin by learning once again from him and from *Totality and Infinity*, for example, how to think what an 'oeuvre' as well as fecundity might be. One can predict with confidence that centuries of reading will set this as their task" (3–4; translation slightly altered).

Indeed, two-thirds of the content of the present volume has never been published before, and what was published has been reedited. Of the present volume's contents, some chapters were published, some were first given as talks and then published, some were only given as talks, and some appear here for the first time in any form.

An earlier version of chapter 1 was previously published as "Levinas, Spinozism, Nietzsche and the Body," in *Nietzsche and Levinas: "After the Death of a Certain God"* (New York: Columbia University Press, 2009), edited by Jill Stauffer and Bettina Bergo.

Chapter 2, "Prophetic Speech in Spinoza and Levinas (and Maimonides)," has never been published. It was first presented as a talk at the University at Buffalo in the spring semester of 2008 when I was invited there for a job interview. Evidently, it did the trick.

Chapter 3, my second publication on Levinas and Spinoza, entitled "Levinas and Spinoza: To Love God for Nothing," appeared in an earlier version in the New School for Social Research's *Graduate Faculty Philosophy Journal: Levinas's Contribution to Contemporary Philosophy*, 20.2/21.1 (Spring 1998), a special issue on Levinas edited by Bettina Bergo and Diane Perpich. I thank them for soliciting my contribution.

Chapter 4 is my earliest publication on Levinas and Spinoza, entitled "Levinas and Spinoza: Justice and the State." It appeared in an earlier version in *Epoche: A Journal for the History of Philosophy*, 4.1 (1996), edited by the very able James E. Faulconer of Brigham Young University.

Chapter 5, "Spinoza's Prince: For Whom Is the *Theological-Political Treatise* Written?," was presented in part as a talk at a small one-day conference on Spinoza and the Political, which I organized under the auspices of the Institute of Jewish Thought and Heritage at the University at Buffalo, on November 6, 2013. Other papers were given by Alexander Green, my new but already esteemed colleague at the University at Buffalo; Warren Zev Harvey, world-respected medievalist now retired from the Hebrew University of Jerusalem; and the well-known, prolific, and genial Spinoza scholar Stephen Nadler.

Chapter 6, "Levinas on Spinoza's Misunderstanding of Judaism," appeared in an earlier version in *In Proximity: Emmanuel Levinas and the Eighteenth Century* (Lubbock: Texas Tech University Press, 2001), edited by Melvyn New, with the assistance of Robert Bernasconi and myself. A part of it, in an even earlier version, was given as a talk at the annual meeting of the Association for Jewish Studies, in Boston in

December 1994. Another part of it was given years later as a talk on June 9, 1999, as my contribution to a small one-day conference on Jewish Responses to Modernity: Spinoza, HaRav Kook, Levinas, sponsored by the Department of Jewish Philosophy at Tel Aviv University, Israel, where I was then a visiting professor. The other speakers were Joelle Hansel, Rivka Horowitz, Aviezer Ravitzky, Shalom Rosenberg, and Yosef Ben-Shlomo, author of *Lectures on the Philosophy of Spinoza*, to which a section of this chapter responds.

Chapter 7, "Thinking Least about Death: Mortality and Morality in Spinoza, Heidegger, and Levinas," was presented in part as a talk on January 19, 2006, at an international conference at the Hebrew University of Jerusalem. I thank the members of the organizing committee: Joelle Hansel, Cyril Aslanov, Marie-Anne Lescourret, Shalom Rosenberg, and Shmuel Wygoda, for the invitation and for an excellent conference. On January 27th, a longer portion of the same paper was presented as an invited keynote address to the entire assembled faculty and student body of St. John's College, in Santa Fe, New Mexico. I would like to thank Ingo Farin, Thomas Scally, David Levine, and Philip LeCuyer, and all faculty and students for their gracious hospitality. This paper was also given on May 21, 2007, as an invited lecture at Regents Park College, Oxford University. This chapter appears in another version, minus Spinoza, but with more on Levinas, published in a journal, and in a book, and most recently as chapter 3 of my own book *Levinasian Meditations: Ethics, Philosophy, and Religion* (2010).

Chapter 8, "Spleen: Spinoza's 'Babies, Fools, and Madmen,'" appears here for the first time in any format, though I have entertained—amused and challenged—some of my philosophy graduate students at the University at Buffalo with some of its contents.

Readers who wish can find a more substantial entry into the present volume in the introduction that follows this preface. Here, having given some personal and bibliographical background, I will conclude by touching briefly on two dimensions of the cultural and historical context of the present volume's confrontation with Spinoza, guided by Levinas, that may enhance its overall sense and account for its continued relevance.

Spinoza lived in mid-seventeenth-century Holland, which was then at the height of its economic, political, and indeed global power. New York was still New Amsterdam. Spinoza was raised in a Jewish merchant family (which came from Portugal and before that from Spain, hence the surname) in Amsterdam. As a youngster he attended Jewish schools, completed his formal studies at twelve, entered the family business (Latinizing his given forename Baruch to Benedictus), did not succeed at it, and then—after being excommunicated from the Jewish community in 1656 at the age of twenty-three—led a retiring bachelor life as a lens grinder while he spent his real life, that is to say, his intellectual life, his life as a philosopher, figuring out, as he believed, the true character of the universe and of the true condition and proper place of humans within it. Spinoza died in 1677 at the young age of forty-four.

His philosophy is usually and quite correctly classified as "rationalist," "pantheist," and "early modern," though of course Spinoza could not have known the latter label. Beyond its chronological meaning, it signifies that his primary concern was to understand the universe in view of the truth of modern science. In response to this concern, he produced a rational pantheism. It is not surprising that when a major shift, change, or reorientation in the world occurs, for example, the rise of Christianity, the Industrial Revolution, or, in this case, the rise of modern science, those who are witness to it often appreciate the differences it makes best, some to celebrate them, some to bemoan them. Spinoza celebrates modern science; indeed, he venerates it more completely, more thoroughly, more radically than any other early modern philosopher. Nevertheless, and not unlike Descartes and Leibniz, he does not break free entirely, or fundamentally really, from the intellectual grip of the premodern past. No one begins *de novo*. Thus, despite his best effort to thoroughly embrace modern science all the way, to affirm efficient causality and the lawfulness of nature in all things, it is still under the tutelage of classical philosophy and medieval theology that Spinoza restricts rational truth—"adequate ideas"—to the eternal, immutable, and necessary, in contrast to the temporal, changeable, and contingent, which are reduced to merely subjective epiphenomena, the self-serving delusions of the ignorant. Such a drastic reduction is the high price of a totalized rationalism, a tax so long exacted by philosophy in alliance with theology that despite his best efforts to think modern science all the way through to the end, Spinoza, almost by intellectual good manners, as it were, continued to pay it—at his cost.

Levinas, whose life spans the twentieth century, was also born into a Jewish family, in Kaunas, Lithuania, which was then episodically a province of Poland or Russia or Germany—shifting borders at the crossroads of larger powers. He was born into the somewhat insular but extraordinarily vibrant and multilayered spiritual-intellectual world of pre-Holocaust Litvak Jewry, raised in a home both traditional and modern. As a bright young man of promise he left that world, going to university in Strasburg, France, and Heidelberg, Germany, studying philosophy, including a year with Husserl and Heidegger, then moving to Paris, becoming a French citizen, engaging fully in "phenomenology" and "contemporary continental" philosophy there, and finally becoming a major philosophic voice of his own. The designation "contemporary continental," like "early modern," refers not simply to chronology, or to a place, but rather to a philosophical outlook. "Contemporary continental" is philosophy that renews the grand tradition of philosophy while rejecting its medieval and classical dualisms, not by an escapist desertion to irrationalism or to a leveling positivism but by taking even more seriously, more rigorously, more deeply, what had previously been devalued, that is, the irreducible phenomena—hence "phenomenology"—and significance of *this world*, the world of change, temporality, embodiment, language, and sociality. Contemporary philosophy no longer pays the price—of prejudice, abstractness, and partiality—of philosophy's theological heritage, though who knows what future philosophers will say of it in turn in retrospect. As Levinas puts the matter: "It has never been more difficult to think."

These brief indications, hopefully illuminating, are doubtlessly at the same time also overly sweeping with generalities. We must take them with the proverbial grain of salt. Nevertheless, they speak to fundamentals. From them we can see already that between Spinoza and Levinas and contemporary thought there lies an abyss and, hence, a confrontation: the "early modern" valorization of another world, call it rational, of laws alleged to be necessary and permanent, eternal, a construct of ideation and its ideas, on the one side, and the "contemporary" valorization of this world, of contingency and change, duration, of sense and sensibility, the concrete rather than the abstract, on the other. It is not a confrontation, as it might seem to some, of mind and body, spirit and matter, but rather a confrontation of two different ways of sorting out these two dimensions, the ideational and the sensational, the spiritual and the material. The rationalist will have body only in conformity with mind, subordinate to rational intelligibility. The phenomenologist, in contrast, will start with and respect their original integrality, the embodied mind, the mindful body.

Because both of these perspectives continue to have their attractions and defenders, Spinoza's rationalism and the critique of Spinoza by Levinas remain *contemporary*. These ideas and outlooks remain viable. No doubt Spinoza's particular conception of science would have to be updated, but his defense of science as the exclusive and ultimate truth, this outlook—often called "scientism" or more often "positivism"—is as alive today as it was in his philosophy. Given the success of science and technology, it is actually far more popular today than in his day, when science was but a fledgling discipline. In this broad sense Plato remains our contemporary, as do Epicurus and Aquinas. Nevertheless, the philosophies of Spinoza and Levinas, and their trenchant opposition to one another, are especially relevant today when more than ever science poses itself as the only and ultimate arbiter of truth, to the detriment of the now-defensive claims of humanism or what Levinas, following Kant, understands as the primacy of ethics.

Thus, too, it is not unfair to utilize Levinas to oppose Spinoza, when only Levinas had the advantage of having read Spinoza while Spinoza of course could not and did not read Levinas. Without dismissing history, the history of ideas is not equivalent to chronological history. Ideas, for all their historical background and coloration, are not reducible to their historical epoch. Spinoza knew very well, without having read Levinas, that his rationalism was radically opposed to humanisms of all kinds. The human, he famously declared, has not the privilege of being a "kingdom within a kingdom." Both Spinoza and Levinas know very well that a reductive science, "scientism," "positivism," means the death of morality and justice. Their conflict, therefore, is a fair one, with both sides informed and armed, and anything but a first-time fight.

Nevertheless there is an important asymmetry. While Spinoza would eliminate morality as we know it, Levinas in no way denigrates science. Further, it is not despite ethics that Levinas defends science, as if in a charitable mood, but rather and precisely because of ethics. To criticize scientism and positivism—to criticize "Spinozism"—is not to criticize science. It is to criticize science going beyond its proper limits, beyond its competence. It is against such hubris that we oppose and Levinas opposes Spinoza, for such excess destroys not only ethics but science as well, and science has a necessary contribution to make toward the creation of a just world.

Despite their radical opposition, it is also true that Spinoza and Levinas share certain significant points of view. Spinoza, despite his fundamental misconceptions, certainly did not get everything wrong. Both are philosophers bound to reason and argumentation. Both have enormous regard for the truths of modern science. Both unflinchingly attack superstition and religious fanaticism. It is in their larger philosophies, however, the worldviews within which these points of agreement make sense, where they radically part company. So while Spinoza integrates all and everything in complete conformity to the logic of modern science as he understands it, Levinas, in contrast, recognizes the transcendence both of human freedom and of the good, the morally good and the just, outside the range of scientific knowledge and yet subtending it, making it possible, indeed justifying science. Thus Levinas writes in the last sentence of the first section of *Totality and Infinity*, where he sums up the two basic claims upon which his book and his philosophy are based: "Thought and freedom come to us from separation and from consideration of the Other—this thesis is at the antipodes of Spinozism" (105).

Though today we in the modern world are challenged by the hubris of science, by positivist rationalization colonizing all registers of life, empowered by capitalist commodification, we should not forget that Spinoza's situation was quite different, though with no less real obstacles and dangers. While our concerns are with the excesses of modern rationalism, Spinoza's were with the excesses of medieval irrationalism. His foes were powerful, entrenched, formidable, and often implacable and vengeful, theological-political forces such as the Holy Inquisition and established religious orthodoxy. The Pope had not only lands but armies. In 1600 Giordano Bruno had been burned at the stake in Rome for his ideas. In 1633—one year after Spinoza's birth—the Roman Catholic Church forced Galileo to recant his heliocentric astronomy as heresy and placed him under house arrest for the remaining eight years of his life. In 1692 and 1693, fifteen years *after* Spinoza's death, twenty-two persons, mostly women, were infamously executed—hung or pressed to death—for heresy by the good Protestants of Salem, Massachusetts. It is not by accident or through mean-spiritedness that the medieval period came to be known as the Dark Ages. Thus, despite our fundamental opposition to Spinozism, in theory and practice, we can at the same time admire the progressive spirit and courageousness of Spinoza's uncompromising defense of science and reason against the close-mindedness and barbarisms of his age. We can thus also understand his intellectual intemperance and exaggerations without agreeing to them.

Humanity is not defined by its blindness or barbarism however persistent they are. Nor is it defined by its rationality, by its sciences and technical sophistication. It even seems correct to say that there is no "definition" of the human, if by definition only the nominative case is permitted. The human would better be conceived in terms of what is dearer, more precious, closer, let us say more humane. Not what humanity is or has but what it can become. Its greatest dignity lies in morality and justice, in the alleviation of suffering and the institutions and protections of justice. Levinas, like the Buddha, places highest priority on the alleviation of suffering. The "method" is not meditation, or not meditation alone, but morality, the compassionate care one person takes for another, to feed the hungry, heal the sick, succor the traumatized, clothe the naked. And morality is not enough, because caring for the one who faces me is not enough. Moral obligation itself demands care for everyone, for all, and hence a truly human responsibility demands of each person to fight for justice, just laws, just institutions, courts of law, unbiased justice, equity, to make the world a place of fairness for all. Insofar as philosophy is the love of wisdom, it is not reducible to scientific knowledge; it is rather more deeply or higher a "wisdom of love," ethics. Science, knowledge, technology, bureaucracy are not faceless. They are necessary for and find their justification in their contribution to a just world. They are not goods in themselves but are *required* by justice, required to provide for the vulnerable, to lend a helping hand, wipe away tears, and bring a smile to the human face. Spinoza never saw this, indeed he denied it.

The conflict between modern rationalism and contemporary thought, and more specifically the conflict between science totalized and science justified, orients the teachings of the present volume. Viewed in such a light, the debate between Levinas and Spinoza is an intellectual and spiritual *gigantomachia*, an argument "in the name of God," as both thinkers would agree, for one a struggle within the true, between true and false, and for the other a struggle between the true and the good. Spinoza exalts indeed idolizes the true, the true without the good, science as a substitute for ethics; Levinas exalts the good, the good above truth but requiring truth, truth serving justice; and I,

I am with Levinas, for this is a debate without neutral spectators as it is debate without exit or escape. My wish is for readers to engage sincerely, intelligently, knowingly, and critically in this argument, for in one way or another it is already the atmosphere enveloping our being, already a conversation in and for which we are contributors and accountable. Responsibility does not begin before or after wisdom, it is wisdom.

Because this is the first book I will see published since the death of both my parents, Sidney S. Cohen and Bette G. Cohen, and thus the first book of mine that they will not see, I want to once again honor their memory, the memory of two individuals, a couple, husband and wife, father and mother, each and together of unfailing love and generosity, of exceptional intelligence and patience, quietly but unfailingly devoted to their family without indifference regarding the larger world—thank you, thank you, I cannot thank you enough. Such words as these cannot capture the love and nobility to which they bear testimony, cannot bring back these great unsung souls who once lived and now are gone, except to the extent that we the living remain inspired by their example to rise to their heights.

I wish also to express a very special thank you to my daughter Arielle, whose mastery of scheduling, her loving insistence, her editorial ear, her ready laugh and good humor, pushed me to finally finish the present book and to send off the manuscript, which for many years languished so near to completion. So too I thank my son Alasdair for his no less positive and constant encouragement every step of the way throughout the years. I am unceasingly amazed and overjoyed that we are family.

The book is dedicated in gratitude to two of my philosophy professors. One, in the memory of Joe Flay, who as I recently learned passed away on June 27, 2014. I am sorry to say that I had not seen him since the heady days of my undergraduate studies at Penn State. It is my loss. He was a teacher of philosophy in the best sense, fully living its dedication to truth, arguing and sharing his wisdom with humility and warmth, sincere, serious yet always with a ready smile—so fitting for an apprentice of both Hegel and Kazantzakis. The other is Don Ihde, director of my doctoral dissertation at the State University of New York at Stony Brook. He too was and remains a teacher of philosophy in the best sense, creator and inspiration of the leading American academic department of contemporary continental philosophy, master of phenomenology, pioneer in the philosophy of technology, advisor, sailor, raconteur, and good-humored and warm-hearted center of a graduate student cohort, my class and others, all of us young and sharing in the challenging conversations, the intellectual growth, the precarious but ever worthwhile spiritual adventure that is philosophy, known to its initiates, magnanimous without fanfare.

—Richard A. Cohen

Abbreviations

Emmanuel Levinas

AT *Alterity and Transcendence.* Trans. Michael B. Smith. New York: Columbia University Press, 1999.

BV *Beyond the Verse: Talmudic Readings and Lectures.* Trans. Gary D. Mole. Bloomington: Indiana University Press, 1994.

CPP *Collected Philosophical Papers.* Ed. and trans. Alphonso Lingis. Pittsburgh: Duquesne University Press, 1998.

DEH *Discovering Existence with Husserl.* Ed. Richard A. Cohen, trans. Richard A. Cohen and Michael B Smith. Evanston: Northwestern University Press, 1998.

DF *Difficult Freedom: Essays on Judaism.* Trans. Sean Hand. Baltimore: Johns Hopkins University Press, 1990.

EE *Existence and Existents.* Trans. Alphonso Lingis. The Hague: Martinus Nijhoff, 1978.

EI *Ethics and Infinity: Conversations with Philippe Nemo.* Trans. Richard A. Cohen. Pittsburgh: Duquesne University Press, 1985.

EN *Entre Nous: The Thinking-of-the-Other.* Trans. Michael B. Smith and Barbara Harshav. New York: Columbia University Press, 1998.

HO *Humanism of the Other.* Trans. Nidra Poller. Urbana: University of Illinois Press, 2003.

IRB *Is It Righteous to Be? Interviews with Emmanuel Levinas.* Ed. and Trans. Jill Robbins. Stanford: Stanford University Press, 2001.

ITN	*In the Time of the Nations.* Trans. Michael B. Smith. Bloomington: Indiana University Press, 1994.
LR	*Levinas Reader.* Ed. Sean Hand. Oxford, UK: Basil Blackwell, 1989.
NewTR	*New Talmudic Readings.* Trans. Richard A. Cohen. Pittsburgh: Duquesne University Press, 1999.
NTR	*Nine Talmudic Readings.* Trans. Annette Aronowicz. Bloomington: Indiana University Press, 1990.
OBBE	*Otherwise than Being or Beyond Essence.* Trans. Alphonso Lingis. Pittsburgh: Duquesne University Press, 1981.
OE	*On Escape.* Trans. Bettina Bergo. Stanford: Stanford University Press, 2003.
OGCM	*Of God Who Comes to Mind.* Trans. Bettina Bergo. Stanford: Stanford University Press, 1998.
OS	*Outside the Subject.* Trans. Michael B. Smith. Stanford: Stanford University Press, 1994.
SM	"Le scandale du mal: Catastrophes naturelle et crimes de l'homme." *Les Nouveaux Cahiers*, 85 (Summer 1986), 15–17.
TI	*Totality and Infinity: An Essay in Exteriority.* Trans. Alphonso Lingis. Pittsburgh: Duquesne University Press, 1969.
TO	*Time and the Other and Additional Essays.* Trans. Richard A. Cohen. Pittsburgh: Duquesne University Press, 1987.
UH	*Unforeseen History.* Trans. Nidra Poller. Urbana: University of Illinois Press, 2004.
US	"Useless Suffering," trans. Richard A. Cohen. In *The Provocation of Levinas*, ed. Robert Bernasconi and D. Wood, 151–167. London: Routledge, 1988.

Baruch Spinoza

CW	*Spinoza: Complete Works.* Ed. Michael L. Morgan. Trans. Samuel Shirley. Indianapolis: Hackett, 2002.
E	*Ethics, Treatise on the Emendation of the Intellect, and Selected Letters.* Trans. Samuel Shirley. Indianapolis: Hackett, 1992.

Letters	*Spinoza: The Letters.* Trans Samuel Shirley. Indianapolis: Hackett, 1995.
TPT	*Theological-Political Treatise,* 2nd ed. Trans. Samuel Shirley. Indianapolis: Hackett, 2001.

Martin Heidegger

BT	*Being and Time.* Trans. John Macquarrie and Edward Robinson. New York: Harper and Row, 1962.
OET	"On the Essence of Truth," trans. R. F. C. Hull and A. Crick. In Martin Heidegger, *Existence and Being,* ed. Werner Brock. New York: Henry Regnery, 1970.

Friedrich Nietzsche

EH	*Ecce Homo,* trans. Walter Kaufmann. In *"On the Genealogy of Morals and "Ecce Homo,"* ed. Walter Kaufmann. New York: Random House, 1969.
GM	*On the Genealogy of Morals.* Trans. Walter Kaufmann and R. J. Hollingdale. In *"On the Genealogy of Morals" and "Ecce Homo,"* ed. Walter Kaufmann. New York: Random House, 1969.
GS	*The Gay Science.* Trans. Walter Kaufmann. New York: Random House, 1974.
PT	*Philosophy and Truth: Selections from Nietzsche's Notebooks of the Early 1870s.* Ed. and Trans. Daniel Breazeale. New Jersey: Humanities Press, 1979.
TWID	*Twilight of the Idols.* In Friedrich Nietzsche, *"Twilight of the Idols" and "The Anti-Christ,"* trans. R. J. Hollingdale. Middlesex: Penguin Books, 1974.
Z	*Thus Spoke Zarathustra,* trans. Walter Kaufmann. In Friedrich Nietzsche, *The Portable Nietzsche,* ed. and trans. Walter Kaufmann. New York: Viking Press, 1966.

The footnotes in this volume are substantive. Bibliographic citations are parenthetical and refer to texts in the list of abbreviations and in the works cited.

Introduction

> The opposite of love is not hate, it is indifference. . . . And the opposite of life is not death, it is indifference.
>
> —Elie Wiesel

There has been somewhat of a revival of Spinoza studies in the past few years, or at least a revival of books about Spinoza and books with his name in their title. Why now? Why Spinoza? Stripped to its essentials, Spinoza's is a scientistic philosophy of science. He attempted to understand science scientifically and defend it against its religious and political enemies. In his day those enemies were far stronger than was science, which was just getting started, or restarted. Thus Spinoza stands at the very beginning of the way of things and doing and thinking that have developed and grown enormously in detail and magnitude ever since. Science and technology have transformed our world. They have become our world. Even those who resist this transformation participate in it. Even those who see farther than them, see them also. Therefore, Spinoza, who with his great mind grasped some of the most essential elements of the transformation and shift between the premodern and the modern world, the medieval world and our world, and understood correctly that the key to this transformation was the rise of modern science, surely his insights can be of value to we who live today in the aftermath of one of the greatest transformations of human life—continuing to our day—about which he was one of the first to take and to think seriously.

We are not driven away, then, by the inevitable shortcomings that Spinoza shared with his fellow early modern philosophers and champions of science. They are of two sorts. One results from the distortion of overenthusiasm, believing science capable of more than it was, great as its contributions to human knowledge and understanding were and are. The other results from the distortion of underappreciation, allowing premodern, medieval standards of truth and knowledge to still influence and determine a thought otherwise thoroughly determined to be modern and only modern. The first error is philosophical positivism, giving science more credit than it is due; the second error is philosophical idealism, binding science to a type and standard of truth it had made obsolete. Spinoza is guilty of both. And despite their great difference, often one reinforces the other. For instance, scientists and philosophers today no longer believe themselves to be seeking or to have discovered *eternal* and *immutable* ideas, truth and knowledge *sub specie aeternitatis*. Rarely, too, in our age of democracy, does one find a scientist or philosopher as disdainfully dismissive of the vast majority of human beings as intractable ignoramuses ("the common people are incapable of understanding higher things"). While we will be forbearing regarding his faults, understanding their origins, we will not be forgiving, justifying errors. Spinoza, therefore, is as interesting to us for what he tried to accomplish as for his failure to accomplish it. That is to say, the question of the meaning of science remains with us, and remains a burning question, for scientific knowing and scientific knowledge permeate our world. We turn to the seventeenth-century philosopher Spinoza, then, for better and worse, to help us more clearly understand ourselves and our world.

Whether due to caution (Spinoza's signet ring was engraved with a rose and the word *caute*, Latin for "be cautious"), concentration, self-criticism, or all three, or some other reason, in his lifetime Spinoza published only one book under his own name. Let that be a lesson to our "publish or perish" academic administrative mentality. And that book was only a secondary one. *Principia philosophiae cartesianae, The Principles of Cartesian Philosophy*, published in 1663, was an exposition of Rene Descartes's new philosophy and a criticism of Descartes for not being Cartesian enough. Today we rather criticize a thinker for being Cartesian, by which we mean dualistic, separating mind and body, idea and matter. In Spinoza's day Descartes was hailed by an enlightened intelligentsia as the greatest, most perceptive, and intellectually powerful defender of scientific rationality—and an analytic method of thinking—in the face of superstition, myth, and arbitrary ecclesiastical authority. From the first Spinoza announced his allegiance to this new thinking, outdoing and upbraiding even its philosopher founder.

Spinoza's only other published book, also published in Latin, like all his philosophical writings, appeared anonymously—or rather under his initials but no more—in 1670, *Tractatus Theologico-Politicus*, the *Theological-Political Treatise*. Regarding the "theological," it can be credited with launching modern "higher biblical criticism" (though there had indeed been earlier, lesser-known books on biblical criticism). This method or approach to textual study is still used today and is of incontrovertible value. Once again, however, one must also appreciate its limits, which Spinoza himself did not. Regarding the "political," Spinoza for the most part follows Hobbes, though there are important differences as we shall see. Because he makes a limited case, whose range and significance we shall be questioning, for freedom of thought and speech, Spinoza is sometimes considered a political liberal or part of the Enlightenment. In a way he is, but it is a way that also includes Hobbes's *Leviathan*, which is credited with having first conceptualized the modern absolute state. Once again, just as in his philosophy of science, in his theological and his political reflections we learn much from Spinoza, both for and against. What is most important, as we shall see, is not so much the positions Spinoza takes but his reasons for them.

Spinoza's chief work, *Ethica Ordine Geometrico Demonstrata*, *Ethics*—the subtitle is *Demonstrated in Geometrical Manner*—years in the writing, perhaps finished by 1674, was circulated to his friends for comment and left by its author with instructions that it be published posthumously, which it was, by his friends in the year of Spinoza's death, 1677, as part of the *Opera Posthuma*, *Posthumous Works*, under Spinoza's initials. A year later it was translated into Dutch, again with Spinoza's initials. The *Ethics* articulates—famously with definitions, axioms, propositions, proofs, corollaries, and the like, in the manner of Euclid—Spinoza's basic philosophy, the philosophy for which he is famous and the philosophy that undergirds his theological and political speculations, indeed all his speculations.

For completeness sake, let us also mention three other "books" by Spinoza that he neither published nor completed, but which are part of *Opera Posthuma*, part of his reception history nonetheless, and which we will be utilizing in the present volume when and to the extent that they become relevant. These are: *Tractatus de Intellectus Emendatione*, *Treatise on the Emendation of the Intellect*, 1662; *Tractatus Politicus*, *Political Treatise*, 1675–1676; and *Compendium grammatices linguae hebraeae*, *Hebrew*

Grammar, 1677. We will also be utilizing Spinoza's extant letters when they contribute to our discussion.

So, what is the root idea or ideas of the *Ethics*, the book of Spinozism, *magnum opus?* Its method and its basis are really one and the same, as they are the same monomania shared by Spinoza and Descartes before him. It is formulated in many ways, for instance in the subtitle of the *Ethics*, but perhaps its clearest expression is in the appendix to part I: "truth might have evaded mankind forever had not Mathematics, which is concerned not with ends but only with the essences and properties of figures, revealed to men a different standard of truth" (58). Only the standard of clarity and distinctness, as Descartes had discovered through doubt, only an intelligibility eternal, immutable, and necessary, and therefore completely self-evident as Spinoza believed to the contrary, only in what Spinoza calls "adequate ideas" are to be discovered the truth of the real; everything else—everything concerned with ends, say—is but ignorance and illusion. Later, in the present volume, we shall examine Spinoza's equation of will and intellect as another key to all his thought. Here, however, we can see how the success of mathematical formalization in Spinoza's day, a tool astronomers put to such penetrating and powerful use in discovering the proper orbits of the planets of the solar system, indeed, to the discovery of the solar system itself, led a brilliant mind like Spinoza's, loving truth to be *misled* into believing that this same abstract and calculative manner of cognizing was the key not only to natural science but to everything, to all of reality without exception, indeed the only reliable way to liberate humanity from its fears, myths, superstitions, illusions, arbitrary authorities, greed, selfishness, indeed from the entire long, senseless, and brutal staggering in ignorance and concupiscence that had hitherto been humanity's unfortunate fate.

We can see today, as the early moderns could not in their day, that the internal logic of such rationalism, its inexorable tendency toward system, was a snare, indeed a Procrustean bed. Not only would such a system be wrong if it were successful, because of all it would leave out and diminish, it also cannot actually succeed by its own standards, succeed, that is to say, in enclosing itself in itself without crack, seam, or remainder. No doubt artificial coherent worlds can be created, by stipulation. Judge Schreiber created one, but it was mad. Libertarians have created one, but it is flat. Spinoza's world, the world of Spinozism, is magnificent by comparison, but it is no less dangerous when taken for the real world.

Three instances of the internal failure of Spinoza's system should be sufficient in this introduction to point to the unresolved and unresolvable conceptual aporia closer analyses would reveal more critically. First, there is the unbridgeable gap between eternity and duration, the unchanging essence of the one substance and the temporality of modes that make up what common sense would recognize as concrete or determinate reality ("we conceive the existence of Substance as of an entirely different kind from the existence of Modes. This is the source of the difference between Eternity and Duration" [letter to Lodewijk Meyer, CW, 788]). Second, there is Spinoza's assertion—untrue even by his own account—of a strict parallelism between mind and body, indeed their equation ("mind and body are one and the same thing, conceived now under the attribute of Thought, now under the attribute of Extension" [E, III, Prop. 2, Scholium, 104–105]; "the order and connection of ideas is the same as the order and connection of causes" [E, II, Prop. 20, Proof, 80]). Even if for the sake of argument one were to grant Spinoza his insistence upon necessity in mind and body, in what sense are the necessity of logical deduction and the necessity of efficient causality identical or, less, even parallel? It is not just hard to figure, it is impossible. Deductive necessity is not causal necessity, and vice versa. Third, there is Spinoza's inherited and adopted theological prejudice—never justified, taken to be self-evident instead—that Nature is perfect: "by reality and perfection I mean the same thing" (E, II, Def. 6, 63). To be sure Spinoza uses the term "God" interchangeably with "Nature," but such semantic trading is no argument. To insist that Nature's laws are eternal, immutable, and necessary, and that together these constitute perfection, and from such insistence to rank entities ontologically according to their nearness or distance from such perfection, these are unjustified theological maneuvers pure and simple, whatever their pedigree. We shall return later to the significance of Spinoza's claim that "to be able to not exist is weakness" (E, I, Prop. 11, Third Proof, 37), which serves as an epigraph to chapter 8 in the present volume. For the moment, I want only to point to the internal inconsistencies, the conceptual failures, that must attend the absolutizing of what is relative, the taking of a part—scientific knowledge—for the whole.

None of the foregoing puts in doubt Spinoza's intellectual good will or his considerable intellectual abilities and accomplishments. Unfortunately, some of the theological dogmas he inherited and adopted uncritically are not up to the task of grasping the nature and significance of modern science. Most Spinoza scholars freely admit the inner failings of his thought. They are due, so I half-jokingly tell my students, to the unfortunate circumstance that Spinoza had not read Kant. The existence of insuperable aporia, in any event, which are central and in no way trivial to his philosophy, coupled with his intellectual self-assurances to the contrary, will help us to understand later a certain emotional disposition in Spinoza that is contrary to the spirit of his thought and contrary, too, to his later public image as the imperturbable sage. Perhaps the same aporia have contributed to the mistaken notion that Spinoza was a mystic. I say mistaken because his rationalist confidence and intent are too clear for their failure to indicate a deeper, more hidden satisfaction with something less, or other.

On its own terms, then, and without the admission, Spinoza's philosophy is a failure. It simply cannot sustain the rationality it insists upon. Yet Spinozism persists. What is important and relevant in Spinoza's philosophy, then, what lends it its continued importance, putting aside its specific and untenable presuppositions, ideas, and their elaboration, is the *intention* of his thought. One might just as well say its *presumption* or, even more boldly, its *pretension*. Let us look more closely at this. What is the rationalist intention of Spinoza's philosophy, and what is its continued relevance today?

Let us approach and delineate an answer by moving from general to specific. In line with all prior philosophies, beginning with Thales, Spinoza's largest intention is to think the whole, to reason about the all. Not to paint each and every unique detail, to be sure, but to grasp the conceptual framework of all that is, its basic principle and its intelligible organization and interrelationships. For Thales "all is water"; for Spinoza, the universe is "one substance." With such an intention, with such high hopes for reason, one can hardly underestimate the dignity of philosophy and philosophers. To grasp the essential structure of the whole of which each and every particular thing partakes and through which each and everything takes its place and makes sense, such would be the grandest aspiration, the greatest *task*, and in some cases the absolute *accomplishment* claimed by philosophy. It is precisely this grandiose aspiration that one still finds today in science, which by its very *telos* seeks and must seek a "unified field theory." Such a goal does not make everything the same, as if apples were oranges, but rather it puts all diversity, the multiplicity of what is, within one ultimate comprehensive equation and thereby makes all things reciprocally and universally translatable. Spinoza's "in the universe there is only one substance" (E, I, Prop. 14, Cor. 1, 40), which is to say the very assertion of a *uni*verse, one reality, united, systematically interrelated, his *amor intellectualis Dei*, are expressions of the grandeur of philosophy. With the additional glory of claiming to have succeeded at it, to have unmasked and elaborated in all its intelligibility the ultimate structure of the real. Though he failed in its execution, it is the grandeur of his intention coupled with his evident self-confidence that he had succeeded, that surely provide one reason for Spinoza's perennial attraction as a philosopher. The grandeur of the intention, the seduction of the rational absolute, despite or perhaps also because of its hubris, remains as another reason for the perennial attraction of Spinozism, beyond Spinoza.

Nevertheless, this reason for Spinoza's attraction, whether correct or convincing or not, is insufficiently specific, is presented at too high a level of generality, since several philosophers other than Spinoza also hold out the possibility of an absolute realized through reason. Furthermore, all such claims are more likely to meet skepticism today than at any time in the history of thought. Fortunately, Spinoza's intention is more specific than aspiring to be just another rational system of the whole. That is to say, the rational whole to which Spinoza aspires is meant to be the result of thinking *modern science* through to the end. For this reason Harry Austryn Wolfson called Spinoza the "first modern man"—not simply because excommunicated from his Jewish community he remained unconverted to Christianity, Europe's first secular man, but more profoundly because Spinoza was the first whose intent was to adopt the perspective of modern science as the one and only and fully adequate explanation of all things. Spinoza's intention is to think the whole as it would be thought if science, scientific knowledge, scientific truth, were the fully adequate and the entirely exclusive way to think all things. Here lies the specific and root intent of Spinozism: scientism, positivism, science all the way down, science all the way up, science without up and down entirely, truth without *telos*.

Philosophy for Spinoza does not supplement science, open to other avenues and forms of knowledge or sensibility in order to situate science within a larger whole. Rather, it totalizes science, shows what a universe in which scientific intelligibility is the only intelligibility would have to be like. Together science and philosophy of science—Spinoza's philosophy—account for the whole, truth eternal, immutable, and necessary, the absolute intelligibility the theological parlance of previous epochs called "God's mind," that in relation to which the scientist's and philosopher's life are an "ethics," in a knowing that would be nothing less than "beatitude." This project, this intention, the great intellectual adventure of modern science supported by the even greater self-interpretation of Spinozism, is what makes Spinoza our contemporary and what remains most important and relevant about his thought today—despite his own failure in this great adventure. Spinoza's was modernity's first uncompromisingly positivist philosophy of the West and of the world. *Deus, sive Natura.* Nature substituted for God. Everything would be Nature. Modern science—mathematical science—is the new Promethean tool to comprehend nature in its truth. All the rest would be illusion and ignorance. Such is the project Spinoza set for himself and expounded in the *Ethics,* and in all his writings. Even the Hebrew language, by means of an orderly grammar, would be tamed and rendered logical!

That Spinoza's philosophy is atheist, despite his protests, was recognized right away. Even his protests, after all, in no way affirmed traditional faith, anthropomorphism, or theodicy. Nor in opposing childish religion did Spinoza affirm an adult one. Rather he proposed a new type of faith altogether, a faith in science, in the truly real, in lawful Nature. Henceforth "God" would have to be conceived according to the mathematical laws of natural science. Certainly, Spinoza understood that such an outlook would only be for the few, the elect intelligentsia, scientists and philosophers. For the masses, the multitude, the many, the horde of ignoramuses, of whom Spinoza is quite unable to disguise his contempt, traditional religion would remain in force. Not because of its truth, which it has none, but because of its *usefulness* to keep these otherwise unruly masses in line, to regulate and tame their inevitable irrationality, their emotional outbursts and bondage, and to provide effective if imaginative sanctity and sanction to the obedience demanded by the no-less-imaginary morality that such fools and madmen must needs obey and that they were incapable of transcending in any event (see chapter 5).

That Spinoza's philosophy is pantheist, this too was quickly recognized. His pantheism and his atheism are of one piece, and both are inseparable from his positivism. That his atheism and pantheism were rooted in scientism, an unbounded defense and totalization of modern science, this—for the cognoscenti—was meant to be the saving grace of his thought, its liberating value, what Spinoza considered its "blessedness." Unfortunately, for we who are critical of scientism, this alleged liberation is achieved with dark blinkers, a narrowing of consciousness that eventually exacts its own terrible revenge, its own crisis of rationality. Despite science's emancipation from superstition, dogma, and intolerance, if it also disregards and dismisses every other register of significance, denigrating everything that lies outside the competence of science, as Spinoza's positivism does, the larger world will come back in distorted form to haunt and undermine even the legitimate accomplishments of science. Science exaggerated is no longer science. Levinas will uncover the limitation of science from the orientation of ethics, the height of moral imperative, the call to alleviate another person's suffering, which for him represents not ignorance and illusion but the irreducible and genuine and most worthy "humanity of the human."

Spinoza reaches his smaller and seemingly more secure world of intelligibility—his rational system—via two basic steps. They are not particularly complicated, even if they are made so by their tortured execution, that is to say, by the "twisting" and "extorting"—to invoke the terms Spinoza throws at the rabbis in the *Theological-Political Treatise*—by which they are passed off as adequate and complete when in truth they are but a Procrustean bed. *First: everything reduced to nature. Second: nature reduced to what is knowable by modern science.* Being is being-known—it is an old story in philosophy, originating with Parmenides, who declared "being and *logos* are one," though its added force in Spinoza comes from the unprecedented analytical power of the modern scientific *logos*. The logical propositions of Parmenides are today replaced by the mathematical formulae of modern science. The outlook of today's positivists remains in basic agreement with Spinoza, even if they would revise his too-logicist conception of science. That is to say, today's positivists, obeying the intention of Spinoza, proclaim the absolute epistemological and ontological hegemony of science: the real is scientific and the scientific is real, and there is nothing else besides. The quibble of these latter-day Spinozists with Spinoza is over the nature not the absoluteness of scientific knowledge.

Levinas will have none of it. "Thought and freedom," Levinas writes in the concluding sentence of the first section of *Totality and Infinity*, "come to us from separation and from the consideration of the Other—this thesis is at the antipodes of Spinozism" (105). These two pillars of Levinas's thought stand in stark contrast to Spinoza. Versus the latter's elimination of the human and its complete integration into nature: (1) the irreducible separation or hypostasis of sensibility and (2) the irreducible moral transcendence or height of the other person. Levinas had already announced these two themes as early as the first page of his 1947 book on time, *Time and the Other*: "To uphold this thesis [that time is intersubjective] it will be necessary, on the one hand, to deepen the notion of solitude and, on the other, to consider the opportunities that time offers to solitude" (39). To deepen the notion of solitude: the irreducible sensuous subjectivity of the subject. Subjectivity as vulnerability, as mortality. The opportunities that time offers to solitude: the irreducible "diachrony"—irretrievable past, "messianic" future—opened up in the face of the other person. Subjectivity uplifted in intersubjectivity. The two dimensions are intimately related: deepening subjectivity heightens transcendence. Heightening transcendence deepens subjectivity.

The human, in myself, in the other, the other in myself, is deeper than Spinoza, deeper than the rationalists (including the empiricists), deeper than their present-day positivist avatars have dreamed. The human is precisely what cannot be reduced to a context, whether atoms and void, double helix, or social or historical *Geist*, even when that context is dressed in the nicest formulae of scientific objectivity. The immeasurability of suffering, of wounds, of hunger, of learning, of enjoyment, of conversation, of the otherness of the other person, these open up in an orientation of moral height, of goodness, greater, higher, nobler than any formulae that would attempt to contain them by placing them in a horizon or reducing them to their context. In taking this orientation seriously Levinas's thought represents a double break with Spinozism, bursting the pretended absoluteness of science from below, by affirming the irreducibility of the independence of subjectivity, and, no less radically, and in relation to such independence, breaking it from above, affirming the priority of the "better than being," the morally good, responsibility for the other and for all others.

That subjectivity originates in the radical independence of sensibility, which thereby contests Spinoza's elimination of the distinctively human "kingdom within a kingdom,"[1] is fundamental to all of Levinas's thought. Its significance has sometimes been underappreciated in view of the transcendence of the other person in the face of which the humanity of the human takes on its highest sense. The former is a phenomenological discovery; the latter, in contrast, is an ethical claim. To appreciate the former, Levinas's account of human sensibility, we must remember to what extent Levinas is one of the great *phenomenological* researchers. Indeed, it is no exaggeration to say that, along with the early Heidegger of *Being and Time*, Levinas was arguably Husserl's greatest student in phenomenology.[2] Levinas's prize-winning book of 1930, *The Theory of Intuition in Husserl's Phenomenology*, not only introduced Husserlian phenomenology to France, but his own phenomenological investigations, especially those found in *Time and the Other*, *Existence and Existents*, and above all the second section of *Totality and Infinity*, display brilliant phenomenological discoveries, which also already challenge the adequacy of the earlier phenomenological studies executed by Heidegger. In any event, Levinas's phenomenological discoveries regarding the constitution of human subjectivity radically contest Spinoza's logical and mechanical theorizing of subjectivity (and also of Hegel's and Sartre's theorizing of subjectivity as negation). Unlike Spinoza's constructions, based upon rationalist presuppositions, Levinas's descriptions are guided by the *evidence* of "the things themselves."

---

1. See E, III, Preface, 102. In the face of the later controversies surrounding the very possibility of Hegel's preface to his *Phenomenology of Spirit*, because the system of the absolute can admit of nothing outside itself, it seems almost like a slap in the face that Spinoza will explicitly deny conceiving "man in Nature as a kingdom within a kingdom" in a *preface*. Should it not rather appear as a truth sufficiently argued through axioms, postulates, propositions, proofs, in any event within the strictest demonstrative logic? To review it in a preface, is this not a concession to the human weakness that Spinoza metaphysically eliminates? But all readers of Spinoza are aware that often the most interesting of his observations occur not within the armory of its deductive apparatus but in the more free-flowing discourses of its scholia.

2. See Cohen, "Emmanuel Levinas," 71–81. And given Heidegger's later shift from phenomenology to ontology and *poesis*, an argument can be made that Levinas was, along with Merleau-Ponty and Michel Henri, the greatest—that is, most original—phenomenologist, after Husserl, of the twentieth century.

But Levinas is not only a phenomenologist. His truck with Spinoza is not simply one truth, one epistemology challenging another. His *ethics* exceeds his own phenomenology. The other person ruptures appearances, exceeds intentionality, because the other person overloads—with moral obligation—the subject with *responsibilities*, raising the subject to a moral agency greater, more demanding, than its capacities. Science—even phenomenological science and all the more natural science—lacks the resources to account for this sort of obligation. The other person is not true, is not even a signification. Rather the other person obligates, makes one responsible. The significance of the other person emerges as what Levinas characterizes as "saying," sincerity, expressiveness, "face," which precedes and *orients* all that is "said": themes, theses, signs, propositions, representations.

Let us underline something else about the relation of phenomenology or science to ethics in Levinas. Ethics exceeds phenomenology, yes, but it remains essential that one pursues phenomenology to its limits. In other words, one does not simply declare, arbitrarily as it were, the superiority of ethics over science. One pursues science all the ways one can, because one seeks truth. And then, in such a pursuit, one sees the necessity for ethics, the necessity of ethics itself, its height, the primacy of its moral exigencies, but also and no less importantly one sees the necessity of ethics for science itself. Thus even positivism is forced—unless it turns into ideology, which unfortunately happens all too often—to experience the error of positivism. Phenomenology, Husserl reminded us time and again, always returns to the beginning, to the presuppositionless, the things themselves. The ground of science is not objects and objectivity but evidence and the illumination of what is evident.

Thus when Levinas encounters at the limits of phenomenological science—the limits of phenomena and the meaning-giving acts of intentionality—the imperatives of moral exigency, their patent comes not from some failure of science but rather from a surplus beyond and above it. For Spinozism, in contrast, reaching the end of science means reaching the end of the universe, beyond which there is nothing but the irrational, the illusory. This, however, sets up the unstable dialectical situation Husserl called the "Crisis." Excluding what objectivity cannot objectify, dismissing everything outside of science as "irrational," what is left out—which is surely not simply irrational and illusory—can only come back in distorted form, lacking all legitimacy, and thus forced to *violently explode* the artificiality of the boundaries Spinozism set up between the "rational" and the "irrational" through a dialectic Freud called "the return of the repressed." Thus in a seeming paradox that is no paradox at all, absolutized science, science totalized in the manner of Spinozism, which at first sight seems to eliminate superstition, dogma, blind faith, and their like, actually and precisely undergirds and exacerbates the mythology of all sorts of irrationalism instead. Scientism, positivism, exclusivist science do not rid the world of irrationalism, they increase and empower it.

When Levinas, as a student of phenomenology, examines human subjectivity to grasp its structures and meanings, he does not presuppose a theory of science according to which in principle everything must conform to a homogeneous causal nature. The methodological point of the phenomenological *epoche* is to rid the scientific investigator of all such realist and cognitive presuppositions. One must rather entertain "the things themselves" in their own terms, letting them show themselves. In contrast, Spinoza knows beforehand that human beings, like all entities, whether stones, stars, or strawberries, are no more than ratios of motion and rest. Thus it is true that Spinoza "thinks least about death" (see chapter 7), because what humans call "death," and respond to emotionally with fear, is in truth really only a larger than usual change in ratio of motion and rest—nothing exceptional there. When the ratio that defines any entity changes beyond a certain magnitude, that thing becomes something else, other ratios take its place. One could just as well say that when salt dissolves it "dies." Again, for the Spinozist, humans constitute no "kingdom within a kingdom." Why all the fuss about morality?!

For Levinas what is indeed special about humans is not a temporarily distinctive ratio of motion and rest but a specific sensitivity bound to sensibility; beginning in sensuous "enjoyment," it is lived through an embodiment always vulnerable to suffering and ultimately ends in the loss that is mortality. Levinas discovers the structure and sense of the *independence* of the human at first in its "separation" from anonymous existence and from other entities through the inner sensitivity of self-sensing. Embodiment is thus not an original sin or fault (see chapter 1) or a prison from which the mind or spirit would rather escape. To be embodied, to "enjoy" sensibility, it is the very condition of humanity. To be sure, embodiment is a complex phenomenon. It is not accurately understood if explained in terms of "sense data," "confused ideas," or "secondary qualities," which are constructs derived from already assuming the primacy of scientific knowing.

The body is not adequately understood if from the start it is a disappointment to knowledge, a merely "stammering thought," a second-class citizen in the state of scientific knowledge. So, too, Spinoza's "substantialist" assumptions, however logical or compelling for an outmoded theology or rationalism, are of no use here.[3] The self-sensing of sensibility occurs through a "passive synthesis," what Maurice Merleau-Ponty in his phenomenological investigations of the same phenomenon named a "fold" in the "flesh of the world," as when one hand touches the other hand without the subject being able to sort out definitively which hand is touching and which touched. It is a motley sensationalism such as Jacques Lacan found in the infant's fragmented body—*corps morcelé*—prior to the syntheses of identification that occur at the ego or "mirror stage." A proper account and appreciation for these phenomena, however, are occluded by the demand for consistency and totality of representational thought, its logicism and objectivism. "By imagining this anesthesia limitless," Levinas writes in *Totality and Infinity*, "Spinoza conjures away separation" (119). Skepticism says, "Nothing is true" and contradicts itself. Analogously, Spinoza would say, "There is no human," at once vanishing *and* expressing himself, there and not there, as if a snake could swallow itself by the tail.

In opposition to Spinozism and to all totalizing rationalization, Levinas deepens the independence of "solitude"—the irreducible independence of human sensuous existence. Looked at from higher-level cultural significations, for instance, the religious register of meaning, he deepens the independence of the human all the way to what he calls "the risk of atheism." Only a being fully capable of denying God, of doing and being without God, can truly affirm God. Levinas thus conceives the subject's independence—its sensibility—free of the clas-

---

3. That interpreting the subject as *substance*—Spinoza goes so far as to interpret the universe as substance; indeed, nothing is more self-evident to him!—is an intellectualist importation to the phenomena itself is a great discovery of contemporary thought, whether or not one agrees with Nietzsche's further claim that the substantial self is a fiction, "owing to the seduction of language (and of the fundamental errors of reason that are petrified in it) which conceived and misconceives all effects as conditioned by something that causes effects, by a 'subject' . . ." (GM, I, 13). We will see later in the present volume that Nietzsche's critique of substance remains closer to Spinoza than to Levinas.

sical logic of "substance and attribute" or "form and content" that, however appropriate they may be to an understanding of craft and manufacture, would already distort an account of the human, conforming to demands of representation but not to the evidence—however "illogical"—of the "things themselves."

The conceptual consequences of taking embodiment seriously in this way are enormous. They are revolutionary for a philosophical tradition hitherto hamstrung by an idea of rationality constricted in clandestine alliance with theology. Because Levinas discovers the first initiative of subjectivity in self-sensing, upon which are built the higher-level constitutive layers of sense such as dwelling, worldliness, labor, and representation, which are elaborated in section 2 of *Totality and Infinity*, when he comes to account for intersubjectivity in section 3 of *Totality and Infinity* and in the whole of *Otherwise than Being or Beyond Essence* (and most of his other writings), an intersubjectivity whose *significance* is from the first weighted with the valence of morality, Levinas elaborates intersubjectivity and morality based in embodiment. That is to say, because the other person is not erroneously reduced to mind, or ratio of motion and rest, or will, or freedom, but rather as a being embodied, hence mortal, subject to wounds and suffering, facing old age and death, in a word, as *vulnerable*, moral obligation is grasped in all its materiality, because, too, at the same time the one who is morally responsibility for the other is also an embodied mortal being, who thus not only viscerally understands suffering, but is one who can materially respond to the other's material needs. Like the Buddha, Levinas has come to teach the meaning of suffering and the alleviation of suffering. The alleviation of suffering is the heart of morality: to give to the other, which is always a giving of oneself to and for the other, the self as giving, as "love of the neighbor," all the way to the possible extremity of "dying for" the other—ultimate expiation of responsible subjectivity. In other words: a body, eyes, hands, skin, tears and laughter, pain and pleasure, hunger and need, are not obstacles to morality, they are precisely what require it and enable it.

Transcendence, alterity in its strongest sense, non-encompassable, *more other even than negativity*,[4] occurs as a *surplus* of obligations, a sur-

---

4. "Transcendence Is Not Negativity," Levinas clearly names one of the subsections of *Totality and Infinity* (40–42); the allusion to Nietzsche's *Ecce Homo* is no doubt quite consciously made.

plus that disrupts, disturbs, overwhelms the self-interest of the self in a responsibility to and for the other person that can never be fully met but that must, all the same, be met as fully as possible. The exigency of helping others trumps the curiosity of knowing, whatever—and despite—the self-composure and self-satisfaction of the latter. One never knows the good, and never can. Goodness demands response out of a "difficult freedom" already beholden to the other person. And yet from such an excessive responsiveness, knowing too finds its reason. Knowledge, contemplation, is not idle curiosity, not the elite entertainment of those with leisure, whether rich like Plato or poor like Spinoza. Nor—and here we are able to answer Nietzsche's challenge—does knowledge lack a *raison d'être*. Knowledge meets a demand, a very specific demand: the demand for justice. Without knowledge there can be no justice, and without justice there can be no morality, and without morality . . . humanity has no significance. But humanity does have significance. Let us unpack these formulae.

Human selves—even in their greatest individuality, their greatest solitude—do not each inhabit inviolate territories, are not disembodied ghosts, imprisoned souls, or pure minds. These are but second-order abstractions, which if asserted as originary or exclusive are but denying their own concrete condition. To be embodied is to be both an entity in the world and to be the vulnerable source point of worldliness. Levinas has grasped that this disjunction is not properly accounted for in the language of intentionality or meaning constitution, whether of a transcendental ego or of the being of beings. Meaning is not first of all a matter of freedom. The difference between self and other cannot originally be grasped in the third person. The I—the me myself—not first a self at all, an entity, a being, or even the being of a being. Rather to be oneself is to be "despite oneself," to be "for the other," which is to say, to rise to moral responsibility. It is a unique structure, recalcitrant to representation, that is to say, to the internal relationality that determines the logic of representation. The surplus—the moral height of the other, the other person as obligation for me—can only be pointed to in the language of morality: to be for-the-other is better than being for-oneself, or more simply, it is *better than being* altogether. Caring is *better* than conatus. Spinoza can win all his arguments, and still lose—be the worse for it. Sacrifice *better* than signification. The key to all of Levinas's teachings, and the deepest source of his radical opposition to Spinozism, lies in grasping the ethical import of these claims, for

Introduction 17

they are claims—truths bound to obligations, impositions, demands, exigencies, "a difficult wisdom concerned with truths that correlate to virtues" (DF, 275)—and not simply propositions. True speech in this sense is not nominative alone, or not nominative at base: it is imperative, accusative, what Levinas has also called "prophetic speech" (see DF, chapter 2). Because the embodied and mortal other suffers, I am first of all—and I first, singularly, and first before my very freedom, under my skin—called upon—called up, elevated, elected—to alleviate that suffering. There is no higher calling, no higher self, no greater dignity than such moral responsibility.

In this way—calling attention beyond the *logic* of representation to the *orientation* of morality—Levinas's thought goes farther, both deeper and higher than that of Spinoza and Spinozism. Phenomenology, for its concreteness, and ethics, for its elevation, are both foreign to Spinoza's thought, indeed they are anathema.[5] Thus, too, we cannot be surprised and much less disappointed that Levinas does not prolong the interminable and fruitless debates about free will and determinism, or mind and body, and the like. Such debates are as defeatist as their premises are erroneous. Besides, Kant saw them all through to their end. Levinas begins in the concrete. His thought is no longer mired in the premises and permutations of abstract notions of freedom and necessity that conform only to the propositional logic of declaration and negation, of being and non-being, oblivious to the real concatenations of sensibility and signification beyond the reach of such language games, and even more so evading the significance, the accusative voice that ultimately gives reason its reason. Spinoza would have been shocked, if only he could have been shocked.

Spinoza—though intending to be the greatest devotee of the new science—forced it into the Procrustean bed of an ancient and medieval logic. Laboring under the Parmenidean sun, he serves the long-dominant tradition of Western rationality that equated being and *logos*. No higher or greater exigency rules or can rule Spinozism than updating an unquestioned inheritance of substantializing and objectivizing truth. Spinoza's philosophy is thus doubly distorted, doubly stigmatized, through its allegiance to scientism and rationalism and the alliance of the

---

5. The recent book by Knox Peden, *Spinoza Contra Phenomenology: French Rationalism from Cavaillès to Deleuze*, whose title alone (I have not yet seen the book) suggests that it deals with this topic, appeared too late for the present volume.

two: truth from science and only from science, albeit the new science, but at the same time that science philosophically comprehended exclusively with the logical tools of an antiquated epistemology. *Whatever is not thus rational is irrational.* Being or non-being, true or false, affirmation or negation, knowledge or ignorance, only the first of these alternatives are real . . . and the rest are madness, immaturity, ignorance, passion, manipulations. Beyond the rational there is nothing. Or worse than nothing, beyond rationality lies *chaos*—the deepest fear of Spinozism, the deepest fear of classical philosophy, as sin is the deepest fear of theology.

For all his apparent imperturbability, for all the debate-stopping QEDs, Spinoza has no answer to Nietzsche's radical challenge: *Why truth rather than lie?* No doubt truth is powerful, especially modern scientific truth, which is power itself. But if we go to the root of Nietzsche's question, which is a question that goes to the root, raising the question of the *value* of truth, does not Spinoza simply assume, out of habit, because it had so long been assumed, that it is *better* to know? And does not this assumption, this "ought," however tacit, however backed by long tradition, contradict the idea of science—science without "final ends," modern science—that his whole philosophy is designed to explain and justify? Surely it does. And such a radical contradiction goes a long way to explain why we find the level-headed Spinoza, the cool, collected Spinoza, despite the much-touted beatitude of pure ideation, raging against ignoramuses, against women, against "babies, fools, and madmen" (see chapter 8).

This contradiction haunts Spinoza everywhere, cracking the great façade of cool rationality. One hardly requires the laborious scholasticisms of a Straussian to see it. Spinoza will protest that truth has no interest, that knowledge is its own reward (see chapter 3). But why must he insist on even this? What does "reward" mean when one says that knowledge is its own reward? All of this, of course, poses no difficulty for Levinas, who shows that the source of truth lies beyond coherence and correspondence, and also beyond the "meaning-bestowing" acts of a transcendental ego, which is the very boundary of phenomenology, or the free "giving" of being or language, which is the boundary of ontology. He shows the source of knowledge—the "said," themes, hypotheses, propositions, and so on—lies in intersubjectivity understood as the "saying of the said," always already a *moral* relation. Levinas willingly admits that such a source of truth is discoverable and expressible only by an "abuse of formal logic," because logic by its own lights precisely effaces its significance. For this reason, too, Levinas agrees with Spinoza's claim that the theological is political, not, however, for Spinoza's reasons, that is, because religion and ethics are for the masses, the ignorant, incapable of free thought, and hence necessarily obedient and slavish. He agrees, rather, because all exclusionary or totalizing systems of thought, driven by the logic of representation, including Spinoza's philosophy, in fact—though not in principle—make up for the artificiality of their closures by a rhetoric that is ultimately only political in the worst sense—authoritarian, vehement, violent—rather than epistemologically justified. To hide their inconsistency and arbitrariness, they must shout down their opponents. Levinas will not abide such violence, including the irresponsibility of truth.

With these considerations in mind, I want to highlight one of Levinas's greatest contributions to philosophy, which is to say, to the world: to have found and articulated the *reason for reason*, the justification that knowledge has always sought but never found because it lies outside its range and resources. Knowledge knows—this is a tautology. And it can reflectively know that it knows—such is epistemology. But in its modern nonteleological form, that is, as modern science, it no longer knows *why* it knows. It has lost its "what for." Having delegitimized final causes, no wonder it has no final cause for itself. Spinoza in his *Ethics* minces no words regarding the error of final causality, because considered positively it is the signal advance of modern over ancient science: "Nature has no fixed goal and that all final causes are but figments of the human imagination" (I, App., 59). Levinas, without reintroducing teleology into nature, will challenge such a view, siding with the ancients, with a broader notion of reason that includes finality, yet without thereby distorting the character of modern science. This is because Levinas acknowledges *justice* as the ultimate goal of humanity, and there can be no justice without knowledge, hence there can be no justice without science—and hence science finds its justification in serving justice. Also, and opposing both Hobbes and Spinoza on this score, Levinas argues that justice is not a function of the State, of power and the political, though of course it requires these for its concrete instantiation, but first and foremost it serves and is required by morality (see chapters 4 and 5). Thus science and philosophy are called to their ultimate purpose and orientation: aiming at the good. Antipodes from Spinozism.

Here is also the place to underscore another position in a debate implicit in Levinas's stance: that in going beyond knowledge toward the surplus of ethics, Levinas, in addition to breaking with the long heritage of scientistic or epistemological hegemony in philosophy, is also breaking with what we can call the "romantic" or aesthetic tradition of thought. To be sure, the latter also broke with scientism, starting in the modern period with Schiller and Schelling or even with Rousseau (it is impossible to put a stop to origins and influences), it continues through Nietzsche, Heidegger, Bataille, and Deleuze. Contra the romantics, having reached the limits of science, Levinas does not turn to the imagination for a new "ground" (or "non-ground") of philosophy. Rather, Levinas supports the primacy of ethics. Here he renews the heritage of Kant, who gave primacy to the *Critique of Practical Reason* in relation to the *Critique of Pure Reason*, and opposes all those post-Kantian philosophers who turned to Kant's third critique, the *Critique of Judgment*, for their ground. Heidegger, for instance, directly after *Being and Time*, in his Kant book, *Kant and the Problem of Metaphysics* (1929), interprets the Kantian schemata—the most enigmatic element of the Kantian epistemological edifice—as temporality, the temporality of Dasein, and ultimately as the temporality of epochal Being, hence as the ground of being, or being as the ground. Bergson, too, for his part, will interpret *duration* in cosmic terms, as the temporality of the universe, a temporal unfolding analogous to artistic creativity, thus also advocating a fundamentally aesthetic route for philosophy. For this reason, too, Levinas launched the greatest and most penetrating criticism of Heidegger, even if Heidegger sovereignly refused to answer. Heidegger had nothing serious to say about the good, about morality, about justice, except to subvert them for the question of being and its homonyms. While Levinas pursues Husserlian science to the extent that he does scientific research (which was considerable, including critiques of Heidegger's earlier phenomenological studies) and in such an endeavor already exceeds Spinozist logicism, unlike Husserl, and beyond all positivism, and while avoiding the siren's call of the aesthetic, he finds that he must go beyond the limits of science in the name of *morality and justice*. It is there, in the demands of justice, justice beholden to morality, that he uncovers the ultimate justification of science, the reason for reason.

To repeat: Levinas finds the reason for reason in neither a more rigorous ratiocination nor a more sensitive *poesis* but rather in a greater responsibility. First in the insuperable priority of responsibility for the other person, that is to say, in morality, "love of the neighbor." Second and as required by moral obligation, in responsibility for all others, that is to say, in justice. The one who faces also faces others, others from whose violence potentially that other must be protected. Hence morality itself demands justice. Or as Judaism expresses this: mercy requires justice, as justice requires mercy. Against Spinoza, then, for Levinas everything that is not rational is not irrational—there is the ethical. There is the rational, to be sure, and its obverse, the irrational, but otherwise than both and beyond their oppositions, and subtending their very possibility, there is the commanding height of the good. "The positions we have outlined," Levinas writes in *Totality and Infinity*, "oppose the ancient privilege of unity which is affirmed from Parmenides to Spinoza to Hegel. Separation and interiority were held to be incomprehensible and irrational. . . . The Place of the Good above every essence is the most profound teaching, the definitive teaching, not of theology, but of philosophy" (102).

Precisely in the transcendence Spinoza can only dismiss as "ignorance" Levinas finds the inspiration of the humanity of the human, the justification of science, and hence the highest treasure of philosophy, the wisdom of the good. There is no irony in Levinas's position, which is straightforwardness itself, "proximity and not truth about proximity" (OBBE, 120), what in *Totality and Infinity* he calls "sincerity" and "teaching" and in *Otherwise than Being or Beyond Essence* he names with such terms as "nakedness," "patience," "substitution," "non-indifference," and "witness," among others. "It is time," Levinas writes, "the abusive confusion of foolishness with morality were denounced" (OBBE, 126). Moral obligation is not irrational, not ignorance, not a stammering thought, for without it humanity would lose its bearings and rationality would make no sense. It is not the freedom of thought, or the freedom Heidegger identifies with being's generosity. Rather, the face of the other inspires a *difficult freedom, freedom bound to obligations, obligations coming from the Other before oneself, coming ultimately from all Others, in an orientation inescapable and from the first oriented by goodness and by right, prior to choice or contract*, and most certainly invisible to Spinozism or, worse, despised by him.

Levinas thus conceives the intelligibility of the intelligible in a radically different manner than Spinoza. The offshoots of Spinoza, call them Spinozism, scientism, or positivism, are still quite alive and well in our day. Not a week goes by without articles in newspapers and journals reporting the alleged and astonishing new scientific discovery of the real basis of what had hitherto seemed beyond science: thinking, morality, justice, love, piety, and the like, are reduced to brain activities, chemical reactions, hormone complexes, synapse connectors, genome segments, and the like, as if such material conditions were *equivalent* to what they condition. I refer readers to the epigraph of Plato at the head of this book: one must distinguish material conditions from that which they condition, for one is not reducible to the other. Doubtless, it is useful for doctors, physiologists, neurologists, physicists, and other researchers and practitioners to know cognitively the inner workings of the brain, to subject it to the most rigorous tests and analyses. But the body the doctor operates on or the scientist studies, and the person who is healed or informed, including doctor and scientist, are not one and the same. It is no fault or flaw that subjects are irreducible to objects; it is the rather the very possibility of objectivity.

The chapters of the present volume contest materialist reductionism, just as they also contest that the grounds of such contestation must be a *poesis*, as if the ground of truth were art, imagination, creativity, as if what is required to overcome Spinozism is a remythologization. The alternative to truth is not the false, the lie, as Nietzsche so wanted, but goodness, goodness that requires truth and enjoys beauty. True and false, after all, are two sides of the same enterprise. Just as we are not freed of scientism by faith, we are not freed from it by aestheticism either, whatever temporary relief both these avenues may seem to provide. Such relief has its own price to pay. Lurking in the blindness of faith, lurking in the aesthetics of "poetic thinking," which shun the standards of truth to opt for oracular pronouncements, lies an unacknowledged alliance with power, as Walter Benjamin understood, the political pageant, elegant uniforms and goose step parades, the pronouncements of the Leader—for power too would free itself from truth, from standards, and distract those it subjugates with awe-inspiring displays of splendor. We did not await the Grand Inquisitor to realize that bread and circuses are ever ready to replace science and independent thinking, that the lures of ideology are seductive. The true life is a moral one, responsibility to and for the other, striving for justice—"difficult freedom."

To remain human—to rise to our humanity, for it is never a given—there is no turning back from knowledge nor should there be. To challenge the hegemony of knowledge is not to eviscerate knowledge but to discover its genuine context and proper purpose. As I have briefly indicated, for Levinas knowledge is necessary for justice (legal and material rights and protections), and justice is necessary for morality (face-to-face), and morality is the *raison d'être* of humanity. The *importance* of knowledge, its *significance* and not only the truth or untruth of its signs, formulae, theses, hypotheses, comes not from the endless horizons of its own research but from the ethical dimension of height. Climate change, for instance, is not simply a fact, a change in the ratio of motion and rest of atmospheric temperature and ocean water levels, say, at a certain moment in geological time. It is this, to be sure, but it is also and significantly an impending disaster for human and all sentient life on earth. It will not be averted by more science or more technology *by themselves*, and certainly even less will it be averted by less science and less technology. The *issue* of eco-disaster is not a scientific or technological question. It is a moral question and a question of justice. It is a matter of humans hurting humans, and humans hurting sentient life in general. If the pain and suffering it portends is to be averted, it will be through the concerted social and political application of moral values, first of all by the moral recognition that humans are more valuable than things or money, that people come first, that each human being counts, as do the lives of other earth inhabitants. Yes, we must understand nature. Yes, we must know it scientifically. But nature is never just a mechanism, organism, or matrix indifferent to us, just as one human is never indifferent to another.

If it seems at times we are harsh on Spinoza, let us not forget the harshness of Spinozism. First of all, criticism is not a matter of harshness but of correct assessment. Second, dehumanization is no mere fillip nor confined to academic debate. What is at stake is the humanity of the human. Furthermore, though it may seem to some readers that we are overly severe toward Spinoza, though I do not think this is the case, and it is certainly not my intention, we also do appreciate what is positive in his thought. Certainly, we are thankful for his battles against the narrow-mindedness of religious and theological prejudice, the extravagances of clericalism, the degradations of religious intolerance, and the unspeakable horrors of religious wars. Spinoza came from a Jewry expelled from Spain and Portugal. He witnessed Christians killing one another over differences in doctrine. Today the world suffers from a murderous Islamic extremism. Spinoza, with his pen, fought such formidable foes in an age when the new science was young and weak and the Church powerful and overbearing. We join

Levinas in admiring Spinoza's uncompromising rejection of superstition and his criticism of anthropomorphic projections and childish dependencies in religion (see chapter 3). Both Spinoza and Levinas support a "religion for adults," even if their visions of such an adult religion are radically opposed, and Spinoza would eviscerate religion.

Also admirable is Spinoza's defense of freedom of thought and freedom of speech, as well as his support of a political separation between Church and State, even if Levinas and Spinoza differ in each instance on their meaning and the reasoning behind them. I cannot say exactly what Levinas would say, but I often find myself arguing that *nothing is more necessary to religion than secularization*. First of all, the secular—because it respects religious differences—stands as a concrete instauration of religious values, foremost by institutionalizing and sanctioning justice and guaranteeing the dignity of each citizen. "Justice as the *raison d'être* of the State:" (DF, 219), Levinas writes, and then continues, poignantly: "that is religion." Or, take one of the most striking sentences from *Totality and Infinity*: "Everything that cannot be restored to an interhuman relation represents not the superior form but the forever primitive form of religion" (TI, 79; my translation), and consider its political implications. While we laud Spinoza's obvious commitment to truth, we are forced to challenge what is also his destruction of truth by restricting it to science absolutized. In the end, the truths lauded by Spinozism turn against the very humanity that makes truth possible and worthwhile. What Spinoza seems to have forgotten is that there can be no truth without truth tellers. Expression and verification are ineradicable conditions of truth.

Levinas's criticism of Spinozist totality—one substance, everything necessary—also unmasks its alliance with the politics of totalitarianism. Philosophers can argue in fifty ways and can insist in even more, but it remains untrue their claim that *freedom is necessity*. Kant unmasked this illusion, and at the same time explained its eternal return. One must reconceive the absolute. Levinas writes of "ab-solution," the absolute not as enclosure, fortress, system but transcendence, openness to the new, response to the unassumable otherness of alterity, which concretely takes place as moral responsiveness to the other person. What is absolute, unsurpassable, unavoidable, irreducible is one's responsibility for another. One may shirk or refuse it, to be sure, because morality—pacific, excessive, "difficult"—is not driven by the necessity of causality or deduction. But one's humanity begins in relation to it. No person is reducible to a part of a whole, a cog in the machine, however much knowledge may demand it be so. Ontology, beings defined by being, structuralism, beings defined by their differential placement, even when converted into knowledge, are not ultimate structures. "Levinas shows," Sean Hand has observed, "that to be or not to be is not the ultimate question" (LR, 7–8). Despite its intensity, despite its push or pull, even despite its occasional triumph, *conatus*—perseverance in being—has no ultimate authority. Better than helping myself is to help the other. Better than my own *Sorge* is to care for others. Nothing trumps moral obligation. Nothing frees me from my responsibilities. Here lies the absolute, always above. Morality, or, more concretely, *the exigency to alleviate the suffering of the other person*, and justice, *the exigency to alleviate the sufferings of all*, the exigencies of mercy and justice, remain better than being, higher, more pressing, more elevated, more precious, even if in the eyes of an absolute science—science blinded by its own truth—these exigencies are dismissed as stupidity, naïveté, foolishness, ignorance, and nonsense. "Divine Spinoza, forgive me. I have become a fool," declares the elderly Dr. Fischelson, in Isaac Bashevis Singer's story, when he finally agrees to marry (32). But it is Spinoza who is the fool, foolish in the solitude of his science. Spinoza, like Kierkegaard but apparently without even a Regina, preferred intellect and ideas, pen and paper, the mind alone, monologue (without words and images![6]), to taking seriously the world of people, of love, family and commitment, of fellowship, community and citizenship, of scientists in addition to science, of philosophers in addition to ideas, of the flesh-and-blood human beings with whom in fact he remained always in dialogue, face-to-face as well as in letters, publications, and manuscripts left for publication. "Who would not prefer to have ideas as children rather than children of flesh and blood?," Diotima asked rhetorically in Plato's *Symposium*—Spinoza took the bait. We can pity him, though he could not pity himself, since he ruled pity out of his system (as later would Sade and Nietzsche).

Contra Spinozism's rigid systemizing and intellectualized indifference to the human, we shall remain impressed—call it naïveté, call it unsophisticated, call it nonphilosophy, what matter—by and shall not

---

6. See TPT, chap. 4: "For it is when a thing is perceived by pure thought, without words or images, that it is understood" (54).

recoil from joining Levinas in acknowledging a deeper wisdom, one more vulnerable, weaker no doubt but greater, higher, nobler, which we find articulated in a citation from Vasily Grossman's great novel *Life and Fate*:

> The private kindness of one individual towards another; a petty, thoughtless kindness; an unwitnessed kindness. Something we could call senseless kindness. A kindness outside of any system of social or religious good. . . . This kindness, this stupid kindness, is what is most truly human in a human being. It is what sets man apart, the highest achievement of his soul. No, it says, life is not evil! (407–408, 409)

The idea—it is an ideal, really—unifying the present volume is to contrast the elevation of such kindness—weak, frail, but ever so precious, not egoism but responsiveness to the other person—to the cold citadel of Spinoza's epistemological, ontological, and political absolutism. Levinas—with the considerable intellectual advantage of having learned from Kant's dialectic and Husserl's phenomenology—contests Spinoza's stunted conception of science and his overestimation of its range and its value. Against the conceptualized system of an abstract mathematical universe, against its digital vision of being and non-being, rational and irrational, true and false, knowledge and ignorance, affirmation and negation, Levinas will defend the surplus of a thicker or messier and certainly more difficult freedom: freedom as responsibility to and for the other and to and for all others. Levinas will contest Spinoza's philosophical system, his *Ethics*, but he will also contest its concomitant political quietism, its incontestable support for the status quo, as found in the *Theological-Political Treatise*. For Levinas there is not sufficient justice in our world to automatically salute the "is," the powers that be, over the "ought." For Spinoza makes his position perfectly clear, that when it comes to the political he values nothing above law and order, the peace and quiet required by contemplation and scientific research. To preserve that order, that peace, no injustice, no tyranny, no outrage is sufficient to risk the chaos that might come from any political change or remedy (see chapters 4 and 5).

Levinas will also radically challenge Spinoza's fundamental attack on religion and more specifically his vicious attack against Judaism, which is no less an attack against Christianity and all religions (see chapter 6). Without the least parochialism, in defending morality and justice Levinas also defends a "biblical humanism" and a "religion for adults"—the universality of religion as open to all and the universality of caring for all others. These living issues, these controversial positions and oppositions, this ongoing struggle between the true and the good, are the concerns that guide the present volume.

Out of Control—why this title? No doubt to suggest a new counterintuitive meaning for the catch phrase. Spinoza is the *control*: totalization, the inexorable logic of a truncated rationality without exit, being and more being without end, perseverance for the sake of perseverance, freedom equated with necessity. More broadly it is the interest of control that turns such rationality into today's world of commodification, no longer an intellectualist but a materialist reduction of all to the one substance: money, pure exchange, a liquid universe where nothing is itself because everything is exchangeable. Spinoza's is Kafka's nightmare in an earlier geometrical incarnation. In any case, whether Spinoza or an updated Bizarro inversion of Spinoza, control stands behind the rationality and rationalization of a universal dehumanization, a mythology pretending to truth with the usual political rhetoric of inevitability, necessity, world historical spirit, to hide its imposition.

Levinas is the way *out*: a metaphysical exit glimpsed as early as 1935 in an essay Levinas aptly named "On Escape," which in *Totality and Infinity* becomes the infinity of the other person—of the human—unassimilable to totality, "a situation where totality breaks up" (24), and named in 1974 as the title of the final chapter of *Otherwise than Being or Beyond Essence*, "Outside." Not negation, not deficit, not some leftover or "not yet" of knowledge, which can be and are recuperated within the operations, procedures, protocols, and structures of control, but a *surplus, not less but more, better than being*, the "saying" of one to another than can never finally be said or reduced to the internal logic of what is said. From *Totality and Infinity*: "The break-up of the formal structure of thought (the noema of a noesis) into events which this structure dissimulates, but which sustain it and restore its concrete significance" (28). Control is never really in control, because despite its sirens' call it never is what it ought to be, or it only *is* when it *ought* to be better.

Not therefore "out of control" in the usual idiomatic sense of sheer wildness, animal vitality, spontaneity free as the wind. Though these Dionysian exaltations, merely destructive as they are, do catch sight of a spirit, ethos, energy, humanity unwilling to submit to chains. Here "out of control" refers to a height, nobility, an orientation, an otherwise better than negative freedom, for which this entire volume argues in presenting Levinas's case. Not negative freedom. Not negation of negation. Not negative dialectics. A refusal beyond and better than negation, a rising to the call to accomplish the positive freedoms of moral responsibility, a difficult freedom. Difficult for the moral agent, to be sure, difficult as is self-sacrifice, but difficult, too, let us remember, for those who would suppress such a freedom, for those who espouse and enforce control! Spinoza as much as admits that such responsibility cannot ever be fully suppressed, even while he tries his best to contain it.

Certainly, then, "out of control" does not refer to a retreat into childish fantasies, wishful thinking, into acquiescence before the "miracle, mystery, and authority" that are the spells cast by Ivan Karamazov's Grand Inquisitor. Spinoza and Levinas both aim to wipe out mythological consciousness, with its seductions and violence. Not an absolute rationality, however, but moral responsibility breaks the spell, demands more than enchantment, rises to humanity's adulthood, to what Kant and Levinas call "maturity." Faith can no longer mean irresponsibility, nonresistance to evil, uncomplaining acceptance of all and everything. Rather, the poor need a shield from the rich, the weak from the strong, the few from the many—this shield, this protection, is justice, the highest calling of philosophy and religion, indeed, of the human adventure. The responsibilities of moral responsibility are out of control because they would stand up to control, as the "power of powerlessness," exerting their exigency on the singularity of a selfhood defined by its dedication to the other and others, selfhood defined by its nobility not its rationality—no matter what power may say or do!

Nor—less thrilling than the oblivion of frenzy, less exaggerated than an escapist faith—does "out of control" mean huddling away from the greater world into what is left of one's garden, *la dolce vita*, a self-satisfied and complacent comfortableness, indifferent to the travails of a larger world in order to enjoy the small pleasures in moderation, Epicurean existence, leaving others—the foolish and foolishly ambitious—to trouble themselves in a larger world that after all cannot be changed. Morality and justice are impossible in such a retreat from the world, which masks the evil of its own indifference in the name of moderation, "common sense," and "realism." The suffering of others is simply ignored. And thus violence, evil, and injustice are not only tolerated but are reinforced, supported, invigorated. An alleged amorality is in fact immorality.

In its own way, then, *out of control* is far more out of control, an upending of oneself in the unending vigilance of responsibility, subjectivity turned inside out by and for others. *Out of control* as the "I must help." "I am called." "Here I am." *Out of control* demands more than the busyness and conniving of self-interest, of accumulating things, property, money, of buying and selling, investing, accumulating. It cuts across the dyadic logic of mine or yours, gain or loss, friends or enemies, beyond and above the so-called business of life, practical, level-headed, a balance sheet of cost and benefit. Shelter, a home, things, belongings, food, fine dining, these are "goods," but not in an indifference to the suffering of others and even less at the cost of the suffering of others. To have property is no less than to have what to give. *Out of control* as generosity, giving to and for the other and all others ultimately without reserve, without end—"dying for the other" as the ultimate structure of morality, "God forbid." One is never done giving, never done with kindness, never kind enough, always guilty, without publicity, without position, without recognition or award—maddening to a system that counts only what can be counted. The true world is unseen. *Out of control* as care for the other incumbent upon the self as its true self, nonsubstitutable, singularizing, an unchosen *election* to service—humanity as service to others. Outrage to economics. Outrage to balance sheets, bottom lines, cost-benefit analysis. Outrage to control systems. Yet their very *raison d'être*. The nakedness of the human, face-to-face, one serving another, alleviating suffering—this is the high sense of "out of control" to which the title of this volume aspires. The present volume is only an aspiration. It is unworthy, no doubt, but hopefully not too unworthy, for its only aspiration is to aim with clarity and intelligence in the right direction.

"To love the neighbor," Levinas comments, "is thyself." Kindness. Love. Compassion. Care. Generosity. Charity. Sacrifice. Responsiveness. Dignity. Responsibility. Humaneness. The words are legion. What they refer to, what they encourage, is what counts. What is *most precious* is called by many names. But in the end the personal name, really the naked unnamable singularity of each person, whatever their name, is what trumps all. Because what is highest has neither name nor identity—never has, never will, yet it is the Archimedean point of the world: alleviating suffering, moral responsibility, upon which all the justice of the world—what Levinas very realistically refers to as "the little humanity that adorns the world" and "the little cruelty our hands repudiate" (OBBE, 185)—is built.

Chapter One

Levinas, Spinozism, Nietzsche, and the Body

Rejection of "Spinozism" means more than a rejection of the philosophy of Baruch Spinoza. It includes the philosophy of Spinoza, but it also comprises the thought of such apparently disparate figures as Hegel, Marx, Freud, Heidegger, and, as I shall argue, Nietzsche. What does Levinas mean by "Spinozism," and what is his argument against it? How is Spinozism manifest in Nietzsche? These are the questions that guide the present inquiry.

Levinas's Rejection of Spinozism

Levinas's opposition to Spinozism and his reasons for it are summed up in the final sentence of the concluding subsection, entitled "Separation and Absoluteness," of the first of the four sections of *Totality and Infinity*: "Thought and freedom come to us from separation and from the consideration of the Other [*Autrui*]—this thesis is at the antipodes of Spinozism" (105). Separation, and the "consideration of the Other" that follows from such separation, stand opposed, radically opposed, to the absoluteness that determines all Spinozism. What does this mean?

The absolute of Spinozism works by denying the *transcendence* of thought and freedom because, *first* of all, it denies the "separation" or radical independence of the human subject. Rejecting transcendence—for reason, logic, *Geist*, power, existence, language—it is thus "monist" or "pantheist," a philosophy of "immanence" and "totality."

Ethics, in contrast, is based in separation, which is to say, the "autonomy" or independence of the subject, the free initiative that constitutes its agency. And owing to this independence of each subject it takes seriously from the start the otherness of one subject in relation to another.[1] For Levinas the irreducibility of each subject and, based on this, of the intersubjective, is a condition for the very "humanity of the human." Spinozism, in contrast, denies the finality and hence the legitimacy of the independence of these dimensions of signification. It denies individual agency and social humanity in the name of a greater totality within which alone they are said to find their meaning. It is precisely this denial that also prevails in the thought of Friedrich Nietzsche, though by embracing the body rather than the mind, it takes a new and distinctive form—closer to our contemporary sensibility—beyond the Spinozism of Spinoza.

First, by "separation" Levinas means the independence of the human subject, interiority distinct from both (1) the amorphous anonymity Levinas calls the "there is" (*il y a*), an *apeiron* of being that threatens the identity, however minimal, of all that is distinct with dissolution from below, as it were; and (2) the radical transcendence of the other person, which calls to and calls forth the subject from above, with the exigency of moral obligation. The initial inwardness of separation must not be understood as a self-positing, as self-consciousness, say, or as an act of representation or judgment, whether affirmative or negative. Instead, Levinas speaks of "created" being, not in the credulous religious sense of a miraculous existence posited *ex nihilo* but rather as being born as hypostatic embodiment, existence in and through a primitive "reflexivity" of self-sensing. The originary base of initiative, agency and free will, then, occurs beginning not with self-consciousness but from out of a circuit of sensing and sensations. It is in this self-satisfaction of the senses, in the instantaneousness of self-sensing, that subjectivity breaks from anonymous being. "For an existent is an existent," Levinas writes in the paragraph prior to the one in which he announces his opposition to Spinozism, "only in the measure that it is free, that is, outside of any system, which implies

---

1. Commentators have noted that ethical transcendence in Levinas means responsibility for the other person, while for Kant it is respect for the moral law, hence more exactly "autonomy" in the etymological sense of this term, assuming that the Greek *nomos* is best translated as "law."

dependence" (TI, 104). The independence of separation, then, sets up an "unconditioned," an absolute, but not the absolute of a larger system within which it makes sense. Rather it is an absolute as independence from anonymity on the one side and any englobing context on the other. It is not the absolute of a well-provisioned fortress but, qua embodiment, of an exceptional vulnerability, sensibility as exposure itself. The embodied subject—if one remains faithful to its phenomenological appearance—is thus at once independent and dependent.

Second, by "consideration of the Other" Levinas turns from separation as the sensuousness of the self's independence from dissolution into anonymous being to separation as the nonsubstitutability or "election" of human responsiveness to another person in moral responsibility to and for that other person. If anonymous being is "below," then the other person is "above," in an orientation or verticality that is originally ethical rather than ontological. Here it is a matter of the transcendence of the other, but more specifically such transcendence qua moral imperative. It is not that the other person must articulate a request, such as "Feed me," or "Lend me some money," but that the alterity or transcendence of the other person appears as irreducibly other or transcendent only through its ineradicable morally obligating quality. The face of the other is already as such a moral command. Encounter with the other, always already a moral imperative, is thus singularizing and asymmetrical. Regardless of how you relate to me, with love or hate, peace or violence, I am always already disturbed by you, disrupted in my homeostasis, troubled out of my self-complacency, bothered in my being-at-home with myself and the world, because in your embodied alterity, your "face"—which is also always a vulnerability—you demand from me a moral responsibility, that in my very being I be for-you. It is important to keep in mind—and we will return again and again to this point—that this structure, despite our occasional reliance on the verb "to be" in discussing it, exceeds ontology. Because human being begins in the separation of embodiment, in flesh and blood, in sensibility, when I encounter the other person, who is thus always a concrete flesh-and-blood being, that other person arises always already as an imperative responsibility for me—a responsibility that cannot be reduced to either my being or the other's being. It is from the other's separation, from the other's independence, from anonymity and from me, that the other transcends my projections and representations and unavoidably disturbs my own self-circuits, from the deepest constitutive layer of self-sensing all the way to higher levels of signification found in worldliness, labor, representation, and knowledge.

The *relation* between I and Other, terms that remain separate yet in relation, the independent subject and the transcendent other, occurs precisely and only as a moral relation, for it is only as a moral relation that radically separate beings can both be respected in their alterity from one another and yet for all that also be in genuine proximity. It is a unique relation that philosophy traditionally misunderstood precisely and paradoxically because of philosophy's own commitment to knowledge. The moral relation *as moral* cannot be looked at from the outside, cannot be comprehended. It occurs in a relationality within which human subjects are always already implicated—commanded—in the first person singular. "I and you" is not reducible to "same and other"—though for knowledge these pairs must be indistinguishable. The peculiar conjunction or valence of morality and singularity is indeed the central "thesis" of Levinas's entire philosophy, though its centrality as its intelligibility comes not as theses, themes, propositions but as claims, impositions, provocations, imperatives. Philosophy insists that knowing must know only as "internal relations," so that the moral relation can only appear to it as an impossible "external relation." But between human beings, internal relation is already an externalization. "Here," Levinas writes, "the relation connects not terms that complete one another and consequently are reciprocally lacking to one another, but terms that suffice to themselves" (TI, 103). As we shall see, this means that Levinas's opposition to Nietzsche is based not on some a priori idealist metaphysics, as one might at first sight imagine, or as a partisan of Nietzsche would certainly prefer to interpret it, but rather on a different conception of the nature and meaning of the human body and embodied sociality. Unlike Levinas's opposition to Spinoza's Spinozism, then, which is an opposition to abstract or intellectualist rationalism, Levinas's opposition to Nietzsche's Spinozism meets Nietzsche on his own grounds, on the terrain of the body.

Spinozism, in any case, constitutes itself by rejecting both elements: separation and transcendence. It does this in one fell swoop by affirming the primacy, indeed the totality, of context over terms, what in Spinoza's case is known as "pantheism." In Spinoza's case, more specifically, the comprehensive totality is taken to be the systematic, universal, and necessary knowledge of modern science; and in Nietzsche's case it is the differential play of will to power. Therein resides the meaning of Spinoza's famous refusal in his *Ethics* "to conceive man in nature as a kingdom within a kingdom" (III, Preface, 102). Spinoza treats humans exactly as he does all other entities: as objects subject to a strict "geometrical" logic. (To be sure, he cannot succeed in this treatment, but all slips and residues are denied, denounced, or hidden.) To deny that humanity is a kingdom within a kingdom, to deny that beyond its distinctness it is somehow special, Spinoza must and does at once deny the independence of the self and the transcendence of the other. Responding to the manner in which these two dimensions had previously been understood, taking this position translates for Spinoza into a denial—based in rational demonstration—of the reality of both free will and morality, with attendant polemics against the ignorance and illusions of those who would assert otherwise. Heir to the rationalist tradition of Western thought, Spinoza bases his denials on the root affirmation: "Will and intellect are one and the same thing" (E, II, Prop. 49, Cor., 96). For Nietzsche, as we know, the independence of the subject, its alleged freedom, is also an untruth, also an error, whose persuasiveness derives from a "seduction of language" (GM, I, 13; 45), a "grammatical error" mistaking the subject-predicate form of a proposition for the substance-attribute character of reality.[2]

How does Levinas respond to such thought? Commentators usually focus on Levinas's emphatic idea of the other person's transcendence, the imposition of the alterity or "face of the other." No doubt such a focus reflects how genuinely striking this idea is and how central it is to all of Levinas's thought. Nevertheless, at the same time we must always also recognize that such transcendence is never an abstract concept, never a "relation" whose sense can make sense independent of its own manifestation or nonmanifestation in the most concrete of all concrete relations, that is, in its ethical sense as *my moral obligation, my responsibility to and for the other person*. That is to say, the "terms" of this relation are two sensuous beings vulnerable to suffering and

---

2. GM, I, 13: "Just as the common people distinguish lightning from the flash of light and takes the latter as *doing*, as the effect of a subject which is called lightning, just so popular morality distinguishes strength from expressions of strength, as if behind the strong individual there were an indifferent substratum which was at *liberty* to express or not to express strength. But no such substratum exists; there is no 'being' behind doing, acting, becoming; 'the doer' is merely a fiction imposed on the doing—the doing itself is everything."

pain, capable of being wounded, violated, ever hostage, as it were, to the slings and arrows of material existence. In other words, the separation of the self, its embodiment, its sensibility, is no less central to Levinas's thought than the ethical transcendence that such a way of existence calls forth. The self, whose origin as a separate being lies in self-sensing, is the condition that, in encountering the other person, is reconditioned, as it were, into the singularity of an asymmetrical moral responsibility to and for the other person. To make a distinction important to Levinas's thought, we can say that the self *originates* in self-sensing but *begins* in responsibility, the latter impossible and unnecessary without the former. Without embodiment there would be no suffering to remedy, and no way to provide remedies. Hands are not only ready or present, they can also beg, as they can also give. First question of ethics: How, without arbitrary fiat, without reducing it to an integral part of a whole, and without resorting to the theological fiction of a "soul," does Levinas defend the independence of the subject, a condition of moral singularity?

Self-Sensing

That subjectivity emerges from anonymous being in and as self-sensing, in and as an embodied way of being both engaged and disengaged in elemental sensations, is perhaps the earliest theme—chronologically—of Levinas's own thought. It appears already in 1935 in an essay entitled "On Escape," when Levinas was fresh from his training in Husserlian phenomenology and saw—as had the whole philosophical world—the brilliant use to which Heidegger had made of it in *Being and Time* to explicate the most concrete, existential significations of worldly human being. In "On Escape" Levinas describes the deepest constitutive layer of the emergent existent in terms of embodiment, and embodiment in terms of the unity of a dual movement or restlessness, at once entrapment, enclosure, self-compression, freighted with its own materiality, backed up against its own being, on the one hand, and rebellion, desire to escape, urge to break from the circuit of its own immanence, on the other. Such an existence that originates in a self-circuit of sensations at the same time wants out. "The necessity of fleeing," he writes, "is put in check by the impossibility of fleeing oneself . . . precisely the fact of being riveted to oneself, the radical impossibility of fleeing oneself to hide from oneself, the unalterably binding presence of the I to itself" (OE, 64). "In nausea," he continues (years before Sartre's novel of the same name), "—which amounts to an impossibility of being what one is—we are at the same time riveted to ourselves, enclosed in a tight circle that smothers" (66). Already, as a good phenomenological researcher, Levinas's account stands as a corrective to Heidegger's. In contrast to the Heideggerian analysis of Dasein, whose deepest significance or "authenticity" is to exist as the opening of an "ecstatic" subjectivity anxious before its own death, and as such already a form of self-understanding open to the revelation of being, for Levinas it is precisely the unbearable but inescapable self-compression, self-entrapment, self-sensing of sensuous embodiment that "*is the very experience of pure being*" (67).

Let it be noted, too, that this difference between Levinas and Heidegger—already clear in 1935—regarding the root sense of existence will make all the difference in separating their respective paths: Heidegger's, which has little to say about embodiment beyond the anxiety before death, single-mindedly pursuing the revelatory character of being, the "question of being" that is opened by Dasein's ecstatic existence; and Levinas's alternative account, always sensitive to embodiment as sensuous existence, which leads, in Levinas's thought, to the centrality of one person responding morally to the mortal suffering and vulnerability undergone by another. Despite the apparent concreteness of Heidegger's analyses in *Being and Time*, it is as though in all his subsequent thinking while there is "mortality" there is no body, no body as locus of suffering, wounds, violence, no unsurpassable vulnerability, in a thought that—pursing philosophy's idealist inclinations—is given over to a hearkening to the "poetic thinking" of being. Already in 1935, in other words, by his attentiveness to the meaning of existence as self-sensing, one can see the grounds for Levinas's commitment to the primacy of ethics over ontology.

After the war, Levinas will again return to this theme, the separation or "solitude" of sensuous subjectivity, extending his earlier reflections in the phenomenological analyses found in *Existence and Existents* and *Time and the Other*, his first two original philosophical books, both published in 1947. In *Existence and Existents* he speaks of self-sensing as "fatigue and indolence" (24). "There exists a weariness," he writes, "which is a weariness of everything and everyone, and above all a weariness of oneself" (24). "Indolence makes one prostrate, idleness weighs us down, afflicts us with boredom" (28). Or employing more traditional philosophical language to describe the structure of this doubled-over sensibility: "There is a duality in existence, an essential lack of simplicity. The ego has a self, in which it is not only reflected, but with which it is involved like a companion or a partner; this relationship is what is called inwardness" (28). Regarding the second moment of separation, the desire for transcendence, *Existence and Existents* goes on to describe the efforts of such a self to escape itself into the world, being-in-the-world across the ecstatic time (projective and retentive), the "temporality" of labor, action, and representation, and finally, successfully, in the transcendent time of sociality. And there lies the segue to *Time and the Other*. *Time and the Other* covers the same ground as *Existence and Existents* and also ends in the liberation from the immanence of embodiment, worldliness and knowledge, via the only relation whose transcendence is genuinely able to break being's adherence to itself, namely, the transcendence of the other person morally encountered. Time as temporality, as *ekstasis*, cannot make this break, but the time of the other person, what in his later thought Levinas will call "diachrony," is able to accomplish this transcendence, whose ultimate meaning lies in morality and justice.

It is only after being prepared by these careful phenomenological studies that in his master work, *Totality and Infinity*, the transcendence of the other person receives its full articulation beyond the epistemological confines of phenomenology, as an *ethical* transcendence. Yet here too in *Totality and Infinity*, the entire second section, entitled "Interiority and Economy," is again devoted to what are now even more careful, closer, and more precise phenomenological analyses of the self as embodied and of the embodied self's futile—in the sense that they remain immanent—efforts to escape its self-enclosure, its immanence, through the world, through labor, activity, and representational consciousness. After once again having laid the groundwork of the independence and solitude of the embodied self, Levinas *then* turns to consider "Exteriority and the Face" (title of section 3), that is, the transcendence of the other person encountered as moral imperative, a transcendence that radically breaks with the circuits of immanence, radically breaks with being and non-being, the parameters of ontology, in a responsibility that rises to a higher, indeed to the highest, calling: to alleviate the suffering of others.

Levinas's second major work, *Otherwise than Being or Beyond Essence*, also returns to the embodied self, but this time to examine and elaborate its new way of being—shamed and responsible—responding to and suffering for the other. Thus the deepening or refinement of Levinas's thought follows the progression of the body or the progression of ethics, each in relation to the other: beginning in embodied solitude, elaborated through the pathways of worldliness, jolted by the face or transcendence of the other, and responding as an embodied responsibility for-the-other toward the other's vulnerability. These are not chronological movements, to be sure, but rather a matter of conditioned and conditioning, where the unconditioned solitary self is "reconditioned," or decommissioned, or deposed, by the "noncondition" of the alterity of the other person. Here too in the moral structure of being for-the-other, undergone in the first-person singular, the language and impact of embodiment remains: the self is traumatized, "turned inside out" by and for the other "as though its very skin were still a way to shelter itself in being, exposed to wounds and outrage, emptying itself in a no-grounds, to the point of substituting itself for the other, holding on to itself only as it were in the trace of its exile" (OBBE, 138). The passivity of the body is not surpassed or overcome in a pure freedom, but now as responsibility the self is a bodily agency responsive because "pierced" by the imperatives of the other, in a "suffering for the other" that holds a place higher than the self-initiated freedom of activity and reflection (Sartre) or the other-initiated freedom of being (Heidegger) or nature (Jonas).

Attentive to the body, to the concrete, not only as existence but as "transascendence" as well, to use the term Levinas borrows from Jean Wahl (TI, 35), such is the moral elevation Levinas calls the "humanity of the human," a life nobly lived, "loving the neighbor as oneself." The human is not defined by its being but by the better-than-being. Morality is not to be enacted as a disembodied spirituality but as a concrete giving, with hands to give, hands to receive, with words to speak, with food to provide, with mouths to feed, exposed skin to cover, and first of all simultaneous with the giving of things as a giving of oneself to the other. Humanity begins in kindness.

The True and the Good: "Dangerous Life"

The true self therefore is not literally true, a function of knowing or self-reflection. Rather it is good. In this way Levinas joins and prolongs the Socratic-Kantian tradition of philosophy whereby ethics rather than science is primary. By "good" Levinas does not mean an innate inclination, predilection, or disposition, or a grace bestowed, which certain philosophers and theologians have hypothesized but never proven and which the recurrent horrors of history, especially the vast and state-sanctioned murders perpetrated in the twentieth century, clearly belie. Rather the good arises through provocation, as response, as the self's efforts to alleviate the suffering of others, as my moral responsibility. On its own, like any other entity, the self would simply continue, persist, and endure, worn down over time by external forces, preserving its forces by repair, or even aggrandizing its powers, depending on what sort of entity it is. As an entity like any other entity the forces of good and evil, justice and injustice, have no inner play. "No one," Levinas has written twice, "is good voluntarily" (OBBE, 11, 138). The nobility of the self, its rising to a being-for-the-other before being-for-itself, comes from exteriority, from the other as command, as obligation on the self, as solicitation of my responsibility. The good is higher than one's own being, better. At the same time, as we shall see, it is through this very goodness that there can be truth, the universal joining of myself and the other across knowledge. The issue of the relation of the good to the true is complex and all of its nuances cannot be presented here in this chapter, but because this matter is important in our understanding of Levinas's critique of Spinozism generally and of Nietzsche's reevaluation of the value of knowledge, the following brief remarks will here suffice to indicate the broad contours of the relation of the true and the good.

Truth in contrast to opinion is justified knowledge, propositions supported by appropriate and sufficient evidence. Beyond the legitimate claims of coherence and correspondence theories of truth, that is, that true statements must indeed correspond with that about which they make their claims, and that they must not contradict one another, propositions which are candidates for truth must also be independently validated by an intersubjective community of truth seekers. That I say something is so, that I have seen the evidence that it is so, is not sufficient for a proposition's truth validation until others too have seen the same evidence and confirmed the same correspondence of claim and reality, and claim and claim. To be sure, the truth of the claim has its own independence, or, more precisely, regarding so-called objective claims, the case to which the truth refers is the case independent of observation and articulation (more distinctly in Newtonian or macro-cases and less distinctly in Heisenbergian or micro-cases), but such independence as a *truth claim* depends in both instances, as in all cases, on supplementary intersubjective confirmation. Regarding "subjective," humanistic, or hermeneutic claims, the necessary interplay between proposition and proposer is even more tightly woven, because such claims directly apply to the one who makes them as a person rather than an object. One might say, then, that with regard to all truth claims, whether naturalistic or humanistic, there is an *inner dialectical interplay* between truth and truth seekers, between truth and human beings we can say more broadly.

Levinas draws our attention to something else, but it is intimately related to the dialectic of truth. It is to the fact that statements, proposition, theses, hypotheses, and the like, neither come out of the sky nor are hidden within "minds." Whether they are proposed as truths or intended for different purposes, statements, including potential truth claims, are first of all *enunciations*, significations said by persons to other persons. Statements may not all be Austin's "performatives," but they are all sooner or later intimately bound to illocutionary acts. There is a *saying* that underlies and charges the *said*. It is to the ineradicable ethical character of this more than linguistic operation—saying—that Levinas calls attention. Enunciation or saying, the discursive character of speech as communication—what Levinas calls its "accusative" dimension—is the source of all that is said, proposed, stated, even if it does not appear within propositions, theses, or themes, that is to say, within what is said. The inaccessibility of saying, which always transcends and yet brings forth the said, functions therefore as a sort of "paralogism," to use Kant's term, except that its orientation is not logical or epistemological but moral, a matter of ethics, of the other's elevation and the self's ennoblement, the good above being. That the "saying" that exceeds the "said" is not and cannot become a theme is certainly a difficulty for philosophical reflection attached to epistemology and perhaps explains its neglect in the philosophical tradition, but this difficulty nowise justifies the exclusion or occlusion of the primacy of saying, qua moral orientation, in the upsurge of meaning.

Communication is not simply a matter of making private thoughts public, as if everything is already accomplished within the confines of something certain philosophers designate "mind," and then empirically brought out of this private domain to be made public to others.

Enunciation is elicited. Why speak at all, what could possibly motivate speech, if everything is really said and done within one's own mind? Speaking would be the ruin of truth not its confirmation. And let us note here, no doubt prematurely, but in anticipation, that for Spinoza "an idea, being a mode of thinking, consists neither in the image of a thing nor in words" (E, II, Prop. 49, Scholium, 97). In contrast to Spinoza's Platonic idealism, communication—saying—is not simply added to truth owing to human imperfection. I cite Levinas at some length regarding this point because it is both subtle and crucial if we are to properly understand how ethics is "first philosophy" and the source of truth.

> Those who wish to found on dialogue and on an original *we* the upsurge of egos, refer to an original communication behind the *de facto* communication (but without giving this original communication any sense other than the empirical sense of a dialogue or a *manifestation* of one to the other—which is to presuppose that *we* that is to be founded), and reduce the problem of communication to the problem of its certainty. In opposition to that, we suppose that there is in the transcendence involved in language a relationship that is not an empirical speech, but responsibility. . . . Communication with the other can be transcendence only as a dangerous life, a fine risk to be run. . . . Here there is proximity and not truth about proximity, not certainty about the presence of the other, but responsibility for him without deliberation, and without the compulsion of truths in which commitments arise, without certainty. . . . The trace in which a face is ordered is not reducible to a sign. . . . To thematize this relation is already to lose it, to leave the absolute passivity of the self. (TI, 119, 120, 121)

The other person as other, the imposition of an alterity beyond what is said but through what is said, signifies prior to empirical speech, solicits our response, which is also beyond what is said, in a communication that leaps, as it were, "as a dangerous life," to use Levinas's formula (one that frontally challenges Nietzsche's "live dangerously"), from one interiority to another, a communication in which one responds to another prior to the certainties of truth, responds to the other as other, that is to say, takes responsibility for the other first, before all self-interest, before true or false. It is in the risk of this moral responsibility—solicitation and response, the "saying of the said"—wherein lies the source of signification, including the rigorously controlled significations that constitute truth, which is required by the larger project of human justice.

Nietzsche's Spinozism

It is profoundly revealing that, how and to what extent, Nietzsche, despite his undeviating and fundamental criticisms of Spinoza's rationalism, enthusiastically embraced Spinoza as his "precursor." To be sure, Nietzsche embraced Spinoza not because he learned Spinozism from Spinoza. As a young man Nietzsche had studied the classics and philology; he encountered other philosophers later and haphazardly. His exuberant embrace of Spinoza, as we shall see in a moment, expresses rather more Nietzsche's belated perception that Spinozism was agreeable to his own thought, indeed a mirror of it, than any labor of Nietzsche in discipleship to Spinoza. In any event, Nietzsche's self-declared genealogical homage to Spinoza finds its clearest and fullest articulation in a postcard of July 30, 1881, to his close friend and former colleague at Basel, Professor Franz Overbeck. Here is the postcard in full:

> I am utterly amazed, utterly enchanted. I have a *precursor*, and what a precursor! I hardly knew Spinoza: that I should have turned to him just *now*, was inspired by "instinct." Not only is his over-all tendency like mine—making knowledge the *most powerful* affect—but in five main points of his doctrine I recognize myself: this most unusual and loneliest thinker is closest to me precisely in these matters: he denies the freedom of the will, teleology, the moral world order, the unegoistic, and evil. Even though the divergences are admittedly tremendous, they are due more to the difference in time, culture, and science. *In summa*: my lonesomeness, which, as on very high mountains, often made it hard for me to breathe and made my blood rush out, is now at least a twosomeness. Strange. (Kaufmann, 92)

The five points Nietzsche names in this postcard can be summed up in one basic principle of agreement: denial of the metaphysical underpinnings of morality. It is morality, of course, that requires a human will or agency subject to judgment, that is to say, a will or decision-making process in some significant sense *free*, unconditioned, uncompelled; and it is morality too that affirms purposiveness, the aim or goal of doing good rather than evil, opposing evil, promoting goodness and justice; toward this end it is morality also that declaims and exhorts the superiority of selflessness to selfishness. Nietzsche is also certainly right about his alliance with Spinoza. In his *Ethics*, Spinoza had clearly argued for the falseness, indeed the illusoriness, of all the metaphysical notions upon which morality is based. All moral notions, hence all ethics in the traditional sense, are but products of deluded imagination, ignorance, not reason. They are unscientific, subjective rather than objective, and only hold sway for the ignorant masses driven by their passions, their bodily desires. Moral notions and their ethical underpinning have no truth-value, as is known by the few, the scientists and philosophers who know better, who, driven by their intellects (*amor intellectualis*), know scientifically (*ratio* and *scientia intuitiva*) the truth that the universe unfolds by strict and unbreakable necessity. A decade and many books later than his postcard, in *Twilight of the Idols* (published just weeks after his own mental breakdown in early January 1889), in one of his last and most unrestrained and extravagant books, Nietzsche again formulates, but in his own name and as his own, Spinoza's position as follows:

> One knows my demand of philosophers that they place themselves *beyond* good and evil—that they have the illusion of moral judgment *beneath* them. This demand follows from an insight first formulated by me: *that there are no moral facts whatever*. Moral judgment has this in common with religious judgment that it believes in realities which do not exist. Morality is only an interpretation of certain phenomena, more precisely a *mis*interpretation. Moral judgment belongs, as does religious judgment, to a level of ignorance at which even the concept of the real, the distinction between the real and the imaginary, is lacking: that at such a level "truth" denotes nothing but things which we today call "imaginings." (55)

Certainly the insight that good and evil are but the illusory products of ignorance was not "first formulated" by Nietzsche, except perhaps in the most literal sense, or perhaps as of a piece with Nietzsche's entire outlook. On this score Spinoza preceded him, to be sure, as did Julien Offray de La Mettrie and the Marquis de Sade. But what matters attribution! While still agreeing with Spinoza's perspective on morality of more than two centuries earlier, Nietzsche has here conveniently forgotten his name. Of course, in a few days in his letter to Jacob Burckhardt of January 6, 1889, Nietzsche will also forget his own name, or rather, famously, he will embrace "every name in history" (Kaufmann, 684).

Nietzsche's Differences from Spinoza

Keeping in mind their fundamental agreement regarding the ignorance and illusion, indeed the nonexistence of morality except as a lie (useful or otherwise), let us look more closely at the divergences separating Nietzsche's Spinozism from Spinoza's. We are guided by Nietzsche's postcard: "Even though the divergences are admittedly tremendous, they are due more to the difference in time, culture, and science." Though there are several divergences, I want first to mention the shift from a theological to a secular world, and second to mention the shift from eternity in Spinoza to historical consciousness in Nietzsche, in order to turn to a third most decisive difference, namely, a shift from Spinoza's logicist or mechanistic paradigm to Nietzsche's vitalist one. While Spinoza is most concerned with scientific truth, Nietzsche is most concerned with healthy and strong life. Indeed, Nietzsche's much-vaunted nineteenth-century appreciation for historical consciousness is itself thoroughly oriented by this third difference, as we find broadcast already in the title and content of one of his earliest writings, his "untimely" meditation on history in *On the Use and Abuse of History for Life*. History, like everything else that is of value to Nietzsche, is of value to the extent that it serves *life*.

From Mechanism to Vitalism

Charles Darwin's groundbreaking study *On the Origin of Species by Means of Natural Selection* was published in 1859. His *The Descent of Man* appeared in 1871. The world-changing influence of these books, not simply their specific scientific theses regarding the origin of humanity and the development of species (Nietzsche never accepted Darwin's doctrine of natural selection, which he considered slavish for being merely quantitative), but their general outlook, their biological rather than mechanistic perspective, had the profoundest influence on the spiritual life of Europe in general and on Nietzsche's thought in particular. Despite his particular grievances with Darwin, there is no question that it is biology—not logic, not mechanics—and even more specifically physiology that is the dominant medium of Nietzsche's thought.

Nietzsche insists repeatedly that in contrast to the deathless abstract ideas of previous philosophers his own thought is a "philosophy of life." In *The Gay Science*, for instance, he writes the following against Spinoza:

> These old philosophers were heartless; philosophizing was always a kind of vampirism. Looking at these figures, even Spinoza, don't you have a sense of something profoundly enigmatic and uncanny . . . mere bones, mere clatter . . . I mean categories, formulas, *words* (for, forgive me, what was left of Spinoza, *amor intellectualis dei*, is mere clatter and no more than that: What is *amor*, what is *deus*, if there is not a drop of blood in them?). (333)

Spinozism as dry bones, empty words, deathless, lifeless, "vampirism." Nietzsche's thought, in contrast, is from the start and throughout always and self-consciously meant as a philosophy of *life*, an incitement to health, vigor, strength, and growth, an attack on sickness, exhaustion, weakness, and decline. For Nietzsche these are not metaphors. His is a philosophy of the body, not of the mind. Body liberated from the cobwebs, skeletons, "categories, formulas, *words*," and all ascetic abstractions of the mind.

To be sure, Spinoza and Nietzsche are both elitists who divide humanity between the approved-of few and the disparaged many. Yet their few as well as their many, as their principles of discrimination, are quite different. Given his commitment to science, for Spinoza the few are those for whom the mind is primary, hence those who are intellectually active, knowers of the truth, scientists and philosophers, while the many are those for whom the body is primary, hence are passive, driven by their emotions and faulty imaginations, swayed by falsehood and moved by illusions. Nietzsche will both reverse this priority, valuing body above mind, and alter the meaning of both, seeing the mind as essentially sick, ill equipped for successful terrestrial life, and the body as a vital multiplicity of forces in contention. Following from this Nietzsche's most decisive evaluation of humanity is biological, a strengthening of "life," life understood as a contest between strength and weakness, health and sickness, growth and decline, vigor and exhaustion: "Everywhere," he writes, "the struggle of the sick against the healthy" (GM, 123).

While he often characterized himself as a *psychologist* to distance himself from what he took to be the ersatz objectivity of previous philosophers, his thought is more profoundly—and Nietzsche explicitly recognized this—that of a *physiologist*. His criticism of Christianity, for instance, is that its cures for ill health and weakness are only "affect medicines," treating only symptoms but not the body. And its greatest cure, which is to interpret suffering as "sin," to add "guilt" to suffering, actually makes humans sicker! To be genuinely cured, so Nietzsche would teach, better to jog by the cathedral on Sunday morning than to sit in its pews. This reversal and revaluation of the mind-body relation accounts for Nietzsche's high-spirited style, his dashes, his exclamation points, his ego, his brio, his tempo—all that Nietzsche calls "dancing." Like Walt Whitman, he wants the body to speak, to sing, to dance. It is no accident, then, that while for Spinoza, with his mechanistic model, the basic character of all things is *conatus essendi*, perseverance in being, *inertia*, for Nietzsche the basic character of all things is *will to power*, a dynamic *aggrandizing* play of forces. It is on this basis, making the will primary and interpreting the will as aggrandizing power, that Nietzsche criticizes Spinoza (and Darwin). In *The Gay Science* he writes:

> The wish to preserve oneself is the symptom of a condition of distress, of a limitation of the really fundamental instinct of life which aims at *the expansion of power* and, wishing for that, frequently risks and even sacrifices self-preservation. It should be considered symptomatic when some philosophers—for example, Spinoza who was consumptive—considered the instinct of self-preservation decisive and *had* to see it that way; for they were individuals in conditions of distress.
>
> That our modern natural sciences have become so thoroughly entangled in this Spinozistic dogma (most recently and worst of all, Darwinism with its incomprehensible one-sided doctrine of the "struggle for existence"), is probably

due to the origins of most natural scientists. . . . The struggle for existence is only an *exception*, a temporary restriction of the will to life. The great and small struggle always revolves around superiority, around growth and expansion, around power—in accordance with the will to power which is the will to life. (292)

We see in these citations the grounding of Nietzsche's thought in life, life interpreted as will to power, as will to expansion, growth, expenditure, always greater power, and its contrast to both Darwin's "survival of the fittest" meaning only progeny and Spinoza's *conatus essendi* meaning perseverance, both of which Nietzsche critically reinterprets accordingly as expressions of will to power, namely, as expressions of a physiology in distress and decline, weak and sick.

Will for Nietzsche is the universal character of all things, organic and inorganic. And this is why Nietzsche remains, no doubt despite himself, a metaphysician. He claims to know and evaluate the whole, even if at the same time he denies the very possibility of such judgments. Everything—each thing and all things—is made up of a struggle. Whatever is represents a temporary holding pattern of striving forces. Not a ratio of motion and rest, perseverance in being until disrupted, but forces held in contention, each force seeking ascendancy, more power, great dominion. It is Nietzsche's idea of a biological image, an image of "life." How Nietzsche knows what *everything* is he cannot say, but he nonetheless and repeatedly says it—or rather proclaims it. Spinoza, too, could not say how he knows that all things are ultimately one substance, or that each thing aims only to persist in its being. Such truths are simply self-evident, unquestionable. "A true idea involves absolute certainty," Spinoza explains; "Truth is its own standard" (E, II, Prop. 43, Scholium, 91, 92). Yet quite clearly Nietzsche's unquestioned truth, that everything is will to power, is not Spinoza's unquestioned truth, that all is one substance.

Given his commitment to life and hence to genealogy, Nietzsche does not ask *what* morality, politics, religion, or philosophy are but rather *who* believes or espouses this or that. The strong believe one thing, the weak another. One set of behaviors and ideas works for the healthy, another for the sick. Nietzsche's well-commented upon "perspectivalism," then, must be understood not simply as the claim that truth is the expression of a finite point of view, a claim made by many philosophers before and after Nietzsche, but also, more profoundly and more Nietzschean, the claim that perspective follows physiology, that perspective is the conscious expression of a certain biological state of health or sickness, strength or weakness. Nietzsche's attacks against Christianity, science, morality, and so much else in high European culture, are at bottom the expression of his rebellion against the asceticism that protects and preserves an *"impoverishment of life"* (GM, III, 25, 154). For Nietzsche the old ideals—truth, eternity, goodness, justice, piety—are just mental expressions of life turned against itself, expressions, in other words, of ill health. In contrast to such asceticism, Nietzsche demands greatness: *"great health"* in individuals and "grand politics" for nations. Nietzsche's positive philosophy, therefore, which rejects truth in the Spinozist sense and goodness in the Levinasian sense, because they are life-denying, products of sick bodies, embraces the lie, imagination, the body, the aesthetic, especially in the spirit of ancient Greek paganism, the spirit of Homer: celebration of victory, superiority, mastery, in war, in politics, in sport, in love, in all things—agon, splendor, and hegemony as greatness.

And this is why Nietzsche supports *art*, the artistic life, with its "will to lie," against religion, morality, and science. As early as 1872, in an unpublished work entitled "The Philosopher: Reflections on the Struggle between Art and Knowledge," pertinent to his differences with Spinoza, he had written: "History and the natural sciences were necessary to combat the middle ages: knowledge versus faith. We now oppose knowledge with *art*; return to life" (PT, 14). The artistic life, the willful lie, display, spectacle, is closest to the will to power, and this is why Nietzsche affirms it. And this is why, despite his agreements with Spinoza, Nietzsche sees in Spinoza, as in all rationalists and theologians, the vampire.

A question arises: affirming the artistic life, does not Nietzsche also affirm freedom of will? If this is so, would it not conflict with his fundamental agreement with Spinoza that there is no free will, and that free will is but the illusion suitable to the ignorant or the sick? It is a tricky question but a revealing one too. It perhaps has no fully satisfactory answer because both Nietzsche and Spinoza are caught in a bind when they deny free will and yet *recommend* that others *should* deny it also. In what, after all, lies the superiority of Spinoza's scientists over the ignorant masses? All one can say, perhaps, is that knowing is *less painful* than ignorance. The same necessary world unfolds for both scientist and ignoramus. Neither chooses anything really that has not already been determined for each. Spinoza promises "beatitude" to the man of science. Nietzsche resorts to the same sort of justification, holding out prospects of health and strength. But to discover that all is will to power, that consciousness itself is simply an aftereffect of will to power, its symptom, is to discover the necessity of the universe, even if that necessity is no longer the causal or deductive necessity of Spinoza's rationalism. Such a discovery, so Nietzsche asserts repeatedly, is "joyful." But is not such joy as determined as sadness and pain? Is this not why in other moments Nietzsche affirms *amor fati*, love of fate, and embraces the eternal return of the *same* as the truest joy?

Nietzsche thus ends up mimicking Spinoza's outlook and recommendation regarding causality, deduction, and beatitude: one should conform to necessity. Freedom lies in conformity. Freedom is necessity. It is philosophy's oldest conceit. For Nietzsche too to discover will to power is to embrace necessity. To embrace the eternal recurrence of all, this too is predetermined or not. Nietzsche writes in *Ecce Homo*, "My formula for greatness in a human being is *amor fati*: that one wants nothing to be different, not forward, not backward, not in all eternity" (258). Again Spinoza: eternity, but now the eternity of the ephemeral! Again, too, the promise of happiness, joy, beatitude. Here is Nietzsche's highest desire and highest joy: "to will eternity." "Joy," his Zarathustra declares, "does not want heirs, or children—joy wants itself, wants eternity, wants recurrence, wants everything eternally the same" (Z, IV, 434).

A life of complete conformity to will to power, without judgment, without regret, willing all and everything to the point that one would will it to recur eternally, such is the life of the overman, "beyond good and evil," beyond the history of ascetic humanity and its anti-natural ideals. "Joy wants the eternity of *all* things, *wants deep, wants deep eternity*" (Z, IV, 436). In contrast to the conformity recommended by Spinoza's Spinozism of the mind and intellect, grounded upon and bound within the intellection of substantial being, Nietzsche's brand of Spinozism demands a conformity of the body to body, aesthetics, and hence exalts imagination, more closely aligned with body than rationality, "liberated" to the nonprinciple of multiplicity, forces in ever-shifting alliances, bottomless production of masks of masks of masks without end.[3]

---

3. The first to underscore the bottomless protean character of Nietzsche's thought and life (the two cannot be separated) was Lou Andreas Salome in her Nietzsche book of 1894. Was it perhaps this same quality that made Nietzsche unsuitable for marriage?

Levinas contra Nietzsche's Spinozism

It is too obvious to emphasize that regarding the points upon which Nietzsche and Spinoza agree, namely, their mutual denial of "freedom of the will, teleology, the moral world order, the unegoistic, and evil," Levinas stands at their antipodes. The new question before us is whether Nietzsche's divergences from Spinoza deriving from changes in "time, culture, and science" introduce differences that somehow buttress and justify Spinozism in Nietzsche's case and enable Nietzsche to succeed vis-à-vis Levinas's opposition to Spinozism, where Spinoza's Spinozism failed. Does Nietzsche's biological-physiological model deriving from the body succeed in creating a new form of "beyond good and evil" naturalism impervious to Levinas's ethical challenge? The confrontation is important not simply as a scholarly exercise, but because Levinas and Nietzsche are both philosophers of embodiment and as such square off against one another at close quarters, within the frame of contemporary philosophy and as our contemporaries, rather than across the untenable dualisms of mind (or soul) and body that separates Spinoza's idealism from them both and no doubt from all non-theological consciousness.

Responsible Body

Just as Nietzsche's adoption of the body in its vitality, interpreted as multiple forces and will to power, in contrast to Spinoza's attachment to the mind and its representation of the world in terms of the unity of substantial being and the persistence of *conatus essendi*, stands as the greatest difference distinguishing Nietzsche's Spinozism from Spinoza's Spinozism, so too Levinas's notion of moral agency as embodied singularity elevated by moral responsibilities for the vulnerable other stands at the farthest antipode challenging the hegemony of the Nietzschean body. Certainly both Levinas and Nietzsche start with the body. But Nietzsche "joyfully" celebrates while Levinas would morally discipline its unchecked spontaneity and animal vitality.

Bespeaking the healthy body, Nietzsche articulates a philosophy of fragmentation, of various underlying forces each pulling in its own direction, with temporary provisional periods of stasis, reflected as surface ideas, images, or desires in consciousness. The imperative of Nietzsche's philosophy is always to go beyond such provisional stasis, to again set in motion the deeper forces that for the time being are held in check, to open up and accept the creative form-giving play—the will to power—that keeps everything in motion, in continual self-overcoming. "The whole surface of consciousness—consciousness *is* a surface—must be kept clear of all great imperatives" (EH, 254). To "love one's fate" is to give oneself over to the evanescent play of will to power whose mobility is the becoming of what is. The Nietzschean self is thus constantly reinventing itself, releasing itself into new energy configurations. Its "overcoming" is a constant shattering of the "idols" of any given conjured unity. It is in this sense that Nietzsche famously labels himself "dynamite" and he who "philosophizes with a hammer"—to explode the seductions of permanence, to exacerbate, release, and celebrate physiological forces. Consciousness must always be awakened, not to higher consciousness but to the depths of untapped bodily energies. The unity of mind is a prison, creates a prison, to escape the body. Thus for Nietzsche, the philosopher—who breaks from such a prison—is "a terrible explosive, endangering everything" (EH, 281). Nietzsche does not aim for progress in the Enlightenment sense of the term, as a cumulative movement of ever-greater self-consciousness as self-knowledge but rather provokes a collapse of precisely such consciousness by means of a release of the body into its own vital dynamism as an open and endless play of possibilities that consciousness retrospectively—always too late—can only grasp as a "schizoid" activity (to use Deleuze's felicitous term). "The last thing *I* should promise," Nietzsche writes in the preface to *Ecce Homo*, "would be to 'improve' mankind. No new idols are erected by me. . . . *Overthrowing idols* (my word for 'ideals')—that comes closer to being part of my craft" (217–218).

Levinas, too, as we have seen, is attuned to the body. His philosophy begins with the emergence of the existent from anonymous existence as an "enjoyment," a "self-sensing," a sphere of immanent sensations content and "bathing" in an elemental sensuousness. Such a description is true to the phenomenological origination of subjectivity as an independent existent. As a phenomenologist Levinas avoids, as Spinoza and Nietzsche do not, importing theoretical constructions—presuppositions really—such as "substance" or "will to power" into his analyses. We also saw that faithful to the evidence Levinas detects within the body's self-sensing not only enjoyment and contentment but also dissatisfaction, disturbance, desire for *escape*, for transcendence. Levinas discovers too that nothing bodily or worldly liberates the self from its own self-enchainment—not being-in-the-world, not instrumentality, not representation, not even being-toward-death. And certainly nothing *ex machina*. The only "answer" to its desire for transcendence must come from an outside truly exterior, beyond itself and beyond its worldly projections, whether practical or theoretical, but not something fantastic either. Such exteriority arrives in the encounter with the face of the other person. Not the visage of the other as phenomenon, but the face as "enigma," as absolute transcendence traumatizing in its exteriority as moral imperative.

We should never forget, then, that the moral encounter with the other, the famous Levinasian "face-to-face," is not some idealist or ethereal revelation. It is in no way abstract, and indeed there is nothing more concrete—it shocks like a trauma, and it shocks me, me in my uttermost first-person singularity as the one who is exclusively called upon to help. It is a bodily event: an internalization of the suffering, needs, destitution of the other person. It is the "other in me," to use Levinas's formula, or the self "for the other." The responsible self is thus "maternal," with the other more inside itself—as moral exigency—than its own self-interested selfhood. This transformation of the immanent body, the spontaneous body, the body as play of vital forces, into the body for-the-other is, as I have indicated, the central topic of Levinas's second major work, *Otherwise than Being or Beyond Essence*. In *Totality and Infinity* Levinas had focused primarily on the otherness of the other person, on the absolute transcendence of the other as moral imperative. In *Otherwise than Being or Beyond Essence*, in contrast, his primary concern is to show that and how such otherness "transubstantiates" or "de-nucleates" the embodied subject into responsible being—responsible body, maternal psyche, bearing the other morally.

Levinas's language, even and especially when speaking about morality, remains visceral, faithful to an embodied existence that suffers, existents who are hungry, wounded, afraid, and at the same time existents with the material wherewithal to help one another, with hands to give as well as to take, goods needed and offered, eyes and ears that listen, mouths that speak. In *Otherwise than Being or Beyond Essence*, for example, he writes:

> The tenderness of skin is the very gap between approach and approached, a disparity, a non-intentionality, a non-teleology. . . . Proximity, immediacy, is to enjoy and to suffer by the other. But I can enjoy and suffer by the other only

> because I am-for-the-other, am signification, because the contact with skin is still a proximity of a face, a responsibility, an obsession with the other, being-one-for-the-other. (90)

And:

> It is the passivity of being-for-another, which is possible only in the form of giving the very bread I eat. But for this one has to first enjoy one's bread, not in order to have the merit of giving it, but in order to give it with one's heart, to give oneself in giving it. (72)

The responsibility of the responsible self, the responsive self, too bodily, too passive to evade responsibility, lies in "its vulnerability, its exposedness to the other" (OBBE, 74). Morality is carnal rather than ethereal. The demands of the other are concrete, real, particular. The other's suffering becomes my own suffering: a suffering for the other's suffering. One does not approach the other with empty hands, or with a cold heart. In this way Levinas is certainly free of a Nietzschean charge that might apply to Spinoza, to have overvalued the mind, the intellect, "ideals," at the expense of the body. But of course, too, Levinas sees in responsiveness the true *greatness*—the glory—of humanity, whereas Nietzsche detects only weakness, sickness, hypersensitivity, and the inability to not respond. Nietzsche abhors above all "pity": to care for the other more than oneself. Nietzsche celebrates self-creation above all. For Levinas, of course, in this respect Nietzsche's is an upside-down world, or a world too real.

What does it mean for Nietzsche to criticize pity? What is the purpose of disparaging the taking of moral responsibility for one's neighbor or the risk-taking and personal sacrifice requisite to create a more just world? Is the "revaluation of all values" Nietzsche proposes really only feasible premised on a prior destruction of all so-called altruistic values? Does it produce anything more than an individual's private self-glorification, in a willful disregard of collateral social damage? Why call this "revaluation"? Where is the "value"? By what imperative, let us ask, *should* humans become events of nature? Is not such a project no less caught in the abstraction, the theorizing, the logic of rationalism and materialism, even if now energized by biology, by the body in place of the mind? Would not a genuine "revaluation of all values," if this expression is to make sense, rather be found, as Levinas teaches, in the true nobility that at once lives up to values and uplifts them—goodness, service, friendship, familial love, justice—to their proper height, incarnating values in one's own behavior and institutionalizing values in a just politics? Does anyone seriously imagine that humanity has even come close to accomplishing the values Nietzsche wants already to destroy? Is not such chaffing rather the expression of an adolescent perspective, irresponsibility itself? Who with a straight face, what mad person could declare that humans are presently so moral and the world presently so just—mission accomplished—that morality and justice, that humanism, have become obstacles, blocking our future, standing in the way of our greatness?

Against Nietzsche, as against Spinoza, it is not conformity to nature, whether substance or will, that is our highest vocation or, for that matter, the condition of our knowledge. Regarding such conformity from a practical point of view, we hardly need to be nudged let alone harangued to greater selfishness, a more animal nature, a more grasping self-interest. These come quite naturally. From a theoretical point of view also such directives, taken by themselves, erase the social conditions of their possibility and success, and certainly their desirability. Nevertheless, Nietzsche was certainly right that intellectual and practical distortions arise when body and desire are left out of account or misrepresented. Taking the body seriously, just as taking time and language seriously, constitute the very innovation, character, and advance of contemporary thought. But in his enthusiasm for body, and time and language, he was still wrong in attacking shame and pity, and the alleged desirability of a "new innocence." We are not innocent, just as we are not defined by our animality. Furthermore, despite the initial excitement of his iconoclasm, the thrill of transgression, shamelessness requires no additional advertising from philosophers. Levinas's insight is far deeper, and certainly far more mature, that we must not lose sight of what is most desirable. This lies not in our vast science, for all its greatness, nor in our technical know-how, for all the power this lends us, nor does it lie in an unrestrained vitality, for all the attraction of such release. What is most desirable, and wherein lies our true nobility, is not an "is" but an "ought," rising to the always difficult freedom of taking responsibility, in compassion for others, in daily acts of kindness, and by engaging in the long struggle for a just world, a world without violence, in community with others, in peace. Pursuing such ends comes not from the affected rhetoric of a fantastic revaluation of all values, which aims only to derail them, but by rising to a revitalization of values truly valuable.

Chapter Two

Prophetic Speech in Levinas and Spinoza (and Maimonides)

> Their national ideal was not "a kingdom of Priests," but "would that all the people of the Lord were Prophets.
>
> —Ahad Ha'am, "Priest and Prophet" (1893)

A remarkable occurrence is narrated in Numbers 11:26–29. The Jews are camped in the desert, years after having escaped slavery in Egypt. Joshua confronts Moses with the accusation that two men are prophesying in the Israelite camp without authorization. In a moment we shall see how Spinoza and Levinas interpret this incident in radically different ways. Here, in four verses, with the usual biblical literary economy, is the entire story:

> Two men remained behind in the camp, the name of one was Eldad and the name of the second Medad, and the spirit [*HaRuach*] rested upon them; they had been among the recorded ones, but they had not gone out to the Tent, and they prophesied in the camp. The youth ran and told Moses, and he said, "Eldad and Medad are prophesying in the camp."[1] Joshua, son of Nun, the servant of Moses since his youth, spoke up and said, "My lord Moses, incarcerate

---

1. Rashi, citing Sifre, records their prophesy: "Moses will die, and Joshua will bring Israel into the Land." In the Babylonian Talmud, Sanhedrin 17a, the rabbis record other versions of their prophecy.

them!" Moses said to him, "Are you being zealous for my sake? Would that the entire people of God could be prophets, if God would but place His spirit upon them!"

One senses right away why Nietzsche, despite his unbending animosity toward religion, so loved the Old Testament as he loved Homer. The greatness of Moses, his spiritual openness, his generosity, and above all his superlative humility, are here once again displayed. It is a glorious moment in human spirituality. Moses is not jealous for prophecy, indeed, quite the reverse: "Would that the entire people of God could be prophets"!

Spinoza contra Prophecy and Prophets
(*Theological-Political Treatise*)

The light of this glory is not to be found in Spinoza. No fear of *ruach haKodesh*, the "holy spirit," breaking out in his analyses. Instead, in commenting upon this same biblical text in the *Theological-Political Treatise*, we find Spinoza's usual strained and pinched reading. His exegesis appears in chapter 17, which is a defense of absolute and undistributed political sovereignty, in a Supplementary Note (no. 36) to a sentence in which Spinoza supports his thesis regarding absolute sovereignty with the historical claim that Moses in fact "held supreme kingship" and was jealous of his "supreme sovereignty" (190). Here is Spinoza's exegesis in full:

> In this passage two men are accused of prophesying in the camp, and Joshua urges their arrest. This he would not have done if it had been lawful for anyone to deliver God's oracles to the people without Moses' permission. But Moses thought fit to acquit the accused, and he rebuked Joshua for urging him to assert this royal right at a time when he was so weary of ruling that he preferred to die rather than continue to rule alone, as is clear from verses 14 and 15 of the same chapter.[2] For he replied to Joshua

---

2. Numbers 11:14–15: "I alone cannot carry this entire nation, for it is too heavy for me! And if this is how You deal with me, then kill me now, if I have found favor

thus: "Enviest thou for my sake? Would God that all the Lord's people were prophets!" That is to say, would that the right to consult God were vested in the entire people, who would thus be sovereign. Therefore Joshua's error lay not in the question of right but in the occasion of its exercise, and he was rebuked by Moses in the same way as Abishai was rebuked by David when he urged David to condemn to death Shimei, who was undoubtedly guilty of treason. See 2 *Sam.* Ch. 19 v. 22, 23. (239)

Spinoza's Moses is another Moses altogether. Despite his apparent largesse in this particular case, which will be explained, he is portrayed as jealous of his singular and exclusive right to prophecy, jealous of his absolute and exclusive sovereignty ("royal right"). For tactical or strategic reasons alone, "the occasion of its exercise," the fact that just at this moment Moses is weary, he provisionally puts off what according to Spinoza's reading would be a perfectly deserved and legitimate punishment of the two unauthorized prophesiers. The referenced analogy to the incident of David, Abishai, and Shimei confirms that this is how Spinoza reads the text, because there David too only provisionally and for strategic reasons delayed punishing Shimei, who had in fact betrayed him and who in fact he later had executed.

Spinoza's exegesis also asserts that independent prophesying was illegal, giving this as the very reason for Joshua's complaint, as if Joshua could not complain without the complaint only having to do with obeying or disobeying the law. This is a particularly forced reading inasmuch as Spinoza has just reminded his readers that Moses had moments earlier (verses 14 and 15) articulated an entirely nonlegalistic complaint to God regarding the burdensomeness of his solitary leadership. Nothing in the biblical text makes Spinoza's legalistic reading compelling. Especially because it seems more likely, that is to say, closer to the plain sense of the verses, that Joshua is reacting

---

in Your eyes, and let me not see my evil." In reply to Moses (Numbers 11:16–17) God tells him to "Gather to Me seventy men from the elders of Israel . . . I will increase some of the spirit that is upon you and place it upon them, and they shall bear the burden of the people with you, and you shall not bear alone." It seems then, contra Spinoza, that God Himself does thereby authorize the distribution of prophecy and sovereignty!

to an unprecedented situation, namely, two Israelites prophesying in the camp without Moses's permission and without, so it seems, prior histories of prophesying. More likely, then, Joshua is responding as we would expect a "servant of Moses" to respond, that is, unsure of how to respond to something so unprecedented and jealous for Moses's authority, while Moses himself, aware as usual of the humility necessary to rule wisely and indeed weary of the burdens of his solitary rule, is not jealous. Thus a more obvious reading would have the young Joshua, who is being groomed for rule and who will later indeed be invested with Moses's mantle of authority, being taught a great lesson in the humility of righteous leadership, in contrast to Spinoza's interpretation whereby Moses's lesson is one of prudence, diplomacy, *realpolitik*, indeed an instance of the deceit necessary to maintain absolute rule in the hands of his own exclusive sovereign authority.

Furthermore, if we may cast a more positive light on Moses's weariness, Spinoza has taken a leap of interpretive liberty to suggests that Moses's rebuke to Joshua, and his exalted claim "Would God that all the Lord's people were prophets!," implies that he, Moses, prefers that prophecy were "vested in the entire people, who would thus be sovereign." According to such a reading—unsupported by the text— Spinoza would have Moses preferring democracy for the Israelites who have just escaped more than two hundred years of slavery in Egypt, not to mention that this reading, as Spinoza most likely knew, goes entirely against Moses's response to the rebellion of Korach and his followers, who earlier in the text had indeed argued for democracy, and whom, for doing so, are severely rebuked by Moses and killed en masse by God.[3] Let us recall, too, that the entire argument of chapter 18 of the *Theological-Political Treatise* is a defense of the "assertion that every state must necessarily preserve its own form, and cannot be changed without incurring the danger of utter ruin" (211). So it does not seem likely that Spinoza is sincere in defending the idea that the Israelites who have been enslaved for more than two centuries should suddenly rule themselves democratically. Again all this makes it far more likely that Moses's exalted claim regarding prophecy is not intended to suggest

---

3. See Numbers, 16:1–17:35. "They gathered together against Moses and against Aaron and said to them, 'It is too much for you! For the entire assembly—all of them—are holy and God is among them; why do you exalt yourselves over the congregation of God?" (Numbers 16:3).

that the Israelites should change regimes from their present monarchy to a democracy, but rather, and contrary to Spinoza, that even under the current monarchy Moses sees nothing wrong, indeed, that he positively welcomes the word of other prophets speaking among the people. So contra Spinoza, it is during his own monarchic rule that Moses welcomes alternative sources of authority—a "division of power," we would now say—sources that would derive their authority not from him but from the same higher authority by which he rules.

This plainer or more obvious reading goes against the central argument of the entire "political" section of the *Theological-Political Treatise* (chapters 16–20), where in a variety of ways Spinoza, in agreement with Hobbes, defends the absolute and undistributed political sovereignty of the state, whether the sovereign regime is ruled by one person, several persons, or an entire population. Given that the *Theological-Political Treatise*, in contrast to the *Ethics*, is concerned primarily with revealed religion and the Hebrew Bible, it is no wonder that Spinoza's ire is directed specifically against prophets. Prophets, after all, are nothing if they are not ethical critics, castigators of kings, authorities, priests, Israelites, and all humanity. Prophecy is a risky and thankless job, and no biblical prophet accepts the load without resistance. But Spinoza, like Hobbes, but unlike Moses, would give all power to the state. It is no wonder then that in the second section of chapter 18, Spinoza remarks "that prophets, men of private station, in exercising their freedom to warn, to rebuke and to censure, succeeded in annoying men rather than reforming them," and that "such freedom brought religion more harm than good, not to mention that great civil wars also originated from the prophets' retention of so important a right" (207). The prophets are neither Spinozist nor Hobbesian. They will not be cowed or shut up by the government. And as for prophets only "annoying men rather than reforming them," Spinoza's reading of the Bible is highly selective, to say the least, unless he somehow had not heard of the Prophet Jonah's great saving effect on the vast metropolis of Nineveh.

Because of his defense of the absolute state, in his exegesis of Numbers 11:26–29 Spinoza wants to eliminate the independence of prophets—then and now. But his elimination of alterative views and alternative bases of authority is far more radical. "No private citizen," he writes unambiguously in chapter 19, "can know what is good for the state except from the decrees of the sovereign" (216). Right is not only a function of the state; it is created by the state. And only the state, sole source of right, knows what is right.

Let us recall too that throughout the "theological" sections of the *Theological-Political Treatise* (chapters 1–15), whose first two chapters are entitled "Of Prophecy" and "Of the Prophets," Spinoza argues that the distinguishing mark of a prophet, the definition of a prophet, has nothing to do with criticism or justice but rather depends on no more or less than a "vivid imagination." To be sure, the prophet's vivid imagination must be accompanied by "signs" and a good moral character, but Spinoza is skeptical of the second and has a political understanding of the third, so his emphasis clearly falls on the first, the "vivid imagination" (170). "[T]he prophets," Spinoza writes in chapter 1, "perceived God's revelation with the aid of the imaginative faculty alone, that is, through the medium of words or images, either real or imaginary" (19). In other words, there is no truth in the words of the prophets. And lacking truth, theirs is mere rhetoric, and against such rhetoric, Spinoza prefers the rhetoric of the state, that is, rhetoric backed by power, ensuring its success by warranting no power anywhere else.

That Spinoza holds the imagination in little esteem in the *Ethics* is obvious. There it is "the only cause of falsity" (II, Prop. 41), in contrast to the scientific truths that derive from knowledge of the second and third kind (II, Prop. 41, Scholium 2). And let us not be fooled: despite certain methodological protestations to the contrary,[4] it is the epistemology and metaphysics of his *Ethics* that guides and provides Spinoza the epistemological and metaphysical standards operative in the *Theological-Political Treatise*.[5] In the *Theological-Political Treatise* no less

---

[4]. Spinoza calls the "true method of Scriptural interpretation" to proceed "by allowing no other principles or data for the interpretation of Scripture and study of its contents except those that can be gathered only from Scripture itself and from a historical study of Scripture" (TPT, 87). But somehow he earlier concluded, presumably using this "method": "Therefore there can be no doubt that all the events narrated in Scripture occurred naturally" (TPT, 79). The latter may be true (and so the *Ethics* affirms), but surely it can not "be gathered only from Scripture itself."

[5]. Just as Spinoza is always aware, based in his philosophy, of the political core and consequences of religion, Levinas is no less aware of the political and religious consequences of Spinoza's philosophical rationalism. So, for instance, in *Totality and Infinity*, Levinas writes: "The difference between the two theses: 'reason creates the relations between me and the other' and 'the Other's teaching me creates reason' is not purely theoretical. The consciousness of the tyranny of the State—though it be rational—makes this difference actual. Does the impersonal reason, to which man rises in the third state of knowledge, leave him outside of the State?" (TI, 252). We shall return again and again to the political consequences of Spinozism.

than the *Ethics*, imagination and thus prophecy are quite explicitly denounced. In chapter 2 of the *Theological-Political Treatise* Spinoza writes: "Those with a more powerful imagination are less fitted for purely intellectual activity, while those who devote themselves to the cultivation of their more powerful intellect, keep their imagination under greater control and restraint, and they hold it in rein, as it were, so that it should not invade the province of intellect" (21). In chapter 1: "the imaginative faculty being fleeting and inconstant, the gift of prophecy did not remain with the prophets for long, nor did it often occur; it was very rare, manifesting itself in a very few men, infrequently even in them" (20). In the same chapter Spinoza notes that "there are no prophets among us today, as far as I know" (10), a claim that must be considered in the light of what Spinoza says in chapter 12, where he writes: "All men, Jews and Gentiles alike, have always been the same, and in every age virtue has been exceedingly rare" (146). It is not difficult to conclude that while Spinoza was all too aware that most humans let their imaginations run rampant, unchecked by intellect, he is skeptical if not entirely critical regarding the uniqueness of prophecy, and in any event concedes—no doubt with relief—only that it was "exceedingly rare." So much for Spinoza's exegesis of Numbers 11:26–29 whereby Moses's noble admiration and support for prophecy is turned into a political machination. For one or for all, prophecy—the "vivid imagination"—is for Spinoza no more than a particularly virulent form of ignorance. A democracy of prophets would be a democracy of dunces. In a word it would be anarchy, of which Spinoza like Hobbes is above all fearful.

In chapter 2 of the *Theological-Political Treatise* Spinoza declares the "moral certainty" of prophecy "inferior to natural knowledge, which needs no sign, but of its own nature carries [mathematical] certainty" (22). This is why in chapter 1 Spinoza declares that "although natural knowledge is divine ["divine," however, in the sense of the *Ethics* ("*Deus, sive Natura*"), meaning the eternal, immutable laws of nature and logic], its professors cannot be called prophets" (9–10), because professors, as Spinoza elaborates in supplementary note 2, teach only what students can also learn by themselves, using their own natural knowledge, while prophets, with their distinctive vivid imaginations (and signs and moral character) teach what can come exclusively only from God ["God" here *not* in the sense of the *Ethics*, of course, but rather the "Lawgiver," "King," "Father," etc., the God of popular biblical faith, i.e., a product of imagination!]. Later in the book, in chapter 11, Spinoza praises the superiority of the Epistles of the Apostles precisely because they are not written by prophets but by teachers and hence are of universal rather than only national import. Here the rationalism of the *Ethics* speaks all too clearly through the exegeses of the *Theological-Political Treatise*.

"Would that the entire people of God could be prophets"—in his nightmares Spinoza could hardly be haunted by a worse specter! All his writings, and certainly both the *Ethics*, written for those who know better, that is, for scientists and philosophers, and the *Theological-Political Treatise*, written for the prudential, that is, wise politicians,[6] defend the primacy of intellect against imagination. The *Ethics*, which Spinoza withheld from publication in his lifetime, was the unadulterated truth, for scientists and philosophers. The *Theological-Political Treatise*, which Spinoza did publish, though anonymously, was for wise rulers, not the truth pure but a manual practical to control the ignorant and unruly masses. To save Socrates from the masses, that is to say, to save himself from the unruly mobs, to discipline and order society so it would not disturb the intellectual order of science, Spinoza must suppress prophets and prophecy above all. His draconian solution is ultimately the same as Hobbes's: the absolute state in principle, the totalitarian state in fact, a political sovereignty holding exclusive authority and hence tolerating no authority outside its own.

Levinas: "It is true that all men are prophets"[7]

Levinas does not agree with Spinoza's definition of prophecy as "vivid imagination," a delineation intended pejoratively, vilifying prophecy as "inadequate ideas," according to the *Ethics*, and manipulation of ignorant masses, according to the *Theological-Political Treatise*. Levinas rather uses the term "prophecy" in a socioethical sense, without divorcing it thereby from its religious status—in fact the reverse is the case. Its ethical meaning or function is its highest religious sense. "Prophecy" is another term Levinas uses to explicate the meaning of the "saying" of the "said," the universal ethical source or significance of meaning that

---

6. See chapter 7 of the present volume.

7. AT, 181.

gives rise to all significations, originating in and indeed hollowing out the responsible singularity and hence also the irreducible multiplicity of the human. Prophecy for Levinas is thus the very dignity of the human.

Levinas uses the term "prophecy" already in *Totality and Infinity*, but it receives a more refined and deeper exposition in *Otherwise than Being or Beyond Essence*. Let us go from one to the other.

In the preface to *Totality and Infinity*, which begins with an extended meditation on the opposition of war and peace—which is another layer of meaning of the opposition of totality and infinity—Levinas characterizes peace as "eschatology." He is no doubt thinking of the etymological sense of this term: the logic or discourse of the end, which is to say, of ends, alluding to Kant's "kingdom of ends." Levinas rejects as superficial and provisional the peace established by military victory and the impositions of power. Such peace is actually suppressed violence rather than positive harmony. Levinas also rejects the more subtle notion of peace as intellectual comprehension of the whole or totality, because it is actually the reduction of its terms to their relations, the suppression of alternatives for the sake of an imposed identity, even if that identity claims to be the identity of identity and difference, and perhaps all the more so in the latter case. Such forms of peace are in actuality regimes of war, temporary victories, violence provisionally held in check, composure but not concord, stasis not peace.

So, too, Levinas rejects as naïve, immature, fantastic, and no less oppressive the popular "religious" sense of eschatology as the miraculous and often apocalyptic end of time and history as we know them. Whether in afterlife or by apocalypse, these realms of peace are but fantasies and as such leave the real world with all its conflicts untouched and unfixed, as Marx made abundantly clear in his fourth thesis on Feuerbach.[8] Rather, what Levinas means positively by peace lies closer to Kant's third formulation of the Categorical Imperative:

---

8. Marx's fourth thesis on Feuerbach: "Feuerbach starts out from the fact of religious self-alienation, of the duplication of the world into a religious world and a secular one. His work consists in resolving the religious world into its secular basis. But that the secular basis detaches itself from itself and establishes itself as an independent realm in the clouds can only be explained by the cleavages and self-contradictions within this secular basis. The latter must, therefore, in itself be both understood in its contradiction and revolutionized in practice. Thus, for instance, after the earthly family is discovered to be the secret of the holy family, the former must then itself be destroyed in theory and in practice" (29).

"Every rational being must act as if he, by his maxims, were at all times a legislative member in the universal realm of ends" (*Foundation*, 57). But Levinas, unlike Kant, is a phenomenologist and not a rationalist. So what he means by the peace of eschatology is not a living toward the end by means of maxims, but a living toward ends by living toward the other person, that is, moral responsibility to and for the other. That such responsibility is not enough for peace, Levinas is quite aware. Responsibility for the other demands justice for all, and hence requires law, scientific knowledge, and philosophy. But unlike Kantian morality, it does not begin in respect for law but in responsibility for the alterity of the other singular person. Peace begins in the face of the other, in prophetic speech, though it does not end there.

Two more citations from *Totality and Infinity* help us to make clear the deepest meaning Levinas assigns to transcendence and hence to prophecy, which is its concrete instantiation.

> To tell the truth, ever since eschatology has opposed peace to war, the evidence of war has been maintained in an essentially hypocritical civilization that is attached both to the True and to the Good, henceforth antagonistic. It is perhaps time to see in hypocrisy not only a base contingent defect of man, but the underlying rending of a world attached to both the philosophers and the prophets. (24)

So, while philosophy and the care for truth is necessary for justice, that is, for universal law, prophecy and the care for the other is necessary for morality, that is, singular responsibility, even if these two realms of signification—truth and goodness—do not and cannot cohere into a comprehensive whole. By attaching itself to the true exclusively, as does Spinoza, philosophy would deny the irreducible status of the good, which lies beyond truth.[9] To be attached to both at once and equally, as it were, is to be torn in hypocrisy and ultimately a disservice to both. Better than a hypocritical pretense or hollow genuflection toward the good, then, would be to admit the primacy of the good, the superiority of genuine peace to the imposed peace of war. It is precisely this that lies at the heart of Levinas's philosophy

---

9. One sees this exclusive attachment to the true not only in Spinoza but also in Heidegger. See OET, 292–324.

and authorizes its appropriation of the term "prophecy" for the saying that is the moral condition of the said.[10]

Levinas continues (and let us not be insensitive to the Kantian orientation of his thought, for Kant preceded Levinas in giving primacy to the ethical):

> Without substituting eschatology for philosophy, without philosophically 'demonstrating' eschatological 'truths,' we can proceed from the experience of totality back to a situation where totality breaks up, a situation that conditions that totality itself. Such a situation is the gleam of exteriority or of transcendence in the face of the Other. (TI, 24).

The situation in which totality breaks up and finds itself conditioned, where even war finds its basis in peace, where morality governs knowledge, is not found by transcendental deduction but rather in the face of the other. If by "situation" one understands a context that can be viewed from the outside, a context in which one is situated, however, then the face is no situation at all but the very rupture of situation, a desituating or deterritorialization. Moral transcendence, the good, occurs in and as the first-person singular responsibility of one person, me, myself, responding to and for another person, you, the one who faces. It is in this sense that later in *Totality and Infinity* Levinas affirms, "The Other is not the incarnation of God, but precisely by his face, in which he is disincarnate, is the manifestation of the height in which God is revealed" (79). To understand this perhaps unexpected and seemingly unjustified introduction of the name God, we must always keep in mind that for Levinas, "Everything that cannot be brought back to [*se ramener à*] an interhuman relation represents not the superior form but the forever primitive form of religion" (79; my translation). Just as for Kant true religion is a community group striving for ethical ends, so too for Levinas it is a "religion of adults" whose *eschaton* or end is goodness and justice. Rejecting religious superstition and fanaticism, on this score Levinas and Spinoza agree. Promoting the ethical, here they radically disagree. For Spinoza what is divine is natural knowledge, while for Levinas what is divine

---

10. While Kant also admitted the primacy of practical reason, which is to say, the primacy of ethics, he did so while at the same time undermining his intent by binding all his thought to the rationality of the *Critique of Pure Reason*.

is the height of the good, its exigency, and all that moves humankind toward such a height.

Beyond these schematic indications, the term "prophecy" plays little role in *Totality and Infinity*. Let us note, however, one subsection of section 3, which is dedicated to defending what Levinas calls a "judgment of God," a suprahistorical moral judgment, against the judgment of the victors, recorded in the history books, the "judgment of history" (240–247), which can also be understood to be a defense of the rights of prophecy, right against might. Certainly, too, Levinas's explicit and repeated invocation in *Totality and Infinity* of care for the "widow, the orphan, and the stranger," utilizing the biblical phrase, or elsewhere referring to the "condition of being stranger, destitute, or proletarian" (75), is also a concern with the continued significance of prophecy. Nevertheless, for an extended discussion of prophecy, one must turn to *Otherwise than Being or Beyond Essence*. It is a book that begins with five epigraphs, two of which are taken from the prophet Ezekiel.

First a general comment regarding these two books. *Totality and Infinity* is concerned primarily with the exteriority, alterity, or *transcendence* of the other person. The alterity of such transcendence occurs as moral obligation. Its medium is language: expression, sincerity, the saying of the said. *Otherwise than Being or Beyond Essence* is concerned primarily with the moral repercussions of such transcendence on the self. The responsible self—always in the first-person singular, I, me myself—"traumatized," "de-nucleated," "put into question," "for-the-other" before being for-itself. Indeed, the responsible self is "turned inside out," through its responsibility for the other, subjectivity as subjection, as "hostage" to and for the other. From the transcendence of the other's saying and from the self-sacrifice of the saying coming out of my own lips, it is here that Levinas invokes the idea of prophecy.

There is in *Otherwise than Being or Beyond Essence* a short subsection entitled "Witness and Prophecy" (OBBE, 149–152). It has to do with prophecy and time, but not with prophecy as miraculous prediction of the future, as one might ordinarily think. The matter is far more complex and far less fantastic. Saying and prophecy—let us think of the terms interchangeably, though we will better see the reasons for this as we go along. Saying occurs not within an a priori or given time frame, as if it were an event within time, but is the ultimate condition of time and as such opens up its own form of time. Since his earliest original writings—*Existence and Existents* and *Time and the Other*—this proposal has been one of Levinas's most profound contributions to philosophy, and the basis of his fundamental disagreement and departure from both Husserl and above all Heidegger. The ultimate structure of time, for Levinas, is neither objective nor subjective; it is intersubjective.

Intersubjective time, time as moral relation, between me and you, is time as rupture and discontinuity, what Levinas calls "diachrony," to contrast it with the synchrony or immanence of the synthesizing or "ecstatic" temporalizing of autonomous subjectivity.[11] Encounter with the other person, in order to be a genuine proximity with that which is other, but not therefore a reduction of the other to the same, short-circuits, as it were, the syntheses that constitute the continuity and identity of the ego's "inner-time consciousness," to use Husserl's expression, the ecstatic temporalizing of its being-in-the-world and openness to being, to speak Heidegger's language. Deeper than identity, for Levinas, is the self as non-identity, the self as for-the-other, put into question by the other, responding to and for the other. A fracturing of the identity of the self-identical self, the "natural" self, to again use Husserl's terminology, occurs as a "saying," first from the other person, as obligation, but also a saying coming out of the mouth of the responsible self introjected with the inassimilable imperative alterity of the other to which it responds insofar as and to the measure that it is responsible. This saying of the moral self is the true inauguration of all meaning, but it remains prior to *what* is said, contents, themes, and the like. My saying, which begins outside myself, overwhelmed and touched off by the excessive impact of the other, a saying whose beginning transcends its origin, this moral response to the vulnerability and suffering of the other, is what Levinas denominates "prophecy."

Little wonder then that in the following citation Levinas comments on Isaiah 65:24 to explicate its sense:

> "Before they call, I will answer," the formula is to be understood literally. In approaching the other I am always late for

---

11. See IRB, 176: "In the very structure of prophecy, a temporality is opened up, breaking with the 'rigor' of being." In my essay, "Miracle of Miracles: More Ancient than Knowledge: Contra Hume," I examine this peculiar time structure in relation to what I present as Franz Rosenzweig's critique of David Hume's critique of miracles, also having to do with prophecy. On the "diachrony" of responsibility, see my article "Responsible Time."

the meeting. But this singular obedience to the other to go, without understanding the order, this obedience prior to all representation, this allegiance before any oath, this responsibility prior to commitment, is precisely the other in the same, inspiration and prophecy, the *passing itself* of the Infinite. (OBBE, 150)

No doubt and in accord with a hermeneutic principle to which he explicitly adheres, Levinas is also calling our attention to the nearby and related verse found at Isaiah 59:21: "And as for Me this is My covenant with them, says the Lord; My spirit that is upon you, and My words which I have put in your mouth . . ." These biblical references are not "proof texts" certainly, any more than citing a philosopher is a proof of veracity rather than attribution. Levinas is a philosopher and not a theologian. But these texts lend weight and help explicate what Levinas wants to say about saying.[12] And that, if I am not mistaken, is that the term "prophecy" serves as a further elaboration of what in *Totality and Infinity* Levinas called sincerity and expression, the face of the other at once as alterity and as solicitation. At the same time it calls attention to the peculiar "maternal" structure of responsibility: the other put into me, *my* words as *for* the other solicited by the other. Here, in this introjection—at once from me and for you—lies the "obedience prior to all representation," the "allegiance before any oath," "responsibility prior to commitment" of prophecy, but of morality as well. *Prophecy* is the touchstone of morality, pacific language, which is to say, of the primacy of morality, because morality is the very priority of any priority, or what I have elsewhere called "the very importance . . . of importance itself" ("Biblical Humanism," 30). In *Otherwise than Being or Beyond Essence*, Levinas speaks of this, the accomplishment of language as saying, language as prophecy, in terms of "glory," a term that we have already invoked: "That the glory of the Infinite is glorified only by the signification of the-one-for-the-other, as sincerity, that in my sincerity the Infinite passes the finite, that the Infinite comes to pass there, is what makes the plot of ethics primary, and what makes language irreducible to an act among acts" (150).

---

12. One could also cite Deuteronomy 30:14, among many other texts: "It [the *Torah*] is no longer in Heaven. . . . But it is in your mouth . . ."

Thus prophecy—emphatic speech, the primacy of speech as the priority of the other—occurs in the speech of all humans, but always only in the singular, second/third person and first person, where the second/third person takes priority over the first, the you/he over the I. It is not simply a structure, however, because it *occurs* always in my first-person singularity, as a trauma, a blow, a disturbance coming from the outside, and more specifically as moral obligation to and for the other. It thus occurs prior to the origin of the self in itself, prior to representation, contract, knowledge, free agreement, deriving from the excessive and inescapable proximity of the other person, the imperative to not desert the other, indeed, to care for the other, as the other-in-me of moral obligation, provoking in me the responsibility to respond and hence provoking all the significations of what should be said and what can be said. As such, prophecy is not an attribute of moral selfhood, something added to a neutral subject. It "is" the non-identity, the "beyond being," the turning inside out that *elects* and as such gives rise to moral selfhood deeper or higher than any self-constitution. Again Levinas: "We call prophecy this reverting in which the perception of an order coincides with the signification of this order given to him that obeys it. Prophecy would thus be the very psyche in the soul: the other in the same, and all of man's spirituality would be prophetic" (OBBE, 149).

To be for-the-other in a moral obedience greater, more glorious, prior to, more important, better than being for-oneself, would be to prophesize. It is also to be human. "That," Levinas writes, "is the resonance of every language 'in the name of God,' the inspiration or prophecy of all language" (OBBE, 152). Thus for Levinas prophecy is not a miraculous predicting, or a divine ventriloquism, as if singularity were but the puppet of an absolute Master, but a humbling responsibility provoked by and responding to the other person. Far from being a calling reserved for the rare and the few,[13] or the product of an overheated imagination, it characterizes the inauguration of all speech and arises as "the very psyche of the soul."

Though he cites the text, unlike Spinoza Levinas does not elaborate an exegesis of Numbers 11:26–29. Its plain sense is consistent with

---

13. See Amos 7:14, where the prophet Amos declares, "I am not a prophet nor am I the son of a prophet, but I am a cattle herder and an examiner of sycamores."

his account of prophecy.[14] We might conjecture that the plain meaning is already so "Levinasian" that Levinas did not feel the need for extended comment, or that his entire philosophy is the commentary. Going beyond Moses's conditional, his subjunctive, for Levinas not only are the Israelites *already* prophets, *all human beings* are already prophets! One rises to one's humanity in prophecy. To be sure, Levinas fully understands that nothing absolutely coerces or guarantees that each and every person will rise to their proper human dignity. But such failures are not simply errors or oversights; they are already unworthiness, callousness, hard-heartedness, and evil in the face of the other person's imperative moral demands. While all humans are prophets, far fewer are moral heroes, Mother Teresa, Gandhi, Dorothy Day, Malala Yousafzai, and the many more unsung moral heroes, taking care of infirm or aged family members, providing for neighbors, helping the stranger, sacrificing themselves without reserve, risking their livelihoods and sometimes their lives for others.[15] Human dignity, the humanity in each of us, is not a definition, a species of a genus, not a given, a fact, or a necessity, but an achievement, an accomplishment, in a word, an election to responsibility. As Levinas taught in *Totality and Infinity*, responsibility increases to the measure—or the immeasure, for it is inordinate—that it is borne.[16]

---

14. In an interview of 1985 Levinas jokingly does indeed refer to this passage, but it is in a context where prophecy is thought in terms of prediction: "Q.: Is there a future for peace? What is the contribution of Christianity to the construction of peace? E.L.: Ah, you are requesting a prophecy from me! It is true that all men are prophets. Does not Moses say in the words of Numbers 11:29, 'That all the people of God be prophets,' and does not Amos go still further, to all of humanity: 'The Eternal God has spoken, who shall not prophecy?' (Amos 3:8). And yet it is difficult for me to make predictions, unless the verses I just cited are themselves favorable prophecies." As one sees from this last comment, however, even when Levinas is "joking" he is suggesting a very serious lesson: that a favorable predictive prophecy is one in which humanity is conceived in terms of prophecy as saying, as moral stature, as responsibility for-the-other before oneself. Levinas, IRB, 226.

15. In the Babylonian Talmud, Sanhedrin 17a, which discusses the incident in the camp described in Numbers 11:26–29, the prophecy of the two prophets, identified as Eldad and Medad, is distinguished as superior, coming "directly from God," to the prophecy of the seventy elders, whose prophecy is mediated by Moses. Furthermore, the prophecy of these two individuals is characterized as continuous rather than sporadic: "All the other prophets prophesied and then ceased to prophesy, but they prophesied and did not stop." See Neusner, 108.

16. "The increase of my exigencies with regard to myself aggravates the judgment that is borne upon me, increases my responsibility." TI, 100–101.

Excursus: The Sage Prophets of Maimonides

A discussion of prophecy can hardly be adequate without considering the writings on prophets and prophecy by Rabbi Moses ben Maimon (1132-1204), known to the world as Maimonides and to the Jewish world as the Rambam,[17] who is generally considered the greatest Jewish scholar of the medieval period.

Though comments on prophecy are dispersed throughout his many writings, two particularly concentrated discussions stand out. First, the second chapter entitled "Prophecy," of his Jewish book, *Introduction to the Commentary on the Mishnayos* (*Hakdama L'Payrush HaMishnayos*) (Lampel, 47–63). Second, in his philosophical book, *The Guide of the Perplexed* (*Dalalat al-Hairin*, better known by its Hebrew title, *Moreh Nebuchim*), wherein part 2, from chapter 32 entitled "Three Theories concerning Prophecy" to its conclusion in chapter 48, is taken up with a discussion of prophecy.[18] Beside the fact of Maimonides's importance as a thinker, his profundity and originality, an additional reason here for considering Maimonides along with Spinoza is that they both agree—contra Levinas—about the primacy of intellect,[19] despite the fact that Spinoza singles out Maimonides in the *Theological-Political Treatise* for extremely harsh criticism. Furthermore, introducing Maimonides also enables us to sharpen our understanding of prophecy in Levinas by seeing how his opposition to both Spinoza and Maimonides on the status of contemplation nevertheless does not deter him, contra Spinoza

---

17. The name "Rambam" is an acronym of Maimonides's Hebrew name: *R*abbi *M*oses *ben M*aimon.

18. Maimonides, *Guide of the Perplexed*, volumes 1 and 2. Also Maimonides, *The Guide for the Perplexed*. There is a vast secondary literature on Maimonides; four useful and accessible studies in English are: Hartman; Seeskin, a very short but illuminating introduction; Twersky, a deeply erudite and carefully reasoned introduction to Maimonides's great Code of Jewish Law; and Halberstal. In Twersky, see especially pages 488–514 ("Philosophy as an Integral Part of Talmud," "Nobility of Philosophical Knowledge," and "Conclusion"). These four books all contest any sharp separation between Maimonides's religious and philosophical works.

19. The eminent Jewish thinker and Zionist Ahad Ha-am (Asher Ginsberg) entitled his penetrating exposition of Maimonides "The Supremacy of Reason: To the Memory of Maimonides," in Simon, *Ahad Ha-am*, 138–182. Ahad Ha-am comments on Moses's exalted declaration in Numbers in a talk of 1893 entitled "Priest and Prophet," in Simon, *Selected Essays*, 125–138 (see pages 135 and 137).

but in agreement with Maimonides, from affirming an agreement with religious Judaism.[20]

Maimonides, because of his great admiration for and his considerable adherence to Aristotelian philosophy, remains a controversial figure within the Jewish tradition.[21] Certainly, as was so later with Spinoza, his account of prophets and prophecy is influenced by his admiration for philosophy.[22] Thus according to Maimonides, when there is a genuine debate about some matter, in contrast to what can be decided by a clear demonstration or a sensible fact, the *argumentative authority* of a prophet is in no way superior to that of a learned sage (Hebrew: *chochum*). The success or failure of a debatable point, in other words, is not decided by the personal authority, even the divine authority, of him or her who is making the argument. While Maimonides accedes to the traditional biblical claim that the true prophet, in contrast to the "false prophet," is one who makes predictions and whose predictions of the future are always correct as well as always being in agreement with Jewish "law" (though the true prophet can also *temporarily* suspend the law in order to better resume it), the prophet nevertheless has no special authority when it comes to Talmudic debate. In a passage now famous in Jewish learning, Maimonides declares: "Should a thousand prophets, all on the prophetic level of Elijah and Elisha, have one sequence of logic, while a thousand sages without the power of prophecy, plus one more such sage, subscribe to the opposite sequence of logic,— *'Follow the majority position!'* (Exodus 23:2); the *halacha* is as those thousand sages plus one, and not as the one thousand prophets" (Lampel, 62).

Aside from having inspired predictive abilities, the prophet for Maimonides has no higher standing than the sage. This point is underlined by Jewish tradition, which has declared that the epoch of the

---

20. It should go without saying that the very terms "religion" and "religious" are problematic. In large measure these are Christian terms, referring to a dimension or part of life given over to the "spiritual," to relation with God (e.g., see Corinthians 1:27). No other world "religion," to my knowledge, makes such a distinction, or makes a distinction so sharp, between things of God and things of the world. Franz Rosenzweig pointed out that there is no term in the Hebrew Bible for "religion."

21. So while Maimonides's *Mishnah Torah* and his Bible commentaries are studied in all orthodox yeshivas, his *Guide for the Perplexed* is generally not.

22. For the controversy raised by Maimonides's adherence to philosophy, see Jospe.

miraculous prophecy of prophets such as Elijah and Elisha has ended. Maimonides does maintain that those who deserve to be called prophets are not simply equal to sages (though their votes are equal) but are in fact exceptionally good sages. The real authority of the prophet, therefore, while in no way preemptive, is that of the *well-educated and perfected intellect*. Spinoza, of course, does not share this high opinion of prophets and goes out of his way in the *Theological-Political Treatise* to show that prophets, for example, Daniel, often did not even understand their own prophecies, were far from always being educated persons, and in no case—with the exception of Jesus—perfected their intellect. What Maimonides, Spinoza, and Levinas do agree about, then, is the need for education and intelligence in those persons who decide upon intellectual matters of importance. Spinoza, however, dismisses all debatable topics, topics with no clear-cut black-and-white answer, as sheer ignorance of self-evident axioms and demonstrations built upon such axioms. History, for Spinoza, like all narrative discourse, contains no truth. (Knowledge of truth "does not demand belief in historical narratives of any kind whatsoever" [TPT, 51].) Maimonides and Levinas, in contrast, recognize that the most important intellectual issues are precisely those that must be intelligently debated and that have no demonstrative or factual conclusion. In this regard we can say that Maimonides and Levinas place Spinoza's Moses above Spinoza's Jesus in the following hierarchy Spinoza sets up in the *Theological-Political Treatise*: "If Moses spoke with God face to face as a man may do with his fellow (that is, through the medium of their two bodies), then Christ communed with God mind to mind."[23]

For Maimonides, then, prophets are rare not because few are chosen by God, as the naïvely religious believe, but because few humans (1) possess the requisite intellectual abilities (and high moral character), and (2) have worked hard enough and succeeded in mastering the vast but prerequisite knowledge of science and tradition. Though not all intelligent and well-educated persons are prophets (which means for Maimonides that the grace of God must also play a role) these two qualifications are required of the prophet. In principle anyone can be

---

23. TPT, 14. More precisely, for Spinoza, because "Christ" is pure intellect, pure scientist, he rises above prophecy itself: "Christ was not so much a prophet as the mouthpiece of God [i.e., of Nature]." TPT, chap. 4, 54.

a prophet, but in reality only a rare few persons combine brilliance and learning and are sages.

But does not such a position accord with Spinoza? Though Maimonides does not limit knowledge to the necessary and universal, as would Spinoza, are not his intellectual prerequisites of prophecy sufficient for Spinoza who, *mutatis mutandis*, need only convert such a medieval sage into a modern scientist? Why is Spinoza so vehemently against Maimonides? It seems the aforementioned conversion is not so easy for him. To answer this question and to understand his venom for Maimonides, we must indeed focus on the distinction between Spinoza's modern rationality and Maimonides's premodern reason. Put in its simplest terms, Spinoza's concept of rationality—which he calls "geometrical"—excludes imagination, while for Maimonides (and Levinas) reason requires it. As I have indicated, while Spinoza would throw history into the garbage bin of ignorance, banking everything upon modern scientific rationality, Maimonides (and Levinas) respects tradition and debate where demonstration and fact are inappropriate.

Spinoza is as unequivocal in the *Theological-Political Treatise* as he is in his *Ethics* that knowledge or truth "does not demand belief in historical narratives of any kind whatsoever. . . . [n]or can the belief in historical narratives, however certain, give us knowledge of God [i.e., the laws of nature]" (TPT, 51). Thus in his book about the Bible he makes it perfectly clear—one hardly need raise the issue of esoteric writing—that biblical narratives have no truth to them at all. While he does "not deny that their study can be very profitable in the matter of social relations" (51), they have no relevance whatsoever with regard to true knowledge. Spinoza could hardly be more dismissive. True knowledge—the "adequate idea"—is all that is real. The universe is its scientific intelligibility. To restate his position in terms of the prophets: "the authority of the prophets carries weight only in matters concerning morality and true virtue, and that in other matters their beliefs are irrelevant to us" (5). Such, indeed, is the central thesis ("the most important part of the subject of this treatise" [164]) of the entire *Theological-Political Treatise*, whose self-declared aim is precisely to radically separate philosophy from theology, truth from belief, freedom from obedience, and science from morality.

> The aim of philosophy is, quite simply, truth, while the aim of faith, as we have abundantly shown, is nothing other

than obedience and piety. Again, philosophy rests on the basis of universally valid axioms, and must be constructed by studying Nature alone, whereas faith is based on history and language, and must be derived only from Scripture and revelation. (164)

Instruction disabusing religion of its truth-claims, confining its leftovers to the privacy of moral conscience, placing it under the anathema of ignorance, are the revolutionary negative tasks of Spinoza's *Theological-Political Treatise*. Only after religion has been exposed and revealed to have no more than a *political* character—dealing not in truth but in obedience—can modern science, which Spinoza always and everywhere positively defends, be freed from its clumsy meddling. Spinoza's interest in the political is instrumental. The state, which also only deals in obedience, is required to stand above religious impertinences, to enforce a peaceful public life, squelching religious squabbling. The purpose of the state, unlike the religious authority Spinoza excoriates, is to guarantee an environment conducive to the scientific life of the few. Only when religion is stripped of its self-delusions, freed of its erroneous belief in itself as truth, can it be tamed and put in its proper place, which is to say subordinated to the state.

It is for this reason, to unequivocally divorce science and truth from religion and faith by relegating the latter to the illusory status of falsehood and ignorance, to the status, that is to say, of the political, that Spinoza radically opposes Maimonides. Maimonides sought truth, but he sought it not only outside of religion but also within it, continuing the project of harmonizing science and religion that, according to Harry Austryn Wolfson, began with Philo of Alexandria. The difference separating Spinoza from Maimonides is not so much a disagreement about adherence to truth, to which they are both committed, as a disagreement about the nature of truth, a disagreement, that is to say, about the nature of reason. Spinoza and Maimonides, on this score, are divided by a "paradigm shift." To put the matter most succinctly: Maimonides's Aristotelian reason includes "final cause," *telos*, while Spinoza's Cartesian rationality does not. So Maimonides naturally takes the purposes that guide humans and that guide human history, and hence morality and political life, to be reasonable, or susceptible to reason, while Spinoza, adhering to modern nonteleological science, does not and cannot.

Given this shift in the character of science, what Spinoza opposes most vehemently is precisely Maimonides's efforts, as Spinoza puts it, "to make Scripture conform with philosophy" (TPT, 165)—"The first among the Pharisees who openly maintained that Scripture must be made to conform with reason was Maimonides" (165). Accordingly, chapter 7 of the *Theological-Political Treatise* blasts Maimonides's approach as "excessive and rash, . . . harmful, unprofitable and absurd" (102). He gives three reasons for Maimonides's necessary failure: (1) assuming of the prophets "that they were outstanding philosophers and theologians," (2) "holding that they based their conclusions on scientific truth," and (3) "that it is legitimate for us to explain away and distort the words of Scripture to accord with our preconceived opinions" (102). Of course Spinoza is as guilty as Maimonides of this third offense, that is, twisting Scriptures to suit his theory. It is really because Maimonides, while aiming for truth, does not share Spinoza's conception of science and rationality, upholding a premodern notion of reason, that Spinoza targets Maimonides above all in his criticism. By his own lights he must attack Maimonides because Spinoza's modern conception of rationality is precisely premised on the exclusion of such elements as purpose, morality, imagination, and historical narrative, vital to Maimonides as they were to Aristotle.

My aim is not to resolve this disagreement. Modern mathematical science has greatly revised its own conception of rationality from the days of Spinoza. What is important for our purposes, beyond the debate between Spinoza and Maimonides, that is to say, regarding our consideration of Levinas, is to see that Maimonides and Spinoza *agree that religion must be made to conform to science*, even if they disagree about the nature of the science to which it must conform.

Levinas certainly also agrees with both Maimonides and Spinoza, and many others, that religion, for its own sake, must be purified of superstition and of mythological reliance on the miraculous interventions of the "ontotheological" God of popular religion. For Levinas Judaism at its best is an "adult religion," a religion of demythologization (millennia before Bultmann) in the name of righteousness. What Levinas disagrees with both Maimonides and Spinoza about is not this but the primacy of reason. True religion is reasonable, to be sure, but it is so because it is based in prophecy as we have seen Levinas interpret it, as the *ethical* presupposition of discourse and signification. Let us add, too, that insofar as Maimonides's conception of reason includes an ethical dimension, as it does, to that extent Levinas is closer to Maimonides than to Spinoza, whose philosophy does not. "Spinozism," Levinas has said, lies at the "antipodes" from his own thought.[24] Not so Maimonides, even if in giving primacy to ethics Levinas is not Maimonidean.

Not a matter of overheated imagination, neither is prophecy for Levinas a function of superior intellect coupled with superior learning, accompanied by moral integrity. Rather prophecy is itself a moral sensitivity, responsiveness, an awakening alert to the needs of the other and of all others. "I do not underestimate the importance of knowledge," Levinas has said, "but I do not consider it to be the ultimate axiological judgment" (IRB, 191). Responsibility and righteousness do not depend on intellect and learning, even if they are the necessary but not sufficient conditions for wisdom.[25] Thus Forrest Gump is a moral person, even if he is deficient mentally and educationally. Is this a scandal for philosophy, that at its root lay an encounter and sensitivity not determined by intellect? So be it. Many times Levinas will refer to the seemingly so small acts of kindness depicted in Vasily Grossman's book *Life and Fate* as instances of the moral rectitude upon which all civilization and philosophy itself is based. Or one might think of the now-famous formula, which is a performative, "*Après vous,*" the "After you," of letting someone else go through a doorway first, again so seemingly insignificant. Yet in it is expressed a perfectly legitimate instance of the kindness, the compassion, the priority of the other person, that lies at the root of Levinas's thinking. This acknowledgment of the exigency and profundity of morality, and hence the priority of ethics in philosophy, does not reduce Levinas's thought to a petty or "bourgeois" philosophy, except for those scoffers who wish to shirk the very responsibility that ultimately *makes sense* of progressive social action, reformation or revolution, if it comes to the latter. No vanguard is above the demands of morality and justice, which are unremitting and overwhelming, indeed infinite. The primacy of morality, and of ethics, indicates the manner and extent to which even the everyday practices of morality take precedence over theory, erudition, knowledge, comprehension, and all the higher intellectual virtues. These virtues retain their eminence but not their preeminence.

---

24. See TI, 105.
25. See Levinas, "L'actualite de Maimonide."

It would be wrong therefore to see in Levinas's thought a romantic or irrational depreciation of intellectual virtues. Rather he insists on their link to moral virtues. It is not at all the same. Indeed, without their link to moral virtues, the intellectual virtues lose their virtue; they succumb to their inner tendency to totality, as Kant laid out so clearly in the "Dialectic" of the *Critique of Pure Reason*. Levinas's writings everywhere evidence a mastery of the difficult and intellectualist philosophical learning of the West. Furthermore, though he was not and never aspired to be a legal judge within Jewish orthodoxy, his learning within the "vast sea" of Talmud is not inconsiderable. Regarding the latter, Levinas explicitly commends Talmudic learning as an apt intellectual resource for honing Jewish moral sensitivity. Moral sensitivity is not a domain independent of intellect, even if intellect is not director as it remains even in Kant. In no way is it the case for Levinas, as it was for Spinoza, that study of history or literature, say, must be purchased at the price of loss of scientific acuity (because for Spinoza to stimulate the imagination is to corrupt the intellect[26]). Furthermore, for Levinas moral sensitivity is not given once and for all but must be constantly improved, refined, deepened, elevated through experience and education. Thus for Levinas, "The human being is not only in the world, not only an *in-der-Welt-Sein* (being-in-the-world) but also *zum-Buch-Sein* (being-toward-the-book), namely, in relation to the inspired word" (IRB, 170). Also, the justice required by morality is in no way a simple matter. Justice requires knowledge, law, universality, precise measurement, agriculture, architecture, communications, distribution systems, polity, technology, administration, and the like. So even if morality is within the compass of all human beings, regardless of intellectual cultivation, it is not therefore detached from intellect and the complex contributions made possible through intellectual development, especially science and technology. "Responsibility for the others or communication is the adventure that bears all the discourse of science and philosophy" (OBBE, 160).

So it is not the prophet as sage, prophecy as sagacity, which represents the highest ideal for Levinas, the ideal of "holiness," but the morally sensitive person, the one who responds most adequately to the

---

26. TPT, chap. 2: "Those with a more powerful imagination are less fitted for purely intellectual activity . . ." (21).

other. Such is the wisdom of philosophy, for Levinas: the wisdom of love—here in prophecy the human rises to holiness. "The only absolute value," Levinas has said, "is the human possibility of giving the other priority over oneself. . . . In my relation to the other, I hear the word of God. It is not a metaphor" (IRB, 170–171). Saying, prophecy, love of neighbor, is thus the highest vocation of humanity. Not theology but morality. "It makes the word God be pronounced, without letting 'divinity' be said" (OBBE, 162). Such is the glory or holiness of prophecy, humanity's highest elevation: the *shema* ("hear," "listen") which is not heard, but which awakens all hearing.

Chapter Three

Levinas and Spinoza

To Love God for Nothing

One of the strangest convergences in contemporary thought is that between Levinas and Spinoza regarding the love of God. Despite the abyss separating their philosophies, both Levinas and Spinoza urge that the proper love for God is one in which nothing can be expected, demanded, or even asked in return. True love of God is one-way, without expectation of recompense. Yet one can hardly imagine two philosophies more distant, more alien, and more opposed to one another than Levinas's ethical metaphysics and Spinoza's rationalist monism. On an issue as important as this, that is, most broadly, the proper relation of humans to God, to know the positions and the reasons for them of these two philosophers, to determine their proximity and their distance here, especially considering how radically they differ on fundamentals everywhere else, prompts the following inquiry into what Spinoza and Levinas mean by putting forward the idea of loving God without recompense.

The locus classicus of Spinoza's position is proposition 19 of part V of the *Ethics*: "He who loves God cannot endeavor that God should love him in return" (211). The proof that follows is brief: "If a man were so to endeavor, he would therefore desire (V, Prop. 17, Cor.) that God whom he loves should not be God, and consequently (III, Prop. 19) he would desire to feel pain, which is absurd" (211). When we turn to the explanatory corollary to proposition 17 of part V, to which Spinoza makes reference, it reads: "Strictly speaking, God does not love or hate anyone. For God is not affected with any emotion of pleasure or pain, and consequently he neither loves nor hates anyone" (210). That God is not affected with any emotion, whether of pleasure or pain, and consequently that God neither hates nor loves anyone, follows from Spinoza's overall rejection of all anthropological characterizations of God as plebian misunderstandings that diminish and therefore negate the perfection of God. For Spinoza, God's will and God's intellect are one, because across the board, "Will and intellect are one and the same thing" (II, Prop. 49, Cor., 96), which is to say that God is nothing other than true intelligibility, that is, Nature as scientifically known in its necessary lawfulness, and not some enlarged human willfulness.

For Spinoza pleasure and pain are "passive emotions" (*passio*). Pleasure comes from moving from lesser to greater perfection, and pain comes from the reverse, moving from greater to lesser perfection. God, being perfect, does not become more or less perfect. Eternal, outside of duration and change, God does not move or differ. Thus God "experiences" or undergoes neither pleasure nor pain. And this is actually the proof for proposition 17 (whose corollary we saw earlier): "All ideas, in so far as they are related to God, are true, that is, they are adequate. Thus God is without passive emotions. Again, God cannot pass to a state of greater or less perfection, and so he is not affected with any emotion of pleasure or pain" (210). Only passive emotions or inadequate ideas can be moved, that is, changed for better or worse. God, who is perfect, never changes, hence—and this is the important and relevant point—the only relation appropriate to God is one also that does not move. This relation, the only one appropriate to God without self-imposed bondage on the part of the human, that is to say, the only relation to God taken in true freedom, adequate, truly recognizing its true object, is Spinoza's famous "intellectual love of God" (*amor intellectualis Dei*). Intellectual love of God, then, is nothing other than "adequate ideas" truly ideated, ideas cogitated as eternal and perfect.

Spinoza distinguishes two sorts of adequate ideas, which he calls "knowledge of the second kind" and "knowledge of the third kind," the latter being the highest, the closest, that is to say, to God. Knowledge of the second kind is made up of universal and necessary propositions, that is, true scientific propositions. Knowledge of the third kind, which is the highest and best kind of knowledge, is made up of true scientific propositions accompanied by intellectual recognition of the whole of which each proposition, or set of propositions, is a part. Knowledge of the second kind, then, is a constituent of knowledge of the third kind, which adds the ingredient of holistic comprehension to that of adequate ideas. God, then, being perfect, is nothing other than complete and final knowledge of the third kind: all true scientific propositions grasped in their totality—nothing less than the complete intelligibility of the universe intellectually comprehended. This is why, by the way, Spinoza's *Ethics*, while presenting knowledge of the third kind, not just science but the philosophy of science, nevertheless still falls short of replicating God's mind: it does not present all true scientific propositions. God's knowledge is complete; human knowledge is programmatic. Proposition 20 of part V makes this distinction clear. The *Ethics* is not the completion of knowledge but the framework of intelligibility within which a scientific *program* follows: "The more we understand particular things, the more we understand God" (214).

Be that as it may, the point at hand is that love of God means grasping true propositions and the unchanging framework or whole, the perfection or comprehensive intellectual character of reality. The thing grasped and the grasping, then, perfection and adequate ideas, have nothing whatsoever to do with "passive emotions" such as pleasure and pain, which are always imperfect since they are the very marks or signals of change. Therefore, to expect pleasure in return for loving God—for knowing God—is to misrepresent or misapprehend God from the very start. Such an expectation would be to "desire that God whom he loves should not be God" (E, V, Prop. 19, Proof, 211), that is, it is a desire to "destroy" Him. So, *Ethics*, part V, proposition 19, with its proof:

> Proposition 19: *He who loves God cannot endeavor that God should love him in return*. Proof: If a man were so to endeavor he would therefore desire (Cor. Pr. 17, V) that God whom he loves should not be God, and consequently (Pr.19, III) he would desire to feel pain, which is absurd (Pr. 28, III). Therefore he who loves God . . . etc. (211)

The only relation possible to God is by means of adequate ideas, perfect unchanging intellectual conceptions, pure ideas without "words or images." Since God is perfect, eternal, unchanging, only perfection is adequate to God. This is also why proposition 18 of part V states categorically: "Nobody can hate God" (210). God cannot be hated, so we learn in the proof, because: "The idea of God which is in us is adequate and perfect. Therefore in so far as we contemplate God, we are active (*agere*). Consequently there can be no pain accompanied by the idea of God" (211). Whatever one hates, it cannot be God. Nor, for the same reason, can whatever one loves, in the sense that one expects pleasure from what one loves, be God either.

Contemplation of God is neither painful nor pleasurable, not only because it is a steady state, but more specifically because it is the steady state of perfection. Although Spinoza speaks of love of God, as we have indicated, one can neither hate nor love God, insofar as either of these are interpreted, as seems natural, as "emotions," hence passivities. However Spinoza is not careful to restrict the meaning and use of the terms "love" (*amor*) and "hate" (*odium*) to the univocal meanings and symmetry found, for instance, in the scholium to proposition 13 of part III, where he defines them as follows: "Love is merely 'pleasure accompanied by the idea of an external cause,' and hatred is merely 'pain accompanied by the idea of an external cause' " (112). Instead he gives to the term "love" a second and higher sense lacking to "hate," namely, its link to *active* rather than passive emotions, thereby sanctioning the obvious rhetorical benefit of his famous "intellectual love of God."

This matter deserves closer attention. In the proof to proposition 58 of part III, we read: "When the mind conceives itself and its power to act, it feels pleasure. Now the mind necessarily regards itself when it conceives a true, that is, adequate, idea. But the mind does conceive adequate ideas. Therefore it feels pleasure, too, in so far as it conceives adequate ideas, that is, in so far as it is active" (139). The perfection of Spinoza's God, like the perfection of Aristotle's Active Intellect (despite Spinoza's obvious animus toward Aristotle[1]), is conceived as pure or unsullied activity, pure intellection, all adequate ideas comprehended separately and together. It is because the mind feels pleasure "in so far as it conceives adequate ideas, that is, in so far as it is active," as we have just seen, that we can understand how Spinoza can claim that the

---

1. For instance, speaking of one of Maimonides's Bible interpretations, in the *Theological-Political Treatise*, Spinoza writes: "But this is mere rubbish. They are concerned only to extort from Scripture some Aristotelian nonsense and some fabrications of their own; and this I regard as the height of absurdity" (13).

mind can feel pleasure in loving God. Indeed, the only way humans can properly desire or love God is through the intellection of adequate ideas, reenacting, as it were, God's mind, participating in this way in the perfect activity that is God. No pain can accompany the idea of God, because pain comes from the passivity of passive emotions and God contains no passivity whatsoever. So the highest form of love, and the greatest pleasure, comes not from improvement or emendation, not from pleasure as increase and pain as decrease of activity, that is, as relative movement, but rather from contemplation, actualization, possession, or reenactment of perfection, the perfect activity that is God.

It is in view of this notion of pleasure and love that Spinoza defines human "beatitude" or "blessedness" (*beatitudo*) as participation in the perfect intellective activity of mind. In the proof to proposition 42 of part V, we read: "Blessedness consists in love toward God, a love that arises from the third kind of knowledge, and so this love must be related to the mind in so far as the mind is active; and therefore it is virtue itself" (223). And with this we are able to understand why there is no reward for loving God, or for any genuine relation to God. There is no *reward* for virtue, blessedness, or the third and highest kind of knowledge, since they are perfection itself. This is precisely what Spinoza says in proposition 42 of part V: "Blessedness is not the reward of virtue, but virtue itself" (223). Thus true love of God is one that expects nothing in return since the love of God is itself the highest "return" love could ever receive. Beatitude loves God, knows as the third kind of knowledge, realizes pure intellectual activity—there can be no higher love, no greater pleasure than such knowing. To expect any reward from God is to succumb to inadequate ideas, passivity, bondage, and thus not to be in relation to God altogether. To expect rewards from God is to miss the highest "reward" of which humans are capable and into which they should strive to realize themselves: actually sharing God's mind by knowing truth.

The scientist, but even more so the philosopher, loves God by knowing truth. Or, one might say, God knows himself, where the scientist knows nature, and where the philosopher knows the whole. These are equivalent expressions for Spinoza.

Levinas, for his part, also argues for love of God without concern for reward or recompense. However his reasoning is altogether different than Spinoza's. His argument, as is quite obvious from the start, does not rely on what for Spinoza is an exclusive adherence to propositional and deductive logic—a "geometrical manner." For Levinas such logic, or rather such logicism is not only always and already derivative but is also blind to its own conditioning. Thus while Spinoza berates everyone who disagrees with him with being ignorant, for Levinas it is Spinoza himself who is ignorant, ignorant in the sense made famous by Socrates: ignorant of his own ignorance. Such ignorance, because it at the same time only sees itself as intelligence, is difficult to refute. Certainly it cannot be refuted in its own terms or on its own ground. There it is irrefutable because rendered incapable of seeing otherwise by the elaborate fortress it has built without doors or windows. Thus, from the start, Levinas *rejects* Spinoza's conflation of intellect and will. The equation of will and intellect, the reduction of the former to the latter, let us remember, is precisely the linchpin of what Spinoza himself understood to be his advance over the confused dualism of Descartes. This Spinoza argued in 1663 in *Principles of Cartesian Philosophy*, the only book he published in his own name, and more briefly in his letter of January 5, 1665, to William van Blyenbergh (letter no. 21).[2] Levinas, as we have seen already, certainly does not oppose reason. Nor does he return to Descartes's rationalist dualism, of which Spinozism is indeed a more logical outcome. But he does, contra Spinoza, insist on the *separation* of reason and will. The issue is decisive; we shall turn to it directly.

Spinoza's famous expression: "God, or Nature" (E, IV, Preface, 153), where the "or" (*sive*) is inclusive rather than exclusive or disjunctive, meaning that the terms "God" and "Nature" can be substituted for one another, depends for its sense and justification precisely on the equation of intellect and will. The Nature that is synonymous with "God" is nothing other than the set of all true propositions. It is that which scientific inquiry uncovers over time but also that which is always already the case eternally and necessarily, and hence what one can also call, using a more traditional language, God's intellect. An obvious counter-question arises: what about mass, materiality, or passivity, in nature? Modern physics has a quick Spinozist response: mass is nothing other than slow energy. What the universe really is, is pure energy, pure activity, even if humans, for better or worse, find themselves bound by parameters such as the speed of light, on the fast side, and absolute zero, on the slow side. Though it may seem theoretically

---

2. See E, 275–280, esp. 277.

plausible at first glance, this answer cannot be correct for a Spinozist. This is because the initial question it is meant to answer simply recurs in another form: what about speed, fast and slow, do not these involve passivity? In other words, to transpose this back into Spinoza's vocabulary, if there is a world of illusion (passivity, inadequate ideas, e.g., fast and slow) and a world of truth (activity, pure intellect, God, energy), what is the ontological status of the former, first of all, and what is the ontological status of their difference? These questions challenge Spinozism not from the outside but in its own terms. Either there is God's mind, that is, intellect, or there is God's mind and something else—and what is the status of that something else? Is it sufficient, in other words, to castigate that something else with vituperative, to call it ignorance, illusion, nonsense, and the like, as Spinoza so often does, as if derogation were nihilation, or is there rather not something terribly wrong with the reduction of will to intellect, as Levinas argues?

Levinas does therefore challenge the Spinozist reduction of will to intellect on the grounds of contingency, of the break, as I indicated in the introduction to this volume, between attributes and modes, even if this is not his ultimate "argument," as we shall see. So, even if the Spinozist knower, the scientist, will *eventually* grasp apparent passivity in terms of real activity, leaving inadequate ideas for adequate ideas, what about those appearances, those evaporated errors, what were they? "The more we understand particular things," Spinoza assures the scientist, "the more we understand God" (E, V, Prop. 24, 214), that is, Nature in its intelligibility, but what about our prior misunderstandings, our uneducated ignorance and the opacity of things? Putting this question in terms of will and intellect: if willing is in reality intellection, as the scientist eventually knows, then what about the initial, provisional, or contingent appearance of will? We know that for Spinoza, as he expresses it in a letter of September 1661, to Henry Oldenburg (letter no. 2): "will is nothing more than a mental construct (*ens rationis*)" (E, 265), lacking therefore any genuine independence or reality. To think the will independent of the mind, then, according to Spinoza, is to have an inadequate idea of the will, an image (*imago*) or fantasy and not an idea. To give credence to contingency, Spinoza informs us in the aforementioned letter to Blyenbergh, is to mistake "comparing," a merely a human weakness, for conceiving the thing "in itself" (letter no. 21, 273), that is, the adequate idea, always and necessarily only conceivable *sub specie aeternitatis*.

Against the rationalist identification of will and intellect, Levinas opposes what he calls "the entire pathetic experience of humanity, which the Hegelian or Spinozist idealism relegates to the subjective or the imaginary" (TI, 217). But Levinas is no romantic. He does not exalt or revalue in "the entire pathetic experience of humanity" an elusive extra-rational moment, the arbitrary or the absurd, the mystical, mad or surreal, the extraordinary as such, as if aberration and uniqueness offered a sufficient resistance or an adequate escape from the englobing machinery of rationalism. Rather, in a resistance that rationalism cannot overcome, the so-called "pathos" of the human bursts the logic of idealism as an imperative "surplus," as the *supra*-rationality of a higher, more elevated exigency, a priority meaningful only as *morality* and *justice* through which the humanity of the human arises, and upon which a nonreductive *logos* must obliquely admit as its condition.

These differences—between intellect and will, and between what in the will resists idealism, that is, the ethical, and what cannot resist idealism, that is, the aberrant or violent—are fundamental, and their consequences are far-reaching. Let us therefore read closely a citation from *Totality and Infinity* wherein Levinas takes up these issues:

> To distinguish formally will and understanding, will and reason, nowise serves to maintain plurality in being or the unicity of the person if one forthwith decides to consider only the will that adheres to clear ideas or decides through respect for the universal to be a good will. If the will can aspire to reason in one way or another, it is reason, reason seeking or forming itself; its true essence is revealed in Spinoza or in Hegel. This identification of will and reason, which is the ultimate intention of idealism, is opposed by the entire pathetic experience of humanity, which the Hegelian or Spinozist idealism relegates to the subjective or the imaginary. The interest of this opposition does not lie in the very protestation of the individual who refuses the system and reason, that is, in his arbitrariness, which the coherent discourse could hence not silence by persuasion—but in the affirmation that makes this opposition live. . . . The protestation against the identification of the will with reason does not indulge in arbitrariness, which, by its absurdity and immorality, would immediately justify

this identification. It proceeds from the certitude that the ideal of being accomplished from all eternity, thinking only itself, cannot serve as the ontological touchstone for a life, a becoming, capable of renewal, of Desire, of society. Life is not comprehensible simply as a diminution, a fall, or an embryo or virtuality of being. The individual and the person count and act independently of the universal, which would mold them. . . . If subjectivity were but a deficient mode of being, the distinguishing between will and reason would indeed result in conceiving the will as arbitrary, as a pure and simple negation of an embryonic or virtual reason dormant in an I, and consequently as a negation of that I and a violence in regard to oneself. If, on the contrary, the subjectivity is fixed as a separated being in relation with an other absolutely other, the Other [*Autrui*], if the face brings the first signification, that is, the very upsurge of the rational, then the will is distinguished fundamentally from the intelligible, which it must not comprehend and into which it must not disappear, for the intelligibility of this intelligible resides precisely in ethical behavior, that is, in the responsibility to which it invites the will. The will is free to assume this responsibility itself; it is not free to ignore the meaningful world into which the face of the Other has introduced it. (217–219)

The human existent, in the separation of its sensible being, stands in an independence from both anonymous being and determinate being, independent in its own right, absolutely, and not only as a relative part of a whole, a piece of a system, self-standing and not merely a deficient form of being or of reason, a merely stuttering reason. "Sensibility is not a fumbling objectification" (TI, 187). Such a will is not reducible to reason except through the latter's imperial or hegemonic but unjustified imposition. Such imposition is essentially tyranny and war—totalization. But neither, in contrast to the many particularistic and essentially romantic "existentialisms" since the appearance of Max Stirner's *The Ego and Its Own*, does Levinas revert to defending the separation of will from reason on the basis of willfulness alone, which would yield philosophies of decisionism, dandyism, the impossible, arbitrarily privileging this or that aspect of the unique individual.

Individuals are without doubt unique and particular, but so are all entities whatsoever that can be distinguished. True individuality is not a matter of fingerprints. Highlighting selected aspects of particularity, however well intentioned, begins and ends in arbitrary choice, and hence if it does not explicitly invite tyranny, it is at the very least susceptible to immorality, selfishness, self-assertion. For Levinas efforts to discriminate will from reason on the basis of the arbitrary are both "absurdity and immorality," the violence of the particular against the violence of the totality, which ultimately reduce to the same violence dialectically divided against itself.

Because his criticisms are not based in the arbitrary and eccentric, and are based in a fuller appreciation of the nature and meaning of meaning than rationalism ever dreamed, Levinas's opposition to Spinozism is far more fundamental. His is not the protest of an annoyed particularity rubbed the wrong way by a reductive but intelligible universality. Rather, against the hegemony of knowledge Levinas poses an alternative significance, not animality, not existence, and certainly not silence, but an "otherwise than being and beyond essence" as ethics. *Responsibility* is the condition of the intelligible, "for the intelligibility of this intelligible resides precisely in ethical behavior, that is, in the responsibility to which it invites the will." We now turn to this ethical intelligibility, to see how it too, all the while in fundamental opposition to Spinoza, demands a love of God without recompense. Let us begin by asking more precisely in what does the "pathetic experience of humanity" consist? Again I want to underline the importance for Levinas's thought not only of the transcendence of the other person, but of the sensibility, the vulnerability of subjectivity.

In section 2 of *Totality and Infinity* Levinas discovers and describes the very first moment in the origin of selfhood, the originary constitution or "hypostasis" of distinct existence, in terms of sensuous "enjoyment" (*jouissance*). Prior to theory, prior to the world of representation and objects (Heidegger's *Vorhandenheit*), and prior to work, prior to the world of instrumentality and tools (Heidegger's *Zuhandenheit*), the distinct existent first emerges in the very sensationalism of sensuality. However blind it is in its deepest constitutive layers of existence to what at higher conditioned levels are constituted as objective and instrumental realities, according to Levinas's careful phenomenological analyses, sensuality originally arises in an independence that is independent precisely as content with itself, self-satisfied, self-sufficient in its sensations, a plenitude of sensations carefree in the plenitude of each instant. Such is the phenomenological evidence, regardless of what logic would or would not allow. "This logically absurd structure of unicity, this non-participation in genus, is the very egoism of happiness" (TI, 118). It is "the very contraction of the ego," "existence *for itself*," "as a 'coiling,' as a movement toward oneself," "a vibrant exaltation in which dawns the self" (TI, 118). "Sensibility," Levinas discovers, "essentially naive, suffices to itself in a world insufficient for thought" (TI, 135). Of course, this happy solitude or isolation of the self "coiled" upon itself, independent in its sensations, is but a "moment," in the Husserlian sense of the term,[3] of selfhood whose second moment is one of dependence. Indeed, the independence of the sensuous, self-sustained in its carefreeness, is but a moment of self-sufficiency in a larger relationality, "worldliness," where such sensations are part of larger complexes of sense and as such are not merely self-sufficient. Sensuous existence is thus also constituted by *needs*, is nourished by what is not itself, nourished by an antecedent world, and is hence uncertain and troubled about the constancy and future plenitude of its own sense of self-sufficiency. "There is here an ambiguity," Levinas writes, "of which the body is the very articulation" (TI, 116). As a sensuous being, in its very being the human existent is vulnerable.

Starting with phenomenological descriptions of a primitive carefree enjoyment and then moving to the troubling ambiguity of the body, in section 2 of *Totality and Infinity* Levinas proceeds to articulate and uncover an entire phenomenology of constituted-constituting layers of "worldly" significations, of labor, economy, habitation, representation, and knowledge. What is of interest in our present concern appears already in the originary and irreducible independence of sensibility, for this meaningful complex is also meaningful independent of reason. "[I]n the eyes of reason," Levinas recognizes, "the contentment of sensibility is ridiculous. But sensibility is not a blind reason and folly. It is prior to reason. . . . Sensibility is not a thought unaware of itself" (138). This is strikingly different from the opening pages of Hegel's *Phenomenology of Mind*, where sensibility is faulted for not being able to articulate itself reasonably. It is strikingly different from Spinoza's *Ethics*, where sensibility is from the start dismissed as unreal because unintelligible according to the unshakable logic of self-evident axioms

---

3. See "Investigation III" of Edmund Husserl, *Logical Investigations*, 436–489.

and deduction. What Levinas is showing, in contrast, is that before reason illuminates sensibility it cannot have already excluded every intelligibility except its own, and instead, and not merely as failure, it must acknowledge the sense of sensibility as sensibility. Sensibility, of its own, and in its own right, and without being merely irrational before the judgment of reason, makes sense outside of reason. To be sure, this sense is not the only sense of sensible existence. It is not even its deepest sense, inasmuch as Levinas will argue that its highest sense, its ethical responsibility, is its "better self." The point at hand, however, is that self-sensing does not evaporate in the light of reason. It is precisely as a sensible and vulnerable existent that the other person calls forth my responsibility to come to his or her aid. And it is precisely as a sensible and vulnerable existent that I am able to do so concretely. Only a being wrapped up in its own sensibility can be disturbed and traumatized by another being wrapped up in its sensibility. Radical transcendence cannot be limited to a being toward my own death, for that is not transcendent enough. More disturbing than my own death is the mortality of the other person. And more wakeful than my own mind is to itself is the wakefulness, the vigilance, the attentiveness, the intelligibility that the other person awakes in me. The other is therefore also teacher, not midwife, who only awakens me to myself, to what I somehow already knew, but like an alarm clock one who awakens me to wakefulness itself, to attentiveness prior to propositions affirmed or denied. "To pass from the implicit to the explicit," Levinas writes,

> a master who evokes attention is necessary. To evoke attention is not a subsidiary work; in attention the I transcends itself. A relation with the exteriority of the master was necessary to engage attention. . . . It first of all teaches this teaching itself, by virtue of which alone it can teach (and not, like maieutics, *awaken* in me) things and ideas. (TI, 69)

Before reason can reconstitute sensibility within a totality, untying the knot, as it were, of sensuous self-sufficiency to produce knowledge, the alterity of the other person must first intervene, must first awaken sensibility, as it were, shock it out of its self-absorption. Without this shock the reflexivity of reason would be but an extension of the coiling of sensibility, which it is not, and which it must repress to claim it is so. This is what transpires in Spinoza, where will is made conformable to reason, and any residue is dismissed. So where in truth intellect is simply conforming to itself, the claim is that it reflects and comprises the will. Precisely such a forced parallelism is articulated, for instance, in proposition 23 of part II of the *Ethics*: "The mind does not know itself except in so far as it perceives ideas of affections of the body" (81). Sensibility for Levinas, in contrast, maintains an independence from reason, an independence respected and articulated by phenomenological description rather than rationalized and eliminated by a logical positivism. Such sensibility—the very existence of the existent—only becomes susceptible to reason by way of a conditioned intervention of intersubjectivity, which is to say, in its ultimate significance, by ethical transcendence.

Ethical intersubjectivity is Levinas's answer to the question of how there can be a genuine or radical intervention in relation to a sensible existence apparently isolated in the circuits of its own self-sufficiency. The needy and dependent character of sensibility may be enlisted to explain how subjectivity comes to be *in-the-world*, but it cannot by itself explain contact with alterity between self-sufficient beings. By maintaining a separation between will and reason, Levinas must then answer a question that beleaguered and finally undermined Leibniz: how do windowless monads interact? Leibniz's answer, "the way of pre-established harmony" is unsatisfactory because, rather than answering the problem, it simply multiplies it: each monad remains enclosed within itself, locked up, solitary, even if for an outside observer it appears as if the monads are all undergoing a coordinated unitary experience. Spinoza's answer, a substantialist monism, though logical, is also unsatisfactory because it refuses to acknowledge the real difficulty, refuses to take seriously the independence of self-sufficient beings, which are instead reduced to the status of "attributes" or "modes" of the one substance. Spinoza, in a word and as we have seen, reduces will to reason, thereby eliminating transcendence.[4] Spinoza would repress rather than answer the problem. Levinas's answer is morality. Morality occurs precisely across an "unrelating relation,"[5] a scandal to representational thought, between two beings irreducible to one another. Morality is proximity: difference in identity, the other in the same, as

---

4. Yirmiyahu Yovel's book, *Spinoza and Other Heretics*, is not accidentally subtitled *The Adventures of Immanence*.

5. TI, 295. Earlier in TI, 80, Levinas had written: "For the relation between the being here below and the transcendent being that results in no community of concept or totality—a relation without relation—we reserve the term religion."

I, me myself responsible to and for you. Thus ethics, the account of morality, would, given the precedence of morality, the height of the good, its unsurpassed exigency, its manner of conditioning signification *tout court*, precede ontology in philosophical priority.

But how, we cannot help asking again and again, can ethics solve a problem that the will by itself would subjugate and vanquish and that reason by itself would totalize and reduce away? Avoiding the war and violence, the suppression of plurality, which would follow from an unrestrained animality or an unblinking consciousness, how is it, we are asking, that two sensibilities, originally independent, can rise to moral obligations through intersubjective encounter, and thereby both surpass animality and recognize the legitimate claims of reason?

Levinas's answer stems from a profound understanding of the meaning of suffering, that is to say, the ethical meaning of suffering. Suffering is not a fact, nor is it an idea—it is first of all a call to action, the solicitation of aid. Levinas has written three articles on this topic, all three also having to do with the Holocaust and the end of theodicy: "Transcendence and Evil" (1978),[6] "Useless Suffering" (1982), and "The Call of Auschwitz" (1986). Because I have already discussed these three essays in detail elsewhere[7] (and recommend that readers look at that discussion), here I will summarize their claims briefly, emphasizing the comparison and contrast with Spinoza that is our current interest. All three essays cover the same three basic components: a phenomenology of suffering and evil, a critique of theodicy, and an ethics of suffering.

Levinas discerns two basic characteristics in the phenomenon of suffering: separation and meaninglessness. Given the phenomenological analyses in *Totality and Infinity* regarding the self-sufficiency of sensibility, what we see in these two characteristics is the reverse side, as it were, the dark side of the happiness or positivity of enjoyment. Like enjoyment, suffering is a "coiling" upon itself. Indeed, the essence or "quiddity" of suffering is that it is always a suffering *of itself, a suffering*

---

6. In CPP, 175–186.

7. "What Good Is the Holocaust? Levinas on Suffering and Evil," a paper given on May 7, 1996, at a conference on Ethics after the Holocaust held at the University of Oregon; in *Philosophy Today*, 176–183; and in Cohen, *Ethics, Exegesis and Philosophy*, 266–282.

of suffering. In this way suffering, like happiness, is not simply a quantitative phenomenon, a matter of magnitudes. Regardless of whether suffering is great or little, the essence of suffering is that it suffers from its own suffering. Unlike enjoyment, then, it is always an unwanted, unbearable, painful disturbance, in a word, excess, too much. Also like enjoyment it is of itself a separation, a riveting of self to self, breaking with anonymous existence. But here separation is also meaningless, "useless, 'for nothing'" (US, 158). Unbearable, "non-integrability," "non-synthesizable," as a "refusal of all accommodation," suffering is a "monstrosity" (CCP, 180). Separate, meaningless, and inescapable, the painful is the unwanted dark relative of enjoyment. Indeed, at this primitive level, "where the dimensions of the physical and moral are not yet separated" (SM, 15; my translation), Levinas equates suffering and evil. Suffering is evil, and evil is suffering. The evil of suffering is sensibility as "enjoyment" of the non-enjoyable; it is, that is to say, the self-sufficiency not of pleasure but of pain, pain doubled back on itself, unwanted but unable to free itself by itself from itself. With the language of morality, however, a new problem emerges. "Good and evil" here are the terms not of an animal sensibility alone, whether in pleasure or pain, but of humanity, albeit a finite and sentient humanity. Suffering as evil imposes a question, really a solicitation: What is to be done, done about the suffering? Just as reason makes every attempt, and in Spinoza perhaps reaches its absolute though misguided apogee, to reduce and absorb sensibility into ideation, here, too, in the instance of suffering as evil, reason will attempt to reduce and absorb the evil of suffering. But it will do so by giving reasons for it, in the ultimate sense providing a theodicy, "justifying" suffering. As Levinas rejects Spinoza's effacement of suffering, he will also reject this defacing of suffering.

Just as Spinoza's philosophy represents an absolute elimination of suffering, indeed of happiness too, the absolute form of reason's reductive approach to suffering is theodicy: justification of suffering and evil by means of divine benevolence. (In a certain sense the latter reduces to the former because the ultimate explanation offered by theodicy is that suffering has no being whatsoever, that it is something else entirely from the perspective of Eternity.) Suffering interpreted as punishment, purification, sign, sacrifice, penitential opportunity, and the like, become a necessary part of the *good*, if not a good itself. In Spinoza suffering is reducible to ignorance, and ignorance is a function of imagination. Hence suffering and evil would ultimately be imaginary, without reality. We have seen that at the level of phenomenological analysis, Levinas rejects these intellectualized efforts to interpret away suffering and evil. For Levinas suffering is intrinsically excessive, unwanted and meaningless; its *evil* is nothing other than this. Reason would rather rationalize suffering away, would rather absorb it into its cognitions, to be sure, but suffering is beyond rationalization, and is independent, self-sufficient, and "non-synthesizable." It is a scandal for reason. But it is a scandal reason can no longer ignore in the face of the horrifying events of the twentieth century.[8] Precisely this is the meaning of the Holocaust for Levinas: "the end of theodicy."[9] "The most revolutionary fact of our twentieth century," Levinas writes, "is that of the destruction of all balance between . . . theodicy . . . and the forms which suffering and evil take" (US, 161). "The disproportion between suffering and every theodicy," he continues, "was shown at Auschwitz with a glaring, obvious clarity" (162).

Levinas takes a further step, and with it he paradoxically moves closer to Spinoza. After the Holocaust, not only is theodicy historically refuted, to propound theodicy is henceforth immoral itself, a heightening of suffering and evil rather than their alleviation. "For an ethical sensibility," Levinas writes, "confirming itself, in the inhumanity of our time, against this inhumanity—the justification of the neighbor's pain is certainly the source of all immorality" (US, 163). The evil of human suffering, its excess and meaninglessness should not in any way be attributed to God, because by means of such an entirely baseless gesture humans pretend to an understanding and justification that they absolutely lack, for one, and because it blames the victims of suffering as if there were some reason or justification for their suffering. Unlike Spinoza, however, for Levinas the brute facticity of suffering, the suffering of suffering in all its apparent meaninglessness, in all its evil, remains. "The philosophical problem which is posed by the useless pain which appears in its fundamental malignancy across the events of

---

8. No doubt Ivan Karamazov is right in *The Brothers Karamazov* to argue that the murder of one innocent child is enough to overturn all theodicy, but experience teaches us that humans seem to be impressed far more by large numbers.

9. It is relevant and interesting that, according to Nehemia Polen's reading, Rabbi Kalonymus Kalman Shapira, "the Rebbe of the Warsaw Ghetto," also came to see the suffering of the Jews during the Holocaust in terms other than Divine reward and punishment.

the twentieth century, concerns the meaning that religiosity and the human morality of goodness can still retain after the end of theodicy" (US, 163). Levinas faces this scandal because unlike Spinoza, who flees into intellectual abstraction, he has an answer to "the fundamental ethical problem which pain poses 'for nothing' " (US, 158).

Theodicy is over. Phenomenology shows that suffering transcends meaning. The Holocaust shows that giving meaning to suffering is not only false but immoral. At this juncture, when suffering seems to be irretrievably mired in the monstrosity of its misery, impervious to all meaning, especially ethico-religious meaning, Levinas makes and applies an all-important distinction. He distinguishes the other's suffering from my own suffering. To give meaning to the other's suffering, to explain away the other's suffering is immoral. But my own suffering is another matter. I too suffer. The key to retaining a religious and moral approach in the face of the evil of suffering lies precisely here, in this distinction between self and other. And the key is that *a self can suffer for another*. This, according to Levinas, is "the only meaning to which suffering is susceptible," namely, "suffering for the suffering—be it inexorable—of someone else" (US, 159).

The other's suffering remains non-sense for me, but precisely for this reason my suffering can be meaningful and moral, if and when my suffering is transformed into suffering for the other's meaningless suffering. "The suffering of suffering," Levinas writes, "the suffering for the useless suffering of the other person, the just suffering in me for the unjustifiable suffering of the Other, opens upon suffering the ethical perspective of the inter-human" (US, 159). And this conversion is not simply a matter of feelings, as if morality and religion could be satisfied with an entirely private existence or with the sentimentality of feelings alone. Much more is involved. All of morality, all of justice, pivots on this transformation of suffering. My empathy, my compassion for the other's suffering, is not my private affair, not simply the "beautiful feelings" of an isolated soul. Rather, it is the original sense of moral responsibility.

For Levinas compassion for the other, suffering for the suffering of another, is the "supreme ethical principle" (US, 159)—"where the primordial, irreducible, and ethical, anthropological category of the medical comes to impose itself—across a demand for analgesia" (US, 158). "The doctor is an a priori principle of human morality," Levinas wrote in *Totality and Infinity* (234). To suffer for the other's suffering is to take on *responsibility* for the other's suffering. Nothing could be more concrete and demanding, nothing could be less fanciful or imaginary. It is to hear the call to do whatever one can to alleviate the other's suffering, whether that relief takes the form of "curative help" (US, 158), medicine, bandages, food, clothing, shelter, employment, or respect, conversation, friendship, affection, or simply company, opening one's heart, joking, or just shared presence. Initiated in my suffering, this responsibility extends infinitely, to all of creation. "The humanity of man," Levinas writes, "is fraternally solidary with creation" (CPP, 185), a "responsibility for everything and for all" (CPP, 184). No wonder then that Levinas calls this morality of compassion and the vast responsibilities and obligations it opens up, from love of neighbor to the institutional demands of a just state, "theophany" and "revelation" (CPP, 185). It "makes the idea of God . . . spiritually closer," he writes, "than any kind of theodicy" (US, 159).

Because the morality of suffering for the other's suffering, alleviating the other's suffering, is not driven by theodicy, its actions are performed "indifferent to remuneration" (CPP, 185). Goodness toward others is good in itself, receiving and requiring "no other recompense than this very elevation" (CPP, 185). "No failure," Levinas continues, "could free one from this responsibility for the woe of the other man" (CPP, 185). Not simply a humanism, if by humanism one means no reference to transcendence, this is theophany and revelation—a "biblical humanism"—because in the taking up of this inordinate responsibility, in suffering for the other's suffering, Levinas sees an adult humanity taking upon itself the very responsibilities that theodicy would rather pass off to an ontotheological God. Levinas insists upon the religion and morality of an adult humanity. Compassionate suffering, Levinas writes, "reveals a God Who renounces all aids to manifestation, and appeals instead to the full maturity of the responsible man" (DF, 143). "The adult's God," Levinas writes, "is revealed precisely through the void of the child's heaven" (DF, 143).

Thus Levinas and Spinoza agree that what is highest and best for humans involves no external rewards. They agree that what is best is so in and for itself. Virtue is its own reward. No divine system of rewards and punishments, here or hereafter, is required to motivate goodness. They both agree that an anthropocentric theodicy represents a human degradation. Both oppose mythology, in and out of religion.

As adults and for adults, they both reject the religion of children in the Sunday school.

But through all this agreement, Levinas and Spinoza remain radically opposed, and especially disagree over the nature and role of compassion in humanity's best relation to God. "In the man who lives by the guidance of reason," Spinoza claims in proposition 50 of part IV of his *Ethics*, "pity is in itself bad and disadvantageous."[10] His proof is simple and consistent: "Pity is pain and therefore in itself it is bad" (E, 182). Levinas agrees that pity is pain. And he agrees too that in itself pain is bad. But contra Spinoza he would not negate pain, would not pretend that it is imaginary, an intellectual error, an inadequate idea. Rather Levinas insists that we remain faithful to the phenomenon of pain, acknowledging its uselessness in itself, but at the same time recognizing that pain can be transvalued, can become good when my own suffering becomes responsibility for the suffering of the other. Suffering and compassion are not simply deficient forms of intellection, imperfections alien and unknown and lacking in being in relation to a perfect God. Rather, suffering for the suffering of the other, compassion, is nothing less than the human route to God. "Only the man," Levinas writes, "who has recognized the hidden God can demand that He show Himself" (DF, 145). Such a demand is one to which humanity must rise to achieve its proper nobility, without expectation of divine help or reward. Meeting this demand, responding to the imperative call of the suffering of the other, through goodness and justice, is precisely the revelation of God on earth, theophany.

For Spinoza, in contrast, relation to God opens after an inexplicable leap away from finitude into the intellectual unity of the *always* of a "past perfect" perfection, a pure ideation without shadow or fatigue, where suffering and evil would have no existence and would never have existed. Despite his religious and ethical vocabulary, Spinoza's is a philosophy of cold intellection and inhuman perfection, not love of God but Nature pure and simple, Nature before and without creation, Nature without end. The highest good—but why call it "good," according to a vocabulary it makes obsolete in surpassing?—is perfect

---

10. E, 181. Of course, regarding the rejection of pity, Nietzsche is in complete accord with Spinoza, as we saw in chapter 1 of the present volume.

intellection undisturbed by anything finite, which after all would only be illusory, without being. Human will can play no role here except to conform to intellect, which it already does in any event, whether through sublation, as in the *Ethics*, or through prudent or ignorant subjection, as in the *Theological-Political Treatise*.

For Levinas, the poignancy of suffering, the cry for help, the tears of innocent victims, the obligation to succor, to aid, to render justice, do not so easily evaporate and are not so easily quieted in such Spinozist dreams of intellectual contemplation. The way of God is not the pure activity of reason enraptured with itself but "to give rather than receive, to love and make love, rather than be loved" (SM, 17). Not to contemplate without reward, as Spinoza would have it, but "to serve without reward" (SM, 17), where serving is its own reward. Responsibility, to serve others, "suffering elevated or deepened to a suffering for-the-suffering-of-another-man" (SM, 16). For Levinas, "the link between God and man is not an emotional communion" (DF, 144) or an intellectual communion. It is the concrete work of moral and juridical responsibility for the other, and all others, from the nearest to the farthest, including all of creation.

Chapter Four

Levinas and Spinoza

Justice and the State

The State, Justice, and Religion

In view of Levinas's fundamental opposition to Spinoza, I want to highlight two propositions found in the penultimate chapter of Spinoza's *Theological-Political Treatise*, chapter 19, because of their profoundly Levinasian character. First: "he who practices justice and charity in accordance with God's command is fulfilling God's law, from which it follows that the kingdom of God is where justice and charity have the force of law and command" (212). Second: "indications of divine justice are to be found only where just men reign" (215). It is the joining of divinity and humanism, Spinoza's mediation of God's attribute of justice through human associations, through the state to be more precise, that appears as the Levinasian note of these propositions.

But then, as we shall see, there is something completely non-Levinasian in the meaning and justification these statements have for Spinoza, also having to do with the state. So right away we know that Levinas would not conclude from them, as does Spinoza, that "devotion to one's country is the highest form of devotion that can be shown" (TPT, 215). Certainly for Levinas devotion to justice is the highest devotion one can have, so great that Levinas will characterize it as "holiness" itself, but nonetheless Levinas does not equate devotion to justice with devotion to the state. The discovery of Levinasian as well as non-Levinasian motifs in Spinoza's political thought, combined with what we know to be Levinas's explicit and unremitting opposition to

Spinozism, motivates the aim of the present chapter, which is to investigate more closely and thereby to more perspicaciously clarify the differences that separate Spinoza and Levinas on the topic of justice and the state, indeed differences that put them into frontal opposition, especially because this topic is dear to both thinkers and important in itself.

What results, as we shall see, is that agitating all their differences, the key or fundamental difference arises not so much, or more accurately not at first glance, from what Spinoza and Levinas have to say about justice and the state per se, but rather it lies in the radically different ways they situate justice and the state in relation to morality and religion, and how they situate these latter, morality and religion, in relation to ontology and metaphysics. It is thus in the deepest philosophical underpinnings, the most basic intellectual allegiances, indeed in the ultimate justifications of the state and state justice, that Spinoza and Levinas radically part company. Their apparent agreement, represented by propositions such as those cited earlier, which support something like a divine humanism wherein state justice is the actualization of divine redemption on earth, do indeed stand out as peaks in their respective philosophies, but they turn out to be peaks of two very distant mountains and peaks of very different shapes and altitudes, if this metaphor can be extended so far. To give two preliminary comparative articulations of the chasm that separates Levinas and Spinoza, which will be unpacked, they are: (1) for Spinoza the state rules religion, while for Levinas religion rules the state; and this is so because (2) for Spinoza ruling is primarily and merely a political affair, while for Levinas ruling is primarily and nobly an ethical affair.

Although they are far apart from one another in so much else, Spinoza and Levinas agree, or at least agree in part, about the nature of justice. For both thinkers justice is to render to each person equally his or her due. It is, in a word, equity. No doubt Spinoza and Levinas disagree about what is due to each person as a member of a polity, but they do agree that justice demands equity in the distribution of whatever it is that is due. For both thinkers, too, law and order, justice or right, in the political sphere are maintained through state institutions and sanctions, and hence require the sovereignty of the state for their effective actualization.

The issue behind the juxtaposition of the terms "justice" and the "state" is the question of legitimacy: the legitimacy of the state, the legitimacy of criticizing the state. I am being careful not say "lawfulness," because the question of legitimacy is a broader one. It is a question of platform, grounds, justification. On what basis can one legitimately criticize state actions? If, on the one hand, all legitimacy derives from the state itself, then the question of legitimacy or criticism relative to the state loses its force because all state actions in the final analysis would be self-justifying. A state would be total in this sense, a totalitarian state, even if the lives of its citizens were pleasant rather than painful. Such an answer is called "reasons of state," or "statism." If, on the other hand, legitimacy does not derive solely from the state, then the question of the relation of such extra-state legitimacy to state legitimacy comes into play.

Our question therefore is not restricted to an inquiry about self-legitimizing statism, but rather, as the use of the term "justice" implies, it is about a specific kind of legitimacy, moral legitimacy, and hence about the status of moral judgment regarding state actions, laws, institutions, diplomacy, and the like. It may be the case, as Hobbes and Spinoza will argue, that state actions are always just, by definition as it were, since there is no justice outside the state, but such a position is not necessarily the case, indeed it is not even *prima facie* the case. Moral judgment, to say the obvious, has to do primarily with neither efficiency nor power but with good and evil, right and wrong. A state's actions are just when they are rightly judged to promote good and unjust when they are rightly condemned as promoting evil. That whatever a state does is a priori good, necessarily good in a moral sense, is in no way a given, as one sees not in Hobbes's and Spinoza's conclusions but in their argumentation, their protests. The heart of the question, then, is to determine the proper standard by which a state's actions, in contrast to an individual's actions, say, are rightly judged good and evil. The question of justice and the state, then, is the question of whether there is or is not a moral platform independent of the state from which one can legitimately judge the state's actions, and in extreme situations from which one can judge the worthiness of the state as such. Of course, too, inasmuch as morality is more than a dream or ideology, such moral judgment should in some realistic sense, whether actual or potential, also be efficacious.

So, on the question as to whether there is or is not a moral platform sufficiently independent of the state such that from it one can legitimately determine whether a state's actions are or are not just,

Spinoza says no and Levinas says yes. For Spinoza what is at stake is not only the claim that the existence and sanction of state sovereignty is one condition for the legitimacy of moral judgments regarding state justice, a noncontroversial proposition to which Levinas and most others would adhere, but rather the claim that the state and the state alone legitimately has final and hence absolute say about its own right and wrong. In view of this position, Spinoza's thought, then, and not Levinas's, as we shall see, is what can correctly be labeled "statist" or even "totalitarian." I mention this point because although many astute readers other than Levinas, such as Edwin Curley,[1] Yirmiyahu Yovel,[2] and, I would even say, Lewis Samuel Feuer,[3] have seen and said more or less the same thing about Spinoza's politics, it seems that many other bright readers,[4] including David ben Gurion, have missed this point altogether and made Spinoza out to be a great liberal opponent of totalitarianism, which he surely is not.

Let us continue our inquiry. For both Spinoza and Levinas the issue of justice and the state must be resolved by determining the nature and hence the limits not only of state sovereignty but also, and of far greater importance, by determining the nature and hence the limits of religion. Despite its widespread disestablishment in the contemporary world, the inclusion of religion in the political equation should not surprise us. If there ever was a moral platform with claims to be independent of the state, or whose very character requires such independence, that platform is religious morality. God, for one, is neither subject nor citizen. Hence, if Spinoza is indeed a statist and Levinas a religious moral opponent to statism, as I think they are, then regarding the question of justice and the state, Spinoza must show how religious morality is irrelevant and a hindrance to state justice, while Levinas must show how it is relevant and a buttress to the same. Let us turn then to religious morality.

---

1. Curley, "Kissinger, Spinoza, and Genghis Khan."

2. Yovel, *Spinoza and Other Heretics: The Adventures of Immanence.*

3. Feuer, *Spinoza and the Rise of Liberalism*; see, especially, "The Impasse of Authoritarian Liberalism," 175–179.

4. Such as Dunner, *Baruch Spinoza and Western Democracy: An Interpretation of His Philosophical, Religious and Political Thought.*

As the etymology of the term "religion" (*re-ligio*) suggests, and as their historical and enduring manifestations reveal, organized religions claim as their basis and authority nothing less than a link to God. Obviously it follows from this self-interpretation that religious authority derives not from the state, since the state, like everything else in creation, is subject to God's mastery, but rather from the peculiar status of religion as the most immediate earthly caretaker or intermediary of the divine (putting aside for our purposes the differing claimed sources and preferred means of transmission for this caretaking that the various positive religions privilege). In a nutshell: because religion is closer to God than the state, its moral authority is superior.

Whatever may be claimed regarding the higher, highest, wider, or widest scope of religious authority in relation to state authority, by its own interpretation religious authority comprises moral authority. I state the obvious, in order to move from it to the following increasingly less obvious propositions: (1) Religion, as linked to God, is in part or wholly, but necessarily, independent of the state. While differing regarding its scope, both Spinoza and Levinas agree to this proposition. (2) Religion necessarily comprises religious morality. Spinoza and Levinas agree. (3) Religious morality is independent of the state. Again, although differing in the scope they attribute to this proposition, Spinoza and Levinas agree. But when it comes to (4) Religious morality is a legitimate base from which to morally judge state actions and states, hence a legitimate base to determine the justice of a state's actions or the justice of a state altogether, Spinoza and Levinas part company. They part company because for Spinoza religious morality as a ground and standard must be considered a strictly *private* affair, one that can be and is overruled in the *public* sphere by state sovereignty, while for Levinas religious morality is the very source and justification of state sovereignty altogether. And here we hit upon the heart of the difference separating Spinoza and Levinas, namely, the differing scope they envision for religious morality.

Spinoza: Knowledge and Power

For Spinoza religious morality is a private affair: "inward worship of God and piety itself belong to the sphere of individual right" (TPT, 212), he writes at the beginning of chapter 19 and refers back to chapter 7, where he wrote: "Inasmuch as it [religion] consists not so much in outward actions as in simplicity and truth of character, it stands outside the sphere of law and public authority" (119). Regarding the public sphere, in contrast, morality is an affair of the state. The state is the final arbiter of justice, and hence cannot be judged externally. "No private citizen," Spinoza writes, "can know what is good for the state except from the decrees of the sovereign, to whom *alone* it belongs to transact public business. Therefore no one can practice piety aright nor obey God unless he obeys the decrees of the sovereign *in all things*" (TPT, 216; emphasis added). In the end, then, state actions are not subject to moral judgment at all. Reasons of state, however cloaked in moral garb, are not moral reasons but statements of self-survival, perseverance in being.

Spinoza limits religion, and hence religious morality, in a two-step process. The first is epistemological and takes place in the *Ethics* and chapters 1 through 15 of the *Theological-Political Treatise*, and the second, built upon the first, is political and takes place in the *Theological-Political Treatise*, chapters 16 through 20

Following Socrates's footsteps, but down a naturalist rather than a moralist path, in the *Ethics* Spinoza reduces positive religion to natural religion. I say "reduce" deliberately because "true religion," as he calls it, turns out to be nothing other than allegiance to the knowledge of natural science, whether that knowledge be partial, which Spinoza calls "knowledge of the second kind" or *ratio*, or all-embracing, which Spinoza calls "knowledge of the third kind" or *scientia intuitiva*. "Popular" (as Spinoza calls it) or unscientific religion, in contrast, is obedience to a fabric of self-serving anthropomorphic imaginings (*imaginatio*) by the ignorant masses (the latter expression, "ignorant masses," being a redundant one for Spinoza). Instead of reason freely affirming truth, which is true religion (in Spinozist "doublespeak"), popular religion is constituted by submission to external authority, which is always by nature irrational and unfree.

The *Ethics*, Spinoza's science of reality, is called an "ethics," an obviously moral term, because science for Spinoza is not merely knowledge taken as one component of life but an entire and comprehensive way of life, indeed the only truly free life. Hence science is true religion, or true religion is science. Here Spinoza joins a long philosophic tradition stretching from Pythagoras to Husserl. As Wolfson has shown most clearly, by casting his lot with the monist and immanent reality known by natural science, Spinoza is able to dispense with all the religious residues, the unresolvable dualisms, that so disturb Descartes's philosophy. The well-known slogan that best sums up Spinoza's conflation of science and religion is *Deus sive Natura*, "God or nature," where the "or" is exclusive rather than inclusive. In true religion, in other words, for the term "God" one can always substitute the term "nature," nature as known by the natural sciences. Thus, the first limitation Spinoza places on positive or popular religion is epistemological: to denigrate it as the imaginary, the superstitious, the passionate, the unfree, in a word, the realm of ignorance, obedience, the non-true.

But life forces Spinoza to retrace Parmenides's *On Nature*. Though the "way of truth" of the *Ethics* is intended as the whole truth and nothing but the truth, the "way of opinion" somehow does not go away. For the few, the knowers, there is "true religion" so-called, freedom, natural science, and the meta-theory of natural science found in the *Ethics*; for the many, the ignorant, in contrast, *and also for the few who invariably must live with the many*, there is the realm of unfreedom, obedience, Church and State, Bible and politics, the subject matter of the *Theological-Political Treatise*.[5] This brings us to the second limitation Spinoza places on religion. The *Ethics*, as we have seen, excludes positive religion from true knowledge, leaving it the sphere of piety and obedience, that is, morality. Upon this basis the *Theological-Political Treatise* will make a further exclusion, now from within the already limited sphere of obedience. It excludes positive religion from public political life, banishing it to the private sphere of inwardness. Just as the *Ethics* denigrated positive religion for the sake of "true religion" or natural science, so, too, the *Theological-Political Treatise* denigrates positive religion, but now, as we have already seen, for the sake of a "kingdom of God" obtained exclusively through *state sovereignty*. As in the *Ethics*, where an essentially nonteleological natural science is glossed in the language of religion, *Deus sive Natura*, here, too, a religious language will be used to gloss an essentially secular or statist politics. Almost any citation from chapters 16 through 20 of the *Theological-Political Treatise* would show this displacement, but the following three from chapter 19 will suffice. The first sentence: "When I said above that *only* those who hold the sovereign power have an overall right

---

5. See the next chapter for a more precise account of for whom the *Theological-Political Treatise* is written.

and that *all* law is dependent on their decision alone, I intended not only civil but religious law; for in the case of the latter, too, they must be both interpreters and guardians" (212; emphasis added). Another: "it is also the duty of the sovereign *alone* to decide what form piety towards one's neighbor should take, that is, in what way every man is required to obey God" (215–216; emphasis added). Or, again: "since it is established both by reason and experience that the divine law is *entirely* dependent on the decrees of rulers, it follows that these are also the interpreters of the divine law" (215; emphasis added). After reinterpreting religion to show that it is itself but a political structure (realm of emotional obedience), and then after subordinating it to political sovereignty (realm of sanctioned obedience), what is left of religion as it is commonly understood is confined by Spinoza to private conscience—"inward worship of God and piety itself belong to the sphere of individual right."

To sum up thus far: for Spinoza religious morality is a purely private affair, an affair of conscience, which at same time if it has a public manifestation, it must—along with all else having to do with religion—be strictly subordinate to the dictates of the state. The state is the final arbiter of justice, solely responsible for "God's kingdom on earth," because the state and nothing but the state defines justice. "Justice," Spinoza writes, "is dependent on the laws of the authorities, so that no one who contravenes their accepted decrees can be just" (260). In all this Spinoza is following Hobbes.

Levinas: Morality and Justice

Levinas reorients the sense of religion in relation to both justice and the state. Levinas and Spinoza, and both thinkers very much within the Jewish rabbinic tradition in this regard, erect bulwarks against religious activism based on alleged immediacy with God. But instead of reinterpreting religion by reducing it to the "freedom" thought by science ("God, or Nature") or privatizing the ignorant remainder of obedience, as does Spinoza, Levinas follows Kant in seeing religion through the lens of social ethics and follows Buber, Rosenzweig, and Rosenstock-Huessy, among others, in understanding society starting with a communications theory, ethically interpreted. Without at all eliminating the sphere of immanence and privacy, for Levinas, in opposition to Spinoza, individual conscience is not simply a private affair. Conscience, too, even in its innermost recesses, as interiority, inasmuch as it is a dimension of morality remains a form of sociality, of relation to the other person. Religious inwardness, then, as moral conscience, is a form of repentance, which is to say of self-expiation and self-improvement, inner purification for the sake of the other.

Spinoza never grasped what for Levinas is one of the central teachings of "Jewish wisdom," and a central feature of genuine reason (in contrast to Spinoza's modern rationality), namely, that spirit and letter, inner and outer, private and public, are inseparable and interdependent. In contrast to Merleau-Ponty, who certainly also knew this structure of intertwining, Levinas shows that at bottom this relationship is an ethical rather than an ontological structure, what we have already encountered previously as the "for-the-other." The humanity of the human arises as the other-in-me, as my responsibility for-the-other before myself, as what Levinas also calls the "maternal" psyche: the self as bearing the other within itself as responsibility to and for the other. Spinoza's way of avoiding the inner conflicts of Cartesian dualism is to have recoiled from the thick or messy intertwining of spirit and matter, and to have tried to reduce matter to mind, conflating idea and thing: "The order and connection of ideas is the same (Pr. 7, II) as the order and connection of things, and vice versa" (E, V, Prop. 1, Proof, 203). Levinas will argue that the failure of Spinoza's reductive idealism in the *Ethics* is manifest in the *Theological-Political Treatise* in its artificial and unwarranted segregation of spirit and letter. Such is one prong of Levinas's several criticisms of the very form of Spinozist rationality.[6] In chapter 6 in this volume we will examine more deeply Spinoza's fundamental misunderstanding of wisdom as understood in the Jewish rabbinical and Talmudic tradition.

---

6. That spirit and letter are inseparable is one of the key points of "Towards the Other" and "The Temptation of Temptation," two of Levinas's "Talmudic Readings," found in NTR, 12–50. On pages 39–40, for example: "I have insisted more than once that the Talmudic spirit goes radically beyond the letter of Scriptures. Its spirit was nonetheless formed in the very letters it goes beyond, so as to reestablish, despite apparent violences, the permanent meaning within these letters." According to Levinas in "The Spinoza Case" (DF, 106–110), by arguing for the separation of letter and spirit in the *Theological-Political Treatise* Spinoza has eviscerated reason and succumbed to an "anti-Jewish" position.

Levinas, in any event, locates the pacific force of morality, the breakthrough of the infinite, in sociality. Inextricably linked to the social, in contrast to Spinoza, for Levinas religious morality is the fulcrum rather than the bane of state justice. To be sure, for Levinas one of the virtues of religion and religious language is not, as in Spinoza, because it can be appropriated for conversion into science and scientific language, but rather because taken in their own terms they open a dimension of the meaningful, the significant, in which terms are bound without identity, linked without synthesizing totalization. Religion succeeds in holding transcendence and immanence together, however, not because of some direct or immediate relation to God, as so-called religious fundamentalists have averred, but rather and precisely because of its irreducible moral dimension. Thus, in opposing superstition and mythology, instead of naturalizing religion away and subordinating its ignorant residue to the state, Levinas raises and ties religion to its proper social and political responsibilities, insists upon "religion for adults," and thereby raises sociality and politics to their moral responsibilities. Instead of redefining the human by reducing it to the natural, as does Spinoza, Levinas revalues the human in terms of a moral-religious sociality and thereby legitimates the justice of the state based on nobility rather than being.

There are also two steps to Levinas's position, but in this case the first is morality and the second justice, rather than first knowledge and second power as we saw in Spinoza. As we know Levinas understands morality as the obligation one has to another or, more precisely, that I, in the first-person singular, have to and for you. Such an obligation, however, is infinite. No one can fully satisfy the needs of even one other person, and of course there are many others. This infinition of obligation is precisely the religious dimension of Levinas's thought: the rupture of immanence, the imposition of radical otherness, heteronomy before autonomy, irreducible transcendence imposing itself. One cannot do enough for the other, and this never-doing-enough, this infinite in the finite that is the upsurge of morality, is the very nobility—or "holiness"—of one's own humanity, in contrast to Spinoza who defines the human by means of *conatus*, perseverance in being, which is the essence not only of human beings but of all beings indiscriminately. Spinoza, as we have seen, assimilates the human to the animal and really to the natural as a whole, as he expressly claims in the preface to part III of his *Ethics* and reiterates in various ways in many other places.[7] In contrast, what it means to be a human "I" for Levinas occurs not by definition but by elevation, a rising to the infinite, the infinite mediated as morality. Humans are distinct because they are distinguished.

Quite unlike the *conatus* of natural beings, morality, religion ("holiness"), and the humanity of the human emerge together. Their signification is not given but established, emerging in the exigencies of inordinate obligations to and responsibilities for the other, contesting the motives of the freedoms of the will-to-know and the will-to-power. Making such a dynamic fundamental, Levinas grounds the human neither in epistemology, for the few, nor in politics, for the many, as does Spinoza, neither in the ways of truth nor opinion. Morality demands that its demands be grasped in their own terms, for morality is neither an ideological epiphenomenon nor an additive function. Its priorities demand priority, establish priority, and as such and only as such are they moral demands. Moral priority is essentially different and exerts an essentially different force than the priorities of knowledge and power. Exceeding and contesting the correlations and circles of a knowing that knows knowledge, and a power that empowers power, morality is moral. If these other complexes in defending themselves end up in circularity, in a certain sense so too does morality. It is good to be good. One cannot ask, or rather there is an inherent fraudulence, danger, or hypocrisy—a moral hypocrisy—in asking the epistemological and/or political question as to whether one is or is not one's brother's keeper—because one already is! The priority of moral priority, however, is neither naïveté nor violence,[8] as a Spinozist (or Nietzschean) would have it. The final word, or the first word, not spoken in a formulation, proposition, thesis, but the "saying of the said," is already *goodness*, already moral *glory*, *holiness*—attentiveness to the other. Moral force is the driving force of all of Levinas's work, the driving force that undercuts and challenges the totalizing claims of epistemology and politics and then reconditioning and reestablishing the claims of science and power on their proper footing, as it were, in relation to their proper height.

---

7. See the preface to part III of the *Ethics*, where in addition to disparaging the notion of a "kingdom within a kingdom," Spinoza also writes: "I shall consider human actions and appetites just as if it were an investigation into lines, planes, or bodies" (103). In chapter 7 of the *Theological-Political Treatise*, Spinoza writes: "I hold that the method of interpreting Scripture is no different from the method of interpreting Nature, and is in fact in complete accord with it" (87).

8. See "The Temptation of Temptation," in NTR, 30–50.

Still, even if one undercuts the usual philosophical and political objections by granting a fundamental status to morality, *morality is not good enough.* Here we begin to see the second step toward Levinas's position vis-à-vis justice and the state and Spinoza. Morality is not good enough not because of some lack but because of an excess: morality contains the seeds, is impressed by the force of demands that exceed even its own infinite demands. Or, to express this in another way: *left to itself morality becomes unjust,* and it does so in a very precise way. Because Levinas conceives morality to be the exigency—unto death—of an infinite obligation to the other person, we are forced to ask and care about other others, others who are other to and for the one to whom I am morally responsible. The other I face may be endangered, mistreated, and otherwise threatened by others whom I do not face. To neglect "the third," as Levinas calls these others, would be to fail *morally,* even if the "reason" for this failure is the very reverse of selfishness, namely, an infinite concern for the one who faces! Here, then, from out of the very moral demand of morality, from my unfulfillable moral responsibility to and for the other person, the question of justice and the state inevitably also emerges. Such is the second step of Levinas's ethics. In a society of two—the one-for-the-other—morality alone would be sufficient. Such is the Garden of Eden, not where complacency and indifference hold sway, ruled by the gravity of nature, but rather where one is helpmeet to the other, where flesh is driven by spirit. It is perhaps as much an erotic as an ethical environment, and perhaps eros always in some way approaches such a dual society. But in our world, exiled from Paradise, as it were, a world which contains many more than two persons, giving everything to one when others too are needy is not just immoral, it is *unjust.* Justice arises, then, not because of the state, a function of reasons of state, as in Spinoza and Hobbes, but rather the state arises because of the requirements of justice, and justice arises and is maintained owing to the limitations in an unredeemed world of religious morality itself. Thus morality for moral reasons demands justice, and justice, to remain just, aims at morality. All of this is absolutely opposed to Spinoza and Spinozism.

And here too at the level of justice and the state, where instead of facing one person all relevant persons must be taken into account (as subjects, as citizens), the normative and religious expression "unredeemed" becomes appropriate. In a redeemed world—and note that this for Levinas is the very definition of a redeemed world and as such the aim and measure of justice—*morality and justice would be one.* That is to say, in a redeemed world doing everything for one's neighbor would deprive no one else of anything. In such a world infinite obligation and equity would be simultaneously and universally fulfilled. In our world, however, this is obviously not the case, which is precisely the mark that our world is unredeemed. Because giving everything to one's neighbor, which is the demand of morality, produces injustice for others elsewhere, morality itself demands its own self-rectification through justice. Justice, of course, requires the state, sovereignty, both to institute and to increase justice by means of laws, courts of law, legislation, sanctions, police, foreign relations, and the like. But now, according to a Levinasian rather than a Hobbesian or Spinozist perspective, the standard of justice lies outside the state in morality, in the proximity of one to another, the one for another. Now justice stands in relation to morality, to the human face, and without being any less just is tempered by and serves mercy. Or, as Levinas writes: "Justice, society, the State and its institutions, exchanges and work are comprehensible out of proximity. This means that nothing is outside of the control of the responsibility of the one for the other" (OBBE, 159). The function of the state is to maintain justice, equal protection, and equal opportunity for all; justice is just to the extent that it serves morality; thus the state must be judged from the perspective of justice, and the perspective of justice must be judged ultimately from the perspective of morality. Thus the state does not create or determine but rather serves justice and morality.

Levinas's model then is radically different from and opposed to Spinoza's. For Spinoza the only alternative to civil society is not moral being as in Levinas, but natural being, *conatus.* Natural being, however, is as Hobbes saw it, wretched and dangerous. This is why outside the state there can be no standard for either justice or morality. Outside the state is war. The origin of the state is not the moral need to rectify morality, as it is for Levinas, but rather to escape the brute violence and fear of the jungle, survival of the strongest and fear of war. Because the state springs from fear, of violence and war, rather than from love, that is, the moral need for justice, nothing has priority over *order* for Spinoza. Any order, just or unjust, cruel or kind, tyrannical or democratic, as we shall see in a moment, is better than no order. *Absolutum dominum.* What is clear is that Spinoza could never say what Levinas has to say at the conclusion of *Otherwise than Being or Beyond Essence.*

"The true problem for us Westerners is not so much to refuse violence as to question ourselves about a struggle against violence which without blanching in non-resistance to evil, could avoid the institution of violence out of this very struggle" (177).

Spinoza does seem to prefer a so-called just state to a so-called unjust state, though his reasons are not moral but prudential: a just state has greater stability and hence provides greater *security* than an unjust state. Security, not goodness, not justice, is the "basis of the state that is its ultimate purpose," the best condition for the maintenance of power,

> is not to exercise dominion nor to restrain men by fear and deprive them of independence, but on the contrary to free every man from fear so that he may live in security as far as it is possible, that is, so that he may best preserve his own natural right to exist and to act, without harm to himself and to others. (TPT, 223)

Security is the *sine qua non* of sovereignty. When Spinoza writes that "the purpose of the state is, in reality, freedom" (TPT, 223), he is not contradicting himself but merely reminding his better readers that the real purpose of life is not to be found in the political realm at all, because it is entirely the realm of obedience. Freedom is found in truth, in science, in knowledge of the true, immutable, and necessary laws of the universe. The function of the state is entirely different: to ensure peace, to enforce public security, to keep the ignorant down, so that they do not interfere with the few who alone enjoy freedom. This why Spinoza has no trouble or shame writing, in words that recall Machiavelli more than anyone else, the following: "Those who govern the state or hold the reins of power always strive to cloak with a show of legality whatever wrong they commit, persuading the people that this action was right and proper" (TPT, 195). Statecraft is a matter of power; morality and justice are what the state says they are and so enforces. No one can judge the state but the state, which is to say, there is no possible moral judgment of the state, and no possibility of an unjust state.

Spinoza's support for justice is no more than a preference, however, because the so-called unjust state, though perhaps less stable than the so-called just state, must be obeyed no less than a just state. In the final account, the unjust state is as right and has as much right as the just state; the terms "just" and "unjust" are simply, as in the previous citation, ideological tools of the powerful to maintain their power. This is why at the end of chapter 18, in line with his reduction of all things to no greater impetus than their *conatus*, their perseverance in being, Spinoza is happy to conclude that "[e]very state must necessarily preserve its own form, and cannot be changed without incurring the danger of utter ruin."[9] Spinoza's greatest fear with regard to the political, a fear consistent with the philosopher's fear of chaos, is not immorality, not injustice, but anarchy. In the end, right is determined by might, and not by morality, and hence is the prerogative of the state itself. Near the end of chapter 19 Spinoza boldly raises the following difficulty regarding his own view: "Now perhaps at this point I shall be asked: 'Then if those who hold the sovereignty choose to be impious, who will be the rightful champion of piety? Are the rulers still to be regarded as the interpreters of religion?'" (219). His only answer, however, is no answer but a counter-question: "To this I ask in return: 'What if churchmen (who are also but human, and, as private citizens, are entitled to have regard for their own affairs) or any others to whom it is proposed to entrust control over religion, should choose to be impious? Are they even then to be regarded as the interpreters of religion?'" (219). No doubt to ask who is to police the police, who is to regulate the regulators, or who is to teach the teachers, is to raise difficult questions; but for all their difficulty, it is hardly adequate, it seems to me, to simply dismiss them in the name, apparently, of a universal unsurpassable selfishness. For Levinas, in contrast, the struggle of forces that constitutes the state is always one to be judged and driven by the difficult goal of justice as a moral standard and never simply as a jungle, a struggle for power and nothing more.

Let us conclude. While both Spinoza and Levinas support justice over injustice, equity over inequity, Spinoza's support is no more than

---

9. TPT, 211. Just a few years later in France, Jacques-Bénigne Bossuet, writing as a Catholic theologian, will also defend the absoluteness of government against any possible dissent or change. "He [Bossuet] takes his worship of the known so far as to say that one must accept whatever form of government is in existence, quoting Romans, XII, 102: '. . . *il n'y a point de puissance qui ne soit de Dieu; et toutes celles qui sont, c'est Dieu qui les a s'établies . . .*'" Citation from Jacques-Bénigne Bossuet, *Politique tirée des propres paroles de l'écriture sainte*, Book II, Article 2, Proposition 12, in Kearns, 126.

prudential because it is based on considerations of power and security alone, and, more deeply still, his prudential support is the expression of a preference based on an ultimate concern for and commitment to scientific knowing for the few only. Levinas's support for justice, in contrast, derives from considerations based neither in knowledge nor power but rather from consideration of the internal dynamics of a higher commitment to religious morality, one that requires equity to rectify the inadequacy of morality in an unredeemed world, that is to say, a religious morality fundamentally a politics of redemption. It is in this sense, where justice and the state derive their authority from morality rather than from knowledge and power, that Levinas is able to agree with the very positive sense in which Mahatma Gandhi once declared that "whoever does not understand that there is no religion without politics, does not understand religion."

Chapter Five

Spinoza's Prince

For Whom Is the *Theological-Political Treatise* Written?

The *Theological-Political Treatise* and Its Three Parts

Baruch Spinoza's *Theological-Political Treatise* (1670) is one of only two books Spinoza published in his lifetime, and unlike the first, *Principles of Cartesian Philosophy and Metaphysical Thoughts* (1663), he published it anonymously. Spinoza's most famous and important work, the *Ethics*, in which he articulates his own philosophy, which is a scientific or rational philosophy of science, the manuscript of which he circulated privately to a limited number of scholars, appeared only posthumously in 1677, as part of the *Opera Posthuma*, much of which Spinoza had left for his Dutch friends to publish. We know from a letter of September 1675 to "the most noble and learned Henry Oldenburg" (letter no. 68), that Spinoza had intended to publish the *Ethics* earlier but "decided to postpone the publication I had in mind," fearful of the harsh public denunciations he expected from "certain theologians" and "the stupid Cartesians" (CW, 935). The relevant point is that the *Ethics*, or at the very least its core metaphysics, was worked out *prior* to the *Theological-Political Treatise*, and it is most probable, too, that Spinoza continued to review and edit it, especially its last three parts, during the five years he was composing the *Theological-Political Treatise*. The significance of this point, as we shall shortly see, is not just chronological but rather lies in the fundamental importance—as philosophical ground—of Spinoza's *Ethics* to the *Theological-Political Treatise*.

From the *Opera Posthuma* we also know that Spinoza wrote but did not complete four additional works. Though there has been some controversy over their dating, it is now generally accepted that two were written prior to the *Ethics* and the *Theological-Political Treatise*, namely, *Treatise on the Emendation of the Intellect* and *Short Treatise on God, Man, and His Well-Being*; and that two were written after the *Theological-Political Treatise*, namely, *Hebrew Grammar* and *Political Treatise*. Not only were none of these four manuscripts published, but unlike the unpublished *Ethics*, none of them were completed either. Their status for Spinoza scholarship, therefore, must take second place to the *Principles*, the *Theological-Political Treatise*, and the *Ethics*. Nevertheless, given the topic of the present chapter, it does not seem wise to ignore the *Political Treatise*, and for two reasons. The first and most obvious reason is because both the *Theological-Political Treatise* and the *Political Treatise* are explicitly concerned with politics. In some instances the *Political Treatise* almost verbatim adopts positions first enunciated in the *Theological-Political Treatise*, but in all cases it continues discussions of topics begun there. The second and also fairly obvious reason is that appearing after the *Theological-Political Treatise* it does not simply repeat the positions taken in the *Theological-Political Treatise* but extrapolates some of them; in particular it provides more extensive accounts of monarchy and aristocracy. Still, and not only because our focus is the *Theological-Political Treatise*, we must not exaggerate the authorial imprimatur of the unpublished and unfinished *Political Treatise*. Thus it will supplement but not direct our analyses.

A final and important point is to be drawn from the unfinished and unpublished status of Spinoza's several manuscripts other than *Cartesian Principles, Theological-Political Treatise*, and *Ethics*. It is a point that emerges most poignantly with regard to the noncompletion of *Treatise on the Emendation of the Intellect*, namely: Spinoza has a problem with pedagogy. The problem is that it is an essential problem, one that he cannot overcome. In this regard let us call to mind Spinoza's repugnance for babies, infants, and women, a topic to which we shall return in full force in chapter 8. In a scholium to proposition 6 of part V of his *Ethics*, Spinoza makes the following telling observation: "If most people were born adults and only a few were born babies, then everybody would feel sorry for babies because they would then look on infancy not as a natural and necessary thing but as a fault and flaw in Nature" (206). Or let us recall that in his Hebrew grammar—unfinished, also unpublished, to be sure—Spinoza tries to explain away the irregularity of Hebrew verbs and other exceptional and obviously historically contingent linguistic constructions.[1] Everything, for Spinoza, must be completed, finished, perfect. Nature is that which is perfectly, immutably, eternally, unalterably lawful. It follows that nothing needs emendation, education, improvement; change and growth are illusions; permanence alone is real. This is what I mean in saying that pedagogy is a problem for Spinoza.

More broadly we can say that Spinoza has a problem everywhere with irregularity, contingency, novelty, in a word, with change. At the metaphysical level this appears in his characterization of substance and its attributes as eternal and necessary, and hence unchanging, and in his understanding of all things as driven not by finality but by *conatus*, perseverance in being. At the political level, as we shall see, this commitment to eternal perfection manifests itself as undeviating support for the status-quo, opposition to any change whatsoever, in principle, "that every state must necessarily preserve its own form, and cannot be changed without incurring the danger of utter ruin" (TPT, 211). So if a monarchy is the present government, then Spinoza must prefer it to any attempt to change to another type of regime. If democracy is the status quo, so too he must oppose any attempts to overthrow it. It is not that Spinoza prefers monarchy, or democracy; it is that he opposes all change. Finally, viewing Spinoza as he viewed himself, that is, as a philosopher, a philosopher who through concentrated and sustained intellection believed he had achieved superior insights, and hence a philosopher with truths to teach, truths not yet appreciated by the world, here his rejection of change manifests itself in his evident difficulty, indeed in the essential impossibility of being able to write a pedagogical book such as *Treatise on the Emendation of the Intellect*. It is the problematic later raised in relation to Hegel's introduction to the *Phenomenology of Spirit*: If the book says everything, as it claims, being a complete (if schematic) account of the whole, then what *in addition* can or need be said in an introduction?

---

1. See Levy; Harvey. More generally, on the rational reformation of life in the early modern period, see Burke, especially 207–243.

To express this aporia in Spinoza's metaphysical terms: if the universe is strictly determined, as Spinoza argues that it is, then there is no improving it, or rather, writing or not writing books, influencing or not influencing readers, awareness or ignorance of truth, preference for one political regime or another, make not a whit of difference in the unfolding of a nature of which humans are an integral but not an exceptional part. Everything unfolds as it "should" means no more nor less than everything unfolds as it must. Granted, the true workings of things are not known to humans, not fully in any event. Regardless, in their ignorance humans substitute wishes for realities, imaginings for truth, and the more so the more ignorant they are, oblivious to and heedless of the necessary order of the universe. Of course, too, their very obliviousness and heedlessness are also a necessary part of a universe unfolding with seamless necessity. Spinoza's is a fatalistic philosophy: whatever happens must happen (see E, II, Prop. 48).

Accordingly, there is an *unresolved* dualism between the eternal and the temporal, between the necessary and the contingent, between substance with its attributes and concrete modes, that permeates all of Spinoza's thought, haunting and undermining the alleged consistency of his metaphysics, most profoundly, but no less haunting and undermining the consistency of his political philosophy (*Theological-Political Treatise*) and his pedagogical therapy (*Ethics* III–V) as well. We recall here what Diogenes Laertius said of the Stoics, who created and experienced the same problem: "It is a tenet of theirs that between virtue and vice there is nothing intermediate,"[2] so "one cannot move from one to the other, each is necessary and each is necessarily what it is."[3]

---

2. Diogenes Laertius, *Lives of Eminent Philosophers*, 231, on Zeno (333–261 BCE), son of Mnaseas.

3. We cannot agree, then, with the alternative position, that Spinoza's philosophy indeed has a well-developed pedagogy, argued by Firmin DeBrabander in *Spinoza and the Stoics: Power, Politics and the Passions*. No doubt DeBrabander is correct, as any reader of Spinoza can see, especially in parts III to V of the *Ethics*, that Spinoza makes recommendations about reducing the debilitating influence of the passions (primarily suggesting that one decommission an unwonted passion by means of a more active passion), but DeBrabander simply ignores the logical and ontological contradictions between the strict or rationally justified determinism of Spinoza's philosophy (*Ethics* I and II), and Spinoza's practical recommendations.

The upshot is that as we read the *Theological-Political Treatise*, this failure at the heart of his thought, showing itself in certain equivocations, will several times be forced upon our attention, especially when we try to clarify and understand what Spinoza means by "democracy" and "freedom." In the *Political Treatise* this contradiction appears not only in the fact of the unpublished, unfinished status of the manuscript but more particularly, regarding content, in the fact that while Spinoza was somehow able to write about the virtues and vices of monarchy and aristocracy, when it came to democracy, which ostensibly or according to many commentators is meant to be Spinoza's preferred political regime, there his pen failed him completely.

So, to continue, just as our concern with Spinoza's books, unpublished and published, is not primarily one of bibliographical, historical-chronological, or scholarly-authorial interest but rather and more deeply a philosophical interest in its theses and arguments, a philosophical interest, that is to say, in his philosophy, which means, as we have seen, considering his philosophy in relation to the conceptual aporia that permeate and perforate it, one must obviously remain cognizant of the same in any attempt such as ours to understand the *Theological-Political Treatise*. That is to say, positively, Spinoza's proposals regarding politics and religion in the *Theological-Political Treatise* are—as he himself makes clear and whose consequences we will make even clearer—intimately linked to his rational or philosophical account of the eternal and the necessary intelligibility of the universe that is articulated in the *Ethics*. To take this approach is not simply to conform to the general and worthy hermeneutic recommendation to read a philosopher's works together and of a piece, which we indeed intend to do. But more particularly it is to satisfy a requirement, and to follow the procedure followed by Spinoza himself in the *Theological-Political Treatise*.

First, then, what is the overall structure of the book? Despite what is announced in its title, which makes explicit two contents or components, the theological and the political, there are actually three distinct and interrelated parts that comprise the *Theological-Political Treatise*. The first and ruling part is not named in the title. Its appearance and preeminence, however, should come as no surprise. It is Spinoza's fundamental philosophy, as found in the *Ethics*. Remember, the *Ethics* was not published in Spinoza's lifetime, so certainly almost all readers, with some few exceptions, of the *Theological-Political Treatise* cannot have known of it. Instead of simply assuming it, as he might have, Spinoza begins the *Theological-Political Treatise* with a summary of its central and pertinent theses. Many commentators seem to have overlooked this. We cannot. So, the tripartite division of the *Theological-Political Treatise* is as follows. First are chapters 1 through 6, based in philosophy, where scientific knowledge of true causes based in "principles and axioms" (20) are distinguished from the merely imaginative and anthropomorphic "rantings of superstition" (21) characteristic of popular religion but also hardly less at work in politics. Second are chapters 7 through 15, "theology," biblical criticism, where theology and science (i.e., part 1 and part 2), faith and philosophy, illusion and truth, obedience and freedom, are shown to have "no relation and no affinity" (164) with one another. Religion, in a word, should not pretend to truth and should not interfere with science's pursuit of truth. Third are chapters 16 through 20, political philosophy, where following Hobbes Spinoza argues that in the world of nonphilosophy and obedience (parts 2 and 3), the state and not religion should have absolute priority, absolute sovereignty, and as such the state is fully justified "to make what decisions it thinks fit concerning religion" (183). Such is the overall structure and such are the basic themes and positions of the text.

The paragraphs that follow, of the present subsection, are intended to provide a somewhat deeper though still quite compressed expository review of the main positions and aims of each of these three parts, the philosophical, the theological, and the political. Though only a summary, this review is strictly required as the necessary conceptual precondition for answering the question that has set the task and title of the present chapter, namely: For whom is the *Theological-Political Treatise* written? We shall turn to this question soon and, let us hope, well prepared.

The first part of the *Theological-Political Treatise*, comprising chapters 1 through 6, while discussing topics theological and political does so by placing such topics in relation to an abbreviated version of the philosophy Spinoza developed in full and *ordine geometrico demonstrate* in *Ethics*. As we know, *Ethics* articulates Spinoza's philosophy of one substance, two (of infinite) attributes, and their multitudinous modes, in their eternal and necessary intelligibility, according to a deductive logic, at the same time claiming to understand nature scientifically according to a thoroughgoing efficient causality without any resort to final ends.[4] Spinoza takes this intelligibility to be the realm of *freedom* not in a political sense, that is, disciplined initiative within a play of forces, but in a *philosophical* sense, that is, the freedom that because knowing necessity knows the inevitable contours and boundaries of the real. Theology and politics, in contrast, the topics of parts 2 and 3, that is, the rest of book, deal not with true or "adequate ideas," as Spinoza calls true knowledge, but the realm of *obedience*, of *political freedom*, willfulness, initiative, choice, purposefulness, hence a practical, relative, or human freedom. It is important not to confuse these two realms, of truth and belief, of necessity and obedience.[5] "The things whose goodness derives only from authority and tradition, or from their symbolic representation of some good, cannot

---

4. "Nothing in nature is contingent" (E, I, Prop. 29, 51); Appendix: "Nature has no fixed goal and . . . all final causes are but figments of the human imagination" (E, I, Appendix, 59). And, regarding freedom of thought (or nonfreedom of thought), let us also cite from Spinoza's proof to proposition 1 of part V of the *Ethics*: "The order and connection of ideas is the same (Pr. 7, II) as the order and connection of things, and, vice versa" (203), despite this claim being one of the most enigmatic and inexplicable claims of the entire *Ethics*.

5. Leo Strauss, in "How to Study Spinoza's *Theological-Political Treatise*" (1948), is also aware that "the first six chapters of the *Theological-Political Treatise*" (199) rely on this very different basis than the rest of the book. Thus he is also aware that they stand on grounds contrary to Spinoza's famous principle of biblical criticism, meant to guide the second section of the book, that Scripture alone be used to interpret Scripture. Thus Strauss writes of chapters 3 through 5, on election, ceremonial law, and miracles: "Spinoza asserts, in striking contradiction to that principle, that the biblical teaching fully agrees with the philosophical teaching, and that any biblical passage which contradicts the philosophic teaching has to be rejected as a sacrilegious addition to Holy Writ" (198). In this way, then, Spinoza is quite guilty, as surely he knew, of what he accuses Maimonides and other medieval biblical exegetes in the second part of *Theological-Political Treatise*, namely, relying not on the Bible to interpret the Bible but on Plato and Aristotle. The difference, of course, is that Spinoza disdains Plato and Aristotle, while he believes that Spinozism, that is, the philosophy of modern science, his own philosophy, is the truth. That is to say, the difference is not that Spinoza alone interprets the Bible by means of the Bible in contrast to Maimonides and the medieval Jewish exegetes who are guilty of relying on an extraneous philosophy; rather, it is that while they *all* rely on auxiliary philosophies, Spinoza relies on what he takes to be a true philosophy and they rely on what he takes to be false ones. Of course they took them for true.

perfect our intellect; they are mere shadows, and cannot be counted as actions that are, as it were, the offspring and fruit of intellect and sound mind" (52). True freedom is necessity; political freedom is obedience.

Indeed, it is precisely to separate philosophy (which means also science) and theology that is the aim and the work of the second part of the *Theological-Political Treatise*, comprising chapters 7 through 15. In contrast to the first part, which is based on self-evident axioms and truths deduced from them, the second is based in "the true method of Scriptural interpretation" (87), which today commonly goes under the name "biblical criticism." Just as in his philosophy Spinoza studied Nature in its own proper terms, that is, as eternal and necessary *truth*, here he studies the Bible in its own proper terms, that is, as language, narrative, figuration, what today literary scholars often call "textuality," that is, not truth but *meaning*. "For the point at issue," Spinoza writes in chapter 7, "is merely the meaning of the texts, not their truth" (88). Thus he proclaims he will interpret the Bible only in terms of the Bible, Scripture only according to Scripture, "to ascribe no teaching to Scripture that is not clearly established from studying it closely" (88), introducing neither alien theories nor forced interpretations, such as those of Maimonides or the "Pharisees," whom Spinoza singles out, calling the reading of the latter, the rabbis, "excessive and rash," and of the former, Maimonides, "harmful, unprofitable and absurd" (102). (Let us note immediately something glaringly obvious to readers familiar with the Bible and biblical hermeneutics: Spinoza's claims for his method, and his claims against others, are laughable or pathetic and certainly false to his actual hermeneutic practice, because his Bible glosses are so often no less and in many instances far more "excessive and rash," artificial, strained, and forced to fit the Procrustean bed of extra-biblical rationalist philosophy.)

In any event, in accord with the textual or hermeneutic approach announced in the second part of *Theological-Political Treatise*, Spinoza there concerns himself with language (Hebrew for the most part, since he is unfamiliar with New Testament Greek), authorship, redaction, historical settings (ancient Middle East), canonization, and the like, in order to explicate the plain or literal sense of the Bible stripped of the allegedly artificial and self-serving glosses of earlier Jewish commentators. Most of Spinoza's explications deal with the Hebrew Bible, though some comment on the New Testament.[6] Though his approach to the Bible is meant to be hermeneutic, and therefore respectful of the meaning of the text, the larger aim of part 2, so Spinoza tells us, is to show that philosophy, science, and truth, on the one side, and theology, religion, and faith, on the other, should be "finally set apart." Indeed, the full title of chapter 15, the conclusion of part 2 of the *Theological-Political Treatise*, reads: "*neither is theology ancillary to reason, nor reason to theology*" (158). In other words, the purpose of part 2 of the *Theological-Political Treatise* is to show (1) that the medieval theological claim that philosophy is "handmaiden" to theology is false; (2) that this confusion is dangerous to theology and to philosophy; and as he will discuss more fully in the third and final part, the political part, (3) that any subordination of philosophy and exaltation of religion is also dangerous to the state as well.

In the third culminating part of the *Theological-Political Treatise*, chapters 16 through 20, Spinoza presents his political philosophy. He defends two basic theses. The first is Hobbesian: the absolute supremacy of political sovereignty, and in particular its absolute sovereignty over religious authority, to "prove," to make good on the claim Spinoza had promised earlier in the preface to the *Theological-Political Treatise*, "that governments are the guardians and interpreters of religious law as well as civil law, and they alone have the right to decide what is just and unjust, what is pious and impious" (7). The second thesis, which

---

6. Because it does include some New Testament figures and stories, Leo Strauss argues that the *Theological-Political Treatise* is addressed to *Christian* readers (Strauss, "How to Study Spinoza," 197). No doubt it is a fact that the *Theological-Political Treatise* was read mostly by Christians. After all it was written in Latin and published in Western Europe, not to mention that Spinoza had been excommunicated from the Jewish community and therefore his writings banned. Nevertheless, the inclusion of the New Testament in its analyses would certainly not be sufficient reason why Jewish readers, or Muslim readers, for that matter, could not have been included in its target audience, or could not in a more liberal environment appreciate its claims, especially given how extensively (and harshly) the *Theological-Political Treatise* deals with Jewish commentators. Strauss, who is no doubt not unaware of such objections, also suggests that Spinoza gave preponderance to Hebrew Bible figures and stories because in Europe in the late seventeenth century: "It was infinitely less dangerous to attack Judaism than to attack Christianity" (Strauss, "How to Study Spinoza," 216). It is a point surely well taken.

at first sight appears non-Hobbesian, is the claim that such sovereignty, despite its absoluteness *in principle*, is best served *in fact* by "granting to the individual citizen the right to have his own opinions and to say what he thinks" (7), to again cite Spinoza's promissory note in the preface. So: absolute state, yet freedom of speech and thought. Let us see how these apparently disparate elements are actually joined.

To indicate the importance of the third political part, and again to underline how the first part undergirds the third part (as well as the second), let us call attention here to the subtitle of the *Theological-Political Treatise*: "*By means of which it is shown not only that Freedom of Philosophising can be allowed in Preserving Piety and the Peace of the Republic: but also that it is not possible for such Freedom to be upheld except when accompanied by the Peace of the Republic and Piety Themselves*" (xlix). Here as always we must be careful to distinguish *philosophical freedom* as Spinoza understands it, that is, knowledge, true ideas, and *political freedom* as it is ordinarily or popularly understood, that is, voluntary action, willing, and choice, preferably with minimal constraints. We must keep this distinction in mind because, as we shall see, Spinoza sometimes equivocates between them to achieve a certain rhetorical effect. In the present case, it is sufficiently clear that the political freedom Spinoza supports in the third part of the *Theological-Political Treatise* is based *not* on a commitment to some liberal principle of human rights, but rather on the *fact* that humans are so constituted that they are simply unable to completely transfer their natural rights to the state, and that therefore the state, consequently, is *unable in fact* to exercise absolute control over human thought and speech. There is a very great difference between positively affirming the principle of human freedom, including freedom of thought and speech, which Spinoza does not, and conceding that the state is unable to completely suppress such freedoms, that such freedoms cannot be completely transferred to the state, and hence that it is wiser, more prudent, more politic, for the state to recognize them insofar as it must (and no farther), which is Spinoza's position. It is hard to believe that many good-hearted commentators—eager to attribute a liberality of spirit to Spinoza that is sorely lacking—have missed this distinction, but there is a very great difference between the *principle* of absolute sovereignty, which Spinoza affirms along with Hobbes, and the *fact* of inability to control, inability to totalize, which Spinoza concedes. We will return to this distinction.

Let us also and finally note, perhaps most importantly, that one must also distinguish the circumscribed *political freedom* that Spinoza concedes in part 3, owing to real limitations in state sovereignty and individual submission, from the *philosopher's freedom to philosophize*, including also the *scientist's freedom to pursue science*, which Spinoza wholly and without reservation supports, which is elaborated in part 1, and which his entire political philosophy—such is my thesis—is designed to protect. While Hobbes defends the state's absolute sovereignty simply to avoid the anarchy and violence that necessarily result when alternative sources of authority are permitted, which is to say Hobbes supports absolute state sovereignty for its own sake, as the only bulwark against war, Spinoza defends the state's absolute sovereignty, defends the public peace that it alone can establish, not for its own sake but as the only way to ensure the sole environment necessary and conducive—public peace—for the philosopher and scientist to pursue truth, which pursuit, and not statecraft, is the only thing worth doing for its own sake. Thus politics for Hobbes is an end, indeed the absolute end, while politics for Spinoza is a means to an end, that end being philosophy and science. Again: part 1, the philosophical part, is the ground and end of part 2, the theological, and part 3, the political, of the *Theological-Political Treatise*.

Paradox of Possible Readers

It is time now to turn to the central question regarding who are the appropriate readers of Spinoza's *Theological-Political Treatise*. We should perhaps ask first why this is a question at all. A book is published; anyone can read it. The question, however, has to do with whom Spinoza wrote the book for or, independent of his intentions, who benefits or can benefit from reading such a book. Furthermore, regarding the appropriate readers of the *Theological-Political Treatise*, what arises is more than a question but rather a conundrum or a paradox really. There are two considerations that together create this paradox. First, paralleling the division that we have seen between the realm of philosophy, that is, knowledge and truth, and the realm of theology and politics, that is, obedience and belief, two realms whose clearly demarked separation is one of the two primary goals of the entire

Theological-Political Treatise, Spinoza also divides the world of people between those who are ruled by their minds, by reason, that is, those ruled by true ideas, who are *few*, and those who are ruled by their bodies, by perceptions, that is, those swayed by passing passions and figments of their imaginations, who are *many*. No doubt the few who are mindful, who cultivate their intellects, have occasional lapses, are episodically distracted by passions, emotions, and the like, insofar as it is difficult to combat and probably impossible for a human being to finally and absolutely calm the passions, even though such dispassion is a prerequisite of knowing truth.[7] Still, in distinguishing knowing and doing, the theoretical and the practical, Spinoza does not refer to two faculties or two alternating types of human activities but rather and repeatedly to two types of human beings: the few truly active truth seekers, that is, philosophers and scientists, and those who are passive and passionate, that is, the masses, the people, the many. As might be expected of a philosopher, Spinoza respects, indeed exalts, the former, the few, because they alone know what is real, and he disdains, indeed despises, the latter, the many, the multitude, the masses.

Spinoza's valuations in this regard are clear and striking, even if in an ultimate or metaphysical sense it can in no way be the *fault* of the passionate many that they are ignorant and corrupted, nor, let us add right away, can it be *praiseworthy* of the knowing few that they are knowledgeable. All is necessary; nothing truly real is good or evil. "Blessedness," Spinoza writes at the end of *Ethics*, or we could say "Knowing," because for Spinoza *to know the truth is blessedness*, "is not the reward of virtue, but virtue itself."[8] Knowing is its own reward, just as ignorance is its own reward—there is no place in Spinoza's *philosophy* for moralizing. So even if we do not yet know exactly who is meant to read the *Theological-Political Treatise*, or why this is a problem, we know already that its subject matter, its announced title, certainly parts 2 and 3 on theology and politics, dealing with the realm of obedience rather than knowledge, has to do with the many, with those who obey their passions rather than having minds freed for and by truth. It may

---

7. See, the famous last sentence of Spinoza's *Ethics*: "All excellent things are as difficult as they are rare" (223). Cf., Plato *Republic*, 435c.

8. E, V, Prop. 42, 223; see also chapter 3, "Levinas and Spinoza: To Love God for Nothing," in this volume.

or may not be a book for the many, as readers, but it is certainly a book about the many. For the few, those concerned not with illusions and delusions but with truth, Spinoza wrote the *Ethics*, which unlike the *Theological-Political Treatise* he did not publish. So, first problem: the *Theological-Political Treatise* seems to be written for the many, or at the very least we can say that it is largely (parts 2 and 3) about topics *outside* the truth-seeking interest of the few, *but* the many are precisely the masses of people who are not led by their intellects and hence cannot be convinced by argumentation and reasoning. We can even ask why Spinoza, philosopher, apparently wasted his time writing such a book, a book dealing with meaning rather than truth.

It will be useful at this juncture to more fully inform ourselves about Spinoza's attitude toward the many. As if forgetful of the dispassionate and blessed philosophy propounded in *Ethics*, coming down, as it were, from the ethereal atmosphere beyond good and evil, indifferent to praise and blame of *Ethics*, when Spinoza speaks of the masses he does so with an undisguised venom and unmitigated scorn. Their human, all too human faults are quite obvious. Instead of seeking truth, driven rather by their emotions, especially by their fears, and carried away by the undisciplined fancies of their imaginations, above all by their vanities, the masses seek transitory and unreal ends such as fame, money, power, luxury, pleasure, and the like, always merely worldly goods. Their aims are low, passing, and unseemly. Their characters are unstable, whimsical, and subject to fashion and influence. In chapter 17 of the *Theological-Political Treatise*, Spinoza writes: "those who have experienced the fickleness of the masses are almost reduced to despair; for the masses are governed solely by their emotions, not by reason; they rush wildly into everything, and are readily corrupted either by avarice or by luxurious living" (187). In chapter 4 he refers to "the great majority in whose lives reason plays little part" (49). On the very first page of the *Theological-Political Treatise*, in its preface, speaking of their susceptibility to superstition, Spinoza describes the masses as "wretched victims of alternating hopes and fears," who "read extraordinary things into Nature as if the whole of Nature were a partner in their madness," for "it is especially when they are helpless in danger that they all implore God's help with prayers and womanish tears. Reason they call blind, because it cannot reveal a sure way to the vanities that they covet, and human wisdom they call vain, while the delusions of the imagination, dreams and other childish absurdities are taken to be oracles of God" (1). The *Theological-Political Treatise* is replete with similar deprecations.

We draw from Spinoza's attitude two points, one relevant to our question directly, and the other relevant to it indirectly, but directly relevant to the further and controversial issue of where Spinoza stands with regard to democracy. First, it can hardly be for these people, for the ignorant unruly masses, that the *Theological-Political Treatise* is written. They are too passionate, too fickle and unstable, too blindly selfish. They disdain reason, will not and cannot listen to it. The *Theological-Political Treatise*, after all and despite its care for meaning (parts 2 and 3) instead of for truth alone (part 1), is in fact driven by the rational truths of Spinoza's philosophy—precisely that to which the masses are blind and impervious. Second, the consistently harsh, unremitting denunciations of the vast majority of humanity—the masses, the multitudes, the people—must surely serve as a red light, at the very least, to cast doubt on any alleged preferential support by Spinoza for democracy as a political regime. Spinoza certainly is not writing for the masses, certainly cares not for them, indeed disdains them, and therefore can hardly be someone with strong or really any democratic political inclinations.

But here is the rub: Spinoza is also not writing the *Theological-Political Treatise* for the few! Philosophers and scientists are properly only concerned with truth, with eternal and necessary ideas, engage only a philosophical freedom, the freedom to conform to necessity, and therefore cannot take seriously, indeed explicitly reject and turn away from all the nonsense that constitutes the realm of obedience, the realm of passion, error, storm and stress, the entire world of so-called political freedom. The few are busy and content with science. Spinoza has written *Ethics* for them. Reason, science, truth, knowledge are the province of the few.

Thus the compelling tenor of our question, indeed its paradoxical nature: If the *Theological-Political Treatise* is written *neither for the few*, who care nothing for its shallow topics, *nor for the many*, who are unable and unequipped to properly care, as Spinoza himself insists on both counts according to the considerations to which we have drawn attention, then *for whom is it written?* For whom indeed can it possibly be written?

Because the division of humanity into the few and the many seems to be an excluded middle, the question of who are the readers of the *Theological-Political Treatise* becomes a paradox. Our perplexity is even more troubling inasmuch as Spinoza's philosophy leaves no place for change, and hence for pedagogy, for improvement, moving, say, from being one of the many to becoming one of the few. The few and the many, the knowers and the ignorant, seem trapped in their respective roles like the predestined elect and damned of Calvinist theology. As for Spinoza's apparent efforts to the contrary, for example, the failed *Treatise on the Emendation of the Intellect,* or the therapeutic recommendations found in parts III to V of *Ethics,* or the point of his exhortatory endorsement of the few and his vituperative denunciation of the many, we must agree with Jonathan Bennett in his *Study of Spinoza's "Ethics"* that an accounting for such countercurrents cannot be carried through in any strictly Spinozist terms. Instead, Bennett shows through close textual analyses that despite itself an unacknowledged teleology haunts—and indeed contradicts—the self-proclaimed nonteleological character of the *Ethics* (Bennett, 240–246). But even recognizing the pertinence and the power of this fundamental criticism of Spinoza's philosophy, with its inability to consistently deny teleology, it does not answer our question regarding the proper readership of the *Theological-Political Treatise.*

Though he certainly has no privilege as a critic of his own work, let us take a look at what Spinoza himself says about who is to read the *Theological-Political Treatise.* His comments appear in two places: (1) the preface of the *Theological-Political Treatise* and (2) letter no. 30, to Henry Oldenburg, then joint-secretary of the Royal Society in England.

From the Preface of the Theological-Political Treatise

After having briefly laid out the aims of the *Theological-Political Treatise,* in the penultimate paragraph of the preface, Spinoza writes the following.[9]

> I would say more, but I do not want my Preface to expand to a volume, especially since I believe its main points are quite familiar to philosophers. To others I seek not to commend

---

9. In the final paragraph of the preface Spinoza declares his readiness to withdraw anything he has written that might "contravene the laws of our country or be injurious to the common good" (TPT, 8).

this, for I have no reason to expect them to approve it in any way. I know how deeply rooted in the mind are the prejudices embraced under the guise of piety. I know, too, that the masses [*vulgus*] can no more be freed from their superstition than from their fears. Finally, I know that they are unchanging in their obstinacy, that they are not guided by reason, and that that their praise and blame is at the mercy of impulse. Therefore I do not invite the common people to read this work, nor all those who are victims of the same emotional attitude. Indeed, I would prefer that they disregard this book completely rather than make themselves a nuisance by misinterpreting it after their wont. For without any advantage to themselves they would stand in the way of others for whom a more liberal approach to philosophical questions is prevented by this one obstacle, that they believe that reason must be the handmaiden of theology. These latter, I am confident, will derive great profit from this work. (7–8)

So, *philosophers* should not read the *Theological-Political Treatise* because "its main points are quite familiar" to them already. The *masses* need not read it because their reading would be pointless or worse: they are impulsive, obstinate, unchanging, and so cannot be freed of their fears and superstitions by means of Spinoza's book or any book or any reasoning. Indeed, Spinoza positively prefers that the common people "disregard this book," because if they do read it they will create a "nuisance" with their misinterpretations. (That the *Theological-Political Treatise* was originally published in Latin and therefore could not be read by the masses is an observation that need not detain us, because surely Spinoza could have anticipated its Dutch translation, which followed immediately its Latin publication.) So according to Spinoza's own remarks it appears the dilemma stands: eliminating philosophers and masses, few and many, there seem to be no others left to read the book.

Except that Spinoza singles out a set of readers who "will derive great profit from this work," namely: "others for whom a more liberal approach to philosophical questions is prevented by this one obstacle, that they believe that reason must be the handmaiden of theology." At last, it seems we have found some appropriate readers: those who mistakenly believe reason is the handmaiden of theology, those who, if they read and rightly understand the *Theological-Political Treatise*, will see the light, namely, that "neither is theology ancillary to reason, nor reason to theology" (165).

Let us state who these readers are in a preliminary fashion: these are readers who are capable of reason, hence they cannot be the masses, but at the same time are intellectually incapacitated because misled by theology and hence are not philosophers. Perhaps we can call them "potential philosophers," *philosophes manqué*, kept from true philosophy only by the mistaken prejudice that reason must serve theology, a prejudice that reading and understanding the *Theological-Political Treatise* will disabuse them of and liberate them from. It is peculiar, however, that while Spinoza claimed that he postponed publishing *Ethics* to avoid the wrath of "certain ministers," here, in contrast, it now seems that he wants precisely theologically inclined persons, persons for whom reason is but the handmaiden of theology, to read the *Theological-Political Treatise*. In this peculiarity lies another clue as to the book's proper readers, to which we will return.

Letter No. 30 to Oldenburg

Spinoza's letter to Henry Oldenburg was written sometime in the fall of 1665, hence five years before the publication of the *Theological-Political Treatise*. I cite the relevant passage in full.

> I am now writing a treatise on my views regarding Scripture. The reasons that move me to do so are these: 1. The prejudices of theologians. For I know that these are the main obstacle which prevent men from giving their minds to philosophy. So I apply myself to exposing such prejudices and removing them from the minds of sensible people. 2. The opinion of me held by the common people, who constantly accuse me of atheism. I am driven to avert this accusation, too, as far as I can. 3. The Freedom to philosophize and to say what we think. This I want to vindicate completely, for here it is in every way suppressed by the excessive authority and egoism of preachers. (CW, 844)

Spinoza's first reason, that the book is written for those who would otherwise give "their minds to philosophy" except that they are blocked by the "prejudices of the theologians," reappears as we have just seen almost verbatim five years later in the preface to the *Theological-Political Treatise*. It is indeed the reason with the greatest weight, and the one that we shall have to take most seriously.

The second reason, namely, to be freed of the accusation of atheism—it suffices to respond that Spinoza was never able to manage this feat, because it is fairly plain to see, not only in the *Ethics* but in the *Theological-Political Treatise* no less, that his philosophy actually is atheist, and hence that the "common people" are correct in their accusation. Unless, that is, we are inclined to follow Spinoza in the stipulative "doublespeak" of his appropriation of such terms as "religion," "God," "blessedness," "atheism," and the like, to conform to a strictly scientific worldview, which we are not, and which renders such religious terms redundant in any event.

Spinoza's third reason in his letter to Henry Oldenburg, to realize the "freedom to philosophize and say what we think," this too seems to reappear five years later as the freedom of thought and speech for which Spinoza argues in the third political part of the *Theological-Political Treatise*. But actually the "freedom to philosophize" is not at all the freedom to "say what we think." It is rather the freedom to say what is eternal and necessary; the freedom to conform to adequate ideas. The political freedom to "say what we think," in contrast, is simply the uncontrollable freedom of thought and speech that no human is able to fully alienate, and no state able to fully suppress. Such inalienable and irrepressible freedom is an entirely different matter than philosophical freedom. Spinoza supports philosophical freedom, which adheres to necessity; he merely tolerates, because he cannot do otherwise, political freedom, which obeys passion. Nevertheless, though to a lesser extent than Spinoza's first reason, the third will help us determine who is the appropriate audience for the *Theological-Political Treatise*, so long as we remain vigilant not to misunderstand what Spinoza means by "freedom to philosophize and say what we think," careful, that is to say, to distinguish philosophical from political freedom.

We note further regarding the three reasons Spinoza gives in his letter to Oldenburg that they are each directed to a different set of persons, two of which Spinoza explicitly identifies. The first, freeing minds from theology for philosophy, is for "sensible people" (*prudentiorum*). The second, defending himself from the charge of atheism, is a response to "the common people" (*vulgus*), that is, the many. And the third, exemplifying and thus vindicating the freedom to philosophize, its audience is ambiguous, as follows from the two senses of freedom, on the one hand directed to philosophers but on the other hand directed to those who want a well-run polity. To unravel these two senses is to discover, as we shall see shortly, the answer to our question. For the present, the letter to Oldenburg, especially its first reason, seems to suggest that the proper readers of the *Theological-Political Treatise* are a peculiar third group, as it were, neither the few nor the many, not exactly philosophers but not the unruly masses either. It points to persons who would otherwise philosophize but are prevented from doing so owing to theological prejudices, persons whom Spinoza here names "sensible people."

Liberal Christian Ministers and Theologians

No doubt based in the latter consideration, some commentators have identified the appropriate readers of the *Theological-Political Treatise* to be liberal Christian clergy of Holland in Spinoza's day. To read the *Theological-Political Treatise* would be a kind of therapy for open-minded ministers and theology students. Reading it, they might perhaps become true philosophers, or failing that, they might perhaps become better theologians. First, learning to no longer confuse theology and philosophy (part 2), in their own minds they would free philosophy from theology and vice versa; and second, socially/politically, no longer demanding theological authority over political sovereignty (part 3), they would no longer support ecclesiastical interference in political affairs. Thus philosophy and politics, freed from clerical interference, could pursue their own proper aims, truth for philosophy, order for politics, and theology, too, freed of philosophical and political pretensions could pursue its own proper aim, which is, as Spinoza sums it up, to obey God by loving the neighbor.[10] To produce such benefits for all, the *Theological-Political Treatise* is written for clergy, ministers, and theology students.

---

10. TPT, 154 (chapter 13): "Scripture demands nothing from men but obedience, and condemns not ignorance but only obstinacy. . . . obedience to God consists solely in loving one's neighbor."

It is this claim, in any event, or this claim in a historicized form, namely, that seventeenth-century Dutch Christian clergy and theologians were the anticipated and proper readers of Spinoza's *Theological-Political Treatise*, which is made by Steven B. Smith in *Spinoza, Liberalism, and the Question of Jewish Identity*, and, following Smith, made also by Steven Nadler, in *A Book Forged in Hell: Spinoza's Scandalous Treatise and the Birth of the Secular Age*. Let us turn briefly to these two books.

Smith addresses our question in chapter 2, entitled "Spinoza's Audience and Manner of Writing." Referring to Spinoza's political-historical context, he points out that: "The chief obstacle to the separation of philosophy and theology is the power of clerical or ecclesiastical authority, which has become an arbiter of opinion" (28). This observation is well worth remembering with regard to Spinoza's entire project, to help us to understand his special concern to limit the authority of religion, most especially too in relation to his particular desire to protect the then-nascent modern sciences. In seventeenth-century Europe the primary threat to independent philosophical thinking and science came from the alignment of religion with power, which is to say, from the power of politicized clerics and their theological influence over government. The disgraceful record of the Church's forceful and often violent opposition to science, from the suppression of Copernicus, to the silencing of Galileo, to the burning of Bruno in Rome, is well recorded in the history books, but in Spinoza's day it was more than a story. It was a looming threatening danger to free thought and publication. No wonder then that Spinoza should want to enlighten clerics and reform religion. "The audience to whom Spinoza appealed," Smith writes, "were those liberal theologians [Smith names the "Collegiant-Mennonites"] among the de Witt camp associated with the variety of dissenting Protestants abounding in Holland" (48). Holland at that time was arguably the most liberal state in Europe, even if by today's standards we would hardly consider it liberal.[11] Johan de Witt, of

---

11. In this regard one might compare seventeenth-century Amsterdam to seventeenth-century Vilnius, as per David Frick, *Kith, Kin, and Neighbors: Communities and Confessions in Seventeenth-Century Wilno*, which shows not that the five Christian denominations in Vilnius (in addition to local populations of Muslims and Jews) *tolerated* one another, which they did not, but rather that for a variety of purposes, commercial, judicial, governmental, and otherwise, they peacefully *accommodated* themselves to one another.

course, along with his brother Cornelis had been assassinated by an angry lynch mob in Amsterdam on August 20, 1672 (perhaps within Spinoza's eyesight). He was the leader of the antimonarchical "liberal" political party in Holland supported by Spinoza and by the dissenting Collegians and Mennonites. So to reform the clerics who inflamed their congregations might mitigate the violence of such mob rule.

Steven Nadler, answering to the same perplexity, the question of who is the intended audience of the *Theological-Political Treatise*, agrees with Smith's historical answer (Nadler, *Book Forged in Hell*, 22–23). He specifies the "theologians" into three subgroups: (1) "those teaching on university faculties"; (2) "religious leaders of the Dutch Reformed Church"; and (3) "preachers" (22). Nadler also includes two other groups: philosophers and the Dutch regents.

As for including philosophers, it is difficult to agree with Nadler for the reasons that we have already given. Namely, except for part 1 of the *Theological-Political Treatise*, parts 2 and 3 deal with narratives, historical events, and beliefs, which have nothing to do with the eternal, immutable, and necessary truths that constitute the intelligibility of the universe and that are the proper subject matter of philosophy and philosophical knowing (since knowing truth "does not demand belief in historical narratives of any kind whatsoever" [TPT, 51]). And as for philosophers reading part 1 of the *Theological-Political Treatise*, which only presents Spinoza's philosophy in a highly abbreviated summary form, philosophers should instead read Spinoza's *Ethics*, which presents his philosophy—eternal, immutable, necessary truth—in its fully articulated elaboration.

Where I do agree with Nadler is with regard to the second group of potential readers of the *Theological-Political Treatise* beyond the theologians, whom Nadler too considers "more important" readers than the theologians, namely, "the Dutch regents, the Republic's relatively liberal elite who governed many of the cities and towns in the provinces." "They," Nadler continues, "also generally favored a tolerant attitude in intellectual, cultural, and religious matters, and are among the 'sensible' people, the *prudentiorum*, whom Spinoza, in his letter to Oldenburg, sees as the work's primary audience" (*Book Forged in Hell*, 23). Here, referring to the Dutch governing elite as potential readers, I think Nadler has indeed made an important observation. But I believe its importance lies less in Spinoza's seventeenth-century Dutch and European historical context, where Nadler places it, and more in Spinoza's overall philosophy, which is to say, to take a broader perspective, its significance has to do with the very relations Spinoza would establish—as the primary goal of the *Theological-Political Treatise*—between philosophy, religion, and politics. No doubt Spinoza was very much aware of his historical context, of the particular theologians and theologies of the Dutch Protestant churches, of the Catholics elsewhere, of the politics of the Dutch regents, of Johan de Witt, and so on. But Spinoza as a philosopher has larger fish to fry, as it were. Leo Strauss has put this point about the relative weight of the history of ideas to the ideas themselves: "Historical understanding, as it is frequently practiced, seduces one into seeing the author whom one studies primarily as a contemporary among his contemporaries, or to read his books as if they were primarily addressed to his contemporaries. But the books of men like the mature Spinoza, which are meant as possessions for all times, are primarily addressed to posterity" ("How to Study," 194–195). There seems little doubt that if Spinoza wrote for the Dutch regents, as Nadler points out, he was also writing for a certain *type* of political leadership. Spinoza, after all, is not a journalist, not one who writes merely for the short term, for the world around him, but rather, and even in his theological-political work, one who has thoughts for the long term. Indeed, has a philosopher since Plato been clearer or more focused in his concern for the eternal beyond the temporal than Spinoza? So, in considering the proper readers of the *Theological-Political Treatise*, we shall return to the Dutch regents, not to the historical Dutch regents, but to the political leader in general, and more specifically to the political leader as Spinoza would have such a person.

First Excursus: The Two Meanings of "Democracy" and of "Freedom"

Democracy

Certainly to understand for whom *Theological-Political Treatise* is written we must understand Spinoza's outlook regarding the nature and quality of his fellow human beings, which is to say, we must understand his views regarding who can profit from his book and who cannot. We have already seen Spinoza's explicit remarks regarding the latter, those who ought not to be readers: philosophers have no need of the *Theological-Political Treatise* and the people, the multitude, are incapable of apprehending it. Regarding the latter we have also seen that Spinoza everywhere expresses a very low opinion of the mass of humanity. For him they are closer to animals than humans, driven by passions, emotions, selfish, looking for rewards merely temporal and transitory, disregarding the argumentation and rationality to which they are impervious. In view of his rather jaundiced position, we are now going to take up for closer examination Spinoza's outlook regarding democracy and freedom. We do so because these are important topics of political philosophy, but also because of the controversies that continue to churn Spinoza scholarship as to whether his is or is not a political philosophy supporting democracy and political freedoms, and hence whether Spinoza is or is not a progressive thinker, whether in his time or perhaps also for our time as well.

Many books and articles, too numerous to enumerate, have been written defending Spinoza the great democrat and defender of political freedoms. In some cases he is presented as the founder of modern democracy. At the same time, astonishingly, many other books and articles, also too numerous to enumerate, have been written arguing precisely the opposite, namely, that Spinoza opposes democracy and severely restricts political freedoms, that his thought is anything but democratic but rather is elitist and even totalitarian. We have already heard for ourselves with what vituperative, with what spleen, Spinoza has written about the people, the masses, the many—and we have duly been forced to wonder whether someone with such disdain can be a democrat or a supporter of democracy. But putting aside our own doubts, we are still forced to wonder how so important an issue can remain so unsettled, how it can give rise simultaneously to such diametrically opposed readings. What is going on? Surely something beyond a plain, straightforward, or clear and distinct position is at work in Spinoza, whether he willed it or not. One need hardly invoke the convoluted rhetoric of "persecution," or the skittish art of "esoteric" writing to see that this is so.

With these questions in view, we turn first to Spinoza's explicit discussion of democracy in chapter 16 of the *Theological-Political Treatise*, and then, regarding freedom, to chapter 20, keeping in mind, of course, that chapters 16 through 20 form a unity, part 3 of the *Theological-Political Treatise*, on the political, which builds on part 2, on theology, and part 1, on philosophy. The immediate answer to our wonder and the source of the interpretive controversy that surrounds

Spinoza's political thought is not hard to find. It derives from a combination of a specific conceptual ambiguity, inherent in Spinoza's philosophy, between the absolute and the relative, or the eternal and the temporal, and the misleading rhetorical slippage that this ambiguity enables and to which Spinoza deliberately resorts, apparently to temper though not to ultimately hide what might otherwise be too dark an aspect of his actual political position. Let us say this again with greater specificity, focusing exclusively on the term "democracy": the source of the interpretative variance at the root of the controversies regarding Spinoza's support or nonsupport of democracy comes not only because (1) he uses the one term "democracy" in at least two sharply differentiated senses, but also because (2) he uses the status of one of these senses, *democracy as the founding moment of all sovereign states*, the political state as such in contrast to the state of nature, to seemingly—but not really, as I shall argue—give his preferential support to the other sense of democracy, *democracy as a particular political regime*, democracy as rule by many in contrast to monarchy, rule by one, and aristocracy, rule by few. Interpreters of Spinoza go wrong, then, when they miss this ambiguity altogether or when they are aware of it but nonetheless unwittingly succumb to the fallacy of ambiguous middle term in judging Spinoza's outlook. In the first case, which is the more egregious or wholesale error, readers miss the two distinct senses altogether and mistakenly thinking there is only one, that is, democracy as a particular political regime, read Spinoza as supporting such a democratic regime, because, so they mistakenly think, Spinoza believes that the state as such is founded democratically, and hence that a democratic regime is the most faithful because it reflects the deepest constitution of a state. Second, if they do catch the two senses but miss the shift in sense from democracy as the constitutive moment of all states as such and the sense of democracy as one possible regime among several, they will mix up what Spinoza has to say about one with what he has to say about the other—succumbing to the fallacy of ambiguous middle term—either to celebrate Spinoza as a democratic thinker or to castigate him for not being a democratic thinker. While it might seem that I will be following the second route, and hence am guilty of the fallacy of ambiguous middle term myself, my whole argument depends on seeing that this is not so and that an anti-democratic reading of the second route is in fact faithful to what Spinoza with sufficient clarify actually does say. So to avoid both of the aforementioned errors, first to make a correct distinction between two senses of democracy, and second to see where Spinoza truly stands regarding them both, that is, to grasp truly where Spinoza stands with regard to democracy, in addition to confirming the pertinent distinctions and comments that have already been made, I invite the reader to judge the faithfulness of the following elaborations.

Spinoza entitles chapter 16 "*The basis of the state; the natural and civil right of the individual, and the right of sovereign powers*" (TPT, 173). Following Hobbes and the well-beaten path taken by political philosophers of his day, in this chapter he highlights and determines the nature and rights of the sovereign state by contrasting it to the nature, rights, and interactions of individuals who otherwise (i.e., without such sovereignty) would be living in a "state of nature." Whether such a state of nature be taken as once real or purely imagined, by this method, this "thought experiment," as I think we are entitled to think of it, political philosophers are able to determine what citizens have given up and what they have given over to live under the rule of a sovereign state. This is the function of "state of nature" theories of the origin of the state: to determine what constitutes the state as such, what distinguishes it from—without excluding the contributions of—the characteristics and organizations that constitute animal life. For Spinoza, as we know, in a "state of nature," a person's right—or really any entity's "right," since Spinoza is not here distinguishing human beings from other entities in nature—is equal to a person's power. In truth, using the term "right" here is already a bit misleading, because what Spinoza means to say is no more or less than that might is might, that the limits of an entity's endurance in being is its endurance in being. A distinct entity, which for Spinoza refers only to a particular ratio of motion and rest, endures as long as that ratio endures. Spinoza's state of nature boils down to the tautology that whatever one can do, one can do, or, more broadly, that all things persevere (*conatus*) in their being. The term "right" here can therefore only mean that so long as a being can persist, it persists. Or, another way to say this, there is no fault or sin or guilt in nature: everything is what it is, and with equal "right." Regarding being, reality, existence, and persistence, therefore, judgments invoking final ends, teleology, Providence, theodicy, morality, or moral justice have nothing whatsoever to contribute.

Spinoza puts this point succinctly in the opening paragraph of chapter 16 as follows: "It is by sovereign natural right that fish inhabit water, and the big ones eat the smaller ones" (TPT, 173). "It is the supreme law of Nature," he writes, "that each thing endeavors to persist in its present being, as far as it lies, taking account of no other thing but itself" (TPT, 174). Here, under the term "endeavors to persist," is the famous *conatus*: perseverance or persistence in being, as the single motor of all and every entity's "right" to be. "Here," Spinoza continues,

> I do not acknowledge any distinction between men and other individuals of Nature, nor between men endowed with reason and others to whom true reason is unknown, nor between fools, madmen and the sane. Whatever an individual thing does by the laws of its own nature, it does with sovereign right, inasmuch as it acts as determined by Nature, and can do no other. (TPT, 174)

Once again, though we are citing from part 3, the "political" part of the *Theological-Political Treatise*, we clearly see at work the philosophy of part 1, the philosophy of Spinoza's *Ethics*. Might makes . . . might; big fish eat little fish; everything persists in its being until it does not, and necessarily so, without praise or blame. Such is the state of nature, indeed, such is Nature.

"Right" in the sense of a judgment about what is alleged to be good, right in a moral sense, arises only with the instauration of the sovereign state, the political state. But here too for Spinoza the so-called "right" of the state, that is, that which one might think to call ethically right in contrast to ethically wrong, or ethically just in contrast to ethically unjust, turns out to be no such thing, but rather, again, to be precisely equal to the state's *might*, entirely independent of independent moral judgment. "Right," in other words, is what the state can proscribe and enforce. *Right is judgment reflecting the state's might.* It is not a matter of ethics as ordinarily understood, of morality and justice in an ethical sense.[12] Because in the constitution of the state as such individuals in principle transfer all their powers to the state—

---

12. In his unpublished *Political Treatise* Spinoza writes: "In order that a commonwealth should be in control of its own right, it must preserve the causes that foster fear and respect; otherwise it ceases to be a commonwealth. For if the rulers or ruler of the state runs drunk or naked with harlots through the streets, acts on the stage, openly violates or holds in contempt those laws that he himself has enacted, it is no more possible for him to preserve the dignity of sovereignty than for something to be and not be at the same time. Then again, to slaughter subjects, to despoil them, to ravish maidens and the like turns fear into indignation, and consequently the civil order into a condition of war" (CW, 697). Concerns of

even if in fact such a complete transfer is not possible—all power in principle lies with the state. Having all might, the state has all "right." Such is Spinoza's theory, following Hobbes. The sovereign political state is absolute, no alternative claim or authority can overrule, contest, or withstand its claim and authority to determine what is right. The state is overpowering, powerful as much as it can be powerful. It cannot make rivers flow backward, square a circle, or turn humans into robots, to be sure, but it can and does have absolute command over its subjects, to order them to behave in whatever ways it wants and of which they are capable. If the state decides to record its citizens' phone conversations and internet activity, or requires each citizen to inform on every other, or to incarcerate, torture, and execute everyone with blue eyes, or who uses the word "cupcake," that is its absolute right, and no citizen has any legitimate grounds outside the state upon which to appeal or protest against such orders.

To be sure, as we have several times underscored, and as Spinoza *concedes* in the next chapter, the theory, despite its absolute precedence and correctness, does not accord precisely with practice:

> The picture presented in the last chapter of the overriding right of sovereign powers and the transference of them of the individual's natural right, though it comes quite close to actual practice and can increasingly be realized in reality, must nevertheless remain in many respects no more than theory. Nobody can so completely transfer to another all his right, and consequently his power, as to cease to be a human being, nor will there ever be a sovereign power that can do all it pleases. (TPT, 185)

Such a statement comes, let us be perfectly clear regarding its sense for Spinoza, as a concession to brute fact, to "actual practice," and in no way as a theoretical justification of limited government. In prin-

---

prudence, not morality or justice, drive political leadership to what so-called morally good behavior they might exhibit and what morally bad behavior they might avoid, as vice versa, exhibiting "bad" behavior and avoiding "good" behavior. Let us recall what Spinoza says in the *Theological-Political Treatise* itself: "Those who govern the state or hold the reins of power always strive to cloak with a show of legality whatever wrong they commit, persuading the people that this action was right and proper; and this they can easily achieve when the interpretation of the law is entirely in their hands" (195).

ciple the power of the state is absolute, even if in fact it is limited because humans are unable to divest themselves of all their powers (actually, as we shall see, they are only unable to divest themselves of the power to think and to speak their minds), or because a state doing "all it pleases" appears impossible or counterproductive given the powers of governance foreseeable in Spinoza's day. The absolute state, though not quite absolute, "comes quite close to actual practice and can increasingly be realized in reality," Spinoza already declares in the seventeenth century. It can hardly be overemphasized, given the willful persistence of certain scholarly misreading on this point, that the limitations of state sovereignty that Spinoza concedes in chapter 17, and again in chapter 20 as we shall see, are provisional concessions of fact but not of principle. Spinoza could hardly have foreseen in the seventeenth century all the possibilities of control open to state totalitarianism in the twenty-first century.

Returning, then, to chapter 16 and the question of democracy: ambiguity comes from Spinoza's use of the term "democracy" to refer both to (a) the original constitution of the state as such, that is, the state in contrast to nature, the idea that everyone is completely subject to its sovereign power, and then also to (b) one type of government, rule by the many in contrast to rule by some or one, that is, democracy in contrast to aristocracy and monarchy. To keep these two very different senses of the term clear and distinct, perhaps it is best to call the former "contract democracy" and the latter "regime democracy." The relevant point is not that Spinoza uses one term in two different ways, but that he sometimes—and sometimes with serious confusion and consequence—shifts from one signification to the other without making clear which of the two he means or that he has shifted sense. Nevertheless, let us also be clear that despite this ambiguity and the occasional semantic slipperiness in its use and the confusion it causes, Spinoza's position regarding democracy is certainly sufficiently clear and unambiguous. The state is constituted by all people, in the sense that all people owe it their absolute allegiance and that the state rules absolutely over all people. Yet regarding whether Spinoza supports regime democracy, in contrast to monarchic or aristocratic regimes, holding such a theory of contract democracy in the constitution of the state determines not at all. If anything, by adhering to such a theory of contract democracy, by giving all power to the state, it seems to suggest that Spinoza would not support regime democracy, because in the latter it is usually the case that majorities rule, and majorities rule precisely because no one knows absolutely what is right. In addition, and no less and perhaps even more convincingly, everything Spinoza says about the people, the multitude, the masses, whom he so obviously despises, indicates that he does not in fact or in principle support regime democracy. Let us continue in our pursuit of greater clarity in just such matters.

An instance found in chapter 16 amply illustrates both the ambiguity of the term "democracy" and the actual clarity the text shows regarding Spinoza's stance toward regime democracy. After explaining that in the shift from nature to sovereign state "everyone transfers all the power that he possesses to the community, which will therefore alone retain the sovereign natural right over everything" (TPT, 177), in the next sentence Spinoza calls such a state a "democracy." "Such a community's right," he writes, "is called a democracy, which can therefore be defined as a united body of men which corporately possesses sovereign right over everything within its power" (TPT, 177). And then, in the next sentence: "Hence it follows that the sovereign power is bound by no law, and all must obey it in all things" (177). Here is what we are calling Spinoza's theory of contract democracy: everyone gives his or her power over to the state, so the state in its original constitution is all-powerful (all powers) and democratic (all persons) at the same time. The argument for this theory of contract democracy is laid out in the next sentence, namely, that the withholding of any natural right (i.e., power) from the state would create "division and consequent destruction of the state" (177). A state divided against itself is no state at all. Division of power is a contradiction of the state contract. Sovereignty must be absolute or not at all. So, "they thereby submitted themselves absolutely to the will of the sovereign power . . . without reservation" (177). Thus Spinoza's explanation and defense of contract democracy: everyone gives and must give all their power to the state, which only thereby, undivided in its power, is constituted as sovereign. The only sovereign is the absolute sovereign. Political sovereignty is "democratic," then, not as one regime among other possible regimes, but in the precise sense that all people give—or more precisely *have already given*—all their power to the state, and that all power is ultimately therefore state power (even if in fact a complete transfer of power yet remains incomplete).

What is truly interesting—and crucial for Spinoza scholarship, that is, for an accurate reading of Spinoza—in this account is not what we have just said about the theory of contract democracy, which after all is taken from Hobbes, but rather that just a few sentences further on in chapter 16 Spinoza uses the word "democracy" in a very different sense, in the sense of regime democracy, without in any way noting or indicating that its meaning has shifted. The new meaning arises just after Spinoza's somewhat assuaging observation that despite the sovereign state's absolute power to do anything at all with complete right, "it is exceedingly rare for governments to issue quite unreasonable commands" (TPT, 178). Unreasonable commands, while irreproachable in absolute terms, are likely to be imprudent, upsetting to the state's *conatus*, its endeavor to persist. Spinoza continues, regarding the sovereign's choice of commands, that it is "in their own interest and to retain their rule, it especially behooves them to look to the public good and to conduct all affairs under the guidance of reason." Reasonable here, "to look to the public good," does not mean, however, reasonable as defined absolutely in the *Ethics*, that is, the strictly determined intelligibility of universal necessity, but rather as good sense, wise choices, prudence. It is in this context that Spinoza again uses the term "democracy." Having established the absolute sovereignty of the state in his theory of contract democracy, Spinoza now invokes regime democracy to contrast the reasonable or wise regime to "tyrannical" regimes insofar as the latter, less likely to be prudent, are less likely to be long lasting. In addition to the shift in the meaning of the term "democracy," notice also, here, that he criticizes tyrannical regimes not for being evil or unjust but for being unstable, not long lasting. So, Spinoza:

> For, as Seneca says . . . tyrannical governments never last long. There is the further fact that in a democracy there is less danger of a government behaving unreasonably, for it is practically impossible for the majority of a single assembly, if it is of some size, to agree on the same piece of folly. Then again, as we have also shown, it is the fundamental purpose of democracy to avoid the follies of appetite and to keep men within the bounds of reason, as far as possible, so that they may live in peace and harmony. (TPT, 178)

In the previous citation the term "democracy" in its first appearance refers to a type of regime, a regime in which an assembly rules by majority. But in its second appearance, though meant to further qualify the regime democracy of the previous sentence, the rule of majorities, actually and explicitly ("we have also shown") refers to the original constitution of the state as such, that is, to contract democracy. Surely there is a great difference between one type or regime of government and the sovereignty of the state as such. Furthermore, the necessity of contract democracy, assuming one accepts the Hobbesian theory thereof, lends no special or privileged status to regime democracy. In any event, the issue regarding regime democracy is one of stability not moral right. On this latter score Spinoza will defend any regime that is in power against any regime that is not, regardless of matters of moral right or wrong, justice or injustice, tyranny or freedom.

So, does Spinoza favor democracy as a political regime? From what we have just read it might seem that Spinoza believes that democracies, in contrast to tyrannies, are more likely to be prudential and hence are more likely to last longer than tyrannies, and hence that Spinoza supports them, prefers them to tyrannies, even if not for nice moral reasons. There is no doubt that for Spinoza the morally neutral "long lasting" serves as a positive criterion. This is because the "standard," as it were, to the extent that one can speak of a standard at all in the Spinozist context rather than simply of being and nonbeing, of all beings is their persistence in being, their *conatus*. An absolute *conatus* would be eternal, and so it is in Spinoza's *Ethics*; in the *Theological-Political Treatise*, however, which deals with the world of change, the standard of *conatus* is "long lasting," the longer the "better." So the criteria for a state's worthiness (again, "as it were," because ultimately only the eternal is real) is its ability to persevere, to last long, hence its stability. But we, attentive readers, must not confuse Spinoza's philosophical preference for longer-lasting governments for a claim that they are *morally better* governments. For us, a long-lasting unjust government might well be worse than a shorter-lasting just government. For Spinoza, that a government may "look to the public good" is purely a prudential issue, entirely a matter of securing public peace and tranquility, and in no way expresses deference to a moral good or a morally desirable justice *as moral*. In this light, then, Spinoza's claim in the preceding citation that "the fundamental purpose of democracy" is "to avoid the follies of appetite" applies no less and indeed equally to monarchy, aristocracy, tyranny, and all and every regime of government qua sovereign government, because it is a claim deriving from contract democracy, that is, from the very constitution of all and every state as such, and has nothing to do with some superiority inherent in a democratic regime.

Given that he wrote very little, and published less, and that what he wrote he wrote carefully, let us ask if Spinoza in his ambiguity is being coy or attempting deliberately to mask his true position. Perhaps he is. Perhaps he is sufficiently esoteric to provide cover for those interpreters who, no doubt with good wills, wish to see him as the great defender of democratic regimes. But even if he is trying to mask his true position, his true position is nevertheless sufficiently clear, as I have shown, that for readers of a truer good will, or perhaps of a greater dispassion, it is unmistakable. In his *Political Treatise*, unpublished to be sure, where Spinoza repeats claims made in the *Theological-Political Treatise* that "the purpose of civil order . . . is nothing other than peace and security of life" (CW, 699), he also explicitly claims that *aristocracy*—not democracy, and not monarchy—is the government which is "absolute, or comes closest to being absolute" (CW, 724), and is the most enduring form of government. And to support this preference Spinoza is there unabashedly anti-democratic, arguing that "to approach absolute sovereignty" the people must "retain no freedom except such as must necessarily be granted by the constitution of the state itself" (CW, 725)—"They [the people] being debarred both from offering advice and from voting" (CW, 725). If there is a regime that Spinoza prefers, then, it is aristocracy, rule by a council of patricians, which he conceives explicitly to be the least democratic of regimes. Of it Spinoza twice says, approvingly, as evidence of its superiority, that when "sovereign power . . . has once been conferred on a council" it "never reverts to the people" (CW, 724). But all this need not be said, and it is useless and wrong to attribute to Spinoza a preference regarding regimes (though it is all too obvious that he abhors democracy), because the government Spinoza prefers most is whatever government actually is ruling, whatever government is currently maintaining stability, regardless of its type, and certainly regardless of what the morally inclined judge to be its moral virtues or crimes. In the political realm Spinoza supports order, because he wants peace above all. And he wants peace above all, not for its own sake but so that philosophers and scientists can do science and contemplate.

With the many reasons for his evident aversion to the masses, there is little likelihood, indeed zero likelihood, that Spinoza has a preferential support for democratic regimes, except of course when they are already in power. The regime he supports is the regime in power. When he did express a preference, in the *Political Treatise*, he supported rule by the few, by a council one of whose virtues is that it is not beholden to the people. Despite this one expression of preference, which appears in an unfinished and unpublished text, Spinoza has no moral preference for any particular type of government. The purpose of government is not public welfare in the contemporary sense but peace and security. This translates into support for whatever regime is the established power, regardless of what type of regime it is, democratic or otherwise.[13] For Spinoza the worst thing in politics, as in everything else, is change. Regime change, therefore, is worse in principle than however tyrannical a regime may presently be. It may not be *prudential* for a regime to disregard "the public good," yes, but if the government does disregard the public good, it is still worse for the public to overthrow that regime. Thus, in chapter 18, Spinoza argues that it was when the ancient Israelites "changed the original form of their state" that "there was practically no end to civil wars" (TPT, 207). For "a people unaccustomed to the rule of kings, and already possessing established laws, to set up a monarchy" was a "fatal" mistake. And lest his readers not grasp his true point, or think that he prefers democratic regimes, Spinoza concludes chapter 18 as follows: "Here, however, I must not fail to point out that there is also no less danger involved in removing a monarch, even if his tyranny is apparent to all. The people, accustomed to royal rule and constrained by that alone, will despise and mock a lesser authority" (209). What is unmistakably clear, and supported everywhere by the textual evidence, is that Spinoza is decidedly not a democrat.

---

13. There were no established democracies anywhere in Europe, or really in the world, in Spinoza's time. All established governments were ruled by one or by a few, but in no case by the many. So from the point of view of historical fact, Spinoza did not support any democratic regime.

Whatever regime has established itself should by virtue of its established status continue—it is just another case of *conatus*. And thus Spinoza concludes chapter 18 with the hardnosed affirmation that we have had several occasions to cite, namely, "that every state must necessarily preserve its own form, and cannot be changed without incurring the danger of utter ruin" (211). It is fully consistent with the deterministic character of his philosophy, with its consequent lack of pedagogy or therapy, that in the political realm we find Spinoza an accommodationist, supporting the status quo whatever it is. If scientific knowledge acknowledges only eternity and necessity in the realm of truth, political prudence acknowledges only established and enduring power in the realm of obedience. Change means chaos, regime change means anarchy, and the philosopher dismisses nothing more than chaos and abhors nothing more than anarchy.

It is time to underscore the other no less compelling reason why Spinoza has no special preference for regime democracy. And here it is not a matter of neutrality, of supporting whatever regime is in power, but rather of positive aversion, indeed antipathy. I refer once again to his unrestrained disdain for the people, the multitude, the mass, the many. His disgust finds voice again and again all throughout the *Theological-Political Treatise*. A sample from chapter 17:

> [T]hose who have experienced the fickleness of the masses are almost reduced to despair; for the masses are governed solely by their emotions, not by reason; they rush wildly into everything, and are readily corrupted either by avarice or by luxurious living. Every single man thinks he knows everything, and wants to fashion the world to his liking; he considers things to be fair or unfair, right or wrong, according as he judges them to be to his profit or loss. Vanity makes him despise his equals, nor will he be guided by them. . . . There is no need for me to go through the whole catalogue, for everyone knows to what wickedness men are frequently persuaded by dissatisfaction with their lot and desire for change, by hasty anger, by disdain of poverty, and how their minds are engrossed and agitated by these emotions. (187)

Given the despicable character of the masses, for Spinoza the "state" is always "in greater danger from its citizens than from the external enemy" (187). Given the free expression of his disdain of the masses, for their ineradicable irrationality, coupled with his explicit support for aristocracy in the *Political Treatise*, one wonders how anyone, by any stretch of the imagination, was ever able to suppose and declare Spinoza to have a preferential support for democracy.[14]

---

14. Lewis Samuel Feuer, in *Spinoza and the Rise of Liberalism*, whose sympathies lie with a liberal and democratic reading of Spinoza, explains Spinoza's "ambivalence" toward the masses as disillusionment following the mob murder of the republican de Witt brothers in 1672 (which, allow me to add, according to Wikipedia, "the Dutch refer to as the 'year of disaster' or *ramajaar*"). See the subsection of Feuer's book entitled "The Masses: Free Men or Slaves?," 192–197. It seems to me, on the contrary, that this historical event contributed to Spinoza's unambivalent contempt for the people, even if it does not fully explain it. Lack of appreciation of the present point—Spinoza's unmitigated disdain for the people—unfortunately compromises many commentaries upon Spinoza's political philosophy. Just because we moderns and we Americans especially are generally well disposed to democracy does not mean that all or even most previous philosophers have shared this sentiment. A relevant example of this distortion at work in Spinoza scholarship appears in Robert J. McShea's *The Political Philosophy of Spinoza*. While he does distinguish between the few and the many, as one can hardly avoid doing when reading Spinoza, McShea asserts that Spinoza's politics are for the "great number of men who fall between the above two categories. The study of politics is mainly concerned with this group; they are 'the people,' they include all who are neither above the need for the state, as are gods and rational men, nor below the level of political life, as are beasts or delinquents. . . . The area between total rationality and total incorrigibility is vast and populous" (92–93). Sensible or even true as such a thought may be, it is nonetheless and importantly not Spinoza's. Nowhere do such distinctions determine Spinoza's thoughts regarding democracy or other political regimes. Another example of distortion, far more egregious, that I hesitate to even mention, appears in the work of Antonio Negri, who somehow reads the *Political Treatise*, despite the fact that the promised section on democracy was never written, as a stalwart defense of . . . democracy (an account of which even Negri admits must be found in the *Theological-Political Treatise*). Negri mistakenly takes the factual inability to alienate an individual's "natural right" of thought and speech to be for Spinoza a positive right. No doubt on the basis of prudence Spinoza on this limitation is more "realistic" than Hobbes, admitting the current incomplete alienation of an individual's free thought and speech, but *in principle*, as we have seen, he sees the state as having absolute and complete sovereignty, and thus in theory he restricts the free thought and speech of the masses—the people—as much as the state wants and can, limited only by considerations of prudence. See, especially, Antonio Negri, "The *Political Treatise* or, the foundation of modern democracy," in Negri's *Subversive Spinoza*, 9–27. I hesitate to mention Negri because his extensive writings ostensibly on Spinoza strike me as being not so much about Spinoza at all but as occasions for Negri to articulate his own positions, to express his own preferences regarding modern democracy, lending them some sort of authoritative aura, perhaps, with the truly ill-fitting "scholarly" cover of a seventeenth-century rationalist philosopher. Negri is entitled to his political opinions, to be sure, but no free ticket to fob them off as Spinoza's.

Freedom

It can come as little surprise that there is no less of an ambiguity at play in Spinoza's use of the term "freedom." The term has a philosophical sense, meaning necessity, and a political sense, meaning willful choice. Because in the *Theological-Political Treatise* he uses the term "freedom" ambiguously, as we have seen him do with the term "democracy," there should be little wonder that many Spinoza scholars read him not only as a great defender of democracy but also and consistently as a no-less-great defender of freedom of thought and speech. To be sure, in a general way we have already seen the reasons why Spinoza's support for freedom of thought and speech in the political arena cannot be based on a genuinely positive and enlightened preference for them, but rather is grounded factually in the impossibility of the sovereign state successfully appropriating or suppressing such freedoms, the impossibility of their complete abnegation. Nevertheless, to properly understand Spinoza's political philosophy, to be clear about his views regarding freedom, in distinguishing, as we will do, between "philosophical freedom" and "political freedom," we must be as careful readers here as we have been earlier. And we must be specific, for though Spinoza's ambiguous uses of "democracy" and "freedom" to a great extent parallel one another, the terms of these two ambiguities are not the same and their differences deserve our attention. Spinoza certainly supports philosophical freedom, the freedom to philosophize, to actualize the intelligibility of eternal, immutable necessity—his life and work as a philosopher, the truth itself, depend on this freedom and actualize it. But such freedom must not be confused with political freedom, to which we now turn.

By now I hardly need to repeat that Spinoza has no belief or hope that the masses of humanity—those who ostensibly would rule in a democracy—have true ideas in their heads or true ideas coming out of their mouths. The masses are mired in their selfish passions and febrile imaginations, with no care for the dispassionate rigors of truth seeking. Yet the sovereign state, despite its absolute sovereignty in theory, finds practically that to fully control the thought and speech of its subjects would be more trouble than it is worth and cannot succeed in any event. But such a limitation is of no serious consequence or if properly managed need not be of serious consequence. State sovereignty need not be threatened by the residue of free thought and speech that subjects cannot abdicate. In fact, if properly managed, if kept within reins, that is, if not considered an alternative base of authority independent of state sovereignty, subjects can be *permitted* free thought and speech. Thus the first sentence of the subtitle of chapter 17: "*It is demonstrated that nobody can, or need, transfer all his rights to the sovereign power*" (185). Explanation: "it should be observed that the government's power is not strictly confined to its power of coercion by fear, but rests on all the possible means by which it can induce men to obey its commands. It is not the motive for obedience, but the fact of obedience, that constitutes a subject" (185). In the realm of political freedom, then, so-called "moral freedom," free choice, free will, and so forth, are useful rhetorical and ideological tools in the state's coercive arsenal. What matters alone are not labels or claimed intentions but obedience. Surely it is easier to control individuals who think they are free, and who in some harmless measure are free, than those who believe themselves coerced.

Is there a counterargument? In chapter 20, the concluding chapter of the *Theological-Political Treatise*, we find the most moralistic pages Spinoza ever published. In them he movingly describes and bemoans the disadvantages to the state, the harm to its security, indeed the harm it would cause to its best citizens, were it to try to completely suppress freedom of thought and speech. Indeed, it is precisely persons who value honesty, people of integrity, the so-called best people, who would be the ones stifled first and suffering the most. In contrast, the suppression of free thought and speech would encourage the worst sort of persons. In Spinoza's words:

> [G]ood faith, of first importance in the state, would be undermined and the disgusting arts of sycophancy and treachery would be encouraged. This is the source of false dealing and the corruption of all honest accomplishments. . . . the greater the effort to deprive them [persons of good faith] of freedom of speech, the more obstinately do they resist: not indeed the greedy, the flatterers and other poor-spirited souls who find their greatest happiness in gloating over their money-bags and cramming their bellies, but those to whom a good upbringing, integrity and a virtuous disposition have given a more liberal outlook. (226)

In addition to "being directed not against villains but against men of good character," and hence in this way being a "great danger to the state," excessive restrictions on freedom of thought and speech "are quite ineffective" because people "who are convinced of the validity of beliefs that are condemned by law will not be able to obey the law" (226). Spinoza gives additional reasons, but the point is clear: excessive restriction of freedom of thought and speech not only cannot succeed in fact, but because it also leaves the worst sort of people unscathed and yet hurts the truly honest and best people, just the people who the state would otherwise be able to coerce with sweet persuasion, as it were, that is, through moral ideology (recall: "Those who govern the state or hold the reins of power always strive to cloak with a show of legality whatever wrong they commit, persuading the people that this action was right and proper" [195]), such repression is altogether counterproductive to securing peace and stability. Such is Spinoza's defense of a limited freedom of thought and speech. At no point, in other words, does he defend freedom of thought and speech because they have intrinsic value. Of course, this is because for Spinoza they have no intrinsic value in the political sphere.

Nevertheless, if we are clear, as I hope we are at this juncture, about the status of freedom at the political level, then we are prepared to also understand that there is a deeper sense outside the sphere of the political but, as we shall see, not entirely unrelated to it, in which Spinoza *does* support freedom of thought and speech. And that is for scientists and philosophers, the few. "This freedom," he writes also in chapter 20, linking political freedom to philosophical freedom, "is of the first importance in fostering the sciences and the arts, for it is only those whose judgment is free and unbiased who can attain success in these fields" (226). Spinoza genuinely and fully supports philosophical freedom, the freedom to know truth, to know the universal and necessary laws of nature. Such freedom of thought and speech constitute the highest vocation of man, if "highest" and "vocation" retain any sense in a deterministic philosophy. In chapter 3—of the philosophical part—of the *Theological-Political Treatise*, had not Spinoza already and unequivocally declared what he declares in so many other instances, namely, that "a man's true happiness and blessedness consists solely in wisdom and knowledge of truth" (35). The political certainly must not interfere in such freedom. And not only must it not interfere, in granting its subjects even a restricted freedom of thought and speech, what it cannot suppress in any event, it is also thereby opening a window sufficient for scientists and philosophers to pursue truth. The blessed, the few, the philosophers and scientists, need to be free, to think and to speak truth. With this recognition, we begin to understand what Spinoza demands of the state and the purpose driving his entire political philosophy.

It is what separates the political philosophy of Spinoza from Hobbes. We have already said it, but it bears repeating. For Hobbes the absolute state is justified by the security it provides. Its purpose is to provide security. Its power is self-justified and has no further end beyond itself. There is only one alternative: anarchy, complete disorder, the war of all against all. The power of the state creates and enforces peace and tranquility, end of story. As for what citizens do, what sorts of lives they lead, what they aim for, these are of no significance except insofar as they might disturb the peace. For Spinoza, in contrast, while the function of the state is also and no less to create and secure peace and security, the latter are not valued simply for their own sake. Rather, peace and security are the necessary conditions, the *sine qua non*, of the life of the mind, therefore of philosophy and science. The highest end of the state for Spinoza is not therefore the state in and of itself but the life of intellect for which it provides the appropriate and necessary environment. Providing security and peace, keeping "the unruly masses" (TPT, 227) under control, makes possible—and finds its ultimate justification in—the true life, the life of the mind. The purpose of the state, in other words, is beyond the state: the state serves philosophy.

Now, with all this said, we are in a far better position to raise again our original question about for whom the *Theological-Political Treatise* is written. It is not written for philosophers, who live the life of the mind, the life of philosophical freedom far from the passions and imaginings of political freedom, including its illusory "free choices," far also from the control and power necessary to keep the masses down and external enemies at a distance. Nor, obviously, is the *Theological-Political Treatise* written for the masses who, incapable of ruling themselves, are incapable of ruling others.

Second Excursus: Why Take Human Laws Seriously at All?

Once again we must approach our destination in a roundabout way. Actually it is less a roundabout way than a matter of drawing attention to an issue, a question really, and confronting it directly, rather than allowing it to enter in and out of our analyses haphazardly and surreptitiously, as it were, as it has been doing in any event. The issue is determinism versus freedom, what we—adopting Spinozist doublespeak—have been calling the realm of freedom, *Ethics*, the intelligibility of philosophy and science, where freedom means necessity, versus the realm of obedience, the theological-political realm, the domain of human choice, moral and political sway and sanction.

Beyond the several audiences and motivations Spinoza gave in the preface to the *Theological-Political Treatise* and in letter no. 30 to Henry Oldenburg, there is a deeper and prior metaphysical question that must be answered: Why would anyone of Spinoza's philosophical persuasion take human laws seriously at all? If, according to the *Ethics* upon which the *Theological-Political Treatise* stands, truth no longer permits taking the human order "as a kingdom within a kingdom" (102), if, that is to say, the real is ordered exclusively according to "adequate" or true ideas, and the order of such ideas is eternal, immutable, and necessary, everything else being merely human illusion, imaginative fancy, superstition, anthropomorphisms, and the like, as is certainly the fundamental claim of Spinoza's philosophy, then to take human laws seriously is no better than describing shadows in a cave or the shapes of passing clouds as if they had real substance, as Plato had already warned long ago. Very simply, the universe does not run by human laws, to which it is indifferent, but by natural or so-called divine ones. Adequate ideas mirror the intelligible or lawful structure of the universe, which in Spinozist doublespeak is also called "divine law" or "God," earning such accolades, presumably, because it is an intelligibility not only eternal, immutable, and necessary but also absolute, total, whole, without other or residue. Science mirrors the intelligibility of nature; there is nothing else. One can hear the excitement in Spinoza's declaration, in *Ethics*: "truth might have evaded mankind forever had not Mathematics . . . revealed to men a different standard of truth" (58). The *Theological-Political Treatise*, however, at least parts 2 and 3, is about another sort of law, laws that are not those of the necessary intelligible structure of the universe but that are *legislated, chosen, products of human deliberation, obeyed or disobeyed rather than necessitated*, whether in the name of God or in the name of a sovereign polity ruled by one, some, or all people. Once again, as with the crucial terms "democracy" and "freedom," a key term of Spinoza, "law," has two meanings and will be used in two different ways: eternal, immutable, necessary, true, "divine" and natural law, on the one hand, and human, contingent, changing, finite, or legislated law on the other.

In chapter 4 of the *Theological-Political Treatise*, in philosophically preparing his readers for parts 2 and 3, Spinoza explicitly addresses this issue, the question of the nature, or more precisely the status of human laws. Their *nature* is the less problematic: they are not what they seem because true laws, that is, natural or "divine" laws, do not come from decisions, choices, deliberations, or legislation. They come from or rather they represent the causality of a fully determined universe.[15] *Ethics*: "Nothing in nature is contingent, but all things are from the necessity of the divine nature determined to exist and to act in a definite way" (I, Prop. 29, 51). There are of course many ways of formulating the necessary intelligibility of the universe; one of the most telling is the equation of will and intellect. *Ethics*: "God's intellect, will and power are one and the same."[16] It is this very thesis that Spinoza in the *Principles of Cartesian Philosophy* turned against Descartes, who had separated will and intellect. Spinoza would have Descartes more Cartesian, fully Spinozist.

But it is precisely owing to this knowledge, and to knowing also that it alone is knowledge, that frees the philosopher from having to read the *Theological-Political Treatise*, which deals in contingencies. Spinoza warned in the *Ethics* that "those who do not know the true causes of things confuse everything" (I, Prop. 8, Scholium, 34). The problem with so-called human or legislated laws is that to think of them in their own terms, as products of free will, of choice, can only be a reflection of *ignorance of their true causes and a source of more confusion*. Therefore the question for the philosopher: Why take them seriously? Why did Spinoza? Taking them seriously is precisely what constitutes the entire domain of the political and of the theological as well, according to Spinoza's political reading of the theological. Taking them seriously is to be duped. But somehow, unless Spinoza has truly lost his way, taking them seriously constitutes the very doorway from philosophy to politics and theology, from the eternal to the contin-

---

15. E, I, Prop. 29: "Nothing in nature is contingent, but all things are from the necessity of the divine nature determined to exist and to act in a definite way" (51).

16. Spinoza, *Ethics*, I, Prop. 17, Scholium, 45. Or, Spinoza, *Ethics*, II, Prop. 49, Cor.: "Will and intellect are one and the same thing" (96).

gent, the hinge joining the *Ethics* and part 1 to parts 2 and 3 of the *Theological-Political Treatise*.

What does Spinoza say for himself on this score? He devotes two paragraphs, providing two answers to this question, in chapter 4. They are introduced with the following sentence: "And although I grant that, in an absolute sense, all things are determined by the universal laws of Nature to exist and to act in a definite and determinate way, I still say that these latter laws [political legislation] depend on human will" (TPT, 48). Spinoza's first answer, his first reason, unfortunately but tellingly is incoherent.[17] Or worse, if it is not incoherent, then the best sense it makes—or can be made to make—is actually to prove the opposite of what it is supposed to have proven, arguing once again for an absolute determinism for which human legislation cannot be taken seriously as such. I do not say lightly that Spinoza's first reason is incoherent. I have long meditated upon it. I have searched the secondary literature, to no avail.[18] For twenty years I have asked my students to unravel this mystery, to no avail. Now is not the time to delve further into this unsolved riddle, except perhaps to say once again that here

---

17. I cite Spinoza's first reason in full: "Man, insofar as he is part of Nature, constitutes a part of the power of Nature. Thus whatever follows from the necessity of man's nature—that is, from Nature as we conceive her to be determinately expressed in man's nature—follows from human power, even though it does so necessarily. Therefore the enacting of these man-made laws may quite legitimately be said to depend on human will, for it depends especially on the power of the human mind in the following respect, that the human mind insofar as it is concerned with the perception of truth and falsity, can be quite clearly conceived without these man-made laws, whereas it cannot be conceived without Nature's necessary law, as defined above" (TPT, 48). The unpublished *Political Treatise* provides no help and makes no progress in solving this conundrum, or even making it clearer. See CW, 683–685.

18. Just to take one instance, but only because one would expect, given the title, that Wolfgang Bartuschat, in "The Ontological Status of Spinoza's Theory of Politics," in *Spinoza's Political and Theological Thought*, would have cleared this matter up. But instead, he relies on what we are about to see is Spinoza's second "reason," that is, that the intelligibility of the real is "not known by the individual" (31), "having an inadequate comprehension" (32). Truth be told, one cannot have one's cake and eat it too: if the universe is strictly determined (if will and intellect are one), as Spinoza's *Ethics* insists, then there is no free will, hence no morality (to all of which Spinoza agrees, in the *Ethics*), and hence human laws—other than that they too appear necessarily, like everything else—are erroneously interpreted as products of choice.

lies yet another manifestation of the incoherence, the noncoherence, of the eternal and the temporal, the necessary and the contingent, that troubles Spinoza's philosophy throughout and as a whole.

Taken with a grain of salt, the *best* I can make of Spinoza's first reason, and I admit it is a forced reading, is that it means to argue that inasmuch as humans are part of nature, humans taking human laws seriously—debating them, legislating them, obeying them, and the like—must also be part of nature, and therefore real, part of universal intelligibility. Somehow contingency too must be necessary. To this, by the way, I wholeheartedly assent: contingency cannot be eliminated, it has ontological status. But that is not how Spinoza would read this concession: somehow for Spinoza contingency is meant to be necessary, not contingent but necessary. In other words, again, Spinoza's first reason makes no sense or contradicts itself. Even according to my best reading, if there is an argument left, which is doubtful, then what it has argued for is very little if anything at all. Because such a reason, if it is a reason at all, would equally justify not only human legislation and free choice but everything humans do and take seriously, such as superstition, adultery, lying, money-making, praying, and in fact anything and everything done in the belief that choice lies at the bottom of behavior. In other words, Spinoza's first reason reduces to saying that because everything that happens, no matter what it is, must happen, attributing false causes to things must also happen, is part of reality, and has being, and hence must be taken seriously. But all these words really say nothing, from a true Spinozist point of view. To "take seriously" can only mean finding true causes. The true causes of false ideas, like the true causes of true ideas, are equally necessary, yes, but this does not make the false ideas true or give to their illusory character reality. So much for Spinoza's first reason.

This leaves us with Spinoza's second reason as his only reason (one that he repeats in the *Political Treatise*), assuming that here we have a genuine reason. I cite it in full:

> We ought to define and explain things through their proximate causes. Generalizations about fate and the interconnection of causes can be of no service to us in forming and ordering our thoughts concerning particular things. Furthermore, we plainly have no knowledge as to the actual co-ordination and interconnection of things—that is, the way

in which things are in actual fact ordered and connected—so that for practical purposes it is better, indeed, it is essential, to consider things as contingent. So much for law taken in the absolute sense. (TPT, 48–49)

Now we are getting somewhere. One takes human laws seriously *as a practical matter* given the *present incomplete state of scientific knowledge*. Because, unlike God or absolute intellect in its complete determination, humans are finite—all humans, the few and the many—and as such are *at this time* ignorant of the totality of "the actual co-ordination and interconnection of things." That is, because our scientific knowledge is as yet incomplete, then for practical purposes we must take seriously some of what seems to us to be contingent in its contingency, and in particular, we must take seriously man-made laws.[19]

Here, then, lies the basis for Spinoza's willingness to take seriously—indeed to write and publish the *Theological-Political Treatise*—the notion of human law, or what in the next paragraph he calls "a rule of life which man prescribes for himself or for others for some purpose" (49).

Such humanly created rules and laws are not *true*, do not reflect the true causes of things, to be sure, but *taking them seriously* is presently a patent requirement of practical life.[20] And readers of the *Ethics* and the *Theological-Political Treatise* know why to take them seriously: because political sovereignty, and the human laws and lawfulness enforced by the state, make possible, provide the security that makes possible the true life, the life of the mind, the life of philosophers and scientists.

---

19. The late great Spinoza and Kant scholar Henry E. Allison argues that precisely his lack of a transcendental argument is what prevents Spinoza, with his mechanistic notion of strict causality, from taking contingency seriously, a lack corrected, of course, by Kant. See Henry E. Allison, "Kant's Critique of Spinoza," in *The Philosophy of Baruch Spinoza*, especially 219–220.

20. I have suggested that Spinoza's justification for taking seriously human laws is temporary or provisional, that is, needed in the time of our present "not yet" completed science. Levinas—in a generous reading (in a review of Sylvain Zac on Spinoza) that attempts to take seriously the independence Spinoza seems to give to the Bible vis-à-vis science—goes further, combining Spinoza's second to his first "reason," Levinas writes: "The impenetrable complexity of things is not contingent, so the Word is not doomed to the silence of the day where 'everything will be clear'" (DF, 113; translation altered).

It is an old story told by philosophers: the well-told lie protects truth; the noble myth provides cover for knowledge; the veil safeguards the true face. The *Theological-Political Treatise* is written to shield the *Ethics*.

Spinoza Shows His Hand

And this is why directly after having stated his reasons for taking human law seriously, Spinoza makes one of the most revealing statements of the entire *Theological-Political Treatise*, if not of his entire philosophy. One sees why Hobbes thought Spinoza so bold, and one wonders why Strauss thought Spinoza so careful. I quote in full:

> However, since the true purpose of law is usually apparent only to the few and is generally incomprehensible by the great majority in whose lives reason plays little part, in order to constrain all men alike legislators have wisely devised another motive for obedience, far different from that which is necessarily entailed by the nature of law. For those who uphold the law they promised what most appeals to the masses, while threatening transgressors with dire retribution, thus endeavoring to keep the multitude on a curb, as far as is practicable. Thus it came about that law was mainly regarded as rules of conduct imposed on men through the supremacy of others, and consequently those who obey the law are said to live under the law and appear to be in bondage. (49)

The few know that the "true purpose of the law" is beyond the state: to protect science. The many, in contrast, who are incapable of knowing truth and are swayed only by their passions, by pleasure-seeking and pain-avoidance, are told that upholding the law brings them material rewards while breaking the law leads to punishment.

It is here, then, that we discover for whom the *Theological-Political Treatise* is written, who are its appropriate readers: not clergy, although it will do them good, but *political leaders*, because philosophers and scientists need them to keep the peace. Like Machiavelli's *Prince*, the *Theological-Political Treatise* is written neither for philosophers, who love only truth, nor for the masses, who are incapable of truth. It is written for clergy, to be sure, but in a limited sense: (1) to keep them from interfering with philosophy and, for the same reason but even more importantly, (2) to keep them from interfering with the supremacy of *political* sovereignty that is the only truly competent guarantor of philosophy's safety. Thus, we have finally reached the answer to our basic question: the primary or best readers of the *Theological-Political Treatise*, its real audience, are political leaders, magistrates, "legislators," as Spinoza has just named them in the previous citation.

The Prince

Who then is a Spinozist legislator? Who is a Spinozist political leader? What are the qualifications? What is their function? To answer these questions, which are really one question, we take our clue from Friedrich Nietzsche. Not by accident. Two hundred years after Spinoza's death, Nietzsche acknowledged Spinoza as his only predecessor for two reasons. They shared a ruling passion for knowledge and they both rejected, in Nietzsche's words, "freedom of the will; ends; a moral world order; non-egoism; evil."[21] Let us add that like Spinoza, Nietzsche also divides the world into two human types. Not into philosophers and ignoramuses, the cerebral and the somatic, mindful and materialistic, as does Spinoza, but rather into two sorts of bodies: the healthy and strong, the master types, the few "lucky hits," on the one side, and the weak and sick, the slave types, who are the many, on the other. Obviously such a division reflects Nietzsche's anti-Spinozist revaluation of the hierarchy of mind and body, that is to say, his valuation of body over mind, and his insistence that mind is an aftereffect of body. But as a division of all humanity separating the few and the many, Nietzsche parallels Spinoza even if his criteria differ.

The clue to understanding Spinoza through Nietzsche comes from section 15 of the third essay of the latter's *On the Genealogy of Morals* (1888). There Nietzsche identifies a third class of humanity, an *intermediate type* between the healthy and the sick, between the strong and the weak, namely, "the ascetic priest." Nietzsche writes:

---

21. See chapter 1 in this volume.

He must be sick himself, he must be profoundly related to the sick—how else would they understand each other?—but he must also be strong, master of himself even more than of others, with his will to power intact, so as to be both trusted and feared by the sick, so as to be their support, resistance, prop, compulsion, taskmaster, tyrant, and god. (125–126)

Transposing this insight back to Spinoza, for whom mind is superior to body: the political leader must be intelligent and knowledgeable, must be smart enough, must care enough for reason, knowledge, and truth, grasp just enough about the true nature of philosophy, to know what only the few can know, namely, that the true life, the blessed life, that beatitude lies only in philosophy and science, and hence also—and this is the key—that *the true purpose of the state is to make the philosophical-scientific life possible.* The political leader is not a philosopher or scientist, is not ruled by mind alone, is not personally and exclusively committed to the quest for knowledge and truth, because the political leader is driven by a will to power, a passion to rule. But, and this is crucial, and this is why Spinoza writes the *Theological-Political Treatise* for such a person, the political leader must clearly recognize the absolute superiority of philosophy, even while not accomplishing it in his or her own person. Only thus, knowing the mind but led by the body, the political leader is preoccupied with ruling others, with legislation, with taking seriously "man-made laws" rather than "divine law" (i.e., natural law), but all the same serves—serves by protecting—the higher life of the mind of philosophers and scientists.

The political leader, then, who is the proper reader of Spinoza's *Theological-Political Treatise,* is an intermediate type, like Nietzsche's ascetic priest but now conceived as an overtly political rather than a religious leader, mediating between the knowing few and the ignorant masses, protecting the former from the latter. Such a prince knows, to return to Spinoza's words just cited, "the true purpose of law" that is "incomprehensible by the great majority," and at the same time such a leader is willing and capable to "have wisely devised another motive for obedience, far different," promising "those who uphold the law . . . what most appeals to the masses, while threatening transgressors with dire retributions, thus endeavoring to keep the multitude on a curb, as far as is practical." These are Spinoza's words, even if they seem extracted from Nietzsche's *On the Genealogy of Morals.* Like

Nietzsche's ascetic priest, for the Spinozist political leader, and here let us cite Nietzsche: "*Dominion over the suffering* is his kingdom; that is where his instinct directs him, here he possesses his distinctive art, his mastery, his kind of happiness" (GM, III, 15, 125).

Thus we are able to solve the "paradox" of the *Theological-Political Treatise*'s proper audience by finding an intermediate type—the type of the political ruler—between the few and the many. Three groups: (1) the few, philosophers, scientists, living the life of the mind, live in true joy, attain true beatitude; (2) the many, torn this way and that by their unruly emotions and wild imaginations, live ignorant lives of confusion and suffering, never knowing the true order and causes of things; and (3) the political leaders, who rule the many but who are spiritually inferior to and ruled by the few, whose proximate task is to control the many, but whose ultimate task is to protect the few, serving truth by duping and governing the many. These are the Grand Inquisitors uncloaked, wearing the ties and suits and uniforms of political leaders. Such leaders, taught by Spinoza's *Theological-Political Treatise*, provide the few with the peace and tranquility necessary for philosophy and science. Such leaders shoulder the greatest burden, bear the greatest responsibility, protecting the Promised Land—pursuit of knowledge, truth, pure intelligibility—without entering it or letting the mobs disturb the equilibrium of the truly blessed, the philosophers and scientists. Their passion is to rule, their art is diplomacy; their proximate reward is power, their ultimate reward is service to what is truly best.

Response to Steven Frankel

Having finally identified the proper audience of Spinoza's *Theological-Political Treatise* as political leaders close enough to philosophy to recognize its worth, but far enough from it to rule the many, I want to address another commentator—Steven Frankel—who, like Smith and Nadler, argues contrarily that "Spinoza addresses himself primarily to clergy and theologians" ("Politics and Rhetoric," 902). I do so for two reasons. First, because in contrast to both Smith and Nadler, Frankel's commentary, like my own, is primarily grounded in textual exegesis and the inner logic of philosophical argumentation rather than going afield to Spinoza's historical-sociological situation. And second, because more than anyone else, with the sole exception of Leo Strauss, whose analyses we will address later, he has directly raised and delved into precisely the same question as the present chapter, as is clear from the title of his article, "Politics and Rhetoric: The Intended Audience of Spinoza's *Tractatus Theologico-Politicus.*"

To avoid misunderstanding and because it is pertinent regarding my response to Frankel, and to Nadler and Smith, let me reiterate that I am not denying that clergy and theologians can profitably read the *Theological-Political Treatise*. Nor would I deny that Spinoza could have had them in mind, in addition to political leaders. Historically, the second part of the *Theological-Political Treatise* was received as a kind of *Urtext* of "higher biblical criticism" (despite the existence of earlier books by other authors with similar theses). Spinoza explicitly anticipates such readers and welcomes them. Nevertheless, where I differ with Frankel, Nadler, and Smith is that I do not share their belief that clergy and theologians are the primary intended readers of the *Theological-Political Treatise*. That audience is the political leader. The political leader who would also learn from Spinoza's book that political sovereignty must not kowtow to clergy and theologians and that to keep the mob down, to keep the public peace, could well and exactly require keeping clergy and theologians in check.

Manuals for political leaders are not so unusual. Spinoza's *Theological-Political Treatise* is a manual for political leaders like Xenophon's *Education of Cyrus*, Machiavelli's *Prince*, or Hobbes's *Leviathan*, but it is written, like the last, its nearest and closest famous relative, after the rise of modern science, committed to that science as the highest form of knowledge and the truth of reality. It is hardly by accident then that the first figure mentioned in the *Theological-Political Treatise* is one of the world's most successful and renowned political leaders: Alexander the Great, world conqueror and student of Aristotle, whom Spinoza faults for having sporadically succumbed to superstition. Spinoza's point is that political leaders must rule over religion (which in showing the way to doing so the *Theological-Political Treatise* reduces to a purely private sphere) and not be ruled by it, even as they must respect philosophy—and provide for the requirements of the community of scholars, the higher Republic of Letters—and not overrule it. Controlling the multitudes, ruling religion, ruled by philosophy, such is the intermediate position of the political leader, reader of the *Theological-Political Treatise*. In the realm of obedience, meaning both politics and religion, politics rules supreme. Better then that clergy and theologians learn their proper place and hold to it, yes, but better still that political leaders know their proper authority and responsibilities, and enforce them.

One limitation of Frankel's account comes from his taking Spinoza a bit too much at his word, that is to say, in not having recognized that the *Theological-Political Treatise*, despite its title and despite Spinoza's hermeneutic claims at the start of chapter 7, divides into three parts rather than two and that the ruling part throughout is the first, the philosophical. Not recognizing this, Frankel proposes the following wrongheaded interpretation:

> The argument throughout chaps. 1 through 15 rests on the authority of the Bible and culminates in the presentation of its true teachings. This organization suggests that even a state founded in accordance with reason must be undergirded by a theology that unified men without undermining reason. Because such a religion does not exist, Spinoza sets out to establish the framework for one in the TTP. (912)

Though we radically disagree, lest we reprove Frankel too sternly, we shall see later in what sense and to what extent Leo Strauss also shares his position. But it is clear already that to create a new religion—or rather to resituate and limit the old religion—is but one of Spinoza's goals, and is an instrumental one at that. We certainly cannot agree with Frankel that the final purpose of the *Theological-Political Treatise* is to theologically enlighten "clergy and theologians," who thus enlightened will then revamp religion, because contrary to Frankel, according to our reading "chaps. 1 through 15" do *not* "rest on the authority of the Bible." Only chapters 7 through 15 do so rest, and even there the authority of the Bible is severely restricted inasmuch as it is sharply separated from and strictly kept away from the knowledge of truth that is found exclusively through science. Far from "undergirding" the state, then, as Frankel would have it, the authority of religion for Spinoza is to be undergirded from below by the authority of the state and trumped from above by the truths of science. In relation to statecraft and science, theology comes out worst of all, indeed with no ultimate authority, either in power or in knowledge.

To save his interpretation, despite its basic flaw of not recognizing the true status of philosophy and the real authority of politics, Frankel ends up multiplying his misunderstanding. For instance, while it is obvious according to the thesis of the present chapter why in his preface Spinoza first speaks of the bad influence of superstition on political leaders, Frankel comes up with the following artifice:

> The reason for this emphasis on the toll which religion takes on the leaders of the state (rather than on the multitude) is rhetorical: because the TTP is addressed to clergy and theologians (as we shall see), it begins with an account of how political leaders manipulate clergy and religion in order to secure their own power. Subsequently, the preface argues that political leaders should not be the high priests, an argument with great appeal for the clergy. (913)

It is certainly wise to be attentive to rhetoric, especially with Spinoza, as we have seen with regard to the play of ambiguity in his use of such crucial terms as "democracy," "freedom," and "law." And also we must be attentive to rhetoric because Spinoza is quite clear that the masses can only be duped and indeed must be deliberately duped. But the reason Spinoza addresses political leaders first in the *Theological-Political Treatise*, with the example of the unhappy effect of superstition on Alexander the Great, is not merely rhetorical, but rather because Spinoza is dead serious about the subordination of religion to the state and wants therefore immediately to signal both who his true readers are, that is, political leaders, and in what and how far their true superiority goes, that is, absolute sovereignty.

It is unlikely that the clergy and theologians of that time, accustomed as they were to political power, would happily learn from Spinoza of their privatization and subordination to the state. No doubt Spinoza would indeed employ rhetoric to disarm the worst of their fears. If the purpose of the *Theological-Political Treatise* is to create a "new religion," as Frankel puts it, that is, a religion without political power and subordinate to political power, it is also no less proposing to create a new politics, a politics above religion but below philosophy and science, at once subordinating religion to politics and politics to philosophy, though these two forms of subordination are quite different. In any event, it is to establish precisely this hierarchy that is the *raison d'être* and the difficult task of the *Theological-Political Treatise*. And to establish this hierarchy it cannot be addressed to clergy alone, or even addressed primarily to clergy. Rather its proper readers are political leaders, that intermediate class of rulers whose power and task is to mediate freedom and obedience, to check religious fanaticism and protect philosophers and scientists from the passions of the mob.

Profile of a Spinozist Leader: Plato's Alcibiades

To illustrate with historical examples the type of the Spinozist leader, one might think of Frederick II, "the Great," of Prussia, during whose reign Kant initiated his Critical philosophy; or of Philip of Macedon, who enlarged Macedonian power and enlisted Aristotle to tutor his son and heir Alexander, or better still of "Alexander the Great" himself, who as we noted is the first figure—a political leader—Spinoza invokes in the *Theological-Political Treatise*; or closer to Spinoza's epoch, Christina, Queen of Sweden (or Elizabeth of the Palatinate, though she never reigned except over an Abbey), who took lessons from René Descartes; or in Spinoza's day, Johan de Witt, the liberal-minded scholar and Grand Pensionary of the Netherlands and perhaps even Spinoza's friend; or of Napoleon, or other such educated political leaders who more or less acknowledged the superior value of philosophy and science even while they led political lives. No doubt none of these actual political leaders, and perhaps no one in human history, has ever exactly fit the mold Spinoza lays out in the *Theological-Political Treatise*. Nevertheless and happily, I think, history and philosophy do furnish us with one great example of the psychological profile, as it were, of a Spinozist leader, even if this leader never managed to rule in the absolute sense of Spinozist sovereignty. That person is Alcibiades. More precisely, for our limited purposes, it is the Alcibiades who appears and is brought to literary and philosophical life for all time in Plato's *Symposium*.[22]

---

22. Machiavelli's preferred exemplar of statecraft, Cesare Borgia, does not seem to have been bitten by philosophy, and is hence more a Hobbesian than Spinozist leader. Perhaps Dionysus and Dion of Syracuse, again as depicted in Plato (Seventh Letter), are other Spinozist leader figures. Spinoza, unlike Plato, is not arguing for the "philosopher-king" but rather, as I have indicated, for the "philosopher-protector." One supposes that Alexander the Great, student of Aristotle and Aristotelians, is another example. Plutarch's account, in his "Life of Alexander," suggests as much: "Aristotle was the man he admired in his younger years, and, as he said himself, he had no less affection for him than for his father. 'From the one he derived

Plato, or if not Plato, whose trip to Syracuse to council his student Dion indicates his political engagement, then certainly his Socrates was a philosopher dedicated to argument, a man of the mind completely and constantly devoted to knowing, to the quest for truth. Such anyway is the Socrates we know from Plato, surely his most celebrated philosophical student. We know that Plato and Alcibiades in many ways resembled one another, and it is clear that Plato was well aware of these similarities too: both aristocrats, both brilliant, both deeply concerned with statecraft, though one, perhaps stunned by his teacher's execution, took the extra-political high road of philosophy, knowledge, and truth, while the other, Alcibiades, entered the lists through the agon of political engagement, power, and fame. We students of philosophy, all of us progeny of that shining ancient Greek triumvirate of Socrates, Plato, and Aristotle, are often prone to forget the great and long-lasting fame, not to mention the political heritage of Alcibiades, adopted son of Pericles. The course and especially the outcome of the entire Peloponnesian War was perhaps more in his hands than in those of any other single person (and the aftermath of the Peloponnesian War, as we know, the geopolitical opportunity it created for Philip and then for Alexander of Macedon, influenced all subsequent Western history and spelled the end of the great age of Athenian philosophy). Indeed, there is hardly a more celebrated or controversial political figure in the ancient Mediterranean world, or one about whom more was written, than Alcibiades.

As is well known, the conceit of Plato's *Symposium* is that of a drinking party. The participants have been invited to the home of the poet Agathon, who is celebrating the victory of his tragedy performed at the just-concluded annual Dionysian festival of Athens. At the party the distinguished guests successively and competitively declaim in praise of Eros. It famously concludes with Socrates's speech, not a speech of "praise" as he tells his listeners, but one of "truth," a speech within which

---

the blessing of life, from the other the blessing of a good life.' But afterwards he looked upon him with an eye of suspicion. He never, indeed, did the philosopher any harm; but the testimonies of his regard being neither so extraordinary nor so endearing as before, he discovered something of a coldness. However, his love of philosophy, which he was either born with, or at least conceived at an early period, never quitted his soul; as appears from the honours he paid Anaxarchus, the fifty talents he sent Xenocrates, and his attention to Dandamis and Clanus" (300).

Socrates tells his listeners of the speech, or really the dialogue and the speech of a certain goddess "Diotima" who had taught Socrates—and thus also all who are present at Agathon's party, as also we readers of Plato's *Symposium*—the true and highest nature of Eros. And that, of course, is the desire for wisdom, which is to say, etymologically and existentially, it is philosophy itself. Socrates and Diotima and Spinoza agree: there is no higher calling than philosophy, philosophy as the search for truth, truth as the intelligibility of all. But in fact Socrates's speech or Diotima's speech does not conclude the *Symposium*, nor, more significantly, is it the only speech in which the *truth* and not merely *praise* is told of Eros or of philosophy. There is a final uninvited speaker who crashes the party and is welcomed by all. It is Alcibiades, and it is he who will give the last speech. His speech in praise of Eros, which like Socrates's speech will not be praise only but truth, tells the truth of Eros, according to Alcibiades's insistence, by speaking not of ideas, as did Socrates and Socrates's Diotima, but of a man: Socrates, the person Socrates, the philosopher Socrates, and in this way—and already tellingly as such—it reveals the truth of philosophy.

The *Symposium* is surely one of Plato's richest and most rewarding dialogues, and here is not the place for a full-blown exegesis, which would require a volume unto itself, or several volumes. Our interest in Alcibiades is spurred by Spinoza's *Theological-Political Treatise*. He is a political leader, but one who not only knows popular religion, and not only knows monarchic, aristocratic, and democratic political regimes, but one also with a far less common knowledge in addition, indeed a rare and rarified knowledge: knowledge of philosophy. Like Socrates again (i.e., in addition to both giving *true* speeches about Eros), Alcibiades arrives late to Agathon's party. For neither personage apparently do the niceties of good manners overrule higher interests, Socrates in ideas and knowledge, Alcibiades in persons and states. But Alcibiades arrives not only late, but very late, and not only very late. Unlike Socrates who is always sober, preternaturally sober, Alcibiades arrives at the party already very drunk from a night of partying, laurel-wreathed like a Dionysian god, with a group of noisy fellow revelers and flute girls. He is a party unto himself or at least the center of parties. Encouraged by Agathon and the other guests, Alcibiades is warmly welcomed and invited to contribute a speech in praise of Eros. He agrees, but like Socrates he changes the rules too. Socrates had already changed the rule guiding the other speakers, insisting that he would not speak in praise but would speak only the truth. Alcibiades follows suit. But unlike the sober Socrates, the drunken Alcibiades insists that everyone's drinking be wildly increased and immediately sets the example by drinking down a gigantic container of wine. But not only will he still speak the truth of Eros, *in vino veritas*, he will do so by speaking about Socrates, speaking the truth about Socrates.

In praising Socrates, Alcibiades is of course praising the highest form of eros and life, the love of wisdom, philosophy. Unlike Socrates who loves wisdom, ideas, Alcibiades loves Socrates, a person, who loves wisdom. This may seem a slight difference, but we can see in it all the difference between the philosopher and the political leader.

Loving Socrates, Alcibiades's love for wisdom is impure, as it were, indeed, as we hear from his own *shameless* words, it is a frustrated love. Frustrated in flesh and blood, to be sure, because what Socrates has to give his students is not the lower love, physical love, pleasure and sensations, even when he is lying naked with flesh pressed against flesh, as he had lain one night with Alcibiades. But frustrated too in the higher sense, for wanting Socrates's body Alcibiades is distracted from what is more important, more valuable, loving Socrates's mind, his ideas, following the philosophical life aiming at truth and knowledge. It is all very clever of Plato. Because Plato has chosen the philosophical life, and is a true disciple of Socrates (and Diotima), which is to say, a disciple of ideas, in the dialogue *Symposium* he shows us the torments of Alcibiades who has not, who has succumbed to the body and to fame rather than having risen to knowledge and ideas. Thus Plato puts into Alcibiades's mouth, and shows in Alcibiades's drunken antics, the self-contempt of one who knows the highest life but does not pursue it, shows the pained admissions of one who driven by the love of power and fame garners the crowd's fickle love, the crowd's passing praise, rather than undergo the higher discipline of truth, philosophy. It is that intermediate state wherein Spinoza identifies the political leader. Alcibiades knows the truth, in other words, knows what is best, but chooses the worse instead, chooses to rule his fellow humans and thus to be ruled by them rather than to submit to the harder, more rigorous, and sober *askesis* of philosophy. He is above good and evil and therefore can rule, but at the same time he remains below true excellence, though he has not forgotten what it is. Alcibiades is drunk with power, drunk with the body. He is a Dionysus who, though he still and painfully knows the superiority of Apollo, cannot tear free of the wild passions. If Socrates is like a Silenus figure,[23] as Alcibiades correctly declaims, that is, ugly on the outside but pure gold inside, indifferent to power, fame, glory, and all the superficial passions, but completely devoted to truth and knowledge, Alcibiades is the same, but he lets himself be driven by the exterior, by the show of beauty, power, fame, glory, and the like, rather than by the hidden treasures of what is hidden to the senses, that is, the mind, ideas, knowledge. The Spinozist political leader, though not a disciple of intellect, appreciates it and respects its devotees, and though opposed to general excess and riot, takes satisfaction in material pleasures and public rewards.

Alcibiades's speech is noteworthy for many reasons, only some of which are relevant to our concern. For one, he knows enough to realize that Socrates constantly deceives others, including the present company of partiers, making them think he loves them in body when he is seducing them to love mind alone, to become philosophers. Agathon, for instance, the refined and beautiful young host of the party, victor at the Dionysian festival, is completely fooled by Socrates, so much so that Alcibiades's true unmasking is to no effect, neither on Agathon nor on the several others at his party who are enamored of Socrates. A master of a rhetoric with which he persuades the aristocrats as well as the demos, here Alcibiades cannot persuade even one person, or a select group of private individuals, in a contest with the philosopher Socrates. Just as philosophy is impervious to politics, truth to power, the political rhetoric of the genuine political leader is unable—even when shameless—to drag down philosophical thought and speech.

The political leader in part resembles the prophet. Both must have a vivid imagination, must be able to sway others with words and images, to the point of duping the many, even if the prophet, like the poet, but unlike the political leader, is not necessarily endowed with keen intellect or even with intellect enough, as Spinoza points out, to understand his own words.[24] Let us listen then to Alcibiades's own

---

23. This striking image—to show dross on the outside, gold on the inside; ugly exterior, beautiful interior; silliness hiding seriousness; "you can't read a book by its cover," and so forth—was again, and in the name of Plato's Alcibiades, utilized by François Rabelais in the "Author's Prologue to the First Book" at the start of his *Gargantua and Pantagruel.*

24. This is Plato's constant criticism of poets: they do not understand what they say. See Plato's *Ion,* among other dialogues. For Spinoza, see TPT, chapters 1 and 2. "Hence it was not a more perfect mind that was needed for the gift of prophecy, but a more lively imaginative faculty" (14).

words or more precisely to Alcibiades's words according to the text of the philosopher Plato:

> He [Socrates] compels me to realize that I am still a mass of imperfections and yet persistently neglect my own true interests by engaging in public life. . . . He is the only person in whose presence I experience a sensation of which I might be thought incapable, a sensation of shame; he, and he alone, positively makes me ashamed of myself. The reason is that I am conscious that there is no arguing against the conclusion that one should do as he bids [and love wisdom], and yet that, whenever I am away from him, I succumb to the temptations of popularity. (*Symposium*, 101–102 [216a])

Again we find here one of Spinoza's intended readers, the Spinozist political leader: cognizant of the height and superiority of philosophy, of the life of the mind, of ideas, but *nevertheless* committed to the life of action, the life of power and public acclaim. Humble in the face of both, of truth and of power.

Continuing along these lines, I will permit myself to indulge in citing from what is likely a spurious dialogue attributed to Plato, *Alcibiades I*, for whether Plato or one of his disciples wrote it, it is not an unworthy dialogue, and, more importantly for our purposes, it accords with what we have just been learning from the *Symposium*. Indeed it is almost too perfect. Speaking to the then-young Alcibiades, Plato has Socrates say the following: "For, as you hope to prove your own great value to the state, and having proved it, to attain at once to absolute power, so do I indulge a hope that I shall have the supreme power over you" (*Alcibiades I*, 735 [105]). Alcibiades, presumably like Alexander the Great, is meant to be a leader, but a leader knowing the true hierarchy: philosophy first, politics second, religion third. Philosophy as the highest life, unsullied by the powers and passions of the theological-political; the theological divested of its philosophical and political pretensions; and the political freed of theological prejudices, freed of theological ideology, disestablished and in full grip of its authority, though always recognizing the superiority of the life of the mind, of philosophy and science, in whose service lies its ultimate *raison d'être*. The task of the political leader in a nutshell: to keep philosophy up and religion down.

Alcibiades is far too caught up in the passions of the body to commit himself fully to the life of the mind. Yet he knows the life of the mind sufficiently to be ashamed to see and to acknowledge its genuine worth. It should be noted that such a character and such an outlook stands in sharp contrast to the other political figures who appear and are put to task in Plato's dialogues, such as Callicles and Thrasymachus, who lack Alcibiades's true understanding of the status of philosophy and instead think philosophy merely something childish or foolish. These are dangerous political leaders who have no idea as to the purpose of the political as such. They are dangerous because power is for them an end in itself. Plato makes us quite aware that despite his admirable appreciation for philosophy, Alcibiades, to his loss, does not pursue it himself. It is unfortunate that unlike Plato Alcibiades is not a philosopher. But this is also exactly what makes him suited to be a political leader, exactly as such leadership is conceived in the *Theological-Political Treatise*. Knowing both, the absolute height of philosophy's search for knowledge and yet succumbing to the relative attraction of the passions, as well as being a man of excellent bodily and mental capacities, Alcibiades is *able to and willing to rule the masses without merely being one of them.*

So qualified and equipped, Alcibiades was able to rule in Athens at times in the party of oligarchs and other times in the party of democrats. Not only was he socially and politically connected and clever enough to command Athens during the Peloponnesian War, he was also able to advise Athens's enemy Sparta, and then also advise Greece's enemy Persia! All this shows that he was a true political leader for whom even patriotism was not the highest value. Aware of the highest truth, he was not bound to a particular regime or city-state or even country. Without actualizing the absolute transcendence that is philosophic love for truth, the beatitude of Spinoza's (or Diotima's) "intellectual love of God," Alcibiades was nevertheless free enough not to be blindly bound by the contingencies of birth or country. And what did others think of him? "For most people," as Thucydides tells us in his magnificent chronicle *The Peloponnesian War*, "became frightened at a quality in him which was beyond the normal and showed itself both in the lawlessness of his private life and habits and in the spirit in which he acted on all occasions" (Book 6, 376). That peculiar quality, that seeming "lawlessness," it seems to me, was Alcibiades's independence, his distance from the realm of obedience, of merely human laws, which derived from his appreciation for philosophy, divine laws, even if it was in the realm of obedience and not freedom that he ruled others and was himself ruled.

Conclusion

Political leaders, those with sufficient drive for power, sufficient intelligence, and the divided identity of an Alcibiades, are not only the perfect audience for the *Theological-Political Treatise*, but the *Theological-Political Treatise* is designed for them. Even regarding the abbreviated version of Spinoza's *Ethics* found in part 1, it provides just enough philosophy to remind them of the world's true orientation but not too much to bore or distract them. Part 1 of the *Theological-Political Treatise* presents only as much of the philosophy of the *Ethics* as is pertinent and needed by men of action, and no more. Thus, too, with regard to theology, the *Theological-Political Treatise* raises just such issues—the nature and authority of prophets, the meaning of chosenness, the meaning and authority of the Bible, and the like—to free political leaders from the ruses of ecclesiasticism, its superstitions and clericalism. Just enough so that, according to the strictures of part 3, they will be liberated to rule with the absolute political authority necessary for real peace and security, and more particularly so that they may without guilt or reservation pacify and control the many who are always and inescapably mired in religious delusion.

Thus we again affirm that the appropriate readers of the *Theological-Political Treatise* are precisely those persons whom Spinoza singled out in its preface and in his letter to Henry Oldenburg: neither the few who are philosophers nor the many who are unruly, but those "sensible people" or potential philosophers who without the liberating perspective provided by the *Theological-Political Treatise* might otherwise, hamstrung by mistaken notions about the true end of political life, submit and succumb to the lower motives and erroneous ideas of religious prejudice. The leader Spinoza would cultivate then is not Plato's philosopher-king. Plato already understood that the philosopher will not want to be king because the philosopher loves higher things than political rule, contemplating the eternal rather than distraction in the temporal. "The knowledge and love of God is the final end to which all our actions should be directed. But carnal man cannot understand these things" (TPT, 51). Rather and agreeing with Plato on this point, the leader Spinoza would cultivate is the philosopher-protector. The freedom of philosophical thinking, under the protection of such a political leader, remains independent of all obedience, of merely political freedom. Perhaps this is why Spinoza understands that the philosopher would obey the political laws that secure peace even if they were not backed by the sanctions with which they in fact must be guaranteed; the political law, in keeping the peace, serves the philosopher:

> Now if men were so constituted by nature as to desire nothing but what is prescribed by true reason, society would stand in no need of any laws. (TPT, 63)

> For, as we have shown, he who does good from true knowledge and love of good acts freely and with a steadfast mind, whereas he who does good from fear of evil acts under constraint of evil, in bondage, and lives under another's sway. . . . Only the wise live with tranquil and steadfast mind, unlike the wicked, whose minds are agitated by conflicting emotions. (TPT, 55–57)

By writing and publishing books such at the *Theological-Political Treatise* the philosopher—Spinoza, who need not be named as author for his authorship is already a betrayal of his true vocation—attempts to train leaders. To train leaders who are first of all political leaders to also appreciate and respect philosophy, and to protect and preserve it from the ignorant and unruly masses, from the wild passions of the mob, whether religiously or politically driven. Spinoza addresses the *Theological-Political Treatise* to potential philosophers *not to make them philosophers* but so that by remaining always potential philosophers—in the sense that they are friends of philosophy, friends of true science—they can best be enemies of all the imaginary and ideological nonsense that arouses dangerous passions, whether religious or political or both, in the masses. Only thus can the public peace be secured, the public peace that is the *sine qua non* of philosophy and science. It is not a matter, then, of supporting one type of government or another, whether monarchic, aristocratic, or democratic, even if Spinoza himself has good reasons to favor aristocracy. Rather and far more important is the aim of securing peace, securing security—so that philosophers and scientists can pursue the truth.

The *Theological-Political Treatise* thus represents Spinoza's best effort to solve the ancient problem of the death of Socrates, the legally sanctioned execution of the philosopher, the honest seeker of truth, including the truth of piety, of goodness, and of justice, who is exposed in the public arena to the perennial and inevitable misunderstanding and irrational emotions of the masses.

Postscript on Leo Strauss's Reading

Earlier I referred to Leo Strauss's 1948 article "How to Study Spinoza's *Theologico-Political Treatise*." Strauss was a great Spinoza scholar, devoting several books and articles to his philosophy and to the question of how it should best be read and understood. It is fitting for me to say more about Strauss's reading of Spinoza, by which I mean more specifically the position he took in the book he wrote in the years 1925–1928 and published in Germany in 1930, which text in large measure makes up the book *Spinoza's Critique of Religion*, which appeared in English translation with the long new preface in 1962.[25] It is to this last book that I turn. Though I usually find the dichotomies upon which Strauss constructs his readings (not only of Spinoza) too stark and abstract to be of much intellectual service, it hardly needs my saying that his reading of Spinoza is often penetrating and insightful, and certainly worthy of response.

More particularly, in relation to my own reading as per the preceding, we share the outlook according to which one must recognize the primacy of the *Ethics* in all of Spinoza's thinking. Thus Strauss too takes the first part of the *Theological-Political Treatise* to be grounded in the *Ethics* and crucial to understanding what Spinoza has to say about church and state in the rest of the *Theological-Political Treatise*. This agreement, indeed, is the point that led me earlier to refer to Strauss's article of 1948. It is also the position Strauss had taken and developed with greater comprehensiveness in his earlier Spinoza book. There, for instance, with regard to the second part of the *Theological-Political*

---

25. Strauss dedicates the book to the memory of Franz Rosenzweig.

Treatise, where Spinoza presents his biblical criticism, Strauss writes: "Spinoza comes to found Bible science as such only after completing his critique of religion. In Chapter VII, 'On the interpretation of Scripture,' he refers back on almost every page to the findings of the previous chapters, which are devoted to critique of religion" (*Spinoza's Critique*, 259). The critique of religion to which Strauss refers is of course the critique found in part 1, but this critique, as I have been at pains to stress, is based in the *Ethics*.

There is another important point of agreement between my reading of Spinoza's *Theological-Political Treatise* and Strauss's earlier reading of it. We both recognize the fundamental status and problematic of the ambiguities of its key terms. I have analyzed these ambiguities in Spinoza's use of the terms "democracy," "freedom," and "law," but of course there are others, such as "God," "religion," "human nature," ambiguities by which Spinoza shifts back and forth between philosophy (which in his book Strauss calls "metaphysics") and politics. Such ambiguities may be either deliberate and prudential strategies of rhetoric, that is, ways of masking and ameliorating dangerous things Spinoza wants to say, for example, criticisms of religion or criticisms of political powers, or they are expressions of deeper conceptual or intellectual aporia, contradictions unresolvable and haunting Spinoza's philosophy.

The ambiguities are indeed problematic, as we have seen, insofar as they gloss over with rhetoric a basic unresolved conflict in Spinoza's thought, between the eternal and the temporal, between substance and modes. Such unresolved conflicts in his philosophy reappear in the register of Spinoza's political thought in the division between the few who know, truth seekers, philosophers and scientists, on the one side, and the many who are ignorant, driven by their passions, swayed by imagined forces, on the other. One attends to the eternal, the other to the temporal; one lives in philosophical freedom, the other in religious and political obedience. Spinoza's philosophical contradictions appear, that is to say, in the lack of *paideia* in his political thought, the lack of any way to move from one group to another, to learn, to make progress, individually or socially. Thus we are able to see that Spinoza always supports the political status quo, not simply because present peace is better than the turmoil of political upheaval, as he tells us in the *Theological-Political Treatise*, but because he opposes change in principle, as one finds in the *Ethics*, where truth is eternal, immutable, and necessary. Thus Strauss writes, and we agree:

Now the antithesis between philosophy and superstition corresponds to the fundamental distinction drawn throughout Spinoza's anthropology—a contrast that ultimately rests on the ontic opposition between the total and imperishable which is *in se*, and the partial and transient which is *in alio*. Between these there is no middle term. . . . For Spinoza there remains only the abrupt antithesis of reason and imagination. (*Spinoza's Critique*, 245–246)

Earlier we referred to Jonathan Bennett, who among others noted the illegitimacy, the inconsistency, of the mix of Spinoza's sharp rejection of final ends *and* his frequent appeal to them, the relentless but philosophically illegitimate *preference* Spinoza has for the few over the many, for adequate ideas over confused imaginings, for dispassionate contemplation over disruptive passions, and the like. Spinoza is filled with preferences, recommendations, prejudices—passionately expressed. But all his exhortations are ontologically voided according to the strict determinism of his philosophy, since everything—intellect and passion, truth and lie, all and everything—is absolutely necessary and cannot be otherwise.

Accordingly, I find it impossible to affirm of Spinoza's philosophy what Nadler, for instance, affirms, namely, "His is a rich and multifaceted system, one that rewards long and careful study. He also basically got it all right" (*Spinoza's Heresy*, vii). While there is little doubt that Spinoza's system is "rich and multifaceted," and while I would agree that it "rewards long and careful study," I am far from thinking that Spinoza "basically got it all right." Precisely the reverse: Spinoza basically got it all wrong, wrong in the sense that we have been learning from Levinas, that is, Spinoza's system is scientistic, reductive, an overreaching of knowledge, and wrong also on Spinoza's own terms, the system is inconsistent from a purely rational point of view. Might not this latter problem in some measure explain why quite unlike Hobbes's *Leviathan*, or Locke's *Two Treatises on Government*, Spinoza's *Theological-Political Treatise* has never had their sort of cache as a political program (in contrast to the widespread influence of its biblical criticism). Even the famous *Pantheismusstreit* of late-eighteenth-century Germany, which involved the cream of Germany's literary, philosophical, and theological elite, was really more about "Spinozism," that is, philosophy as pantheistic, than it was about the principles, axioms, theses, and nuances of the philosophy Spinoza articulated in the *Ethics* and certainly not at all about the political thought and recommendations found in the *Theological-Political Treatise*.

Given the preceding substantial agreements, where and why do I part company with Strauss? Our difference is considerable, for it has to do with our differing ideas regarding the ideal reader of the *Theological-Political Treatise*. In the present chapter I argue that the appropriate readers of the *Theological-Political Treatise* are not only theologians and clergy but primarily political leaders: capable and intelligent persons within the realm of obedience who are bitten by philosophy but nonetheless remain driven by their passion for power. Such persons need to be freed of misguided theological prejudices, girded thereby in their authority, and at the same time impressed with their responsibility toward philosophy, the highest end, an end outside and above the realm of obedience altogether. I have invoked Alcibiades—Plato's Alcibiades more specifically—to illuminate the psychological profile, the torn identity, as it were, of such a leader. I have also mentioned other historical figures, such as Philip and Alexander of Macedon, Frederick the Great, Johan de Witt, and Napoleon. The ideal political leader can bridge the metaphysically unbridgeable gap dividing the few and the many as per Spinoza's worldview. That such figures are impossible from a strictly philosophical point of view, I am willing to admit. That they are necessary for Spinoza's politics and necessitated by his having a philosophy such as he has, *Ethics*, and a politics at the same time, this is my thesis.

For his part, Strauss argues for a different middle term—also probably impossible within the Spinozist philosophy. And that middle term, quite different than my own suggestion, is *liberal religion*, religion that is neither the true knowledge reserved for the few nor the imagined superstitious ideology of the many. Frankel too, as we saw, was sympathetic to such a view. No doubt Spinoza does defend a new liberal conception of religion, by virtue of his critique of superstition coupled with his arguments to privatize religion vis-à-vis state sovereignty. But agreeing about this does not put us in agreement with Strauss altogether, as it did not put us in agreement with Frankel. "Religion," Strauss writes, "stands midway between philosophy and superstition" (*Spinoza's Critique*, 246). By "religion" as a middle term Strauss means what he has called "liberal religion," which is to say religion based in universality, similar therefore to the universality Kant specifies in ethical terms and calls "true religion" or "pure religious faith" in contrast to the particularisms of "clericalism" or "ecclesiastical faith" in his *Religion within the Limits of Reason Alone*.[26] Strauss in the name of Spinoza's liberal religion means *beliefs based in a common anthropology*, in contrast to everything bound to words, images, "symbolic representation," "authority and tradition," all of which, as we have seen, "are mere shadows" (TPT, 52) for Spinoza. For such religion "obedience to God consists solely in loving one's neighbor" (TPT, 154), joined to beliefs consistent with this core imperative, what Spinoza boils down to a small set of essential "dogmas of the universal faith" (TPT, 161), such as God is one, that He is just, that He is omnipresent, and the like, which Spinoza enumerates on one page of chapter 14 of the *Theological-Political Treatise* (162).

There is no reason to doubt that Strauss is pointing to something important when he delineates a Spinozist sense of "religion" standing between "knowledge" and "superstition." After all, old-fashioned religions themselves oppose what they call superstition, sorcery, witchcraft, and the like, just as they also explicitly base themselves in faith, in miracles and the supernatural, rather than purely naturalist knowledge. Nevertheless, it seems to me that Strauss credits Spinoza with a far more enlightened or liberal picture of religion than the vision of religion that Spinoza actually proposes in the *Theological-Political Treatise*. First of all, there can be little or no doubt that the primary aim of parts 2 and 3, especially part 3, is to ground all real power, all real force and sanction, all public authority, in the state, in political sovereignty, and to deprive religion of precisely the same. The theological has nothing to teach philosophy, the two being entirely separate, and in the realm of obedience, where all theology is located, it must always and everywhere defer to the political—such are the prime theses of the entire book.

Or to put this in yet another way: the meaning of Spinoza's confinement of religion to the realm of authority and obedience, separating and excluding it from the realm of freedom and truth, the realm of science and philosophy, is that the religious is in reality but a form of politics, of obedience, authority, rule. This is quite explicit

---

26. See, especially, book 4, "Concerning Service and Pseudo-Service under the Sovereignty of the Good Principle, or, concerning Religion and Clericalism," in Kant, *Religion within the Limits of Reason Alone*, 139–178.

in Spinoza's completely secular explanation of the meaning of Jewish "chosenness." In chapter 3:

> Thus the Hebrew nation was chosen by God before all others not by reason of its understanding nor of its spiritual qualities, but by reason of its social organization and the good fortune whereby it achieved supremacy and retained it for so many years. . . . Therefore their election and vocation consisted only in the material success and prosperity of their state. (38)

Which means, and Spinoza draws this conclusion, that when the Jews lose their political independence, their sovereignty, they are no longer "chosen." "Therefore," Spinoza writes, "at the present time there is nothing whatsoever that the Jews can arrogate to themselves above other nations" (45). What Spinoza exposes in the *Theological-Political Treatise* is that religion is in fact but a type of politics, one that Spinoza wants to see subordinated to the state, to a political sovereignty freed of theological trappings, that is, disestablished, which he believes can only be done if religion is stripped of all overt political power and banned from all public influence, that is, privatized into individual conscience. Thus Spinoza is quite harsh toward religion, hardly a proponent of what we today think of as "liberal religion," even if he is less harsh than the Marquis de Sade, who wanted to root out and annihilate religion entirely, including individual conscience.[27]

While Strauss appears to be aware of Spinoza's reduction and subordination of religion to politics and the state respectively, his account of religion, and the status he accords to religion, nonetheless do not adequately reflect these positions. Spinoza does not set for religion the task of mediating between philosophy and politics. By my account, such is the task of the political leader the *Theological-Political Treatise* is meant to train. It is he or she who mediates between philosophy, respecting and protecting it, and religion, which is suppressed and privatized by the absolute and indisputable power of the state, which

---

27. See de Sade, "Dialogue between a Priest and a Dying Man," 163–175; and, in *Philosophy in the Bedroom*, the intercalated pamphlet "Frenchmen, one more effort if you wish to become republicans," 296–339.

such a political leader rules. Strauss's account of religion cannot be fitted to explain this required dynamic. That is to say, it cannot explain how religion, with no possible notion of the true, can serve as an intermediary between the few and the many when only political power is capable of managing the latter for the sake of the former. Only a clearheaded politics, knowing both above and below, can restrict religious authority and prevent mob rule from disturbing the peace required by contemplation. That Strauss grasps that such a function must be satisfied is clear, from what we have already said, as it is further made clear in the following citation, which I introduce because in addition it shows Strauss admitting the failure, or at least the problematic—or "obscure"—character, of his own proposal.

> Even though religion is more in accord with reason than is superstition, religion has no rational means to prove its superiority over superstition, for it is grounded in "mere experience." If religion wishes to defend itself against superstition, it cannot invoke truth, take its stand on the inner right of love over against hatred, but only on the will of God. Religion thus presents itself as a combination of elements that stem from reason and from superstition. Its aim stems from reason but its means stem from superstition. The bond between these remains obscure. (*Spinoza's Critique*, 248)

The failure of religion as a middle term, then, comes because it has no actual ground in reason but in its entirety is but a type of obedience, despite its declared precautions and the apparent distances it takes from what it will call superstition. Reason can distinguish itself from superstition and criticize superstition, but religion can at best only do the former, and even that it can only do in rhetoric and pretense but not in reality or theory. It cannot appeal to truth, but only to faith, even if to a "liberal" faith extolling works as the legitimate expressions of faith.

Kant and Levinas are able to overcome the aforementioned failure by conceiving liberal religion not in terms of ontology, in which it remains mired in irrational faith, but in terms of ethics, whose imperatives are universal. In this way, binding religion to ethics, its possibility and intelligibility can be admitted by reason, though with difficulty. Though Spinoza seems in many ways to lean in such a direction, for instance in his apparent support of religion as works rather than faith alone—"only by works can we judge anyone to be a believer or unbeliever" (TPT, 160)—he ultimately retreats from it, declawing and restricting religion, as we have seen, to private conscience, banning it from the public square entirely. Strauss honestly admits as much. Restricting and confined as it is, Spinoza's religion still cannot resolve religious conflicts because it is unable to invoke reason and truth. Even Spinoza's preference for a religion of works over a religion of faith cannot be and probably is not ultimately justified on religious grounds, and it seems the weaker position on political grounds insofar as it is hardly consistent (though not entirely inconsistent) with the complete privatization of religion Spinoza's philosophy demands.

Finding the intermediary term in the *political leader*, in contrast, enables us to understand—as the example of Alcibiades shows us—how a person can have genuine and lasting insight into the true nature of reason, the true value of knowledge, of wisdom, science, truth, and yet, as a finite person not fully live up to such an insight and choose rather to rule and be ruled by passions, that is, the passion for power. Such a leader does not necessarily have to *use* a subjugated liberal religion (or even a manipulated old-fashioned religion) to control the masses, although from a purely practical-political perspective no greater ideological prop to political power has yet been devised than God and religion, as even such nonreligious political leaders as Robespierre and Stalin at certain times realized. (Usually patriotism-nationalism, another highly effective ideological tool, is aligned with religion so used.) There are certainly other tools in the political leader's arsenal of control: if religion is the opium of the people, as Marx called it, patriotism is surely at least its marijuana, nationalism a kind of heroin, and perhaps consumerist self-interest crack cocaine. No need to push this metaphor too hard. The type and force of propaganda varies according not to purely rational or abstract criteria but to the particular historical-cultural experiences of the relevant society and polity. The point, as Spinoza has explicitly stated, is that political leaders must be willing and able to use what they will—truth or lie—to maintain security, and to maintain their power. Religion has worked well in the past, but who knows what will work best in the future. It has no privilege as a political tool, and it is nothing other than a political tool.

To recognize the proper reader of the *Theological-Political Treatise* as a political leader also underscores the special orientation it has that is lacking, say, to Machiavelli or Hobbes. Political leaders, so Spinoza is teaching, must respect and protect science and philosophy. This is their special assignment, their special task, the justification of their rule. As I have indicated, here we do not have Plato's philosopher-king. But that is exactly Plato's teaching: we shall not have, we cannot have a philosopher-king. Rather, and in this Spinoza joins Plato, the king, the political leader, who cannot for that very reason be a philosopher, must be a philosophy-protector. The philosopher cannot be king, because he is absorbed in higher things, but in the best possible world the king can have been touched by philosophy. And it is such a king, an enlightened king, or rather a would-be king as one of a group of peers, *primus inter pares* in an aristocracy of such leaders, an enlightened *council of rulers*, that Spinoza would have rule. As Spinoza observes in the *Political Treatise*:

> And out of a hundred men whom fortune raises to office hardly three are to be found who are singularly gifted with skill and understanding, it will come about that the sovereignty will be in the hands of, not a hundred, but no more than two or three men who excel in mental power and who will easily contrive to gather everything into their hands, each of them, ambitious as is the way of humans, preparing his path to monarchy. (CW, 723–724)

To awaken and provide guidance to such leaders, a mere handful, but the best, leaders true to intellect and to power, Spinoza has written and published the *Theological-Political Treatise*.

Chapter Six

Levinas on Spinoza's Misunderstanding of Judaism

This chapter was first entitled "Levinas on Why Spinoza Is Bad for Judaism." Such a title would have disconcerted some readers, and not just because today one rarely hears an overt moral judgment, much less a blanket overt moral judgment, not to mention a negative blanket overt moral judgment, in any academic venue. Spinoza is meant to have been initiated; he is one of the greats, an untouchable. There is more. Because Spinoza is now ranked in the pantheon of "great philosophers," because he is the only person of Jewish heritage to be so ranked, and because he is clearly conversant in the Hebrew Bible, in the Hebrew language, and familiar with some great Jewish commentators such as Maimonides, it is usually taken for granted that he must somehow be "good" for Judaism, someone whom Jews should be proud of, perhaps the greatest Jewish contributor, and no doubt the most famous Jewish contributor, to the long and high dialogue that constitutes the history of philosophy. Hence that he must be respected if not revered as one of the pillars of Western spirituality as a whole. Why then did the rabbis of his own Amsterdam community, one of the most liberal Jewish communities then extant, excommunicate Spinoza in 1656 when he was only twenty-three years old? What is the famous Spinoza really saying about Judaism, and about religion more generally? Let us keep our heads clear.

In the previous chapter we have already engaged the preceding question in the course of a close examination of the *Theological-Political*

Treatise, which asked and answered another question, the question for whom is the book written? In the present chapter, guided by Levinas's reading of Spinoza, we will ask and answer a question that has previously often not been asked with sufficient seriousness and often not been answered with sufficient depth and learning. And this is why Levinas is our guide and why I am guided by him: he knows the history of Western philosophy and he is learned in Jewish tradition. There are few who are so versed. Therefore Levinas has a sufficient vantage point both as a philosopher and a Jew to raise and to answer the question of Spinoza's understanding vis-à-vis Judaism. Levinas will find that Spinoza falls short. We will try to understand why Levinas thinks this is the case, and thus the title of the present chapter: "Levinas on Spinoza's Misunderstanding of Judaism." The chapter is not a court hearing for a case of excommunication. That has been done. Rather it is a scholarly examination and results in a scholarly judgment. It is text based. Most certainly it is offered for readers to decide on its accuracy, validity, and probity.

Unlike many scholarly topics, this one is extra-sensitive. Indeed it throws us willy-nilly into a field strewn with spiritual land mines. Philosophers care about getting philosophers right. Levinas does, I do, and I expect readers to also. Jews care about Jews and Judaism, getting them right. Levinas does, I do, and again I expect readers to also, whether Jewish or not Jewish. To discuss Judaism, after all, is to discuss Christianity and Islam as well, and in some sense it is to discuss all religions, indeed to discuss everything of significance and the significance of significance. No doubt the same can be said of philosophy. And yet with the greatest good will coupled with a lifetime of study and learning, with regard to such an ancient, deep, and still-living intellectual and spiritual tradition, there is too much diversity, too great and too varied differences of opinion, including unbridgeable differences in the very manner of engagement, that no one interpretation, no one reading, can possibly capture all that can be said, leaving nothing out, slighting no point of view, stepping on no toes.

Let it be said from the start that by "Judaism" what is meant here is certainly not one among several contemporary Jewish "denominations," for example, "Reform," "Renewal," "Reconstruction," "Conservative," or "Orthodox," to name a few. Rather it refers to any form of Judaism that retains its identity in continuity with its specific tradition, including especially in the latter the cluster of writings that comprise Judaism's historically cumulative intertextual interpretive tradition.[1] From this point of view one might prefer to say that there are many "Judaisms," in the plural. I will not be using this locution, but it must be understood that under the term "Judaism," in the singular, there is enormous room for interpretative variation, though not infinite room. I think that here Wittgenstein's notion of "family resemblance" is useful, no doubt more suited to what we are referring to by "Judaism" than "definition" or "essence," but no doubt too there are ways of using the latter terms that are equally flexible and inclusive.[2] It is not a matter of words but of what they refer to, and I hope I have made my point sufficiently clear regarding the present meaning of the term "Judaism" for that.

The present chapter title, "Levinas on Spinoza's Misunderstanding of Judaism," is of course already an answer to the basic question of the present chapter, as it is also to the question of the original title that has not been used. Spinoza misunderstands Judaism. And his misunderstanding is bad for Judaism. The two are connected: he is bad for Judaism because his misunderstanding is so fundamental. It is a strong thesis, and more especially in the face of the far more popular view of Spinoza as intellectual master and authoritative spokesperson of Judaism. He was neither.

Before turning to Levinas's reasons for this thesis, which is the main task of the present chapter, I want first and briefly to review certain insights and implied criticisms of Spinoza developed by Harry

---

1. So, for instance, the Hebrew Bible is a "Jewish" text not by virtue of the text itself, the black letters on white pages, for this same text is certainly a Christian text for Christianity, a Christian text when read in the light of the New Testament and Christian theology. It becomes a Jewish text by virtue of a "Jewish" reading" of it, for example, (and this applies to all contemporary denominations of Judaism) a reading informed by the "Oral" Torah, the Midrash and Talmud and their commentaries.

2. It would be amusing if it were not too tiresome to count how often self-proclaimed "antiessentialists" with great opprobrium apply the strictest essentialist reading to whatever "essentialism" they happen to be excoriating precisely while remaining blind to the same or worse essentialism of their own outlook. So, for instance, while adhering to the usual and narrow-minded *Wissenschaft*, philological or text-critical methodology in Jewish studies, they will attack alternative phenomenological, hermeneutic, or structural approaches for what? Essentialism!

Austryn Wolfson and, though even more briefly, by Yosef Ben-Shlomo. Neither interpreter, however, despite the propriety and profundity of their Spinoza studies, goes to the heart of Levinas's criticism.[3]

Two preliminary qualifications. First, with regard to the fact that although I speak of Judaism and its wisdom, there is no way in fact to capture all of Judaism in one interpretation; this pluralism and excess is not *for Judaism* a limitation. As we shall see later, especially in the final section on exegesis, Judaism celebrates diversity of interpretation, diversity of reading, multiple paths, without however losing a complete grip of itself. In this regard even and especially Jewish "fundamentalism" is almost precisely the opposite of Christian fundamentalism insofar as the most traditional, the most so-called orthodox readers of Jewish texts are precisely those scholars who know more commentaries, more interpretations, a greater variety of readings, and not less, and certainly not one so-called "literal" reading. No form of Judaism, from the most liberal to the most conservative, tolerates such a notion of literal reading. For traditional Jews God Himself does not tolerate such a notion. The issue regarding Spinoza is whether or not he has gone too far. Is his reading so eccentric, so alienated, and alienating regarding the Jewish heritage of readings that he has left the wide precincts, the vast ocean of Judaism altogether? And if so, as the rabbis of Amsterdam obviously thought, then why? Second, it should be understood, but I will say it explicitly, that what is said positively about Judaism in the present chapter in no way implies that other religions do not also have positive beliefs and behaviors, no matter their different terminology and emphases. I am not saying all religions are the same, for this is empirically untrue. But my studies and my experience have shown me that the great religions of the world do not differ because one of them sees something, some insight, some truth, a certain revelation, that the others do not. Rather they differ because each has its own specific traditions, languages, rites, practices, and each places a different weight or emphasis on the very same dimensions that they all see and that Levinas will articulate in the name of Judaism. Salvation and redemption, in a word, are found in all religions. No doubt also

---

3. In this chapter, Levinas's criticisms of Spinoza are taken primarily but not exclusively from the three essays Levinas wrote on Spinoza: "The Spinoza Case" (published in 1956), "Have You Reread Baruch?" (published in 1966), both of which appear in DF, 106–110 and 111–118, and "Spinoza's Background," published in 1982 in BV, 168–173.

each world religion contains an exclusivist faction of the faithful who would and do vociferously deny precisely the universality that I have just asserted. But even in their denial, in the fact that every religion has just such a faction of naysayers, they but show once again how very much they are all fundamentally in sympathy.

Harry Austryn Wolfson

In the final chapter of his great two-volume work on *The Philosophy of Spinoza*, Wolfson distinguishes four "acts of daring," as he calls them, by means of which Benedict Spinoza overturns the religious medieval worldview and inaugurates the modern secular period. In each instance, two incommensurable and hierarchical realms, one divine and the other mundane, are reduced to the one realm of a uniform and homogeneous Nature. In each of these acts of daring, too, we will discover good reasons to see how Spinoza has radically misunderstood Judaism.

In his first act of daring, according to Wolfson, "by declaring that God has the attribute of extension as well as thought, Spinoza has thus removed the break in the principle of the homogeneity of nature" (333). Spinoza denies God's transcendence. No longer absolutely other, either in thought or in extension, God would no longer transcend absolutely. He would thus no longer be the God of monotheism, God considered not as creature, as in the ancient polytheisms, but as Creator, absolute mystery, invisible, beyond space and time, metaphysical, eternal.

In the second act of daring, according to Wolfson, "by denying design and purpose in God, Spinoza has thus removed the break in the principle of the uniformity of the laws of nature" (335). Wiping out three of Aristotle's four causes, efficient causality would be the only causality. The universe, the real, being, Nature, would have prior causes but no final end. Thus not only God as Creator, but God as Revelation and Providence is eliminated.

In his third act of daring, "Spinoza's insistence upon the complete inseparability of the soul from the body, has thus removed another break in the homogeneity of nature" (Wolfson, 336). The soul—or, we could say equally, the intellect or the will, since they are the same for Spinoza—would be nothing more than a parallel reflection of body.[4] In effect, then, there would only be body. Though more profoundly, the truth is the reverse: what counts as body for Spinoza is only what parallels the mind, that is, intelligibility, strict lawfulness, necessity.

From either point of view, the soul as divine spark, as "image and likeness of God," as something exceptional, special, is eliminated.

And finally, in his fourth act of daring, "Spinoza's insistence upon the elimination of freedom of the will from human actions, has thus removed another break in the uniformity of the laws of nature" (Wolfson, 339). Without free choice, the morality of obligations and duties—Jewish morality—becomes absurd. Thus Spinoza effectively eliminates morality, and hence also justice. Morality, like religion generally, would thereby be reduced to a form of ignorance that is ignorant of itself. Or, as we have just seen in the previous chapter, morality along with justice would become the prudential tool of cynical masters, with no source of and no appeal to authority beyond the sovereign state.

Such a philosophical point of view, pantheist or naturalist, it comes to the same, would certainly be bad for a Judaism that according to its strictures would no longer be able to affirm, as Spinoza no longer affirms, indeed as he absolutely denies, the transcendence of God, truth in history, the exceptional status of the human soul, and the independence and efficacy of morality and justice. It is hardly controversial to say that all conceptions of Judaism that are even minimally coherent, no matter how eccentric, consider the elimination of some or all of these elements as an attack on Judaism. Thus, on Wolfson's analytical account alone, Spinoza is bad for Judaism. Levinas, for his part, was familiar with Wolfson's analyses at least as early as 1937 and did not disagree with them.[5] Nor, I think, would Levinas disagree with the evaluation of Spinoza vis-à-vis Judaism that follows from these analyses, even though Levinas's own conception of God's transcendence, divine providence, the soul, and the efficacy of morality also differs significantly from the medieval conception of the same that Spinoza rejected. The opponent of your opponents is not necessarily your friend.

Yosef Ben-Shlomo

At the conclusion of the last of his thirteen *Lectures on the Philosophy of Spinoza*, Yosef Ben-Shlomo briefly presents five oppositional "differenc-

---

4. E, II, Prop. 7: "The order and connection of ideas is the same as the order and connection of causes" (66).

5. Levinas published a review, entitled "Spinoza, philosophe medieval," of Wolfson's *The Philosophy of Spinoza*, in the *Revue des etudes juives*.

es" between "Spinozism and . . . monotheism of the type of Judaism, Christianity or Islam."[6] In each case only one of the two alternatives can be correct. As with Wolfson's list of Spinoza's four acts of daring, if Spinoza is right then Judaism is wrong and if Judaism is right then Spinoza is wrong. In his presentation, Ben-Shlomo refrains from making overt evaluations, but it is perfectly clear all the same that adopting Spinoza's viewpoint is contrary to Judaism. The first three points of difference—that Spinoza's intelligible God is without personality, that his pantheist God is without transcendence, and that his necessary world is without freedom[7]—are close enough to Wolfson's four points

---

6. All five points are elaborated on pages 122–123, so in the following I will not document citations.

7. Ben Shlomo's first three points of difference are: First, for Judaism, based in the Bible, God is personal. "This is a God," as Ben-Shlomo puts it, "with willpower, who demands various things of man, gives him commandments, and one is able to worship and love Him in a personal way." What Spinoza presents, in contrast, "is a concept of an impersonal God," a purely rational or scientific intelligibility. God, for Spinoza, is reality and, more deeply, the truth of reality, "adequate ideas." He is nothing less than the systematic whole of true ideas. Spinoza's God, therefore, neither loves nor wills. Nor, in return, do humans serve or love Spinoza's God. Humanity's only link to the philosophical God of Spinoza is knowledge. Indeed, true knowledge is nothing other than the "mind" of God.

Second, for Judaism, God creates the world in an act of free will. The Creator God is thus separate from (though not indifferent to) the world. And the world is separate from God. Furthermore, for Judaism, the human "soul, too, is not part of God; it can only worship God, or even 'adhere' to Him." For Spinoza, in contrast, God is not apart from the world or the soul, just as they are not apart from God. This is because for Spinoza God does not freely will creation. (Let me interject here that it is rather difficult to say positively with any precision how, according to Spinoza, the finite world is related to perfect intelligibility. The two best possibilities, it seems to me, though both have their problems, are: (1) "expression" [see Deleuze], that is, that the finite is the expression of the infinite, even though such an approach would require an unacknowledged anthropocentrism both Spinoza and Deleuze prefer to vacate; and (2) "actualization" [see Hallett], that is, that the finite is the actualization of the infinite, even though making the notions of "actuality" and "potentiality" so central would reintroduce a metaphysics that Spinoza aimed precisely to leave behind. Be that as it may, there is no doubt about the correctness of the second point of difference. For Spinoza, there is no Creation in the Jewish sense).

Ben Shlomo's third difference follows from the second. Insofar as the world is created, and hence is contingent for Judaism, it is amenable to human free will. For Spinoza, in contrast, "God or Nature" (*Deus, sive Natura*) is necessary. Thus for Spinoza "there is no place for freedom in the sense of free choice between various possibilities." Because there is free will, "Judaism regards man as responsible for his deeds ethically." For Spinoza, "this idea is absurd."

that here I will concentrate on Ben-Shlomo's fourth and fifth points of difference.

The fourth has to do with ethics. Judaism conceives of ethics, he writes, in terms of "obeying God's command, as an *obligation* which is imposed" on humans. "Defiance of this obligation is regarded as non-ethical." Spinoza in contrast, who rejects both free will and ethics, obviously has "no such concept as an obligation." For Spinoza, whose philosophy is based on reality, knowing what *is*, and not on morality, achieving what *ought* to be, "there is only a striving for power, and the one who is strong is 'moral.'" In this regard, we can see that for Ben-Shlomo too Spinoza and Nietzsche are in agreement, both being "beyond good and evil."

For Ben-Shlomo the fifth point of difference, however, "is the most important in the results and conclusions which stem from Judaism and which are not included in Spinoza's philosophy." It has to do with "the importance attached in Judaism to the factor of time in general and to historical time in particular." "To Spinoza," Ben-Shlomo writes, "there is no importance to history. There is importance to the state, and that is why Spinoza has a political theory, but he has no philosophy of history." Again we saw exactly this in the previous chapter: history has no truth; power and hence "justice" are matters of state. Finding reality and truth exclusively in "adequate ideas," as he conceives them, Spinoza is interested only in the necessary, immutable, and eternal. His philosophy presents reality, as he says, *sub specie aeternitatis*. Ben-Shlomo: "Spinoza does not accept the Jewish and Christian view that man can and must change the course of history on the road to redemption, and thereby participate in God's plan. In this, Spinoza is 'Greek': the concept of redemption remains to him a concept of salvation that only applies to the individual." I would add, in support of Ben-Shlomo's comments, that we should not be misled by Spinoza's use of the term "beatitude" to characterize what he calls "intellectual love of God." For that matter, we should not be deceived with any of Spinoza's appropriations of religious terminology. In truth, both "intellectual love of God" and "beatitude," according to Spinoza's conception, mean nothing other than a vision of complete knowledge, science, or "adequate ideas" in their totality.[8]

---

8. Ben-Shlomo, for his part, prefers a *mystical* reading of Spinoza, whereby the scientific and systematic character of knowledge (the ongoing research of "knowledge of the second kind"; Kant's "understanding"), along with its ostensive (but

There is little doubt that Levinas would agree with the validity of all five of Ben-Shlomo's points of critical difference from Spinoza. He would also agree, I think, to the relative importance of the fifth difference regarding time and history. For Levinas, Judaism is deeply committed to time and history, not simply as historiography, however, but as a juncture of ethics and history that Levinas, in the name of Judaism, calls "holy history." Judaism for Levinas is precisely lived as an ethical-religious commitment not only to the salvation of individuals alone or individually, nor only to the redemption of the Jewish people, without disparaging the nobility of its election, but finally and most deeply, and based in Jewish election, the mission of Judaism is precisely its commitment to the collective redemption of all humankind. Judaism, in its every fiber, in every nuance of its every behavior and belief, in its very bones and sinews, as well as its pots and pans, is a commitment to the redemption of humanity through the concrete work of morality and justice through time and history. As such it must and can only reject Spinozism categorically.

That the wide chasm separating Spinozism from Judaism, as indicated by Wolfson and Ben-Shlomo alone, makes manifest a profound, indeed an unbridgeable, antagonism, is already evident. Such opposition to Judaism was already sufficiently evident more than three hundred years ago in Amsterdam. Nonetheless, it is important for us to recall the points of separation in their specificity, as per the aforementioned, since they remain, despite the dangers they pose for Judaism, intellectual temptations to this day. Naturalism, pantheism, scientism, positivism, and thus Spinozism remain great temptations. There is much in their favor, even if ultimately Spinozism fails as a philosophy as it fails in its representation of Judaism. We must therefore remain mindful of the differences just elaborated, which are of themselves important, but also because taking the positions he takes in their regard provides the philosophical background to the additional points

---

pre-Kantian) vision of the whole ("knowledge of the third kind"; Kant's "reason") is interpreted as mystical union with God. While I can see why one might be tempted by such a reading, that is, because it makes what sense it can of a philosophy that at bottom is incoherent, nevertheless I entirely reject it, because Spinoza, as is clear from all his writings, wants only to be a philosopher of science, an advocate of science and science alone, science as comprehensive totality—such for Spinoza is the ultimate intelligibility, such is the "divine" mind, even if critical readers of Spinoza can see that he was unsuccessful and unable to justify such a scientific program.

of difference to which we now turn, points of no lesser antagonism, though perhaps of even greater relevance and urgency with regard to our question about Spinoza's understanding of Judaism.

Levinas

Going further than the previous presentations of "acts of daring" and "differences," Levinas also opposes Spinoza both as a philosopher and in the name of a recognizable Judaism.[9] Levinas neither divorces philosophy and religion nor sets them in opposition, as does Spinoza, though of course they are different. Levinas's criticisms are launched from three angles. The first has to do with Spinoza's conception of Judaism in relation to Christianity. The second has to do with Spinoza's conception of Judaism in relation to the state. The third and most important, upon which the first two criticisms are ultimately based, places Spinoza's presentation of Judaism, as found primarily in the *Theological-Political Treatise*, in relation to the Jewish or Talmudic idea of Jewish wisdom that Spinoza believes he is criticizing, and Levinas

---

9. The first two of the following criticisms of Spinoza recall the similar and forceful criticisms of Spinoza made by Hermann Cohen in "Spinoza uber Staat und Religion, Judentum und Christentum." The all-important criticism of Spinoza, however, the one upon which the first two are based, is Levinas's third criticism, and it is here that Levinas parts company with Cohen. In a nutshell, the difference is that whether he wills it or not, Cohen (like Kant before him, and Cassirer and Strauss after him) remains wedded to an epistemological framework, while Levinas's thought is based quite otherwise in an ethical metaphysics. In addition, Levinas's philosophical launching point to ethical metaphysics is not Kantian philosophy but phenomenology. This, too, is an important difference separating Levinas from Cohen. "Contrary to the neo-Kantian method," Levinas writes, "which reconstitutes the transcendental from the logical and the scientific, and through this very process forgets the horizons which are lost precisely because scientific results can only be purchased at the price of the forgetting of these infinite horizons—phenomenology, which does turn toward them, makes possible the expression and the perfecting of the logical itself" (DEH, 137–138). It is important to remember, also, that at Davos in 1929 Levinas supported Heidegger's revitalization of the imagination and not Cassirer's more careful Kant scholarship. Of course Cassirer was the better Kant scholar, more faithful to Kant. The issue, however, despite Cassirer's commendable intent and approach, was not limited to Kant scholarship alone but also touched on the larger question of the nature of philosophy, that is to say, the impact of phenomenology on scientific philosophy.

contends he has misunderstood. This last criticism, then, is a very serious charge against Spinoza, even if rarely mounted in the secondary literature, because it challenges Spinoza's very competence—about which he is so regularly praised—and hence his authority, his legitimacy as a faithful interpreter of the Judaism he would criticize. Indeed, all three criticisms challenge Spinoza's competence as an accurate interpreter of the Judaism he would criticize.

A Christianized Judaism

Levinas criticizes the attacks on Jews and Judaism found in Spinoza's *Theological-Political Treatise* for the partisan bias, the parochial Christian interpretation of Jews and Judaism that they reproduce but never admit. The Judaism Spinoza attacks, in other words, is the Judaism that Christian theology has fabricated for its own purposes, which certainly from the start of Christianity have always included a certain degree of anti-Jewish polemic. Christianity was born from the womb of Judaism. All its key early figures are themselves Jews, including Jesus himself and his mother Mary, but also Joseph, Peter, James, Matthew, Mark, the High Priest, all the disciples, Paul, and so on. Little wonder, then, that in forging its own distinct identity Christianity envisioned an inadequate Judaism, one that Christianity brought to fulfillment, the "New Israel," in a consummation that the old Judaism malignantly rejected. As scholars, however, we must not confuse Christianity's Judaism or Islam's Judaism or Mormons' Judaism, regardless of the role these constructions play within each of these religions, with Judaism's Judaism. But this, according to Levinas, is precisely what Spinoza has done. His "Judaism," the Judaism he attacks so viciously, is Christianity's "Judaism."

That Spinoza does engage in a vicious ideological assault against the Jewish people, their sages, and Judaism in the *Theological-Political Treatise* is obvious enough to the unbiased observer. Or perhaps it is only obvious to persons knowledgeable about Judaism, or at least to persons who do not share Spinoza's prejudices. For these reasons, and because Spinoza is so often depicted in the saintly image of a dispassionate scholar and certainly as an expert witness for and against Judaism, I will offer some examples to jog readers' memories. Spinoza hardly misses an opportunity to demean and berate the ancient Israelites. He calls them "ignorant" too many times for citation. Spinoza wants to hurt closer to home. Far from being the people of God they think themselves, or that others mistakenly take them for: "The Israelites knew scarcely anything of God, although he was revealed to them" (TPT, 31). In chapter 3, Spinoza enlightens us that when Moses addressed such people, he had to condescend "to the immaturity of their understanding" (36). In chapters 5 and 13, Spinoza speaks of their "limited intelligence" (68, 157), so dim that only the most simpleminded pedagogy can penetrate it. Again, everywhere and always Spinoza characterizes the ancient Israelites as an unruly horde of ignoramuses, simpleminded, childlike, slavish, and otherwise too obtuse and primitive for truth or reason.

Nor should it come as a surprise that Spinoza's animus toward the rabbis—the rabbis of the Talmud, the biblical and the Talmudic commentators, who in fact created and shaped all post-biblical Judaism, hence the Judaism of the Jews today and in Spinoza's day—is greater than his disdain for the Israelite masses. Their Scriptural commentaries, for example, so Spinoza informs us in chapter 7, are driven not by the search for truth or even for God's will but by "ambition and iniquity" (86). Of the rabbinical commentators who seek to reconcile narrative discrepancies in the Bible, in chapter 9 Spinoza unmasks what he sees at work: "The Rabbis run quite wild, and such commentators as I have read indulge in dreams, fantasies, and in the end corrupt the language altogether. . . . I do not know whether these views proceed from folly and a feeble-minded devoutness or from arrogance and malice" (121–122). In chapter 10, Spinoza denounces "the audacity of the Rabbis" (129) who, in this case, debated whether to exclude Proverbs and Ecclesiastes from the biblical canon. The rabbis cannot get it right, whether they claim to respect reason or to reject it is all the same for Spinoza, as we see in chapter 15: "Thus they will both go wildly astray, the one spurning reason, the other siding with reason" (165). "Who but a desperate madman would be so rash as to turn his back on reason?" (171). In the same chapter, Maimonides, as a rabbi who respects reason, is singled out for special abuse. Earlier in chapter 7 Spinoza had already caustically dismissed Maimonides's interpretive efforts as "license . . . as excessive and rash" and concluded there that "this method of Maimonides is plainly of no value" and "we can dismiss Maimonides's view as harmful, unprofitable and absurd" (102). No less harsh and dismissive remarks appear in chapter 1, where Spinoza attacks Maimonides's work as "mere rubbish" and calls his approach "the height of absurdity" (13). Do please keep in mind that this same

Maimonides is considered within Judaism—then and now—to be in the highest rank of all its scholar sages, comparable, say, to the stature of Thomas Aquinas within Roman Catholicism. To be sure, Spinoza is not singling out Maimonides alone, nor is his venom reserved for the rabbis alone, although they do take the brunt of it. In the preface of the *Theological-Political Treatise*, Spinoza first warned his prospective readers against the words of all clergy, which he there characterized as self-serving and "arrogant ravings" (4). As for the religion of the people, their "prayers and womanish tears, . . . delusions of the imagination, dreams and other childish absurdities are taken to be the oracles of God" (1). What to conclude from all this? It is clear, for one, that we do not need a particularly high-strung or Straussian sensibility to detect Spinoza's quite obvious derision and scorn toward religious believers, toward clergy, and even more particularly toward the ancient Israelites and the Talmudic rabbis ("Pharisees") and commentators.[10]

Contrary to the stated method of the *Theological-Political Treatise*, that is, to examine Scripture only in the light of Scripture,[11] it is clear, as we have shown in the previous chapter of the present volume, that the *Theological-Political Treatise* is actually based, for its argumentation

---

10. That the major figures of early Christianity were for the most part Jews no longer surprises us and perhaps is taken for granted. But for centuries such was not the case. Kant, too, as he explicitly writes in *Religion within the Bounds of Reason Alone*, thinks of Christianity not so much as arising out of Judaism but as arising in a complete leap away from Judaism, as an entirely new and completely different religion. In Nazi Germany the majority of Christians convinced themselves that Jesus was an Aryan. See Susannah Heschel's excellent book on the latter topic, *The Aryan Jesus: Christian Theologians and the Bible in Nazi Germany*.

11. TPT, 5–6: "I deliberately resolved to examine Scripture afresh, conscientiously and freely, and to admit nothing as its teaching which I did not most clearly derive from it. . . . I show in what way Scripture must be interpreted, and how all our understanding of Scripture and of matters spiritual must be sought from Scripture alone, and not from the sort of knowledge that derives from the natural light of reason." Also, in chapter 7, TPT, 87: "In this way—that is, by allowing no other principles or data for the interpretation of Scripture and study of its contents except those that can be gathered only from Scripture itself and from a historical study of Scripture." We have shown in the previous chapter of the present volume that in fact, and quite contrary to the previous declarations, Spinoza interprets Scripture in the light of his own rationalist philosophy. And why should Spinoza not proceed on the basis of reason, "reason, the greatest of all gifts and a light divine" (TPT, 167)?

if not in some measure for its venom as well, on Spinoza's rationalist philosophy, whose fully developed form appears in the *Ethics*. Spinoza is basically attacking the rabbis and the ancient Israelites for not adhering to modern science. Yet there is another exterior factor that perhaps better accounts for Spinoza's particular venom than this explanation. Levinas's claim, his criticism, is that Spinoza has not only imported his scientific philosophy—but speaking more specifically to the actual biases and denunciations unleashed in the *Theological-Political Treatise* against the Jews and Judaism—he has also imported a triumphalist and supersessionist Christian theology.

Let us not fall into a simplistic view of Levinas's criticism. Spinoza defends Christianity and attacks Judaism, true, but his defenses of Christianity often appear *pro forma*, and in any event—as he is surely aware—his attacks on Judaism cannot ultimately be deflected from Christianity. In other words, for Spinoza the rationalist or naturalist pantheism of the *Ethics* works as much against Christianity and the New Testament as it does against Judaism, the Hebrew Bible, and the rabbinical commentaries. Nevertheless, of course, Spinoza clearly spends the preponderance of his critical efforts against the latter and tries as much as is reasonably credible to exempt Christianity, usually with a supersessionist interpretation by which an alleged Christian science is contrasted to Israelite ignorance, and sometimes with an excuse as weak as simply claiming ignorance.

Still, there are attacks that pertain only and particularly to Judaism. And it is exactly here that the rub occurs. These attacks by Spinoza are launched not against the Judaism Jews had lived and known for centuries, even under Christian oppression, but against a version of "Judaism" constructed internally and theologically by a polemical Christianity. It is a version of "Judaism" Spinoza might have inherited from his own family's converso experience in Portugal, one he would have heard firsthand after his excommunication, especially given his close associations with Christian theologians, but one too that any Jewish member of a Jewry sojourning within Christendom, a Spinoza in Holland, say, would certainly also be familiar with as well. So either Spinoza knew Judaism truly but deliberately and meanly glossed it through a Christian lens to better attack it, or, as we shall see is indeed the case, he misunderstood Judaism and mistook the Christian polemical construction for the thing itself. What one cannot doubt is that in the *Theological-*

Political Treatise Spinoza attacks Judaism with the very same polemics with which Christianity had been attacking its construction of "Judaism" for more than a millennium. Thus in the *Theological-Political Treatise* for Spinoza Christ is infinitely superior to Moses, the Apostles are qualitatively superior to the Prophets and Pharisees, and Christian universalism and spiritualism are an unprecedented advance over Jewish tribalism and carnality, among others, all the usual canards. But now from the mouth of a Jew! But what sort of Jew?

No doubt this was especially disturbing to Levinas, as a philosopher and as a Jew, the perverse spectacle of another philosopher and Jew, Spinoza, reiterating and endorsing the time-worn Christian polemics against Judaism. No doubt for this reason Levinas calls Spinoza's position a "betrayal." Let us flesh out the examples. Spinoza: "Christ was sent to teach not only the Jews but the entire human race" (TPT, 54). The teachings of Christ's Apostles, so we are told in chapter 11 of the *Theological-Political Treatise*, are universal and akin to natural knowledge; the Prophets, as well as the Law of Moses, in contrast, are merely tribal, products of the imagination, of merely human origin. So, too, the wisdom of Christ—and notice, though it may seem a small point, that Spinoza insists on calling the Christian Savior "Christ" and not "Jesus," just as he constantly calls the Jewish sages "Pharisees" and not "rabbis" or "sages"—the wisdom of Christ is purely intellectual, while Moses' remains bound to the flesh. And the Jewish God is not only corporeal but merely a local and tribal deity. "And surely this fact," so Spinoza declares in chapter 4 of the *Theological-Political Treatise*, "that God revealed himself to Christ, or to Christ's mind, directly, and not through words and images as in the case of the prophets, can have only this meaning, that Christ perceived truly, or understood, what was revealed. For it is when a thing is perceived by pure thought, without words and images, that it is understood."[12] No doubt such a claim, that

---

12. TPT, 54. Compare this to E, II, Scholium 2: Christ seems to have "knowledge of the third kind." Its source lies in the *Ethics*; see E, II, Scholium, 97: "I urge my readers to make a careful distinction between an idea—i.e., a conception of the mind—and the images of things that we imagine. Again, it is essential to distinguish between ideas and the words we use to signify things. . . . Then one will clearly understand that an idea, being a mode of thinking, consists neither in the image of a thing nor in words. For the essence of words and images is constituted solely by corporeal motions, far removed from the concept of thought."

pure thought is without words and images, reflects Spinoza's rationalist philosophy found in the *Ethics*. But that the *Theological-Political Treatise* attributes pure thought to Christ and impure thought to Moses, or that the latter propagates merely tribal and carnal teachings, these and most of Spinoza's polemics against Judaism and Jews merely replicate theological prejudices, biases, hatreds, misrepresentation on the dark side of Christian apologia—no matter how often repeated or commonplace such biases may have become in Christendom. Did Spinoza forget Jeremiah 22:3? "This is what the Lord says: Do what is just and right. Rescue from the hand of the oppressor the one who has been robbed. Do no wrong or violence to the foreigner, the fatherless or the widow, and do not shed innocent blood in this place." Did he forget Micah 6:8? "He has showed you, O man, what is good and what the Lord requires of you; to act justly and to love mercy and to walk humbly with your God." Can we really take Spinoza as a scholarly, objective interpreter of the Hebrew Bible? Do not the Hebrew prophets teach and do not the rabbinical commentators read them to teach a universal ethics? *Credibilis non est.*

Of Spinoza's attacks against Judaism, we are certainly cognizant of the historical fact that in seventeenth-century Europe it was far safer, far more prudent, to attack religion by attacking Judaism than by attacking Christianity. Certainly also more dangerous for a Jew to attack Christianity. But we are no less cognizant of the historical fact that prior to Spinoza, no Jew—short of conversion to Christianity, which so many Spanish Jews did under pressure in 1492—was ever quite so willing to travel so far down such a route, a route of distortion, misrepresentation, and endangerment for Jews, than Spinoza. Can we say for certain that it is not anti-Semitism, despite its intellectualist veneer?

It is not surprising, then, that Levinas is appalled both by the rhetoric and the substance of Spinoza's Christian distortion and denigration of Judaism. Levinas distinguishes two problems. First, to be sure, Spinoza's attack is false. It targets not the Judaism of the Jews but what is in fact merely a biased, indeed a Christian, theological misrepresentation of Judaism. But second, Spinoza's attack poses a special danger for modern Jews. Given their long experience living within Christendom, Jews had been long familiar with these very distortions and their missionary subtext and were thus for the most part inured against them. Yet in Spinoza's attacks, Levinas discerns two new dangers to Jews, to contemporary Jews. First, as we have pointed out, insofar as Spinoza was born Jewish and despite his excommunication never converted to Christianity, there is something like a Jewish imprimatur to the Christian distortions he expounds. While for reasons just given Jews are not easily fooled, in Spinoza's case the Christian theological distorted picture of Judaism now seems to have the endorsement of someone who is a truly learned Jewish scholar, independent of whatever the excommunication might signify. Whether some or many Jews were taken in is hard to measure, but Spinoza's picture of Judaism certainly had real repercussions in the thought of influential Christian philosophers such as Hegel and Kant. Hegel, as we see from the epigraph at the beginning of the present book, was well aware of the limitations of Spinoza's philosophy, but this does not at all mean that he was equally aware of the distortions—which after all fit the image of Judaism Hegel learned as a child and which in any event are replicated in his lectures on religion—that he could hardly know plague Spinoza's representation of Judaism. Kant's basic and for the most part negative picture of Judaism, for instance, especially in its relation to Christianity, as found in the fourth book of his *Religion within the Limits of Reason Alone* (1793), is certainly at least as much influenced by Spinoza, who clearly despised Judaism, as it is by Mendelssohn, who was a great advocate of Judaism.[13] So the first warning Levinas raises is that Spinoza is a danger because he appears to provide a Jewish imprimatur, a Jewish testimonial, for what would otherwise be yet another and usual—and ineffectual—Christian attack on Judaism. Thus Spinoza provides support to contemporary secular-minded Jewish thinkers and activists who, for a variety of reasons, still look for a Jewish stamp of approval in their denunciations of religion in general and Judaism in particular.

---

13. And this is not even to raise the question of to what extent Mendelssohn's picture of an enlightened Judaism was itself influenced by Spinoza. There is much literature on this subject. See, for instance, Julius Guttmann, "Mendelssohn's *Jerusalem* and Spinoza's *Theologico-Political Treatise*." One cannot doubt, however, that Mendelssohn was an advocate of Judaism, while Spinoza, such is the thesis of the present chapter and such is Levinas's thesis, was quite the reverse.

Second and related, but cutting more deeply, because Spinoza's real argument with Judaism is an argument against religion per se, and thus an argument against both Judaism and Christianity (and all other religions as well), and is an argument that derives from the pure scientistic rationalism of his *Ethics*, his attack on Judaism in the *Theological-Political Treatise* is dangerous because it gives a *secular rationalist and scientific* certification to what are really *Christian* distortions of Judaism. Such distortions that were spiritually deflected by Judaism for centuries, are now reborn, as it were, and reanimated in our day, such is Levinas's view, in the name of a secular and scientific rationalism that many modern Jews find attractive and that in many ways—and most certainly without Spinoza's metaphysics and his anti-Jewish venom—*is legitimately attractive*.

Thus the danger, so Levinas warns, that modern Jews, inspired by and for the sake of the great and noble themes of an enlightened humanism, feel they can and indeed must attack as "primitive," "regressive," or "reactionary" the Judaism that in fact they have misunderstood via Spinoza's representation of it. Certainly Levinas supports no primitivism in Judaism or in any religion—quite the reverse. But under Spinoza's spell he is fearful that modern Jews will be seduced into believing that Judaism is nothing more than an embarrassing relic, not only obsolete but stupid and primitive. The great danger of Spinoza, then, is that he functions as a Christian Trojan Horse, as it were, in the Temple of Judaism, offering the "gift" of a theologically distorted image of Judaism in place of the genuine article. The danger is that, like Spinoza himself, certain liberal or modern Jews—Jews assimilated to secular rationalism and ignorant of the wider resources of traditional Judaism—attack "Judaism" as if it were in fact the image that Christianity created of it and attacked in the first place.[14]

Such Jews—and non-Jews as well—in unwittingly affirming the specifically internal Christian distortion of Judaism, also as a key part of that same distortion, affirm the theological dogma of Christian super-

---

14. One finds this double distortion—attacking a Christian picture of Judaism as if one were attacking Judaism itself—in liberal opinion and in the popular press, to be sure, but one also finds it in the scholarly works of such avowed Spinozists as Yirmiyahu Yovel and Ze'ev Levy.

session of Judaism. "It was by prefiguring Jesus with Judaism," Levinas writes in "The Spinoza Case," "that Spinozism managed to introduce a movement into irreligious Judaism which, when it was religious, it opposed for seventeen centuries. . . . Thanks to the rationalism patronized by Spinoza, Christianity is surreptitiously triumphing, bringing conversion without the scandal of apostasy" (DF, 108–109). Spinoza's distorted and degraded depiction of Judaism in the *Theological-Political Treatise* would be responsible (of course only in part) for the sorry result that "[t]he inner thought of Western Jewish intellectuals bathes in a Christian atmosphere" (DF, 109). To make good on his criticism Levinas of course must show how and to what extent Spinoza misrepresents Judaism. But here is already an instance: Spinoza's supersessionist Christian polemic against Judaism, wherein Judaism is represented as merely tribal, carnal, and spiritually blind to universalism, to humanity as brotherhood, Jews filled with hatred of others rather than love, and so forth, that is to say, the usual Christian theological polemic. But Christianity's "Judaism" is not Judaism. Spinoza has sorely misunderstood and sorely misrepresented Judaism.

Levinas's first criticism of Spinoza—that his vision of Judaism is false and distorted, indeed a Christian polemic in the mouth of a Jew—has a further refinement. Spinoza's betrayal comes not only because he attacks Judaism from a Christian perspective, a Christian theologically constructed "Judaism," but as well because such a distortion is based not in a historically accurate account of *Christianity* but rather from a thoroughly idealized one. Very simply, Spinoza presents Judaism in the worst possible light and Christianity in the best. Such is a danger and temptation that ideally the academic study of religion is meant to overcome. It is certainly a greater danger for religious partisans: not to judge another's religion exclusively by its historical reality, especially its failures and shortcomings, while comparing and judging one's own religion exclusively by its ideal image and historical successes. For Levinas Spinoza's betrayal of Judaism is compounded by such a bad faith, by precisely this sort of partisan duplicity. The *Theological-Political Treatise*, in short, contrary to its self-proclaimed objectivity and independence from external theory and theology, must be recognized for what it actually is: an *apologia*. It is thus a theological *and* a political work in the worst possible sense: at once biased and self-serving and doubly distorted to boot. It presents a falsified Judaism, one seen through the doctrinal and denigrating filter of a triumphal Christian supersessionism (reinforcing Marcionist tendencies in Christianity[15]). *And* it presents a falsified Christianity, one seen through the rose-colored lens of Christian apologetics. On behalf of Christianity, let me suggest that it can surely muster a higher, more accurate, and respectful posture, first because Christianity is in large measure a continuation of Judaism, comprised mostly of Jewish elements, and second, because Christianity is itself not a monolith or wedded to such negativity because like all world religions it has the broad spiritual and intellectual resources for a more accurate and self-affirming grasp of its relation to Judaism as well as to other religions (as witness, e.g., Vatican II and *Nostra aetate* of the Roman Catholic Church).[16]

---

15. Professor Levy, in *Baruch or Benedict: On Some Jewish Aspects of Spinoza's Philosophy*, on page 82, considers Levinas's charge of Spinoza's supersessionism in "The Spinoza Case" and boldly asserts that it is "unwarranted" and hence "simply not true." Levy writes: "Spinoza's sympathy toward Jesus' moral teachings nowhere implicated a belief in the revelatory nature of the Gospels. He did not endorse the Christian view that Judaism (the Bible) prefigured Jesus, nor the outlook, propounded later, among others, by Lessing, that Christianity represents the penultimate stage before philosophical truth or philosophical reason." As much as I respect Professor Levy and have gained from his book *Baruch or Benedict*, I do not see how he can justify his opposition to Levinas and his defense of Spinoza on these points, that is, the absolute superiority of philosophical truth to Christianity (and Judaism) and supersessionist superiority and the revelatory import of Jesus and the Gospels in relation to Judaism and the Bible. Regarding the latter point alone, in chapter 1 of the *Theological-Political Treatise*, Spinoza writes: "I do not believe that anyone has attained such a degree of perfection surpassing all others, except Christ. To him God's ordinances leading men to salvation were revealed not by words or by vision, but directly, so that God manifested himself to the Apostles through the mind of Christ as he once did to Moses through an audible voice. . . . In that sense it can also be said that the Wisdom of God—that is, wisdom that is more than human—took on human nature in Christ, and that Christ was the way of salvation" (64). Again, in chapter 4: "Now what I have said applies only to the prophets who laid down laws in God's name, but not to Christ. With regard to Christ, although he also appears to have laid down laws in God's name, we must maintain that he perceived things truly and adequately; for Christ was not so much the prophet as the mouthpiece of God. . . . Christ was sent to teach not only the Jews but the entire human race. Thus it was not enough for him to have a mind adapted to the beliefs of the Jews alone [as were the minds of Moses and the Hebrew prophets]; his mind had to be adapted to the beliefs and doctrines held in common by all mankind, that is, to those axioms that are universally true" (108).

16. Kant in *Religion within the Bounds of Reason Alone*, notes that religions with sacred texts, or let us add, texts treated with utmost reverence—such as Judaism,

Statism

With the notion of bad faith we arrive at Levinas's second basic criticism. Because of his narrow and absolute adherence to modern scientific rationality, as found in the *Ethics*, Spinoza not only distorts and hence misunderstands Judaism in the name of a distorted and hence misunderstood Christianity, but he distorts and hence misunderstands Judaism in the name of a distorted and hence misunderstood account of the state and its proper role and authority. We have examined much of Spinoza's political philosophy in the previous chapter in the course of discovering for whom he wrote the *Theological-Political Treatise*. Here we want to follow Levinas's critique of Spinoza's account of the state inasmuch as it represents a radical misunderstanding of Judaism.

For Spinoza, as we have seen, a person's highest loyalty—quite otherwise than the intellectual "freedom" of the few—must be directed neither to God nor religion, nor to family, friends, or community, but rather to the state. And for that matter, when the issue is loyalty, which is to say obedience, the few also must be obedient to the state (though they know the true reasons while the multitudes are deceived). Spinoza's discussion of politics in the concluding five chapters of the *Theological-Political Treatise* has divided commentators into two opposed camps. One reading has Spinoza genuinely defending a liberal state, hence defending the individual's political freedoms.[17] The other reading (which is also my own), in contrast, sees him only apparently defending a liberal state, as a diverting rhetorical flourish, but in realty justifying the absolute and therefore totalitarian authority of the state, regardless of its particular form of government (monarchic, aristocratic, democratic) as the best way to secure not political freedom but the peace and stability, the "security," as Spinoza so often says, that enables the few to enjoy philosophical freedom, that is, to do science and philosophy.[18] Proponents of each of these opposed readings

---

Christianity, Islam, Buddhism, Hinduism, Confucianism, Taoism, among others— are especially enabled, through hermeneutic ingenuity, to continually revisit, revise, and develop their spiritual outlook as they progress toward more enlightened, that is to say, toward more moral and just worldviews.

17. Three examples of the "liberal" reading of Spinoza: Feuer, see especially "The Impasse of Authoritarian Liberalism," 175–179; Dunner; and Karshap.

18. Sir Karl Popper has made a strong case for the "totalitarian" reading of Spinoza; but also see Curley.

cite relevant passages from the *Theological-Political Treatise*, often taken from the same paragraph. So, for instance, in the fifth paragraph of chapter 20, to support the liberal view, we hear Spinoza saying: "Thus, the purpose of the state is, in reality, freedom." But in the very same paragraph, to support the totalitarian view, we hear Spinoza saying: "Its [the state's] ultimate purpose is . . . to free every man from fear so that he may live in security as far as is possible."[19]

I am calling attention to this interpretive divide, which we already discussed in the previous chapter, not to once again explain the semantic and rhetorical ambiguities that Spinoza utilizes to keep it alive, or to explain the deeper conceptual reasons for its appearance, nor also to show once again that the totalitarian reading is clearly the one that captures Spinoza's true position, but in the present context in order to note that Levinas's political criticism of Spinoza, while not unaware of these considerations, nevertheless cuts deeper and at a different angle. What disturbs Levinas is Spinoza's "statism," the idea that human allegiance should be given to the state *above all* and thus, in particular, to the state above religion. To be sure, we have also already examined this matter in chapter 4 of the present volume, on justice and the state. But here, again, we shall pursue it in relation to Judaism. One citation from chapter 19 of the *Theological-Political Treatise* should suffice to remind us of what it is that disturbs Levinas: "There can be no doubt," Spinoza writes, "that devotion to one's country is the highest form of devotion that can be shown; for if the state is destroyed nothing good can survive, everything is endangered, and anger and wickedness reign supreme amidst universal fear" (283). By elevating state authority above religion Spinoza not only dismisses civil society, he also dismisses the political experience and long and thoughtful political perspective of Judaism. To be sure, the Jews in Europe in Spinoza's day and for more than a millennium beforehand had no state of their own, and it was not until 1948 that they regained political sovereignty in the land of their ancient Palestinian commonwealth. Nevertheless, despite its absence or misrepresentation in Spinoza's writings, Judaism has had much to

---

19. TPT, 292–293. A better citation to support the totalitarian reading, but taken from chapter 18, would be, 279: "Every state [including the tyrannical state] must necessarily preserve its own form, and cannot be changed without incurring the danger of utter ruin."

say in political philosophy, across many texts and a long experience, not least of all because its political worldview was formed over the course of nearly a thousand years of its experience of sovereignty in its ancient Israelite commonwealths. And that worldview, in contrast to Spinoza's demand for the public expulsion of religion and its privatization to the individual conscience, expects rather in both the public and private spheres an integral unity of the political and the religious, never severing one from the other. This is because for Judaism, as for Levinas, religion is always a social phenomenon, a community bond, and—beginning no later than the biblical prophets and certainly then for the rabbis of the Talmud and its commentaries—never detachable from morality and justice. As such the political finds its justification in the ethical-religious and becomes tyrannical without it.

Given the unfortunate but historically real and terrible excesses committed by European states in the name of Christianity or as officially established Christian states, up to and including Spinoza's time, it should not altogether surprise anyone, however, that he would propose suppressing religion altogether in wanting to establish public peace, and therefore that he would, following Hobbes, elevate state sovereignty to an absolute to do so. Undivided loyalty must be given to the state and the state alone.

Spinoza's solution to the problem of divided loyalties between religion and state is threefold. First, he requires their separation (disestablishment of religion); second, the state rules supreme and without any alternative source of authority in all matters of public life, including matters of religion; and third, to facilitate these requirements, religion is confined to individual private conscience. The *problem*, then, to which Levinas points, is that Spinoza's "solution" loses sight of the proper role of religion and certainly of the role of religion as Judaism conceives it, namely, as the prod to a redemptive politics, a politics whose meaning derives not from power alone, which is mere tyranny and war, but from the great unmet project of creating a just society for all. Such a perspective of course views Judaism in an altogether different way than any perspective that separates "religion" and "nonreligion," or "things of the spirit" from "things of Caesar," as has often been the case for Christian self-interpretation. Judaism would not be a separable dimension of life, for instance the "spiritual" versus the "carnal," but rather an integral aspect, an inextricable significance permeating all dimensions of life, private and public, personal and social, in a word, a "way of life."[20] Spinoza, in contrast, holds a theological rather than an existential vision of religion. The result is that he excludes redemption from politics and politics from redemption, ending up—or perhaps having begun—with a Machiavellian power politics, on the one side, and an eviscerated ethereal religion, on the other.

Spinoza's doubly distorted attack on Judaism in part 2, the theological part of the *Theological-Political Treatise*, and his marginalization of religion in part 3, the political part, must also be understood in relation to the secular and scientific rationalism of part 1, which is to say, in truth, in relation to the *Ethics*. From such a perspective religion must be suppressed and marginalized by the state for two reasons. First, religion is basically constituted not by reason but by the imagination and is therefore the domain of falsehood and illusion. For Spinoza, truth is found exclusively in science, not even in "words and images" but in pure ideas, pure intellection, and it is reserved for the few. Politics, for its part, having to do with the distribution of power and the organization and regulation of the many, is also outside of the realm of truth. But politics, unlike religion, does not claim to be true. Its realm is obedience not knowledge. But that, for Spinoza, is also the domain of religion, regardless of its false self-interpretations. Because the state cannot brook competition in obedience, it must suppress religion.

There lies the second reason religion must be marginalized by the state. Religion claims truth for itself. Spinoza criticizes religion not only for its ignorance and factual errors but also for its claim to any provenance let alone priority over truth. For Spinoza, any such claim *over* science is really "political," a power play, a matter of control and not intellection. Religion is one type of politics, politics in the name of God. Spinoza would banish it. In contrast to Spinoza and much of Christian medieval thought, however, Levinas does not conceive of religion, and certainly not of Judaism in an exclusively theological manner, that is, as a logic of being, or a logic of highest being, or even as a logic of faith. For Levinas, as we have seen in earlier chapters, religion and Judaism are at bottom constituted ethically. Contra Spinoza, their claim is ultimately neither one of truth nor one of power but a moral claim, a call to moral responsibility, and building upon such responsibility, they proclaim the

---

20. A point about Judaism stressed in the nineteenth century by Rabbi Samson Raphael Hirsch, who rejected what he saw to be the Reform effort to strip Judaism of its full integrity by defining it as a particular compartment of life, the religious.

great tasks of justice, social justice, that is, redemption. "Justice," Levinas writes in "Messianic Texts," "precedes and conditions visible splendors" (DF, 86). Precisely such religion, precisely its ethical authority, is pilloried throughout the *Theological-Political Treatise*. For Levinas, however, seeing religion as the bulwark of a morality and justice above and tempering power, Spinoza's entire project is anathema: "separating the reign of God from the reign of Caesar. This reassures Caesar" (DF, "Place and Utopia," 101). To be sure, Spinoza very well wants to reassure Caesar!

Just as in the previous chapter we found two meanings each to the terms "democracy," "freedom," and "law, based ultimately in Spinoza's philosophical differentiation between science and non-science, one can distinguish in the *Theological-Political Treatise* two forms of "religion," one of which itself has two forms. So on the side of non-science and obedience there is the *popular superstitious religion* Spinoza opposes and the *controlled internalized religion* he would institute; and on the side of adequate ideas and science, there is what we might call *scientific "religion,"* which doublespeak he invents, science glossed with the vocabulary of religion ("God or Nature," "beatitude," "mind of God," etc.), and the *popular superstitious* mystification he opposes. Part 1 of the *Theological-Political Treatise* elaborates scientific "religion," part 2 deconstructs popular religion, and part 3 advocates controlled religion.

The worst form of religion is the popular form, which for Spinoza is comprised of fears and superstitions, ambitions and trickery, where illusion and fantasy masquerade as truth. It is made up of "the delusions of the imagination, dreams and other childish absurdities" (TPT, 50). It is the object of Spinoza's constant scorn and invective. Levinas also rejects such religion. Indeed, going further and in radical opposition to Spinoza, he sees *Judaism* as opposing such religion precisely in its opposition to mythological consciousness. Thus for Levinas the proper opposition to popular or superstitious religion, which both Spinoza and Levinas reject, is not a resort to state power, as Spinoza would have it, not its confinement to private conscience, but its replacement by "adult" or nonmythological religion—for instance, Judaism.

What is the basic nature of the religion that Spinoza can accept in its severely confined form? We have called it *controlled internalized religion*. In the *Theological-Political Treatise* Spinoza will call its legitimate claims—legitimate in the realm of obedience—the "Word of God"[21] in

---

21. See, especially, TPT, chapter 12.

contrast to the lessons taught in biblical narratives and the imperatives of the Mosaic codes. It is religion made up of a handful of simple, basic, and self-evident moral precepts, a religion easily grasped by individual conscience, but a religion fully subservient in its public manifestation to the authority of the state. With barely hidden relish Spinoza parades its simplicity, its nonintellectual character, for example, in the title of chapter 13, which begins "*It is shown that Scripture teaches only very simple doctrines and inculcates nothing but obedience* . . ." Or even more pointedly, in the last sentence of the first paragraph of the same chapter: "Scriptural doctrine contains not abstruse speculation or philosophical reasoning, but very simple matters able to be understood by the most sluggish mind" (TPT. 153). No doubt Levinas would agree that the simplest persons are quite able to be moral, to love their neighbors, to share scarce bread, to put others before themselves, and the like. Because they show and glorify graphic instances, albeit literary, of such acts of kindness, Levinas often refers to the writings of Dostoyevsky or to Vasily Grossman's *Life and Fate*. But it is clear that the valence, the orientation, the position of such morality in the overall scheme of life and reality is radically different in Levinas than in Spinoza. Levinas certainly does not confine religious morality to individual conscience marginalized from public life. Nor, for that matter, does he think the religious task of establishing a just world easy or superseded by state security. Nor, as we have seen, does he think morality mere foolishness.

Finally there is Spinoza's notion of *scientific* religion, as it were, the rationalist science of eternal, immutable, and necessary laws of Nature glossed in the popular religious language that such science precisely makes obsolete. "Spinozism," Levinas writes in "Have You Reread Baruch?," "was one of the first philosophies in which absolute thought also tried to be absolute religion" (DF, 117). Hegel will later bring such an ambition to its conclusion.

Popular religion knows neither that it is a politics nor that politics is the rule of power alone, absolute sovereignty. As we saw in chapter 4 in the present volume, politics for Spinoza is in essence what has come to be called "Machiavellian," the organization and regulation of power relations devoid of and unguided by intrinsic moral values. Spinoza unmasks religion and unmasks moral values as well: both lack truth, both lack intrinsic value, both are merely utilitarian. "Words," Spinoza says plainly in chapter 12, referring to the words of Scriptures and of religion and morality more generally, "acquire a fixed meaning solely from their use. . . . Thus it follows that nothing is sacred or profane or impure in an absolute sense apart from the mind, but only in relation to the mind" (207). For Spinoza, only Machiavellian politics and hence politics freed of religion, or limiting religion to *controlled internalized religion*, can prevent the even worse politics, the politics of fanaticism, politics ruled by *popular superstitious religion*, which follows from taking ethical and religious values and confusing them with truth or with the legitimization of power.

Here then is the second criticism of Levinas: Spinoza not only misrepresents Judaism, religion, and science, he also and for the same reasons misrepresents the legitimate tasks of politics. Politics, for Levinas, is not defined by Machiavellianism. By excluding and marginalizing religion for the sake of the absolute state Spinoza ignores Judaism's fundamental mission—articulated by the prophets, developed by the Talmudic rabbis and commentators—that politics is not merely brute obedience but uplifting obedience to morality and justice, hence a politics of compassion and redemption. This was also Ben-Shlomo's fifth point of difference discussed earlier, namely, Spinoza's attack upon redemptive politics.

Not surprisingly, Spinoza's politics are of a piece with his Christianized picture of Judaism. He reproduces the "outsider" political point of view of Christianity, born in flight from Rome, escaping into a politically harmless spirituality, the otherworldly Kingdom of God, while leaving unchallenged the real historical power of the state of Caesar. In contrast, as we have indicated, Jewish politics—with all its flaws, its backsliding, its immorality, its injustices (which the prophets broadcast loud and clear)—derived from nearly a thousand years of home rule, of actual political sovereignty in ancient Israel, where politics, economics, civil society, military, monarchy, family, and education were joined together in an integral whole; call it "religion," if you will.[22] On this crucial contrast between Judaism and Christianity—or Judaism and Spinoza, or Judaism and Augustine—regarding politics, Levinas writes in "The State of Caesar and the State of David":

---

22. If this amalgam of all the elements of everyday life, holy days, tithing, army service, monarchy, priesthood, courts, Sanhedrin, Temple sacrifices, among others, is "religion," then it is religion in the sense that "being Japanese" is the Japanese religion, whereas what is called "Shinto" in the world religions textbooks is a construct conforming only to a Christian—and nineteenth-century European university religion studies—notion of compartmentalized "spirituality."

> In the Judaism of the Rabbis, in the centuries immediately preceding the birth of Christianity, as in post-Christian rabbinical doctrine, the distinction between the political order and the spiritual order (between the earthly City and the City of God) does not possess the clear-cut character suggested by the evangelical expression "Render to Caesar the things that are Caesar's, and to God the things that are God's." In Christianity, the kingdom of God and the earthly kingdom are separated yet placed side by side without touching and, in principle, without contesting each other. They divide the human between themselves, and do not give rise to conflicts. It is perhaps because of this political spirit of indifference that Christianity has so often been a State religion. (BV, 177)

Without equating religion and politics, Levinas in the name of Judaism, contra Spinoza, will insist on their interrelation, their inextricable proximity, that is, on the rule of justice as guide to the rule of law. Such, in any event, is the task of redemption, and redemption is the traditional mission of Judaism. One would never guess it from Spinoza.

As a philosopher of science Spinoza's concern is truth and the protection of truth. His task is not to redeem the world but rather to know it in its truth, and to protect such knowing from all that he believes would subvert it. What Spinoza wants to preserve and protect, above all, is the life of the philosopher, the life of the savant-scientist, he who requires the "use of reason without restraint."[23] Given the century of religious wars that preceded his own time, given his family's experience of religious intolerance in Spain and Portugal and his own experiences in Amsterdam, all compounded by his immature grasp of Judaism, it is really not too surprising that for Spinoza—as for many early modern thinkers—the greatest threat to the free use of reason came not from the state, as we are often prone to think today, but

---

23. TPT, 293. I think this expression: "the use of reason without restraint," is telling. Apart from moral considerations, can reason even be reasonable without restraint? Does a thought that, at the extreme, only thinks itself, also lack restraint? "Autonomy," being a law unto itself, would be a discipline compared to the use of reason without restraint.

The point of view of the solitary philosopher is also the angle from which Gilles Deleuze, in *Spinoza: Practical Philosophy*, glorifies Spinoza (and Nietzsche).

from religion. For this was true in his day. Thus the primary aim of the *Theological-Political Treatise* is to defend neither a liberal nor a tyrannical politics but rather to redefine both politics and religion in such a way that the independent free thinker can live in peace and not be silenced, tortured, or killed in the public square. It is in the single-minded and narrow-minded manner of his pursuit of such an aim, however, that Levinas sees Spinoza misreading and betraying a long prophetic and rabbinical tradition of universal social compassion, and the ethical-redemptive politics required by that universal social compassion. Politics would not be exterior and opposed to religion but rather required by religion, in the service of religion, not repressing but realizing religion's deepest quest for morality and justice on earth—the prophesied this-worldly messianic "kingdom of God."

For Levinas the philosophical root of Spinoza's statism is identified in Wolfson's fourth act of daring, "Spinoza's insistence upon the elimination of freedom of the will from human actions." The elimination of free will is no mere afterthought or side show in Spinoza's thought. Indeed it is central, and Nietzsche admired it as such two centuries later. One finds it, for instance, in the corollary to proposition 49 of part II of the *Ethics*: "Will and intellect are one and the same thing" (96; Scholium, 97–101). One finds Spinoza arguing it extensively and in direct confrontation with Descartes in the five pages of the scholium to this same proposition. It is captured succinctly in the preface to part III, in Spinoza's famous rejection of the idea of "man in Nature as a kingdom within a kingdom" (E, 102). In a letter of September 1661, to Henry Oldenburg, again criticizing Descartes, Spinoza writes: "The will is nothing more than a mental construct (*ens rationis*)" (E, letter no. 2, 265). It appears in the *Theological-Political Treatise*, at the beginning of chapter 16, in Spinoza's distinction between humanity's true conformity to the iron rule of "natural laws" and humanity's obedience to human legislation, wherein "the validity of an agreement rests on its utility" (240). I would not belabor this point, since no one disputes it, but I emphasize it here nonetheless because of its political consequences. To reduce will to reason is, for Spinoza and for Levinas, tantamount to eliminating the independence and excellence of the entire domain of morality and justice, that is, the domain of that "kingdom within a kingdom" the proper name of which is given by Levinas as "the humanity of the human." Of course it is precisely on this point, and on this point foremost— the independence and excellence of the human—that Levinas resists

Spinoza. "Idealism completely carried out," Levinas writes, "reduces all ethics to politics."[24]

For Levinas and a Jewish tradition both popular and refined, that is, rabbinic Judaism, morality and justice, far from being illusory, deficient, or secondary modes of being, constitute the very "first signification, that is, the very upsurge of the rational."[25] For Levinas and rabbinic Judaism to be responsible to and for another human being, especially those most vulnerable, "the widow, the orphan, the stranger," is no dream, illusion, or diversion. It is no luxury, and no ignorance. Nor is it mere slavishness. Rather, it is the very first and most human of imperatives. Precisely in morality, in moral imperatives, so Levinas argues contra Spinoza, humanity is constituted at its very best, at its highest and most desirable. And humanity for Levinas, though certainly not for Spinoza, lives as an aspiration, inspired by the Good beyond being.

Levinas's criticism here of Spinoza's statism is no less a challenge to its more sophisticated twentieth-century versions, including the structuralism of Claude Levi-Strauss and the ideology critique of Louis Althusser. "We must remember," Levinas writes in "Ideology and Idealism," in criticizing Althusser, "Spinoza, that great demolisher of ideologies, still unaware of their name" (OGCM, 6). As with his criticism of Spinoza, Levinas attacks the debilitating notion that morality and the quest for justice are no more than "ideologies," meaning mere surface phenomena that can be explained *away* by a more scientific thought by

---

24. TI, 216. Levinas continues, TI, 217–219: "This identification of will and reason, which is the ultimate intention of idealism, is opposed by the entire pathetic experience of humanity, which the Hegelian or Spinozist idealism relegates to the subjective or the imaginary. The interest of this opposition does not lie in the very protestation of the individual who refuses the system and reason, that is, in his arbitrariness, which the coherent discourse could hence not silence by persuasion— but in the affirmation that makes this opposition live. . . . If, on the contrary, the subjectivity is fixed as a separated being in relation with an other absolutely other, the Other, if the face brings the first signification, that is, the very upsurge of the rational, then the will is distinguished fundamentally from the intelligible, which it must not comprehend and into which it must not disappear, for the intelligibility of this intelligible resides precisely in ethical behavior, that is, in the responsibility to which it invites the will. The will is free to assume this responsibility itself; it is not free to ignore the meaningful world into which the face of the Other has introduced it."

25. See footnote 24 for larger context.

means of deeper structures or superstructures. For Levinas, in contrast, putting ideals above motivations—hence reversing Spinoza—is not the expression of false consciousness, the deluded ideological surface of a material substructure, or a predictable and conformist differential option within a larger dominating linguistic structure. The "saying" of the other, or the "saying" of the moral agent in response to the other, are for Levinas irreducible to the "said." In his essay entitled "Ideology and Idealism," where the previous reference to Spinoza occurs, Levinas writes: "If we believe Althusser, Ideology [saying] always expresses the manner in which consciousness's dependency in regard to the objective or material conditions [the said] that determine it—and which scientific reason grasps in their objectivity—is experienced by this consciousness" (OCGM, 4–5). For Levinas, in contrast, the epistemological reduction of saying to the said—objectification, reification, Spinoza's intellection—precisely occurs by erasing the moral priority of saying over the said, precisely by the pretense of defusing responsibility, obligation. Structuralism and ideology critique, exactly like Spinozism, are guilty of their inability to take seriously the pacific force of an individual's moral obligations and responsibilities, and of the forceful call to justice, that actually makes such "sciences" possible in the first place.

Morality, irreducible to the rational, provides the very *rationale* for the rational and the *significance* of signification. Contrary to the long and venerated tradition of the primacy of *episteme* in philosophy, manifest no less in theology whether for knowledge or for faith, Levinas claims "ethics as first philosophy" (LR, 76–87). Divorcing science from the social, politics from the religious, and the religious from an effectual ethics, Spinoza distorts them all. Because his thought is a thoroughgoing but blinkered rationalism, Spinoza ends up defending a Machiavellian politics, politics as pure power, whether sweet or brutal, and attacking religion, whether popular and superstitious, or private and conscientious, rendering it in both cases ineffective. Spinoza propounds these positions because he has fundamentally misunderstood the proper nature and role of *values, ends, ideals*, the *orientation of height*, in epistemology, in religion, and in politics.

Rationality without Wisdom

We arrive finally at Levinas's deepest criticism of Spinoza from the point of view of Judaism. It is that he misrepresented and misunderstood the links binding reason, morality, religion, and politics that Judaism, or more properly, that rabbinical Judaism from the Talmud through modernity manifest in its debates and discussions, its mandates and mitzvot, its self-reflections and practices, even lacking full political sovereignty of its own. By misunderstanding the *wisdom* of Judaism, in other words, Spinoza misunderstood the aim of politics (*Theological-Political Treatise*) and the nature and role of knowledge (*Ethics*). Contrary to popular belief, Spinoza was a very poor student of Jewish wisdom.

But surely this does not tell us enough. Certainly his supporters, but also his critics, have praised Spinoza for his profound knowledge of Judaism. It is certainly this that originally distinguished Spinoza as a biblical critic. He is not only Jewish by birth, family, and education; he is also thoroughly versed in the Hebrew language, in the Bible, in Talmud and rabbinic commentaries—what else makes for expertise in Judaism?! On what basis can Levinas claim that Spinoza misunderstood it? The answer is to be found in one word: Talmud. Contrary to popular belief, and contrary to the many scholars, Jewish and non-Jewish, who have without independent verification repeated the same popular belief, Spinoza misunderstood Judaism because *he neither learned nor grasped the wisdom of the Talmud*, the very sensibility that defines rabbinic Judaism, which is to say, defines every stream of postbiblical Judaism.[26] For Levinas the Talmud—understood quite broadly as the wisdom found in and through Talmudic discussions, Talmudic hermeneutics, and Talmudic sobriety, the "world of the Talmud" as one says "the world of Plato," but also any similar sensibility found elsewhere outside of Judaism, in other religions, other cultures, in world literatures, in short, in civilization—is not just a set of books, or even less a set of laws, but it is rather the very heart and soul of Judaism, its very life.

Levinas is not the first, and not alone, in having recognized Spinoza's debilitating lack of scholarly qualifications.

Explanations for Spinoza's Misunderstanding. Before turning to Levinas's conception of Talmudic wisdom and the clear evidence that Spinoza never understood such wisdom, let us first speculate how and why Spinoza was so deficient. It has nothing to do with the quality of his intelligence, whose superiority is proven in all his writings. It has

---

26. With the exclusion of the Karaites, who also far earlier rejected the rabbinic commentaries, (but nevertheless had their own commentaries), and who in Eastern Europe eventually rejected Judaism altogether.

nothing to do with the quality of his knowledge, per se, of Hebrew, Hebrew Bible verses, or of science and mathematics for that matter. So, too, it has nothing to do with the quality of his knowledge, per se, of the new philosophy inaugurated by Descartes. What, then, is the problem?

Yirmiyahu Yovel, without in any way agreeing with Levinas's assessment or evaluation of Spinoza, has emphasized the importance of Spinoza's Converso background (*Marrano Patterns*). For more than a century Spinoza's family, which had publically converted to Christianity under pressure of the Catholic Inquisition and the governments of Spain and Portugal, had to daily prevaricate and masquerade as Christians. Could it not be, then, with such a heritage, a family so long cut off from normal Jewish community life, that Spinoza came actually to believe in the Christianized construction of "Judaism"? Perhaps Spinoza actually believed that Judaism was indeed reducible to the Old Testament, reducible to Christianity's distorted image of the Hebrews, reducible, that is to say, precisely to the false and distorted picture of the Israelites, the prophets and the sages one finds in the *Theological-Political Treatise*. Perhaps also he had lost touch with the distinctive Talmudic sensibility of Jewish life and thought. Blame his Converso background. Perhaps there is a certain truth to this, but as we shall see, there is another more compelling explanation.

It turns out that despite his indisputable intelligence and mastery of Hebrew and the Hebrew Bible verses, and his many references to medieval commentators,[27] Spinoza had never been trained in Talmud. At first glance this seems so unlikely, but it turns out to be true. In fact, it turns out that Spinoza's formal training in Judaism ended at the age of twelve, when he had to leave school, never to return, to join the family business. Levinas specifically invokes this explanation, that Spinoza simply had no Talmudic training, referring to the recent historical research in Holland of Vaz Dias and van der Tak, regarding the

---

27. Levy, *Baruch or Benedict*, 18: "The list of Hebrew writers in the TPT, in any case, is impressive. Spinoza refers to Abraham Ibn-Esra, Abraham Ibn-Daud, Jehuda Alphaquer, Josephus Flavius, Joseph ben Shem-Tov, Gersonides, Bonaiuto dei Rossi, Philo of Alexandria, David Kimchi, Rashi, Nachmanides, and, evidently more than anybody else, Maimonides." No doubt Spinoza was also familiar with the work of Hasdai Crescas, who also challenged traditional formulations of "free will." While Levy's list certainly includes some major Jewish scholars, as evidence of erudition in Talmud studies, however, it is not particularly impressive.

details of seventeenth-century Jewish life in Amsterdam. Their research casts serious doubt on the traditional but in fact presumptive and hagiographic biographical account of Spinoza's great learning. The community records are extensive. No record, however, shows Spinoza's name on the list of advanced Talmud students. No record indicates Spinoza ever in any way studied under Amsterdam's preeminent Talmudic scholar, Rabbi Morteira.[28] For Levinas such a revision of the legend "certainly does not compromise" Spinoza's reputation as a Hebrew-language scholar or as someone familiar with the Bible. "It would tend," Levinas writes in "Spinoza's Background," "to put into question only the width and depth of his Talmud practice" (BV, 168). The word "only" here is deceptive; there is nothing limiting, in Levinas's view, about the "width and depth" of "Talmud practice." Still, Levinas admits that this historical research, despite the real doubts it supports, is not by itself sufficient to establish the level of Spinoza's own acquaintance with the Talmud.[29] The best evidence, in the final account, cannot be based in conjectures about his family background or his youthful learning but in what Spinoza actually says about Judaism, the knowledge of Judaism that Spinoza displays explicitly in his writings.

Of the level of Talmud studies in Amsterdam in Spinoza's day, but more so referring to Spinoza's own training or lack of training in Talmud, his understanding of Talmudic wisdom, as witnessed by his written characterizations of Judaism, Levinas writes in "Spinoza's Background":

---

28. Steven Nadler, in his recent life of Spinoza, confirms this negative assessment of Spinoza's Talmudic training: "Vaz Dias has shown that Spinoza was not, in fact, attending the highest class, or *medras*—that taught by Rabbi Morteira and including advanced lessons in Gemara and readings in rabbinic and philosophical literature—when he should have been, in the early 1650s. . . . Nor is he listed in the registers for the preceding or subsequent years [relative to 1651]. . . . As his name appears nowhere in the registers for the *talmudim* [students] at Ets Chaim for the years 1647–50 (5407–5411), there is no evidence that he attended even the fifth grade" (*Spinoza: A Life*, 80–81).

29. In the course of writing about contemporary assimilated Jews, Levinas does cast certain aspersions on Spinoza's teachers: "Do they still know that our great books, which are increasingly ignored, reveal a Synagogue that in no way tries to act as a blindfold? That Spinoza, in his Jewish studies, perhaps only had teachers of little caliber? Alas! Hebraism, in our day, is such a rare science that one can only imagine it nondescript or mediocre" (DF, 109).

It is not at all certain, then, that Spinoza's environment was favorable in the domain of Talmudic science. This is significant beyond its biographical importance. In the critique that the *Theologico-Political Treatise* makes of it, rabbinical exegesis of Scripture is, as it were, separated from its Talmudic soul, and consequently appears as a blind and dogmatic apologetic of the "Pharisees" who are attached to the letter (but who are quick to give it an arbitrary meaning) and as a forced reconciliation of obviously disparate texts. . . . It is here, more than by consulting documents, that the suspicion of a lack of knowledge is born. As far as a Spinoza is concerned, it is more likely to be this than any misappreciation or lack of understanding. (BV, 169)

Certainly Spinoza was intelligent enough to learn and understand Talmud. But he did not. And this is evident, such is Levinas's charge, in his writings, published and unpublished. Levinas's charge is serious and damning for an allegedly objective critic of Judaism: nowhere in the *Theological-Political Treatise*, or elsewhere, in any of his books or letters, does Spinoza show in his characterization of Judaism that he has understood the wisdom of the Talmud. In the *Theological-Political Treatise*, for instance, and this would be obvious to scholars with even a limited grasp of Talmudic wisdom and hermeneutics, "Scripture is, as it were, separated from its Talmudic soul."

The issue, let us be clear, is not really to explain why Spinoza lacked an understanding of the Talmud. To the possible causes mentioned previously one might add, as some scholars have noted, the Marcionist influence of his Collegiate associates, or perhaps an Epicurean disposition, or an unacknowledged malice and vengeance for his excommunication. These are topics for historians and psychologists. More important for the conceptual issues that are our interest, to decide if Spinoza has gotten the Judaism and religion he attacks right, is that in every aspect of his work Spinoza "betrays" Judaism without ever having presented an accurate, fair, or much less a deep understanding of it. No doubt his misunderstanding philosophically derives also from his exclusive attachment to scientific philosophy. From whichever direction, however, whether from the side of an accurate grasp of Judaism or an accurate grasp of the limitations of science, the result is the same. Spinoza's Judaism is not Judaism's Judaism, which is to say, it is not rabbinic Judaism, or what Spinoza would call "Pharisaic" Judaism.

It is an internal and theological Christian claim that the basic difference between Judaism and Christianity is the difference between the Old Testament and the New Testament. This is certainly not how Jews or scholars view the matter. Jews and Christians both have the same Old Testament, sacred scripture for both religions. But they have different new testaments: the New Testament of Christianity and the Talmud of Judaism. It is simply false—however much a commonplace of the Christian perspective—to distinguish Judaism from Christianity as if Judaism has only the Old Testament and Christianity the Old and the New. Retaining the New Testament but subtracting the Talmud, Spinoza's Judaism perforce ends up the "Judaism" of the Old Testament constructed by Christian theology, which actual Judaism never was and which actual Judaism, to the best of its limited abilities, always resisted. Levinas makes no such mistake, either regarding Judaism or regarding wisdom. For Levinas, going much further as a philosopher, and without betraying Judaism, the wisdom of the Talmud is not restricted to the Talmud or Talmud study but includes, as he says, every "authentic expression of the human," hence all of world literature, "because all literature is inspired" (BV, "Spinoza's Background," 171). Spinoza's betrayals, his bad faith, and his misunderstandings—of reason, of ethics, of politics, of religion, of Judaism—can thus be traced back to one primary source, his profound lack of understanding of and appreciation for the different (or shall we say "superior"?[30]) wisdom of the Talmud.

Talmudic Wisdom

Here is not the place to elaborate in any great detail the unique character of Talmud or "Oral Torah": its textual layers of Mishna, Braita, Gemara; its division into Aggadah (narrative) and Halakhah (law);[31]

---

30. To characterize the superior rationality Spinoza did not understand, Levinas uses the term "different." I have taken the term "superior" from Leo Strauss, who at the end of his 1965 preface to his own book on Spinoza, completed in 1928, *Spinoza's Critique of Religion*, calls it both "superior" and "pre-modern." In the concluding paragraph, admitting that he no longer reads Spinoza in 1965 in the manner in which he read him in 1928, and after having shown the atheist and self-destructive consequences of Spinoza's rationalism, Strauss writes: "The victory of

the role of Midrash (stories), Kabbalah (tradition), Takkanah (enactments), and Minhag (custom) in its elaboration; the logical and semantic peculiarities of its unique hermeneutics, such as are articulated, for instance, in Rabbi Ishmael's "Thirteen Rules of Interpretation"; or the manner and effect of Responsa (letters) and its codifications (Mishne Torah, Tur, Shulchan Aruch). Scholars with far greater expertise than my own are entitled to make these clarifications. Nor is this the place to adequately demonstrate—historically or conceptually—the extent to which the Talmud's sense and sensibility have come to permeate and determine all forms of postbiblical Judaism and Jewish life. Nonetheless, within the limits of these disclaimers, I do want to distinguish four dimensions of a hermeneutical or exegetical sensibility and sensitivity, which I have elsewhere called "ethical exegesis," which together constitute the broader sense of reason or wisdom, closer to the ancient Greek senses of these terms, in contrast to Spinozist rationality. While I am the one analyzing an integral Talmudic wisdom into these four components, to better understand this wisdom, it is this same Talmudic wisdom that for Levinas is the key to Judaism as a whole, and the lack thereof that undermines Spinoza's credibility vis-à-vis Judaism utterly. While I am presenting these four characteristics or aspects as elements of Talmudic exegesis, their actual relevance goes beyond the reading of texts, just as Talmudic wisdom is not restricted solely to texts, because it permeates a style of life, a way of life that is also ethical and holy. Spinoza jettisoned all four, as he jettisoned Talmudic wisdom, in the name of mathematical scientific omniscience.

Four dimensions, aspects or characteristics of Talmudic exegesis, or of reason or wisdom in its fullness, are as follows: (1) a productive

---

orthodoxy through the self-destruction of rational philosophy was not an unmitigated blessing, for it was a victory, not of Jewish orthodoxy, but of any orthodoxy, and Jewish orthodoxy based its claim to superiority to other religions from the beginning on its superior rationality (Deut. 4:6)." Strauss continues: "I began therefore to wonder whether the self-destruction of reason was not the inevitable outcome of modern rationalism as distinguished from pre-modern rationalism, especially Jewish-medieval rationalism and its classical (Aristotelian and Platonic) foundation" ("Preface," 172–173). Deuteronomy 4:6: "Keep them [the Lord's statutes and judgments] therefore and do them; for this is your wisdom and your understanding in the sight of the nations, who shall hear all these statutes, and say, Surely this great nation is a wise and understanding people."

31. On the division of Oral Torah into Halakhah and Aggadah, see, for example, Hansel, 273–282.

integrity of spirit and letter, or of body and soul; (2) a necessary pluralism of persons and readings; (3) truth aligned with virtue, wisdom that is existential or self-transformative; and (4) authority, or the renewal of a living ethical-religious tradition.[32] Spinoza, rejecting any positive role for imagination, history, and persons, (1) separates spirit and letter, siding with "ideas" independent of "words and images"; (2) rejects a plurality of persons and readings for a systematic logic of noncontradiction; (3) radically separates truth from virtue, fact from value, explanation from understanding, relegating the latter to the false and illusory; and (4) rejects the authority of history and tradition in the name of a *mathesis universalis, sub specie aeternitatis.* Between the rich and variegated world and wisdom of Talmudic Judaism and the *more geometrico* of Spinozist rationalism, then, we have, to use Levinas's term, two philosophies at "antipodes" from one another. However only one is human and alive; the other is robotic and artificial. Spinoza's is a logical system of control, stasis, suffocation, death, while responsible life with its open future, its debates, its progress and setbacks, the struggle for justice, is out of such control. In the following I want very briefly to elaborate the four characteristics—elements of exegesis but no less elements of life—of the Talmudic world and wisdom to highlight their contrast to the narrowing of reason manifest in Spinozist rationalism.

Productive Integrity of Spirit and Letter

Levinas acknowledges an integral or dialectical unity of spirit and matter.[33] For text interpretation, this translates into a positive regard for

---

32. It should be noted from the start that Levinas's "interpretation" of rabbinical exegesis is in no way idiosyncratic, wishful thinking, or invented. For a very fine account along the same lines of the living and authoritative dialectic operative in rabbinical exegesis—called "Intrinsic Inspiration" (lxv)—in contrast to both strict literalism and loose liberalism, see Loewe, especially lv–lxxxi. For a similar account of the four characteristics of Levinas's understanding of Talmudic exegesis, see also my introduction, "Humanism, Religion, Myth, Criticism, Exegesis," to Levinas's NewTR.

33. For Daniel Boyarin, as for Levinas, this notion of the integral unity of body and soul, matter and spirit, is both a content thought and lived and a root principle of hermeneutics. Boyarin will speak, as the title of his book indicates, of "carnal Israel." "That is, for rabbinic Jews, the human being was defined as a body—animated, to be sure, by a soul—while for Hellenistic Jews (such as Philo) and (at least many Greek-speaking) Christians (such as Paul), the essence of a human being is a soul housed in a body" (5).

spirit *and* letter, meaning *and* text. Like the symbol that "gives rise to thought" for Ricoeur, the letters of Torah give rise to spirit, call out for commentary.[34] Spirit, for its part, despite its flights remains rooted in letters, in a textual richness that is one of the marks of sacred literature, or of literature taken in a sacred sense. Always adhering to this integrity, Talmudic exegesis succumbs neither to an impossible literalism of the letter, which Levinas derides in "Contempt for the Torah as Idolatry" as the "negation of all spirituality and the source of all idolatry," nor to a no less impossible detachment, an abstract or free-floating interpretation, which Levinas dismisses as "pious rhetoric . . . in which ambiguity, amidst unverifiable 'mysteries,' always finds a convenient shelter" (ITN, 63). Literalism and spiritualism are both merely subjective, liable to willfulness, to unregulated self-projection, rather than inspired readings, reading inspired and animated by texts. In exegesis, by contrast, "through the apparent attachment to the letter, there is the extreme attention paid to the spirit of the biblical text and a hermeneutic which puts a passage . . . back into the context of the totality of the Bible, with a view to deepening" (BV, "On Religious Language and the Fear of God," 91). It is not merely one letter, after all, to which a reading is attached; nor only one text; rather each letter and each text is interconnected to an entire literature and tradition of intertextuality. To bind spirit to letter, then, just as to awaken spirit from letter, are already great sources of disciplined creativity, in a creativity that is neither willful nor unregulated. The rabbis, in a word, are not "running wild," as Spinoza sees them.

This exegetical deepening through the dialectic of letter nourishing spirit and spirit nourishing letter is at the antipodes from Spinoza's narrower approach to the Bible, a Bible that, after all, as Spinoza writes in chapter 13 of the *Theological-Political Treatise*, mimicking Paul, is comprised of "letters that are dead" (230). Of the rabbinical readings, in this instance that of R. Yehuda Alpakhar, Spinoza—who dismisses all textual, semantic and semiotic difficulties, differences, complexities, and nuances with his *idée fixe* countercharge of "contradiction"—can only say: "I am utterly astonished that men can bring themselves to make reason . . . subservient to letters that are dead. . . . This is not piety, but mere folly" (230). For Levinas, in contrast, the interpretive subtleties of the rabbis

---

34. In Sotah 47b, the Torah is said to "beg from house to house to house" in order to get students. Cited in Montefiore and Loewe, 668.

sum up the efforts made over thousands of years to go beyond the letter of the text and even its apparent dogmatism, and to restore a wholly spiritual truth even to those passages in the Scriptures called historical or ritual or ceremonial or thaumaturgical. In its scope and lucidity this undertaking has no precedent, but it is guided by the letter of the text, an extraordinary letter since it nurtures and demands this effort. This accounts for the prestige . . . enjoyed by the Talmud. . . . And it is on this issue that [we] part company with Spinoza. (DF, "Have You Reread Baruch?," 116)

The source point of intelligibility need not be confined to self-evident axioms nor its trajectory straitjacketed by logical deduction.

Pluralism of Persons and Readings

Jacob Neusner, writing on Torah and Midrash, cites the dictum: "'If it is empty—from you,' that is, if you find no meaning in a verse, the fault is yours" (*History and Torah*, 18). Levinas agrees, insisting, in the name of Talmudic exegesis, that each person has his or her part in the Torah. Such exegesis not only yields but *requires* multiple readings, multiple interpretations, and multiple readers. Such multiplicity is not the product of oversight, ignorance, inattentiveness, willfulness, or mental lapse, as a Spinozist would assert in affirming univocal formulae that only stipulation and mathematical construction can hope to achieve but in truth do not.[35] Rather such pluralism of meaning is a product of and a tribute to the pluralism constitutive of human society, a pluralism of independent persons reflected in Talmud and Talmudic exegesis. That is to say, it is a testimony to the *ethical* basis

---

35. Many contemporary philosophers, from Merleau-Ponty to Paul Feyerabend, have argued for the essential role of imagination—or metaphor—in strictly scientific discourse. For a clear and well-argued defense of this view, without retreat into philosophical skepticism and in the light of the question of religion relevant to the present chapter, see the very fine book by Janet Martin Soskice, *Metaphor and Religious Language*, especially, 112–117. Although Soskice recognizes the importance not merely of meaning and reference in the use of metaphor but also, following Hilary Putnam, the essential role of speakers and historical context, she does not draw, or does not explicitly draw, as does Levinas, the ethical implications inherent in exegesis.

upon which social pluralism rests. "Each one of us Jews," Levinas once declared in "Judaism and Christianity" before presenting a public interpretation of Judaism, and without any false modesty, "retains his freedom of expression. We do not have, despite the rigor of the Law, any orientation dictated by the synagogue; neither obligatory nor even just official" (ITN, 161). "If the Talmudic saying is so strange," Levinas writes, "it is not because it would take pleasure in stating in a complicated way what can be expressed in a simple way. On the contrary, it is because it leaves a multiplicity of meanings to its saying, because it calls for several readings of it. Our role, precisely, consists in looking for them" (BV, "Cities of Refuge," 37). Regardless of the depth, brilliance, sincerity, erudition, and wisdom of one's own religious outlook, no one reader—no interpreter, no person, including learned rabbis of such genius as the Vilna Gaon Elijah or Moses Maimonides—can appropriate a definitive oracular mantle or close down the horizons of interpretation opened by Talmudic wisdom. Without endorsing all readings willy-nilly, the Midrash teaches that millions of interpretations of the Torah, more even for non-Jews than for Jews, were given and legitimated at Mount Sinai.[36]

Contra Spinoza's intellectualist monism, the essential pluralism of the Torah means and reflects the irreducible fact that each human being retains his or her right of expression because that expression is not extraneous to truth, is not a merely subjective interference, or the source of merely secondary imaginary qualities, or a "mere opinion." Rather, expression, commentary, dialogue, partnership in learning, questioning, validating, arguing, debating, are the necessary "manner" or "way" in which truth comes to be, grows, develops, enriches itself, becomes better, since truth cannot be true without reflecting rather than suppressing its actual conditions, including its moral birth in the "saying of the said." Thus revelation itself requires multiple readings and readers. Levinas observes in the essay "Revelation in the Jewish Tradition":

---

36. According to Midrash the Torah at Sinai was given to 600,000 souls, for each of whom it was received differently; it was given with at least four ways of interpretation ("PaRDeS": plain, allegorical, homiletic, mystical), yielding 2,400,000 readings; it was given even then to the seventy nations, yielding 170,400,000 readings; all of which is to say that there are innumerable legitimate readings, each necessary for a complete understanding of Torah; which is to say that the Torah is inexhaustible.

The Revelation has a particular way of producing meaning, which lies in its calling upon the unique within me. It is as if a multiplicity of persons . . . as if each person, by virtue of his own uniqueness, were able to guarantee the revelation of one unique aspect of the truth, so that some of its facets would never have been revealed if certain people had been absent from mankind. . . . I am suggesting that the totality of truth is made out of the contributions of a multiplicity of people: the uniqueness of each act of listening carries the secret of the text; the voice of Revelation, in precisely the inflection lent by each person's ear, is necessary for the truth of the Whole. . . . The multiplicity of people, each one of them indispensable, is necessary to produce all the dimensions of meaning; the multiplicity of meanings is due to the multiplicity of people. (LR, 195)

As Levinas understands it, in Jewish wisdom, in the revelation proper to religion "there is included a semantics that is absolute, inexhaustible, ever renewable through exegesis" (ITN, "From Ethics to Exegesis," 112). Rabbinical debate and disagreement, multiple even incompatible commentaries, then, are essential to revelation. "The innumerable sides of the absolute Truth live in the bosom of rabbinical debates or disputes, avoiding dogmatism, avoiding heresies" (NewTR, 87). "Their diversity, their very contradictions, far from compromising the truths commented upon, are felt to be faithful to the Real, refractory to the System" (OS, "The Strings and the Wood," 130). Revelation thus extends through the pluralism of persons[37] and readings throughout history right up to the present, as Levinas notes, recalling the celebrated insight of an eighteenth-century rabbi for whom "the slightest question put to the schoolmaster by a novice constitutes an ineluctable articulation of the Revelation which was heard at Sinai" (LR, "Revelation and the Jewish Tradition," 195). "[F]aithful to the Real, refractory to the System"—surely an anti-Spinozist slogan.

---

37. In Ta'an, 7a: "A Rabbi said that as fire does not burn when isolated, so will the words of the Torah not be preserved when studied by oneself alone. Another said that the learned who are occupied in the study of the Law, each one by himself, deserve punishment, and they shall become fools." Cited in *A Rabbinic Anthology*, 107.

Virtue or Existential Self-Transformation

This third characteristic of the Talmudic life of Judaism is closely related to the second. The dialectical or dialogical dimension of exegesis is not merely a spectacle, seen at a distance, in the third person. Nor is it a game like those of college debating clubs, where contents take second seat to scoring points and the debaters perform as lawyers rather than interested parties. Rather Talmud dialogue—debate, argumentation, questioning—transforms and is meant to transform its interlocutors in the first person. "I" and "you" (including the "you" who speaks through the text[38]), are thus not the same and cannot be understood in the same way, as "one" and "it," or the "self" and "other person," which is to say from the outside, objectively. Exegesis, in contrast to scientific criticism, lives because it touches and engages the lives of those who engage in it. The activity of knowing involves passivity, receptivity, vulnerability, the impact of a relation with another person. To some measure it is this difference that undergirds the hermeneutic distinction between understanding and explanation, self-reflection and objectivity, humanism and natural science, even if its significance escapes Spinoza or is suppressed by him. The significance of a text—*inseparable from exegesis*—is neither a subjective projection, as if the self were inviolable and imposed itself on the text, nor an impossible literalism, as if the self again remained untouched but somehow miraculously discovered something completely outside itself, revealed to someone unmoved and unmovable beside the text. Rather, the sociality that lies at the heart of signification, and conditions truth, is an existential enterprise, an intertwining of inwardness and exteriority, the meeting of passivity and activity, vulnerability, which emerges in and affects the interaction that is exegetical reading. Written Torah cannot be separated from Oral Torah without becoming "dry bones," just as Oral Torah cannot

---

38. It is interesting in this regard that in orthodox yeshiva exegetical circles sometimes a revered sage-author becomes known and (re)named by the title of his primary book (e.g., Rabbi Yisroel Meir Kagan (1838–1933) is known after his book as "Ha-Chofetz Chaim"(The "Will to Life"), Rabbi Meir Simcha HaCohen (1843–1923) is known as "Ha-Or Someyach" (The "Joyful Light"); very often important religious books (Midrash, Talmud, commentaries, codes) are spoken of as if they were live personages, for example, "The Midrash says . . ." or "The Mishnah Torah says . . ." rather than "Maimonides says . . ."

be separated from Written Torah without producing "beautiful souls," both of which are abstractions alien to the readers and writings they claim to elucidate. For Judaism there simply is no Written Torah without Oral Torah, no Old Testament without its constant renewal in rabbinic exegesis. It is interesting that until the modern epoch, Jews always printed their Hebrew Bibles with multiple commentaries surrounding the biblical text. These were not expendable supplements but necessary limbs, indeed additional mouths, eyes, ears, of the very text they extended because in and through them one discovered its meanings.

The distinction between explanation and understanding is inadequate because it does not make sufficiently explicit the ineradicable *prescriptive* dimension of meaning. For Jewish wisdom not only the wisdom learned but the very learning is also an ethical venture. Regardless of the immediate practical consequences of the *content* of Torah learning, which in fact is often entirely impractical and irrelevant (at least *prima facie* or *in praesenti*), for instance debates regarding Temple sacrifices, the learning itself is valuable, permeated by values. It was "study," Levinas writes in "Judaism and Kenosis," "that was considered valid as *association*, as covenant, as sociality with God—with his will, which, though not incarnate, is inscribed in the Torah" (DF, 120). If I may indulge in extended metaphor: Torah is the recipe; exegesis is the cooking. Meaning, then, is the food, the holy sacrifice; and it is we who are nourished. In any event, the point is that exegesis is satisfied neither with detached knowledge nor with blind faith, but it promotes a moral way of life and serves as a way toward that way of life, a combination of truth inextricably bound to behavior and behavior inextricably bound to truth: "a difficult wisdom," as Levinas has said, "concerned with *truths that correlate to virtues*. . . . This study is the highest level of life where knowledge is no longer distinguished from imperatives and practical impulses, where science and conscience meet, where reality and justice no longer belong to two distinct orders" (BV, "Cities of Refuge," 47; emphasis added).

Authority or the Renewal of a Living Tradition

Ethical self-transformation or wisdom is linked, for Levinas—but for sociology as well, to the fourth and perhaps most important characteristic of Talmudic exegesis, which functions as a concrete regulative principle, namely, organic connection to a surrounding and trailing and projective ethical-cultural-historical tradition.[39] Perhaps the term "mores" comes closest to such a complex of weights, measures, significations, significance, of present, past, future, duration, and diachrony. While interpretations are innumerable and inexhaustible, they are nonetheless rooted in past interpretations, in past texts, in texts that have a past, but a past that traverses the present, makes for its presence, while aiming at a future. Thus the wisdom of the individual is matched and regulated by the wisdom of a community and its traditions. Singularity and salvation are thus bound to sociality and redemption. Levinas in "Cites of Refuge" notes: "In return for personal access to the truth and to Scripture—which is probably the *raison d'être* of the very multiplicity of human beings aroused by the scintillating infinite of the *one* truth—there is recourse to the tradition which is renewed only when it is received beforehand" (BV, 48).

Thus the liberty of multiple readings is guided by the authority and diversity of tradition. Or, phrased differently, the wisdom of

---

39. In the preface to their recent book, *Thinking Biblically: Exegetical and Hermeneutic Studies*, authors Andre LaCocque and Paul Ricoeur write that "the factor . . . the exegete most takes into account has to do with the connection between the text and a living community" (xii). They label this factor "textual dynamism" (xiii). Regarding the difference between a Jewish reading and a Christian reading of the Old Testament, one must wonder, however, what the authors were thinking when they wrote: "The First Testament is not abolished by the Second, but reinterpreted and, in this sense 'fulfilled'" (xiv). Does this mean, as I would hope, that both New Testament and Talmud "fulfill" the Old Testament each in its own way, one Christian the other Jewish, but both legitimate? Unfortunately this hope finds little support. The allegedly "Jewish reading" LaCocque and Ricoeur make explicit in fact remains almost entirely within the Christian theological construction of a Jewish reading, that is to say, confined to the Old Testament and almost completely unaware of Talmud. Such an approach is all too usual in Christian circles, even in academic departments of religious studies, which really should know better, and even by "enlightened" and "tolerant" theologians, including so-called "post-Holocaust" theologians, who also should know better. In the light of this exclusion one must wonder what the authors of this particular book mean when they claim that the New Testament is on the "same trajectory" as the Old Testament but is "considerably ramified." On firmer scholarly ground, however, LaCocque and Ricoeur do advise that "the Christian reading is not taken as a substitute but, rather, as an alternative to the traditional Jewish reading" (xiv). Is it too much to expect scholars of religious studies who study Christianity to make good on such advice and learn a modicum of the actual "traditional Jewish reading," even if only to better understand the variegated Judaism endorsed, practiced, praised as well as castigated by Jesus and his immediate disciples according to New Testament sources?

the individual and the wisdom of the community mutually nourish and grow with one another. Sometimes the individual stands out and directs; sometimes the community, without preestablished harmony or immutable categories in either case. Sometimes change is swift, sometimes slow; sometimes one subgroup changes faster and another slower or imperceptibly, sometimes it is the individual, sometimes the family, sometimes a study group, sometimes a school, sometimes a movement, all within the same broad community. Once again, in such a mix the dangers of radical subjectivism and objectivism are avoided:

> There is, moreover, a means of discriminating between personal originality brought to bear upon the reading of the Book and the play of the phantasms of amateurs (or even charlatans): this is provided by the necessity of referring subjective findings to the continuity of readings through history, the tradition of commentaries which no excuse of direct inspiration from the text allows one to ignore. No "renewal" worthy of the name can dispense with these references. (LR, "Revelation in the Jewish Tradition," 196)

Or more briefly: "To belong to a book, as one belongs to one's history!" (OS, "The Strings and the Wood," 129). Thus even God, according to the Midrash, must and does abide by human decisions, but only to those decisions that are made "in the name of God" (*b'shamayim*)!

There is no original word, but no obsolete word either—such is the unity of humankind, such is the unity of Torah. Exegesis, beyond deduction and demonstration but without countermanding them, is not some wild and nefarious manipulation and self-serving distortion of meaning, as Spinoza thought, because he wanted to bury reality, time, and history in the possible, eternal, and lawful, taking orders from an immutable mathematical science. Rather, attuned to the unpredictable unfolding of the real, Talmudic exegesis is a continual reanimation, a permanent awakening, and as such, as a diachronic process, the very revelation of revelation. It is mistaken therefore to conceive of revelation as once and done with, locked up in the "once upon a time," which in truth reduces it to fable and myth that only satisfy a childish consciousness. Exegesis, like revelation (the two are inseparable), is once and forever, to be sure, but only as once again, again and again. The voice heard at Mount Sinai, deafening from the start, must be constantly modulated to the human ear. One goes "back" to Sinai but only by moving forward to it for the first time, hence in a constant return that no less is renewal. Prophecy is indeed a heightened imagination, as Spinoza said, but it is not merely that; it reaches both higher, vertically, toward the good, and extends wider, across the multiple universality of humanity, than Spinoza dreamed.

No doubt I am here presenting something of an idealized picture. No one can be unaware that in history and today still, in actual Jewish communities, there have been narrow-minded rabbis, intolerant rabbis, as well as triumphalist rabbis, and there have been rabbis, and not just theologians, who have forbidden the reading of banned books (Spinoza's books are still banned in certain quarters of the Jewish world!) or have ordered the burning of opponents' books, excommunicated one another, and the like. Rabbis too are human, and the Jewish community has not always been at its best; we do not pretend otherwise. In fact the Bible is itself a record of Jewish backsliding and recalcitrance, perhaps unique in the world as a sacred text in this regard. Spinoza, too, for all his philosophical hauteur, wrote in the penultimate sentence of the *Theological-Political Treatise*: "I know that I too am human, and may have erred" (230). Nevertheless the picture I am presenting of exegetical reading and life, while an ideal, nonetheless presents an ideal that has remarkably often, with remarkable success, and in good measure, been put into practice. And it remains alive to this day in the vibrant and intense back and forth search for wisdom between texts, commentaries, teachers and students, in the study halls of many *yeshivas*—Jewish schools of higher Talmudic learning—around the world. In contrast to the reserved quiet that blankets a university or public library reading room, and the sharp hushes at the slightest breach, the nearly deafening din of multiple intense debates ringing through the typical yeshiva or synagogue study hall of today gives poignant testimony to the continued committed and relevant reality of Talmudic exegesis.

Science is always contemporary science, in the sense that historical truths, even truths once but no longer affirmed by science, have a very different status than the current truths of science. The development of morality and justice occurs otherwise. The latest scientific truth might be a completely new discovery, never conceived before. But with regard to the strictures of morality and justice, we were not born yesterday. Several thousands of years of moral experience and hence moral wisdom are not merely behind us, a thing of the past, in the dustbin of history, but live on as impetus for us, as guide, exigencies still pushing, like loving parents—as Socrates called the law—to become the moral beings we strive to be, for ourselves and for our children, today and for the future, building on the wisdom of the past. So too we already know—without knowing it exactly—our highest goal. It is justice. No higher love guides us, to aim for a just society, a society in which humans can be kind to each and all, humans, sentient creatures, the universe in all its diversity.

"The Bible," Levinas writes in "On Jewish Philosophy," "*signifies* for all authentically human thought, for civilization *tout court*, whose authenticity can be recognized in peace, in *shalom*, and in the responsibility of one man for another" (ITN, 172). "We must isolate the ancient examples," Levinas has written, "and extend them to the new situations, principles and categories which they contain" (LR, "The State of Israel and the Religion of Israel," 262–263). As he says in "Revelation in the Jewish Tradition," which I cite in conclusion: "We can now appreciate in its full weight the reference made by the Revelation to exegesis, to the freedom attaching to this exegesis and to the participation of the person listening to the Word, which makes itself heard now, but can also pass down the ages to announce the same truth in different times" (LR, 195). Morality, justice, human history are neither false nor meaningless. Across the alternations of the time of conversation and history humanity retains its distinctiveness, at its best when renewing its past in aiming for a better future. Science is not an end in itself, and can only pretend to be by a cold and haughty—a dehumanized—close-mindedness. It is not the all, which, according to Ecclesiastes, "is vanity." The elevations of ethics, kindness, alleviation of suffering, the long labors of justice, these can only be dismissed at cost, for they give meaning to life and give meaning to science. Spinoza may deny it, but to do so he must deny his own humanity and the humanism of Judaism.

Chapter Seven

Thinking Least about Death

Mortality and Morality in Spinoza, Heidegger, and Levinas

Introduction: Life and Death

Herodotus, in chapters 32 and 33 of the first book of his *Histories*, tells of Solon's response to the question of his then host, the Persian king Croesus, regarding who is the happiest of all humans. We know, of course, that Croesus—powerful, wealthy, intelligent, military conqueror, absolute sovereign—expected to be the type or perhaps even the person named in the wise Solon's answer. But Solon did not oblige the king. He responded instead: "Call him until he dies not happy but fortunate" (16). It is an answer circumspect and cautious with a divine or at least a posthumous disinterest: one must await the end, the final closure, before one is able to pronounce judgment on the entirety of a person's life. Happiness—not passing pleasures and pains but a complete summing up, a "final judgment" as it were—is a function of totality. It depends on death and the verdict of survivors, the judgment of history, or perhaps only of a God, who because able also to read one's inner thoughts alone knows a person wholly, inside and out.

King Croesus was disappointed, to say the least, by this response and rewarded the wise Greek Solon with "neither largess nor honor" but "much indifference" as a result of it. Herodotus in his own wisdom continues the tale—lest we think Croesus's inhospitable rebuke merely the haughty reflex of a well-stroked vanity unaccustomed to and angered by deflation—by providing Croesus's reason: "he thought that a man must be an errant fool who makes no account of present good, but made men always wait and mark the end."[1] For Croesus apparently one can already, here and now, within an ongoing and unfinished earthly life, despite its uncertainties, its lack of guarantees, despite what might come later on but is not yet, enjoy sufficient well-being, success, and good fortune to be called happy, and rightfully so. Good times, good fortune, pleasures, who knows exactly what, eating, drinking, making merry, loving, being loved, but no doubt also of economic success, familial joys, convivial friendships, perhaps even public service and distinctions, not to mention personal and private spiritual accomplishments, these are for the sovereign Croesus the stuff of happiness, sufficient if not perfect, isles of contentment heedless of the whole. Only "an errant fool" would spoil the happiness of present blessings with morbid thoughts of mortality, finitude, uncertainty, instability, the unpredictability and fragility of the human condition. Happiness does not await death.

Here then already in this ancient report of an exchange occurring millennia ago, we find demarcated two great and rival orientations toward death—but actually they are two great and rival orientations toward life! On the one hand there is life lived under the sign of its closure, life gripped by its own mortality, become being-toward-death as its deepest signification. One thinks of the ancient Egyptian cult of death, of pharaohs born from childhood into a lifelong construction of tombs, sepulchers whose monumental remains today testify to a culture of death now itself dead. One thinks too of a certain Christian asceticism, fixation upon the afterlife, afterworlds, and to a spiritual love for a crucified God at the expense of human love and loves. On the other hand there is the life lived under the sign of a creative vitality, earthly plenitude, worldly pleasures, of desires met, where in a flesh inseparable from spirit, and a spirit inseparable from flesh, word and deed bound to one another, a life lived with family and friends, in communities, in the world of today as the heritage of yesterday, of ancestors, and as an inheritance for future generations, is celebrated across time

---

[1]. Herodotus, *Histories*, 17. Of course, later, in chapter 86 of book 1, King Croesus reconsiders the value of Solon's wisdom in view of his own defeat, the loss of his empire, and his immanent death at the hands of King Cyrus.

and history and in time and history. One thinks, for instance, of the incarnate this-worldly social spirituality of mainstream Judaism, or of the Epicureanism or bourgeois lifestyles that spread with the growing prosperity of today's postindustrial world, or of the social gospel of the Christianity of Walter Rauschenbusch, or the all-embracing Hindu activism of a Mohandas Gandhi, for whom religion, ethics, and politics are inextricably intertwined. For life lived in the grip of death, living as also dying, of the totality impossibly seen from the outside (eternity seeing time, the afterlife judging this life), or for the life lived to the full, in the fullness of time and history, with its infinite obligations, tasks, temptations, the open futurity of life producing more life with no end in sight—one sees quite well how the meaning of death and the meaning of life are inextricably bound to one another and how, at the same time, the sense of their intertwining is neither simple nor straightforward.

One thing is certain, however, that the defining characteristic of "contemporary" philosophy in contrast to all previous epochs of philosophy, whether ancient, medieval, or modern, involves a positive embrace rather than flight from the passage, duration, the temporality of time. Time is no longer envisioned and dismissed as an obstacle blocking truth or eternity or beauty, or whatever absolute one would set above it. Rather, it is the very means to whatever ends are taken to be highest. Love, for instance, is not distracted or diverted by the finite sensuous body; it is enacted through its desires, in collusion with them, higher as well as lower. Morality is not obeyed despite the body but because of it and by means of it. An intimate sense of the temporality of time is experienced as mortality, in death and dying, as human finitude. The so-called eternal soul is no longer a foreign visitor inexplicably "imprisoned" in the mortal body; the mortal body is the home of the human, of all that is best as well as all that is worst, for embodiment and hence mortality are the very conditions of all that humans are and aspire to.

Spinoza, therefore, in the very form of his intellectual devotion to the eternal is not our contemporary. Indeed, he is perhaps the most unrelenting, the most uncompromising proponent of a thoroughly modern (but not contemporary) vision of the scientific essence of philosophy: of life conceived purely through rationalist representation, purely by means of a propositional, deductive, universal, and necessary logic, continuing, but now inspired by mathematics, by Cartesian analytics, an abstract cognitive reduction of being to logic. No doubt, too, as we are better able to see and say with hindsight, the entire project of modern rationalism, dazzled by the clarity and distinctness of mathematics, was itself a diminution, a narrowing of horizons, in comparison to the broader range of the *logos* as *reason* to which the ancient Greek philosophers were attached. We have previously mentioned Aristotle's "four causes" in relation to Spinoza's but one cause, "efficient causality." But for this reason, too, at the ruination, as it were, of past philosophical developments, having narrowed and pruned the *logos* of Greek reason to a caricature of its former greatness, reducing the world and thought to the abstract clarity and distinctness without shadow found in mathematical axioms and demonstrations, Spinoza's philosophical efforts and especially his failure, provide us what is perhaps the sharpest contrast to better highlight what is new and distinctive and true in contemporary thought.

Thus we—we contemporaries—are not surprised that Spinoza denies to mortality any significance, for it is a denial completely in accord not only with the entire thrust of classical philosophy's sacrifice of time to eternity, but even more in accord with Spinoza's reduction of classical philosophy to the abstractions of logic and mathematics. Our first interest then is to present an accurate exposition of Spinoza's rational disposal of death. What also interests us in this regard is that at first glance Levinas too seems to deny the importance of mortality, even if his denial is radically different than Spinoza's. His seeming denial, however, must be understood less in relation to Spinoza, his antipode, than to the more celebrated reflections on death of his predecessor, his contemporary, his fellow phenomenologist and philosophical protagonist, Martin Heidegger. Levinas rejects Heidegger's account of mortality. It is Heidegger above all in contemporary thought, however, who has given to mortality an irreducible and central significance. This is true of his early writings, especially *Being and Time*, and of his later writings, in which humans are named as the "mortals."

In an interview of 1982, entitled "The Philosopher and Death," Levinas has this to say about the preceding: "Spinoza will say, as you know, that philosophers should think of nothing less than of death. Heidegger, by contrast, is the one who pursued philosophical thought's reference to death the farthest" (AT, 155). Levinas stakes out his own position "between" these two thinkers in the same interview: a phenomenologist opposed to Spinozist rationalism, an ethical thinker opposed to Heideggerian ontology. Negatively, a few sentences after the previous citation (citing Jean Wahl and from his own lectures of 1946, published in 1947 under the title *Time and the Other*), Levinas continues: "Heidegger calls the extreme possibility of death 'possibility of impossibility.' Without wishing to play on words, I have always thought that possibility implied a human power, whereas dying is 'unassumable': it is rather 'an impossibility of possibility.'"[2] On the positive side, in the same interview Levinas declares: "I think that *the Human* consists precisely in opening oneself to the death of the other, in being preoccupied with his or her death. . . . But above all, it is no longer just a question of going toward the other when he is dying, but of answering with one's presence the mortality of the living. That is the whole of ethical conduct" (AT, 157–158, 164). Heidegger and Levinas both object to Spinoza: death cannot be abstracted away by thought. And Heidegger is certainly right to emphasize the centrality of death as morality. But Levinas stands against Heidegger: the human mortality that counts most is not my own but the other's, whose mortal frailty I must care for and whose life I must protect and save.

Here, then, in their broadest strokes, are the three positions we will examine in turn in the following: Spinoza: death is nothing to knowledge, therefore the philosopher thinks least about it. Heidegger: mortality is *Dasein*'s essential way of being, anxiety in being-toward-death. Thus death is also nothing less than *Dasein*'s gateway to the most urgent and central of all issues, the "question of being." Levinas: indeed, humans are mortals, frail, subject to deprivation, illness, outrage, and wounds. But it is not my own death that I must take most seriously, as Heidegger suggests, but rather the other's death, the other's mortality and hence vulnerability, for such concern for-the-mortal-other is "the whole of ethical conduct," the very humanity of the human. We see then that it is not at all the case that Levinas thinks least about death like Spinoza. Rather, he thinks it completely otherwise than Spinoza but still least in the way Heidegger thinks about death. In contrast to Spinoza, Levinas takes mortality very seriously—Levinas is a contemporary philosopher, like Heidegger. But it is the other's death, the other's mortality, the other mortal vulnerability, that has

---

2. AT, 155. TO, 70, fn. 46; Levinas has this to say: "Death in Heidegger is not, as Jean Wahl says 'the impossibility of possibility,' but 'the possibility of impossibility.' This apparently Byzantine distinction has a fundamental importance."

priority over my own being-toward-death and mortality, and it is precisely through this asymmetrical priority of the other's death that my own subjectivity—singularized in responsibility to and for the other—finds its deepest meaning as moral and just.

Spinoza: To Not Think of Death

Proposition 67 of part IV of Spinoza's *Ethics*, now famous, states: "A free man thinks of death least of all things, and his wisdom is a meditation of life, not of death" (192). We know already that by "free" in this proposition Spinoza means "philosophical freedom," freedom of thought, which is nothing other than the eternal, immutable, and necessary intelligibility of what is.

We learn from the proof for this proposition that Spinoza is talking less about death as dying, per se, or even as the last moment, the moment of perishing, than about the *fear of death*, a person's existential-emotional attitude toward his own mortality. The proof reads: "A free man, that is, he who lives solely according to the dictates of reason, is not guided by fear of death (IV, Prop. 63), but directly desires the good (IV, Prop. 63, Cor.); that is (IV, Prop. 24), to act, to live, to preserve his own being in accordance with the principle of seeking his own advantage. So he thinks of death least of all things, and his wisdom is a meditation upon life" (192).

So Spinoza's "thinks of death least of all things" is really an admonition to think philosophically, to think in the abstemious rationalist manner Spinoza thinks, that is, to cognize or conceive truth rather than to imagine or emote. To think as such, then, is to not fear, and hence to not fear death. The admonition or observation is therefore but a specific instance of the more general admonition or observation that rules all of Spinoza's thought, namely, to think rationally about all things, to convert all the objects of consciousness into rationally justified thoughts, into "adequate ideas," but especially—in pursuit thereof—to cognize away the emotions that above all distract humans from truth and reality. Indeed, unlike parts I and II of the *Ethics*, which lay out Spinoza's intellectual truths, parts III to V are dedicated to subduing and conquering the emotions and imagination for the sake of intellection. To the extent that Spinoza's work expresses *admonitions* (despite the contradiction we have noted about such a possibility in a deterministic philosophy) in addition to being a set of observations, a dispassionate report of truth "in the geometrical manner," it is precisely and constantly the admonition to think, to cognize, to conceive, and thus to stay within the circuit of intellection, of thought thinking itself. Above all to be avoided is sinking into one's emotions, to be passively engaged by them, swayed or moved by them rather than to activate and be activated by the truth. Thinking sets one free, because true freedom is found only in thinking, thinking the necessary. Best of all would be not to emote at all, since to emote is to be swept up in emotions, swept up and hence swept away. We will elaborate further on this last point in chapter 8.

What is Spinoza's remedy against emotion? Emotions, which always only produce *enthusiasm*, the passivity of being carried away, can be demoted, deflated, disengaged, by thinking them through, discovering their efficient cause, by cognizing and hence converting them into rational truth. One thereby sees their *falsity* and hence their *unreality*, which for Spinoza following a long philosophical tradition beginning with Parmenides are one and the same thing. Emotions, after all, including the fear of death, are products of the undue influence of imagination and have nothing whatsoever in them of genuine ideation and hence reality, except to lead ignorant persons astray from knowledge and reality. Positively, then, Spinoza's whole message regarding death is contained in his advice to pursue "a free life, that is, he who lives solely according to the dictates of reason" is deluded no more by emotions. The truly free person is under the sway of no emotions whatsoever, is rather pure intellect, pure unadulterated cognition of truth—Spinozist beatitude.

Despite its obvious ostrich-like denials, we must take this manner of thinking more seriously than an aberrant idiosyncrasy of Spinoza alone or of his philosophical peers who also adhered to the same narrow early modern form of rationalism. This is because it expresses—even while overstating—the still-current dehumanized or vampire essence of "scientism," the belief that scientific knowledge, the set of all true propositions, or what Spinoza calls knowledge of "adequate ideas," is the one true explanation of all things in their ultimate reality—and the rest is but sound and fury signifying nothing. Such a reductive manner of thinking, even if no longer garbed in Spinozist form, is very much still with us. Today one does not even "think," rather brain synapses flare up and subside.

To be a free person, someone guided by reason, is to live in conformity to what is real, that which is revealed to rational knowledge and to rational knowledge alone, eliminating all contributions of wild imagination, of untamed emotion, of mere sentimentality, which have to do only with subjective illusions, falsehood, non-being. Such being the case, let us ask how Spinoza defines death, not the fear of death that is emotional and imaginary, but death—the termination of life, perishing—as understood by reason. What is death as something purely rational and hence in its true reality, assuming, for the moment, that death has sufficient reality, is sufficiently rational, to be understood by reason at all.

In fact Spinoza does define death, earlier in part IV of the *Ethics* in the scholium to proposition 39. To fully appreciate this definition of death we must first examine the proposition to which it is appended. The proposition reads: "Whatever is conducive to the preservation of the proportion of motion-and-rest, which the parts of the human body maintain toward one another, is good; and those things that effect a change in the proportion of motion-and-rest of the parts of the human body to one another are bad" (176). The notion of "proportion of motion-and-rest" is of central importance in Spinoza's system of thought. It is by means of this notion that the individuality of all material entities whatsoever are determined as distinct, and not merely the individuality of the human body. We have earlier been made aware that for reason or rationality as Spinoza understands these terms (in contrast to certain equivocations found in Descartes), humanity is not, as he says in the preface to part III of the *Ethics*, "a kingdom within a kingdom." Rather, humanity—individual humans, human society, human history, human civilization, and so on—must in its *truth* be understood as an integral and unexceptional part of nature, which is everywhere "always the same."[3] For modern science, unlike ancient and medieval science, all of nature, indeed all of reality, is homogeneous; there are no heavens or hells or "other worlds" whatsoever.[4] Homogeneous, however, does not mean an undifferentiated universe,

---

3. E, 102. "Nature is always the same, and its force and power of acting is everywhere one and the same. . . . I shall consider human actions and appetites just as if it were an investigation into lines, planes, or bodies" (102, 103).

4. See Koyré, *From the Closed World to the Infinite Universe*.

the "night in which all cows are black." Individuals are distinguishable from one another else they would not be individuals. But how are they distinguished? We have already seen Spinoza's answer: "proportion of motion-and-rest." Humans, like all "Bodies are distinguished from one another in respect of motion and rest, quickness and slowness, and not in respect of substance" (Part II, Proposition 13, Corollary, Scholium, Axiom 2, Lemma 1, 72). So, an identifiable something, a something distinct—which is also a something that, in accord with Spinoza's theory of *conatus*, perseveres in being and whose only impetus is to so maintain itself—is what has a particular and an identifiable "proportion of motion-and-rest," along with its impetus to maintain that proportion.

All this having been said, we can now return to the scholium to proposition 39, that is to say, to Spinoza's definition of death, to the rational truth and reality of death and not merely to some imaginary and arbitrary fantasy: "I understand a body to die when its parts are so disposed as to maintain a different proportion of motion-and-rest to one another." Not "my" death. Not a specifically "human death," mortality, in contrast to the perishing of other sentient beings, or even to the destruction of a material entity. Rather, death as no more and no less than a quantitative shift in an identifiable ratio of motion and rest sufficient to undo that ratio and hence to undo that identity. It is not a minor shift, an adjustment or modification let us say, which can occur to the same entity, but rather a shift in the proportion of motion and rest large enough, of sufficient magnitude, to produce a *different* proportion of motion and rest, that is, a different entity. Death is nothing other than such differing, the breakup and reconfiguration of an enduring ratio.

This definition leads Spinoza—ever so devotedly following what he believes to be the purely logical and necessary consequences of his propositions—to a result so peculiar, so at odds with common sense, that he spends the rest of his scholium on its elaboration. I will allow Spinoza to speak for himself; his next two sentences: "For I do not venture to deny that the human body, while retaining blood circulation and whatever else is regarded as essential to life, can nevertheless assume another nature quite different from its own. I have no reason to hold that a body does not die unless it turns into a corpse; indeed, experience seems to teach otherwise" (177). What is he talking about? That a human can "assume another nature quite different" clearly is meant to refer to radical changes in a living body, a body "retaining blood circulation and whatever else is regarded as essential to life." Some changes are sufficiently radical for Spinoza to equate them with death, that is, with his definition of death, that is, a change in an entity's ratio of motion and rest such that it is no longer the original entity but another or part of another or parts of many others. Just as the *living body* dies when it becomes a *corpse body*, the body can also undergo sufficient changes to warrant considering it another body in the same way, that is, as having died. But what does this mean, what are we talking about more exactly? I will turn to Spinoza's own two examples in a moment; first let us reflect further to figure out just what Spinoza is saying.

What Spinoza means is that an entity, such as a living body, being defined by a specific proportion of motion and rest, becomes another entity, another body, when that proportion changes beyond a certain point. In human parlance, regarding the life of human bodies, humans call such a drastic change "death." Spinoza, however, having adopted a thoroughly scientific outlook, integrates such human language and perspective into a larger naturalist scientific view whereby all things, all definable entities, are individuated by and change through variations in their identifying "proportion of motion-and-rest." What we humans call "death," then, is in truth properly but a change in the "proportion of motion-and-rest" such that the defining equilibrium of one body is sufficiently transformed such that it can no longer be considered as, and no longer is, the same body. It "dies," becomes another body or bodies, defined as having their own unique ratios of motion-and-rest. No doubt this view makes sense in relation to the human living body that becomes a corpse, because we know the corpse rots, is eaten away by maggots, decomposes, and turns, as the Bible puts it, into "dust." But as we have heard, though not fully made clear, Spinoza is actually accepting as true something more, because he follows the full logic of his definition regardless of contrary common sense or hallowed conviction. For Spinoza it is possible for a human to "die" without turning into a corpse. How so?

The two examples Spinoza gives from "experience" are, first, "a certain Spanish poet who was seized with sickness, and although he recovered, he remained so unconscious of his past life that he did not believe that the stories and tragedies he had written were his own." And second, "a man of advanced years" who comparing himself to his infancy and hence to infants, "believes their nature to be so different from his own that he could not be persuaded that he had ever been a baby if he did not draw a parallel from other cases" (177). I will be returning to these cases in the following chapter. Let us turn here to the sick Spaniard. Presently having no conscious memory of his previous literary self, Spinoza is saying that the truth is that that formerly poetic Spaniard "died." The poetic Spaniard and the sick Spaniard are two sufficiently different entities, owing to the difference in consciousness, so that while we might casually say they are two different persons, for Spinoza they are literally two different persons, such is the reality, the truth: the poetic Spaniard died, the sick Spaniard lives—these are two different beings. They are as different, so Spinoza's reasoning teaches, so different fundamentally, in their respective definitions and identities, as discontinuous from one another as a living body and a corpse body, that one can properly be said to be dead while the other to live. Not being a Spinozist, I am unable to not wonder if the Spaniard's mother or wife or child would agree. Would his creditors agree? No doubt a radical change has occurred, and no doubt it has serious consequences—but is it really equivalent to death? Spinoza will have none of our "common sense" or "settled convictions"; he is scientist first and last. The Spanish poet is dead; long live the sick Spaniard.

So, death for Spinoza is change of identity. And identity is determined solely by a differentiated and enduring ratio of motion and rest. The very use of such an unscientific, ordinary language term as "death" is already far too great a concession to anthropocentrism, a concession to the dissimulations of the imaginary and the emotional. One must remain rational: whether the change is from a living person to a corpse, as we ordinarily think of death, or from a living person with one identity to another living person with a different identity, has no import with regard to what Spinoza believes to be the rational core, the truth, the reality, of what would otherwise be a vague and untrustworthy notion of death. "It sometimes happens," Spinoza states in the same scholium, "that a man undergoes such changes that I would not be prepared to say that he is the same person" (177).

Arguably more questions are raised by Spinoza's definition of death, or of identity change, than are resolved by it. At what point is a quantitative change in "proportion of motion-and-rest" sufficient to be counted as a qualitative change? How is this to be determined? Who decides? Presumably frozen water, ice, is something qualitatively different than liquid water, a fluid, but is cold water something essentially different, another entity, from hot water? At what point is memory loss equivalent to loss of personal identity? More generally, at what point is one ratio another ratio? Spinoza might answer that our presumptions are already false, that hardness and softness, solidity and liquidity, like hot and cold, are merely imaginary differences, merely subjective and arbitrary constructions, tricks of language or grammar perhaps, as Nietzsche thought, without rational truth or being. He would say the same of "personal identity," pleading that our present ignorance of human biochemistry is no excuse for making an exception. He would answer that throughout all these illusory changes, from solid to liquid and vice versa, the water—a set ratio of hydrogen and oxygen, as we now know—indeed has not changed, has not lost its identity, and hence remains identifiably the same. He would say that when the hydrogen atoms separate from the oxygen atoms, when the compound is decomposed, then indeed, with the emergent new and different ratios of hydrogen atoms within themselves (of their electrons, neutrons, protons, etc.), and of oxygen atoms within themselves (the same), the water has "died," has lost its identity, is no more, and other material entities, the ratios of motion-and-rest called "hydrogen" and "oxygen" are now there instead. And so too with humans, who are no exceptions, no kingdom within a kingdom. Spinoza's challenge: a lion eats a human, we call him dead; a person goes mad, is there anything more than sentiment and custom that prevent us from calling his pre-mad personhood dead?

But is Spinoza's willingness to regard human identity changes, changes in consciousness, death, sufficient to assimilate humans into nature? Is there really equivalence between H_2O and individual humans? Does not Spinoza's admission that a certain level of amnesia, as in the case of the sick Spaniard, warrants distinguishing two persons, then certainly lesser levels of memory loss do not. How decide the level? Can it ever be a purely rational judgment? If the Spaniard forgets where he left his sword, is he a different person? What about if he cannot remember the name of his second cousin, or of his mother? If he is blinded and can no longer see? If he loses one arm in a swordfight, is it enough, or must both be cut off, or his legs as well as his arms? If the Spaniard get blind drunk one night, is he someone else, and if so, only for that night? Surely Spinoza is playing fast and loose with the notion of human death. Change in "proportion of motion-and-rest" cannot serve as he wishes it to serve. Is it not more likely that it is for reasons such as these rather than anything more scientific or intellectual that Spinoza concludes his long scholium with the following sentence: "But I prefer to leave these matters unresolved, so as not to afford material for the superstitious to raise new problems" (E, 177). But be sure, despite Spinoza's wont, we will continue raising new problems, without superstition.

Death is that about which Spinoza thinks least and of which he has no fear because it is nothing exceptional. Indeed nothing is or can be exceptional in the totality without exit of the immutable, eternal, and necessary intelligibility that is the true nature of the universe for Spinoza. Death has no sting, not mine, not yours, not anyone else's, not my pet's or yours, because none of these are special in any way. Every entity is but a node in the web of strictly necessary causes and deductions. Nothing interrupts, nothing disturbs, each thing is what it is, and all unfolds of necessity. "It is impossible for a man not to be part of Nature and not to undergo changes other than those which can be understood solely through his own nature and of which he is the adequate cause" (E, 156).

Change can only come to an entity externally, as it were, because each entity has no other internal impetus than to persist. And yet at the same time change cannot be external, can only be the effect of a prior cause in a sequence without interruption or break. The Spaniard had to go mad; it was not an accident, nothing haphazard, mere chance. To be sure, Spinoza "supports" persistence, continuity, equilibrium, and opposes change. "Each man," Spinoza writes, as if making a recommendation when in fact he is only describing a necessity, "as far as in him lies, should endeavor to preserve his own being" (E, 164). Perseverance is a matter of course; no "should" is involved. Destruction, or more exactly, redistribution of proportions of rest-and-motion, is also a matter of course. As for particular individuals, John, Fido, or TWA, which come and go, because "all particular things are contingent and perishable," we "have no adequate knowledge of their duration" (E, 85). To be sure "God" knows, which is to say, the intelligibility of the universe is one of strict necessity, even if we finite minds, we human minds, scientist and philosophers, do not know. Death is thus replaced by the identity changes that are constituent elements of causal sequences that are strictly necessary, even if the precise sequence of such changes are presently unknown to finite minds like our own.

The true life, in other words, is the life of necessity and permanence, the "life" of the mind, of perfectly clear and distinct ideas, "adequate ideas" exclusively—eternal ideas, immutable reality *sub specie aeternitatis*. It is here that Spinoza is able to declare, at the same time endorsing Socrates's reasoning in the *Phaedo* (from which, as Kojève notes, Plato conspicuously absents himself): "The human mind cannot be absolutely destroyed along with the body, but something of it remains, which is eternal" (E, 213). Such is the solace of the rationalist philosopher who affects to obliterate death while alive to the extent that his mind cognizes adequate ideas. And thus Spinoza offers the following consoling words: "death is less hurtful in proportion as the mind's clear and distinct knowledge is greater" (E, 220). Death as something special is merely a fiction of imagination and emotion, an unhappy phantom of ignorance and feeblemindedness. We detect behind this intellectual resoluteness, behind Spinoza's chipper advice not to fear death because it is unreal, the whispers of an ancient consolation, voiced by Parmenides, who is perhaps only repeating an even older idea from India: "For never will this be proved, that things that are not, are" (qtd. in Barnes, 158). Death has no sting because death is not.

A final observation needs to be added regarding Spinoza and death. The reason Spinoza, the scientist, the philosopher, or the "free man," thinks least about death is because such a person has escaped into the eternal realm of intellect and idea. There what "unfree" humans—non-philosophers, non-scientists—take to be something special and fearful, *sub specie aeternitatis* is but a piece of a homogeneous nature where ratios change according to a necessary causality, even if that causality is not yet entirely known by finite human intellects. The additional point I want to underscore is that in not thinking about death neither does Spinoza think about life. Spinoza's rationalism is mechanical, or what I have been calling "abstract," made up only of logical deduction in the realm of intellect and efficient causality in the realm of matter. In neither case is there room for life, which is to say, growth, irreversibility, genesis, regeneration, reproduction, fecundity, or an infinite future.

Thinking life as life, biological, organic, growing life, life as an irreducible dimension of the real, so important to Aristotle, did not enter or reenter into contemporary philosophy until the "vitalist" philosophy of Henri Bergson.[5] His notion of "duration" was meant to

---

5. See chapter 1, "Bergson and the Emergence of an Ecological Age," in Cohen, *Ethics, Exegesis and Philosophy*, 27–52, where Philo, Spinoza, and Bergson are taken to be hinges in a four-part historical-conceptual periodization of philosophy.

correct the deficiencies not only of mechanistic or abstract representational thought, such as Spinoza's, but also the "hylo-morphism" of Aristotle and Aquinas. In any event, it is as true to say of Spinoza—contra Spinoza's own self-characterization—that he thinks *least about life* as to say that he thinks *least about death*. He simply has no room for the biological as an irreducible category in his thought. Life and death, like good and evil, or just and unjust, cannot figure as "adequate ideas" within his rational system, hence they must be illusory, fantasy products of imagination, figures of charged emotions, no more than sorry expressions of the ignorance of the unlearned and unruly many. While it is true that Spinoza was excommunicated by the Amsterdam Jewish community, it is also true that intellectually Spinoza is quick to chop off and excommunicate whatever refuses to fit nicely into his Procrustean bed of rationality. Unfortunately, as with the original Procrustean bed, much real blood is spilled by the resulting exclusions. Spinoza thinks least about death, but for precisely the reasons that make his entire philosophy dead, inert, stillborn. He calls it "eternal." Could it not with equal justice be called lifeless, frozen, robotic, abstract, or escapist? Certainly from the perspective of contemporary philosophy it is so. To die while living is hardly a life at all. Pascal thought he was wagering eternity against the briefest of times, but in fact he was wagering all the time of one's life against a thought, and a merely wishful one at that.

Though we are about to turn to Heidegger, a philosopher who thought most about death, let us first, in a teasing anticipation, insert a citation from Levinas regarding Spinoza and death. Levinas too will advise going beyond fear for one's own mortality, but he does so in a way entirely otherwise and in radical opposition to Spinoza, as well as to Heidegger. In *Totality and Infinity*, Levinas writes: "Contrary to the Spinozist tradition, this going beyond death is produced not in the universality of thought but in the pluralist relation, in the goodness of being for the Other, in justice" (301–302). Antipodes from Spinoza; we will soon see more precisely what is entailed in such a claim.

Heidegger: My Mortal Being

In the sharpest contrast with Spinoza, perhaps no philosopher has thought more about death or brought death more to the center of philosophy than Martin Heidegger. Indeed, the turning point of his magnum opus, *Being and Time*, the awakening of an individual to philosophy, to "thinking," to the "question of being" itself, is the instant when *Dasein* in a revelatory mood (*Stimmung*) of anxiety (*Angst*) recognizes that it is going to die, that it is a dying being not just at the end but all the time, and thereby understands with the greatest existential force that its future is only *possible* and not necessary. "It ["Death, as possibility"] is the possibility of the impossibility of every way of comporting oneself toward anything, of every way of existing. . . . Being-towards-death, as anticipation of possibility, is what first *makes* this possibility *possible*, and sets it free as possibility" (BT, 307).

Far from being abstract, time itself, the future as possibility, is a function of mortality, of being-toward-death, which while giving a certain priority to the future, appropriates a self-presence always already specified by a past, a past which is itself, and as projecting a future, embedded in the unfolding of historical—or what Heidegger calls "epochal"—being. Time and history are complex structures, but it is clear that facing death represents the great moment of awakening to their import and way of being.

Dasein in its very being is a being-toward-death (*Sein zum Tode*). This felt recognition lies at the core of Heidegger's existential account of subjectivity: only in and through anxious being-toward-death—one's "ownmost non-relational possibility" (BT, 307)—does the human subject come to itself in its genuine being, become "authentic" (*eigentlich*). To try to avoid such a realization, to flee or escape from what is in truth an anxiety in the face of being-toward-death, this, and not Spinozist ignorance, is what would count as an inauthentic (*uneigentlich*) way of being: losing oneself in the irresponsible anonymity of what "everybody" does, of what "they" say, the swirl but also the mediocrity of everyday life. But so too to flee to the mind, to lose oneself in abstract representational thinking, in theorizing, contemplation, in a system such as Spinoza's, say, is also a flight from death, flight from facing being authentically. Heidegger's thought, rooted in a positive and existential embrace of mortality, while not at antipodes from Spinozism in the manner of Levinas, is in its own way also at antipodes from Spinozism. It will see in theory not truth but flight from being. It will see in "thinking least about death" not "beatitude" in the eternal intellectual order of the universe but flight from truth.

Because there is already an enormous secondary literature on death and mortality in Heidegger, here I will provide only a brief sketch of their main significations. Indeed, asking some readers' forgiveness, for this brief sketch I will borrow a subsection on Heidegger from a chapter, entitled "Thinking Least about Death—Contra Heidegger," from my previous book, *Levinasian Meditations* (58–61). I will add comments here and there referring to Spinoza.

(1) Death is "ownmost"—nothing is more one's own than death. Possessions, home, friends, pets, gardens, ideas, can all be alienated, but not one's own death. For Heidegger the human subject is "individuated," becomes its "authentic" or "genuine" self, properly occupies the *Da*, the "there" of *Da-sein*, "existence" or "being-there," in being-for-death. While Heidegger in a certain sense like Spinoza rejects the human as a "kingdom within a kingdom," he does this not to integrate the human into homogeneous nature but to characterize human willfulness—including flight into theory—as superficial. To be one's own being is to recognize that Dasein is "given" by Being. Nevertheless, to attain such recognition first requires also acknowledging the irreducible and individuating status of mortality for *Dasein*. For Heidegger it is as "mortal" that humans are given by being and play their role in the disclosure of being.

(2) Death is "nonrelational"—in being-toward-death the authentic subject has broken from all abstract relations with others: "all its relations to any other Dasein have been undone" (BT, 294). This is why sociality is itself suspect in Heideggerian thought. "*The 'they,'*" as Heidegger calls the anonymity or nonsubject of everyday social life, "*does not permit us the courage for anxiety in the face of death*" (BT, 298). Thus it is not the mass congenital stupidity, a succumbing to bodily desires and imagination, as with Spinoza, but escape from death, fleeing one's own anxious mortality, that seduces most people most of the time, and in some measure all people some of the time, to escape into the oblivion of mass mentality.

(3) Death is "not to be outstripped"—in being-for-death Dasein understands death as the inescapable, unavoidable, most certain future, in a certainty that "demands Dasein itself in the full authenticity of its existence" (BT, 310). Only a theorizing outlook—out of touch with its own mortal existence—such as Spinoza's philosophy, his scientism, can mistakenly believe that death can be theorized away and assimilated to identity change, or, more broadly, to homogeneous nature as a system of deductions and causes. There is no avoiding death because at every moment Dasein in its existence, in its very being is being-for-death, mortal. For Heidegger death cannot be outstripped even if one flees it—because even in fleeing it, its dominance remains. Fleeing death, in other words, is yet another way to be-toward-death, an inauthentic

way. But whether realized authentically or inauthentically, death can never be theorized away, expunged by ideas.

(4) Death reveals Dasein as "possibility"—facing the "*possibility of the impossibility of any existence at all*" (BT, 307). Dasein sees itself as a projection into possible futures. We saw this in the first citation from Heidegger in this chapter. Obviously, then, Heidegger does not call upon "eternity," as does Spinoza in conformity to all classical thought, as an alternative to possibility. Possibility is itself no mere theoretical abstraction but finds its concrete signification for Heidegger in each Dasein's deathbound, finite temporalizing and in a community's epochal "historicizing."

(5) Being-toward-death is disclosed through the mood of anxiety (*Angst*)—"Being-toward-death is essentially anxiety" (BT, 310). Radically opposed to Spinoza's attack on emotion and imagination, for Heidegger it is precisely through a mood, through anxiety specifically, that mortality is revealed and has its proper sense. Theory, suppressing mood, loses touch with death—and so Spinoza would have it always and everywhere (what Levinas calls Spinoza's "unlimited anesthesia"). Husserl's phenomenology broadened the horizon of thought, of what counts as legitimizing evidence, to include emotion, and it is into that horizon that both Heidegger and Levinas travel, a route explicitly barred by and to Spinoza's intellectualist rationalism. For Heidegger, then, the phenomenon of death, its irreducible meaning, can only be captured and its significance recognized in the mood of anxiety, despite the inability of Spinozist theorizing to admit any such thing. Heidegger explicitly states that while theorizing knows "perishing," it cannot comprehend "death" or "mortality," which each Dasein undergoes in the first person.

(6) Being-toward-death is a disclosure, illumination, indeed an ontological prehension. Dasein as being-toward-death *understands* in the sense Heidegger indicates in the introduction to *Being and Time*: "Dasein . . . is ontically distinguished by the fact that, in its very Being, that Being is an *issue* for it. . . . Understanding *of Being is itself a definite characteristic of Dasein's Being*" (32). No such "understanding" is even possible to Spinoza, except to be immediately dismissed as illusion and ignorance.

(7) Finally, because being in the anxiety of being-toward-death is not a self-understanding Dasein is able to maintain constantly, once and for all, as it were, after realizing itself at least once in such a way Dasein then lives in alternating states attuned to or fallen (*Verfall*) from such self-understanding. For this reason Heidegger characterizes authentic

Dasein in *Being and Time* as "resolute" (*entschlossen*). In his later thought he gives up this term because it is too willful, and characterizes Dasein's mortal openness to being as a "letting be" or "release" (*Gelassenheit*). Either way, against Spinozist "freedom" of logical thought, a freedom that is equivalent to logical and causal necessity, Heidegger acknowledges a "passivity," a "freedom of essence," as receptivity, attunement (*Gestimmtheit*), hearkening to the significance of being's historical move. In both cases, willfulness or free choice is rejected as merely epiphenomenal, but in Heidegger's case it is replaced with historical-epochal "generosity" while in Spinoza's with strict necessity.

Heidegger and Levinas, in their sharp differences from Spinoza, reflect all the differences that divide classical from contemporary thought, which is to say they take seriously embodiment, temporality, language, and history; which Spinoza does not. Body, time, discourse, and history are no longer denigrated as errors, illusions, missteps, or sins, to be surpassed in the name of spirit, ideas, and eternity, but they are recognized as the very means by which humans think truly and live fully. Mortality is therefore not dismissed along with all that is finite. Inexorable, ineluctable, it is our very being, irreducibly meaningful. For Heidegger mortality is not only the key to the individuation and mindfulness of human beings; it is nothing less also than the revelatory portal of being itself.[6]

---

6. It is hardly controversial, and I am certainly not the only one to see in being-toward-death the linchpin of Heidegger's thought. In a lecture of the 1950s, Leo Strauss contextualizes the point as follows: "Yet while according to Plato and Aristotle *to be* in the highest sense means to be *always*, Heidegger contends that *to be* in the highest sense means *to exist*, that is to say, *to be* in the manner in which man *is*: *to be* in the highest sense is constituted by mortality." I mention this not so much for its own sake but rather to draw attention to another quite telling remark Strauss makes in the same lecture: "Only a great thinker could help us in our intellectual plight [of historicist relativism]. But here is the great trouble: the only great thinker in our time is Heidegger." Leo Strauss, "An Introduction to Heideggerian Existentialism," in Leo Strauss, *The Rebirth of Classical Political Rationalism*, 37, 29. Strauss died in 1973; it is a pity, to say the least (and surprising, too, given his intellectual sensitivity and erudition), that he was apparently unaware of Levinas's thought and therefore unaware of its greatness as an alternative to Heidegger, that is to say, as an answer to Strauss's "intellectual plight" (a better answer, I think Strauss might well have come to see, than his own somewhat skittish affiliation to "natural law" theory).

Having reduced reason to a rational calculus in thrall to modern mathematical science, when Spinoza distinguishes three types of knowledge, the most human, most finite of them is dismissed as sheer irrationality. "Knowledge of the first kind," merely opinion or fantasy, is a tissue of imaginings without reality. "Knowledge of the first kind is the only cause of falsity; knowledge of the second and third kind is necessarily true" (E, II, Prop. 41, 91). "Knowledge of the second kind," which Spinoza calls "reason" in the strict sense, is made up of "adequate ideas of the properties of things" (E, II, Scholium 2, 90), which is to say, it is made up of ideas of causal necessity. Such is what we would call scientific knowledge, the knowledge discovered by the natural sciences. "Knowledge of the third kind," finally, which Spinoza also calls "intuition," knows "the essence of things" (E, II, Scholium 2, 90). Here is the philosopher's knowledge of the whole, the system, the intelligible totality—that is, Spinoza's *Ethics*—within whose framework the ongoing research of scientific knowledge (knowledge of the second kind) is pursued. All real knowledge is theoretical.

For Heidegger, in contrast, what he considers "the essence of reason" or "thinking" is not determined by or as representational thought or theory. Theory, which Heidegger dismisses as mere "calculation," is an evasion of and obstacle to genuine thinking. It is always only a second-order or derivative discourse, grounded first of all in praxis. But insofar as the instrumental world of praxis is ultimately for the sake of Dasein, its deeper ground lies in the "issue of being," which is the authentic way of being of mortal Dasein. Thus hermeneutics, the taking of "this as that," or what in the later Heidegger is called "poetic thinking," is the only approach suitable to reveal the truth of being. Spinoza, of course, dismisses all the latter as mere "words and images," "narratives," products of ignorance having nothing whatsoever to do with truth or being.

Instead of shedding its existence, its mortality, in the intellectual exclusivism of deductive logic and causal necessity, Dasein's deepest way of being, its very existence, its time and place, temporality and history, is a disclosive prehension: "fore-conception" (*Vorgriff*), "fore-having" (*Vorhabe*), and "fore-sight" (*Vorsicht*). The details of Heidegger's account of disclosure, of *aletheia*, are not our concern here. The point is that truth in its deepest sense is not found through subsumption of subject and predicate, or conformity of proposition and reality, or the coherence of the noncontradictory, and the like, which all operate within and structure a merely representational-propositional logic. Rather, *Dasein* in its very existence is the "issue" or "question" of being, the opening through which the "ontological difference" between beings and their being finds its voice, a voice resonating with time, place, and history.

So for Heidegger truth or reason are only derivatively limited to the correspondence of ideas with reality, or, in Spinoza's case, with the intellectual vision of the equivalence of reality with necessary and eternal ideas. Rather they arise more originally as *disclosure*, revelation, openness, which in the final account means truth and reason are given through *ontological difference* as the very "question of being." Mortality, then, ultimately raises and signifies the question of being.

Thus while Spinoza's notions of reason and truth are rationalist, a calculus of deductions and causes, Heidegger's is hermeneutic, aesthetic, prehensive, listening to what is as it gives itself, prior to all theorizing. Hermeneutics is aesthetic in the sense the ancient Greeks (and Kant) gave to this term: the manifestation of sensible manifestation, the show or shining of what is—whether through nature, art, sport, war, politics, or thinking. No wonder then that Spinoza's and Heidegger's conception of death, as their conceptions of life, and of the meaning of meaning in relation to truth, have so little in common.

Levinas: Dying for the Other

Levinas understands death and dying at the intersection of phenomenology and ethics. Following Husserl he tries to grasp its sense phenomenologically as far as phenomenology goes. But he discovers that to understand it truly requires admitting an ethical sense that does not properly fit into the framework of "intentionality" and "constitution" so basic to phenomenology. Furthermore he discovers that the ethical sense subtends the phenomenological sense, conditions it, even if phenomenology cannot elucidate such conditioning in the descriptive scientific language of phenomenology. Just as being is ruptured by ethics, the "is" by the "ought," which as such exerts a higher exigency than knowing, so too phenomena are ruptured by the "enigma" of the face of the other person as moral obligation, as elicitation of moral responsibility, and ultimately as a call to justice for all. Though Levinas and Heidegger both develop their original thought as existential students of Husserlian phenomenology, and hence both reject the unexamined presuppositions of methodological adherence to the abstract propositional logic that orders the rationalism of a Spinoza, say, there is nevertheless an enormous divide, indeed an opposition, separating the moral exigencies that ultimately drive Levinas's thought and the ontological-hermeneutic thinking that underwrites Heidegger's. What we will see is that though he disagrees with both Spinoza and Heidegger, Levinas also has an original and profound vision of the significance of death, indeed he discovers in relation to mortality the deepest significance of morality and justice.

Three texts will guide us, though we will refer to others as well. First, from the third part of *Time and the Other*, published in 1947, two contiguous subsections entitled "Suffering and Death" and "Death and the Future" (68–73). Second, from the third section of *Totality and Infinity*, published in 1961, two contiguous subsections entitled "The Will and Death" and "Time and the Will: Patience" (232–240). And third, a short lecture of 1987 given at a colloquium on Heidegger's thought, appropriately enough, and published as an article in 1988, which was reprinted in Levinas's collection *Entre Nous* under the title "Dying for . . ." (207–217).

Levinas's "Dying for . . ." is for the most part an exposition and critical analysis of Heidegger's notion of being-toward-death in its relation to the sociality of "being-with" (*Mitsein*) others, as elaborated in *Being and Time*. It is a remarkable text, not only for its positive and original contributions but also because it shows a philosopher of great and rare originality at the height of his intellectual maturity and creativity, after more than half a century still responding with great care and attention to Heidegger's early and most brilliant phenomenological work. It is a great show, and for us a great example of intellectual respect, probity, and humility, without in the least compromising Levinas's originality or his specific criticisms of or his frontal opposition to Heideggerian thought. It is too bad, we can only shake our heads, that Heidegger apparently had no similar regard, for he did not once respond or even mention the radical and sustained critique of his thought that Levinas had been elaborating in lectures, articles, and major books of philosophy for more than forty years of Heidegger's active intellectual life. Actually, we will be in a better position to understand in concluding that this asymmetry too speaks to the very difference dividing their respective philosophies, one oracular, the other conversational. In any event, on the concluding two pages of "Dying for . . . ," after his extensive analysis of Heidegger's account of death, Levinas presents an excellent summary of his own quite different thoughts on the meaning of death.

A fourth and relevant text readers may wish to consult is the transcript of an interview of Levinas conducted by Christian Chabanis in 1982, published the same year under the title "The Philosopher and Death" and now found in a collection of Levinas's shorter writings entitled *Alterity and Transcendence* (153–168). Though unlike the first three texts, which are publications by Levinas, this one is the transcript of an interview, it has the remarkable virtue nonetheless of presenting a clear and succinct reiteration of the entire multilayered account of the meaning of death that Levinas had elaborated from his earliest to his last philosophical reflections.

We have seen that Spinoza dissipates death within homogeneous and lawful Nature. While embracing science, affirming scientific knowledge, indeed supplementing its quantitative formulations with phenomenological or descriptive science, Levinas rejects scientism, that is, the exclusionary totalization of science, as one finds in Spinoza. Scientism, which is a metaphilosophy, must be distinguished from science, which is knowledge based in evidence. No doubt the heady enthusiasm of scientism is easier to explain in Spinoza's day, when the new mathematical sciences were just making their way and first presented bold, even astonishing, discoveries in astronomy, physics, and mathematics especially. The authority of myth, the trickery of superstition, the deceptions of religion, the randomness of folkways, the injustices of feudalism, and the like, would all fall—such was the enthusiasm—before the irrefutable truths of science that were open to all intelligent persons. To understand the historical reasons for Spinoza's scientism, however, is not to justify or condone it.

Today there can be no such excuses. Today we see that science is a double-edged sword, illuminating and darkening. Today when metaphysicians of science try to convince us they are discovering the "genes" that make humans moral, or the "cerebral synapses" that cause poetry or love or loyalty, we should be alarmed. "The only decision which, in such conditions," Georges Bataille wrote insightfully in "Andre Breton: Ode to Charles Fourier," "would not be completely ridiculous is to say to what extent scientific research has deprived this stable world of truth" (155). We can only agree with such a diagnosis. I will not here repeat Husserl's analysis and warnings in the *Crisis*, where he diagnosed a world gone mad—Nazis, Italian and Spanish fascists, Soviet dictatorship—owing to a science boastful in its narrow-mindedness, where no truths, no meanings, nothing would be acceptable, true or real, outside the confines of a quantitative "objectivism." But I will cite Levinas: "When knowledge takes on an ecstatic signification," he writes in *Totality and Infinity*, commenting on the intellectual highhandedness, the hubris, indeed the imperialism of knowing that knows only itself, thereby turning what is really a limitation, as Kant understood, into an absolute license and bludgeon, "it issues in Spinozist unity, relative to which the I is but a thought. And the alleged movement of transcendence is reduced to a return from an imaginary exile" (274–275). All would be dream and illusion, superstition and chicanery, ideology and false consciousness, error and ignorance, until scientifically weighed and certified. Quantity would be the only password, mathematics the savior of the real. But thankfully—so Husserl taught in the name of phenomenology, and so Levinas teaches, moving beyond phenomenology, in the name of ethics—all is not so easily contained and dismissed in the all-inclusive categories of science and formal logic; all is not either rational or irrational, on or off, one or zero, positive or negative, being or non-being. There is the better than being, which cuts across and orients both.

Levinas radically challenges the two key elements of Heidegger's account of death: first that the deepest meaning of death is the finitude of being-toward-death, and second that what is disclosed to Dasein in being-toward-death is its highest vocation as the question of being.

Let us say that it is quite natural for two students of Husserl to disagree with one another. Husserl, after all, conceived of phenomenology as a science, as the work of teams of investigators, researchers all intent on rigorously describing the essence of various chosen topics rigorously, with the greatest clarity and distinctness, and of course subject to correction and revision by other phenomenological scientists. In a certain sense a phenomenological study is at once a description of the phenomenon under study and a manual to instruct other phenomenologists how to discover the same significations. I do not think that Levinas would disagree with such a picture of phenomenology, or would he think of his own phenomenological analyses as excluded from criticism and revision by alternative or further researches. Heidegger, however, thoroughly reinterpreted phenomenology. As early as the introduction to *Being and Time*, he had come to see its core not in terms of Husserl's rigorous descriptive science, with teams of like-minded and correcting researchers, but rather as hermeneutic ontology, one that eventually led to the primacy of "poetic thinking," the poetic thinking, as it turns out, of the especially sensitive and receptive thinker (who, as it turns out, was Heidegger himself). We know that Husserl was deeply upset with this development, seeing in it a betrayal of phenomenology's scientific aspirations. Ernst Cassirer criticized Heidegger directly for just this—loss of verifiability, of epistemological standards—at Davos in 1929. Despite these developments, despite his reinterpretation of phenomenology as "fundamental ontology," in the book by which he made his name in the philosophical world, *Being and Time*, one finds careful phenomenological analyses still recognizably close to the Husserlian scientific model, even if they are cast by Heidegger into an ontological framework said to be primary. Such, for instance, are the analyses of "ready-to-hand" and "present-at-hand," "the they," "ecstatic" temporality, and, let us add, Heidegger's account of being-toward-death. At a certain level, then, as we shall see, Levinas's alternative account of death and dying is a straightforward phenomenological critique of Heidegger's phenomenological account. As such it is a corrective, better "science" in the phenomenological sense, more accurate, more precise, clearer, more distinct descriptions of the phenomenon.

But Levinas also parts company with Husserl, in seeing the true basis of phenomenology outside of phenomenology, not in ontology, to be sure, but in ethics, in the "better than being." From this perspective, Levinas will fault Husserl *and* Heidegger for remaining within the orbit of knowledge and being, even if knowledge for Heidegger has become hermeneutic-ontological and for Husserl it remains descriptive-representational. For Levinas the ultimate structure of death is not *disclosure* at all—whether its revelation is best captured by natural science, by descriptive phenomenology, or by hermeneutic ontology. Death is not a revelation, not a disclosure, not any type of knowing. Its deepest meaning is ethical, the *moral exigency* exerted by the other person, my responsibility for the other's mortality. Thus the first significance of death is not my finitude, even if such finitude be interpreted as the gateway to being itself, but the other's finitude, the other's mortal vulnerability and suffering. The ultimate structure of morality, and the highest meaning of mortality, lies thus in the possibility—surely unwanted—of "dying for" the other.

With this overview in mind, let us now turn to look at the several layers and many nuances of Levinas's account of death, highlighting its phenomenological significations as well as its ultimate moral structure. Because in my previous book, *Levinasian Meditations*, I have also presented Levinas's account of death,[7] the following will borrow from there, though in a more abbreviated form, sufficient, it is my hope, for our present comparisons. I have divided Levinas's unitary account into nine elements, dimensions or layers of sense, the first few very clearly predominantly phenomenological, the latter ethical. They are all always present, even if the last two, "dying for . . ." and "justice" give ultimate weight and meaning to mortality, penetrating through all the layers, indeed uplifting them.

Suffering

For Levinas mortality does not first announce itself in the mood of anxiety. Rather, it is first intimated in the phenomenon of suffering, "in the suffering," as Levinas says in *Totality and Infinity*, "called physical" (238), which in *Time and the Other* he had identified as "the pain lightly called physical" (69). How is this so?

The acuity of suffering comes from the enforced *passivity* of the sufferer. Pain is always a doubling up of pain: there is pain and like a shadow there is also its inescapability, which as part of pain increases its painfulness. On this horizon of bodily pain, wretched in its insurmountable enchainment to itself,[8] appears the fear of a complete enclosure, suffocation, or total compression. What is announced in such an extremity, at the far end, as it were, of the acuity of suffering, of flesh forced to suffer insufferably from itself, is death. Obviously not all pains, for instance the relatively minor suffering of a paper cut or a cough, raises the fear of death—though who will not admit

---

7. See chapter 3, "Thinking Least about Death," in Cohen, *Levinasian Meditations*, 57–79, 331–333.

8. This notion of "enchainment to oneself"—"a kind of dead weight in the depths of our being" (OE, 60)—is the central theme of Levinas's 1935 essay entitled "On Escape." Already in that early text Levinas had written: "Nevertheless, death is not the exit toward which escape thrusts us. Death can only appear to it if escape reflects upon itself" (67).

to "foolishly" fearing even death in such minor bruises and ailments? In suffering, Levinas writes in *Time and the Other*, there arises "the call to . . . the proximity of death" (62). "The whole acuity of suffering," Levinas reiterates in *Totality and Infinity*, "lies in the impossibility of fleeing it, of being protected in oneself from oneself; it lies in being cut off from every living spring. And it is the impossibility of retreat" (238). "In suffering," Levinas continues, "the will is defeated by sickness. In fear death is yet future, at a distance from us; whereas suffering realizes in the will the extreme proximity of the being menacing the will."[9]

Indeed, as we shall see, death is never *present*, but it is in suffering, and not in fear-of or being-toward death, that the will is menaced: "The supreme ordeal of the will [or "of freedom"] is not death," Levinas writes, "but suffering" (TI, 238). For this reason, too, like Merleau-Ponty, taking seriously the ambiguity of a body at once subjective and objective, of embodiment as a being burdened with oneself in one's own sensibility, Levinas must reject the imported notion of a pure "necessity," Spinoza's causality, as well as the immaculate freedom of Sartre's "for-itself." "Suffering remains ambiguous: it is already the present of the pain acting on the for itself of the will, but, as consciousness, the pain is always yet to come. In suffering the free being ceases to be free, but, while non-free, is yet free" (TI, 238). Such a formulation, such a situation, upsets the niceties of logic, to be sure, as it certainly upsets the objectivist ambitions of Spinozist rationality, but it nevertheless and accurately describes a will inescapably both independent and dependent, at the edge of shutting down upon itself, collapsing into inertness.

Mystery

Common sense understands that death is unknowable. If a dead person "comes back," with or without an "after death experience" story, so I have taught my students, then that person was not dead in the first place! Dead means never coming back. Without such an absolute limit "resurrection" would hardly be a miracle, and "reincarnation" without possible proof. In *Time and the Other* Levinas develops the sense of this

---

9. TI, 238. Here is the place to mention Michael J. Hyde's fine book, *The Call of Conscience: Heidegger and Levinas, Rhetoric and the Euthanasia Debate.*

absolute "gone and never coming back." The inscrutability of death must be understood beyond the dichotomy of known and unknown, that is to say, beyond the categories of knowledge altogether. The point, very simply, is that knowledge is not its proper medium. Levinas therefore calls death a "mystery."[10] "It is not unknown but unknowable, refractory to all light. . . . I have characterized this event as mystery because it could not be anticipated—that is, grasped" (TI, 76–77). In contrast to Spinoza this recalcitrance does not mean that death—death as human mortality—is a mere figment of the imagination. Rather one must attempt to understand, despite the obvious inherent difficulties, this "beyond knowledge," this "outside of any grasping," in its positive significance. It is not unknown; it is mystery. What is the difference?

In *Totality and Infinity* Levinas reaffirms and elaborates the significance of the impenetrable mysteriousness of death. "Death is a menace that approaches me as a mystery; its secrecy determines it— it approaches without being able to be assumed, such that the time that separates me from my death dwindles and dwindles without end, involves a sort of last interval which my consciousness cannot traverse, and where a leap will somehow be produced from death to me" (235). It follows, as Levinas points out in a footnote to this passage, that human mortality cannot be understood as Heidegger thought, as "the possibility of impossibility." For the latter it remains within the grasp of comprehension, reaching its ultimate ground as the understanding or question of being. Rather death is "the impossibility of possibility" (an expression Levinas attributes to Jean Wahl), something essentially out-

---

10. TO, 75. Gabriel Marcel, whom Levinas knew personally, first gave this term legitimacy in contemporary French thought, but he ended up leaving its meaning rather vague. His Gifford Lectures of 1949–1950 at the University of Aberdeen were published in two volumes under the title *Mystery of Being* (volume 1: *Reflection and Mystery* [whose final chapter is entitled "Presence as Mystery"]; volume 2: *Faith and Reality*). He also takes up the notion of "mystery" in his *Metaphysical Journal*, first published in French in 1927 and then translated into English (with Marcel's help) by Bernard Will and published in 1952. One of Marcel's efforts to provide what he calls a "definition" of the term "mystery" occurs in a volume collecting several of his writings in English translation, edited by Manya Harari, which appeared under the title *The Philosophy of Existentialism* (1956). In the first essay, entitled "On the Ontological Mystery," written, Marcel informs us, in 1933: "A mystery is a problem which encroaches upon its own data, invading them, as it were, and thereby transcending itself as a simple problem." Mysterious indeed.

side of or beyond all human capabilities whatsoever. "This apparently Byzantine distinction," Levinas notes, "has a fundamental importance" (TI, 70 fn. 43). It goes without saying that Spinoza is indifferent to such a distinction, having already rejected its viability and possible validity.

Passivity, Weakness

To speak of possibility or impossibility in an existential sense is to speak of time. Before turning to time, however, let us first note that mortality entails the "passivity of the subject" (TO, 70). Again, we are already outside of Spinoza, or on the wrong side. In mortality, in the approach of death, in the dying person's sinking into the inescapable sensed compression of suffering, "in the crying and sobbing," as he puts it, Levinas sees the end of the subject's liveliness and verve, the end of its willfulness, "the end of the subject's virility and heroism" (TO, 72). Perhaps this is why, as an unavowed compensation, Heidegger emphasized "resoluteness," precisely because mortality is the end of resoluteness, a weakness, feebleness itself. Dying, according to Levinas, is a "supreme irresponsibility. . . . infancy" (TO, 72). Or as Levinas expresses this in a formula he will later repeat in *Totality and Infinity*, "in the face of death one is no longer able to be able" (TO, 78). The subject in approaching death through suffering and illness, in dying, is weakened, emasculated, debilitated, incapacitated—rendered passive.

As I have indicated, Levinas's recognition of passivity directly rejects Heidegger's claim that authentic Dasein be "resolute" (*entschlossen*) in its being-toward-death, that in contrast to the pusillanimous and anonymous crowd the individuated Dasein must, as Levinas puts it, "have the courage" of its "anxiety before death." Heideggerian resoluteness, however, is not simply a proud militancy or virility, it is also an expression of the fundamentally disclosive character that Heidegger attributes to being-toward-death. "Being toward death in Heidegger's authentic existence," Levinas notes, "is a supreme lucidity and hence a supreme virility. . . . Death in Heidegger is an event of freedom, whereas for me the subject seems to reach the limit of the possible in suffering. It finds itself enchained, overwhelmed, and in some way passive. Death is in this sense the limit of idealism" (TO, 71). Death does not reveal; it is a mystery; it closes the self in itself, in its own suffering, all the way to shutting it down.

Futurity

While the passivity, incapacitation, irresponsibility, and intimation of death felt in physical and emotional suffering, in injury and illness and humiliation, all establish the intimate mortality of the human, for Levinas death as an experience of the subject nevertheless remains *always future* and hence exterior to the self-presence that constitutes the embodied human subject. In *Time and the Other*, Levinas cites the adage of Epicurus, "If you are, it is not; if it is, you are not," to approve its recognition of the "eternal futurity of death" (TO, 71). "Death," Levinas writes, "is never now. When death is here, I am no longer here, not just because I am nothingness, but because I am unable to grasp" (TO, 72). Again, death is not just incomprehensible; it is beyond comprehension, beyond grasp, outside of knowing and disclosure. It is true that for Heidegger also the primary temporal dimension of death is its futurity, but for Heidegger this does not derive from its aspect of "not yet," it's being "something still outstanding" (an interpretation Heidegger explicitly considers to be an inauthentic construal of the futurity of death[11]), but rather from Dasein's comportment, its being-toward itself as being-toward possibilities. For Levinas, in contrast, not my projection in possibilities, but death itself is never now, is always to come, always outstanding, always future, disturbing the subject's self-projections, breaking the subject of its project of projecting.

Totality and Infinity will also affirm the absolute futurity of death, but, as we shall see, for Levinas the meaning of that futurity must be associated with the other person, and beyond that with all others, which is to say, in its ultimate signification, with the as yet unmet demands of justice.

Postponement

Because death is always future Levinas will say life is lived in the "meantime"—not toward-death but before-death, prior-to-death. The palpabil-

---

11. BT, 293: "The Interpretation in which the 'not yet'—and with it even the uttermost 'not-yet,' the end of Dasein—was taken in the sense of something still outstanding, has been rejected as inappropriate in that it included the ontological perversion of making Dasein something present-at-hand."

ity of this meantime can become quite evident in the reaction some people have when faced with the imminent threat of death. "Prior to death," Levinas writes in *Time and the Other*, "there is always a last chance" (73). Levinas invokes Shakespeare: "Like Hamlet we prefer this known existence to unknown existence" (78). Levinas comments upon a more obvious instance from Shakespeare's *Macbeth*, citing Macbeth's defiant words when facing Macduff in combat, after Macduff has revealed that he is "not of woman born," when therefore all hope seems lost, Macbeth cries out: "yet I will try the last" (73).

In *Totality and Infinity* Levinas speaks of this interval between death and the self as the time of "postponement."[12] It is time as duration, the passage of time, ecstatic temporality but based, as we see, upon the deferral of death, the "not yet." "The postponement of death," Levinas writes, "in a mortal will—time—is the mode of existence and reality of a separated being that has entered into relation with the Other. . . . In it is enacted a meaningful life which one must not measure against an ideal of eternity, taking its duration and its interests to be absurd or illusory" (TI, 232). The allusion to Spinoza is unmistakable. It expresses the difference between modern and contemporary philosophy. We see in this citation also an announcement of the other

---

12. A book that purports to be on the topic of death and responsibility in Levinas, Dennis King Keenan, *Death and Responsibility: The "Work" of Levinas*, in fact focuses more narrowly on the time of "postponement." And even here, dealing with what is only a component of Levinas's far more complex account of death, Keenan confines himself (and therefore his readers) to the usual fanciful and filigreed cleverness of a deconstructive "reading," influenced especially by Derrida's *The Gift of Death*. Typically, then, Keenan misreads Levinas's faithful descriptions of ambiguities inherent in incarnate freedom as if Levinas were naïvely guilty of "contradictions," as if logic ruled phenomenology. And so too does Keenan's "reading" manage to discover that Levinasian responsibility is guilty of—of all things, surprise—irresponsibility!

For a more serious criticism, recall Levinas's comment in a 1985 interview, "Violence of the Face," with Angelo Bianchi: "I have often wondered, with respect to Derrida, whether the *difference* of the present which leads him to the deconstruction of notions does not attest to the prestige that eternity retains in his eyes, the 'great present,' *being*, which corresponds to the priority of the *theoretical* and the truth of the theoretical, in relation to which temporality would be failure. I wonder if time—in its very dia-chrony—isn't *better* than eternity and the order of the Good itself" (AT, 173). See chapter 10, "Derrida's (Mal)reading of Levinas," in my book *Elevations: The Height of the Good in Rosenzweig and Levinas*, 305–321.

person, so important to Levinas's philosophy. We see this conjunction of postponement, the not yet, and the alterity of the other person again in the following citation, also from *Totality and Infinity*: "The will, already betrayal and alienation of itself but postponing this betrayal, on the way to death but a death ever future, exposed to death but not *immediately*, has time to be for the Other, and thus to recover meaning despite death" (236). It is within this meantime, in this last chance that lasts a lifetime, entirely dismissed by Spinoza as illusion, inadequate idea, imaginative fantasy, and diverted to ontological disclosure for Heidegger, in this time of postponement, that the whole dimension of human meaning opens up, for it is in such a "not yet" that the other person appears. In this meantime of "being against death" (236), as Levinas calls it, alluding this time to Heidegger, in the meaningful life it makes possible, the mortal subject lives in a time where there is time. Death may be approaching, it may even be immanent, but until it arrives, the I always "has time."

The Grim Reaper

One of the most original, profound, and consequential insights of Levinas's entire philosophy, one that Levinas began elaborating as early as *Time and the Other*, is the claim that *time itself is neither objective nor subjective but intersubjective*. This idea was intimated in the preceding citations taken from *Totality and Infinity* where Levinas spoke of postponement as a "time to be for the Other," or even more directly in the assertion that time "is the mode of existence and reality of a separated being that has entered into relation with the Other." Death is not only the future always yet to come but never arriving, but as such its transcendence is *like nothing so much as*, is *tantamount to*, is *as if* it were the approach of another human being. Shortly we will see more fully the significance of the approach of another human being, that is, its ethical significance, here regarding death we read in *Totality and Infinity*:

> In the being for death of fear I am not faced with nothingness, but faced with what is *against me*, as though murder, rather than being one of the occasions of dying, were inseparable from the essence of death, as though the approach of death remained one of the modalities of the relation with

the Other. The violence of death threatens as a tyranny, as though proceeding from a foreign will. The order of necessity that is carried out in death is not like an implacable law of determinism governing a totality, but is rather like the alienation of my will by the Other. (234)

Again the reference to Spinoza, to the "implacable law of determinism governing a totality," is unmistakable, as is Levinas's rejection of such a conception. But of prime interest, and what is most remarkable, is not Levinas's criticism of Spinoza, but what he is affirming: death approaches from the future like nothing so much as the approach of another human being, as if or as though death came as murder.

Let us first explicate Levinas's use of the expression "as though" here. It is not simply the mark or the rhetorical gesture of simile or metaphor. It has rather to do with phenomenology, with the discovery of meaning, and more precisely with the discovery and description of "essence." Essence, in the phenomenological meaning of the term, must not be confused with substance, a notion which itself presupposes distinctions between form and content, subject and attribute, presuppositions alien to rigorous phenomenological investigation led by "the things themselves." Nor is "essence" in phenomenology a politically incorrect ignorance of time and history and the broader cultural-historical contexts that contribute to signification, such as today's so-called "anti-essentialists" break their lance upon. Rather and far simpler it refers to the "invariable" core of sense, if such a thing can be discovered, without which something is something else. The phenomenologist, unlike the Platonist or theologian (or "anti-essentialist"), is certainly under no obligation to think this "invariable" as "eternal." We saw in Spinoza that all entities are ratios of motion and rest and that a particular ratio is the invariable core that makes one thing one thing and another thing another, for example, the poet Spaniard one person and the sick Spaniard another, or a potato not an orange. Unlike the phenomenological notion of essence, however, which is or aims to be derived from careful examination of "the thing itself" without any presuppositions, Spinoza's definition of an entity's identity in terms of a ratio of motion and rest is both stipulative and presupposes an entire metaphysics. It is in this context, by means of the "free variations" or "free fantasy variations" exercised by the investigating phenomenologist to whittle down to the indispensable core or "essence" of whatever subject matter is being studied and described, that Levinas assimilates the always outstanding futurity of death with murder, that is to say, with the transcendence of another human being. Death is always postponed, its futurity never becomes present, hence is always transcendent. But how do we understand "transcendence," what is its "essence"? Nothing is more radically transcendent than the transcendence of the other person. The latter is thus the source point, the ground zero, as it were, for all possible meanings of transcendence in all registers of sense. Hence the transcendence of death takes on its sense of transcendence, indeed of absolute transcendence, from the limit case of absolute transcendence, namely, the transcendence of the other person. Thus the futurity of death is like nothing so much as murder, which is to say, death coming from the incomparable alterity of another person, mysterious, ungraspable, unwanted, and irreducibly transcendent. And therein, phenomenologically explicated, lies the real meaning of the legendary "grim reaper" image. And therein, too, is the passage from Levinas's account of death, phenomenologically approached, to his account of death within an ethical perspective, because the transcendence of the other person, the very "essence" of transcendence, surpasses the resources of the phenomenological notion of essence itself, because its meaning is ultimately not amenable to knowing but already demands ethical responsibility first.

With such developments we have clearly arrived at a philosophy, an intelligibility, based in the imperative, the interrogative, the accusative, rather than the nominative or denominative, an approach Edith Wyschogrod named "ethical metaphysics," and I have called "ethical exegesis," which is radically alien to and critical of both Spinoza and Heidegger. Let us review our route. Death is first intimated in pain, as a fear of a sensible passivity even more passive than suffering, to the point of inertness. Yet it never comes, never closes down completely. A living being, however much it may suffer, is not dead, not yet dead. It may wish to die, under torture say, or in the face of extreme pain, but so long as it is alive it suffers and is not a mere thing. Death never arrives, the meantime is inescapable, and life goes on in the time of postponement. From whence, however, comes this sense of a futurity that never arrives, a futurity always future and never present to even the most ecstatic or futurally projective present, *a-venir*, to come? Levinas's answer: such a sense can only come from the absolute and irreducible transcendence of another person. The other's time is not my own; the manner in which the other person has passed and is still to come in relation to me opens up the ultimate sense of the always "yet to come" futurity of the future and the immemorial pastness of the past, transcending and yet disturbing my present. The futurity of death is thus *like*, or *as though*, or *tantamount to* the transcendence—the futurity—of another person. Thus death comes like murder.

And with this signification we are forced to break with phenomenology and shift to the proper sense of what has broken it, and for Levinas the proper sense of the intersubjective relation is from the first always already a relation of moral obligation and responsibility. What is always future are my responsibilities to and for the other. What has always already passed is the "too late," the remiss, the guilt of my not having already fulfilled them. Hence philosophy must shift from science alone, shift from disclosure to goodness, shift to ethics as first philosophy. How does this break appear in Levinas's developing account of the significance of mortality?

The Doctor

Death, far from being reducible to change in ratios of motion and rest, but far also from an ownmost nonrelational way of being, arrives from the outside, which is to say its significance occurs within and colored by a social context, and as such it cannot be separated from ethical significance. Death comes, as if murder, but so too comes or can come the doctor who in the meantime can provide aid, healing, medication. From *Totality and Infinity*:

> The solitude of death does not make the Other vanish, but remains in a consciousness of hostility, and consequently still renders possible an appeal to the Other, to his friendship and his medication. The doctor is an a priori principle of human mortality. Death approaches in the fear of someone, and hopes in someone. . . . A social conjunction is maintained in this menace. (234)

Death does not disabuse the subject of its social engagements but rather heightens their significance: death comes like murder; the vulnerability of mortality renders possible an appeal to help, solicitation of the other person as healer, helper, in trust and responsibility.

In the meantime of mortality, in the ever future futurity of death, hope remains for "the doctor," that is to say, for aid, for treatment, for a cure, for alleviation of pain, for solace. Life, which regenerates and reproduces itself, has no internal end and can in principle go on forever. Perhaps the extraordinary ages, the longevity, of some of the earliest biblical figures—Methuselah, Jared, Noah, Adam, Seth—calls attention to just such a "without end"? Or we can think of avant-garde medical research into genetic longevity and life-extending drugs. Humans do not have the immortality of the pagan gods; to be sure, we remain vulnerable, mortal, but the always future futurity of death, its radical exteriority, inspires an unquenchable hope. In all this we find intimations and confirmations of Levinas's idea that death comes to the self from the outside, and it comes to the self from the outside not, as Spinoza thought, "like an implacable law of determinism governing a totality" but, *as though it were murder*, from a radical exteriority. In other words, for Levinas there is no natural death. Not because all entities, organic and inorganic, do not change ratios, but because death is not internal to organic entities, and in principle a human life can go on forever. Death strikes us down from the outside, like murder. And thus too "the doctor is an a priori principle of human mortality."

Morality: Dying for the Other

But there is another side to death: if all death comes as murder, from the outside, it is not only my death that comes as murder, so too does the other person's death come as murder. This consideration—that the other too suffers, that the other too is vulnerable, subject to pain, illness, wounds, humiliation, outrage—brings Levinas to an even deeper sense of mortality, namely, the other's death for which I am responsible: the subject as responsible for the other's suffering, the other's mortality. The first mortality is not my own but the other's, the other's mortality as my responsibility, my responsibility to alleviate the suffering of the other person and ultimately to ward off the other's death.

The imperative of the face of the mortal other, Levinas writes in "Diachrony and Representation," "commands me to not remain indifferent to this death, to not let the Other die alone, that is, to answer for the life of the other person, at the risk of becoming an accomplice in that person's death" (TO, 108). The face of the mortal other, so

Levinas teaches, first "appears"—it is an "enigma" before it is a "phenomenon"[13]—in the moral imperative "Thou shall not murder," which is the "condition," as it were, of appearing. Two significations of the term "murder" arise immediately: shame at the vital spontaneity of my own powers that are capable of murdering the other; responsibility for the protection of the other from murder, not only from me but from any source, from illness, from wounds, from natural disasters, from others, and so on. The other's mortality—the "Thou shalt not murder," which is the very face, the exceptional vulnerability of the other as other—thus sets off the entire ethical domain, the entire world of imperatives, obligations, responsibilities, which Spinoza would eliminate as sheer ignorance and to whose exigencies Heidegger is condescending and finally indifferent. To not murder the other I must tend to the other's suffering, to the other's mortality, and support and do everything in my means to avert the violence that produces the death of the other. "Thou shall not murder," which is also the "face" of other person, is thus the least abstract event in the world, indeed nothing is more concrete, nothing more demanding, because all the exigencies of the world arise directly and indirectly from its imperative mortal command. To alleviate the suffering, to protect from violence, to forestall the dying of the mortal other—everything depends on such imperatives.

The face of the mortal other, the "Thou shall not murder," ultimately demands of the self that utmost responsibility that in his later writings Levinas describes as "dying for the other." It expresses the ultimate structure of morality, and the root of all significance. All caring for the other is self-sacrifice, to some extent, putting the other first, but its ultimate sense derives from the ultimate form of self-sacrifice, the sacrifice of the self for-the-other, giving one's own life to save the life of another. The greatest foolishness in the eyes of a Spinoza, a monstrous form of *conatus* if it can be said to be *conatus* at all, is the final and highest sense of "glory" for humanity. This sense is doubtless what Merleau-Ponty had in mind when he wrote shortly after the end of World War II: "The heroes are all dead."

In the moral extremity of this notion, "dying for the other," Levinas discovers the ultimate sense of mortality, and no doubt also

---

13. See CPP, "Phenomenon and Enigma," 61–73.

the ultimate sense of morality, living for and caring for others—"to not let the other die alone." Such sacrifice expresses the highest humanity of the human. As he writes in his 1988 article entitled "Dying for . . .": "the human, in which worry over the death of the other comes before care for self. The humanness of dying of the other would be the very meaning of love in its responsibility for one's fellowman and, perhaps, the primordial inflection of the affective as such" (EN, 216). And another citation from the same article, which has Heidegger in mind:

> The priority of the other over the I, by which the human *being-there* is chosen and unique, is precisely the latter's response to the nakedness of the face and its mortality. It is there that the concern for the other's death is realized, and that "dying for him," "dying his death" takes priority over "authentic" death. Not a *post-mortem* life, but the excessiveness of sacrifice, holiness in charity and mercy. This future of death in the present of love is probably one of the original secrets of temporality itself and beyond all metaphor. (217)

Justice beyond Death

"Dying for" the other is the ultimate meaning of mortality and morality. But it is nonetheless not the last word to be said about death, precisely because it is not the last word of ethics. The last word must be given to *justice*, because justice rectifies morality and as such provides another dimension, indeed the final meaning of "dying for." The moral person is capable of dying for the mortal other to save the life of the other. The just person is capable of dying for all mortal others, which is to say, for the freedom and equality, the laws and courts, the health, housing and education, the social welfare, and all the political, economic, and social institutions that are required to make possible, guarantee, and protect a moral life in society at large.

To die for another though an ultimate self-sacrifice is *not enough*, because there is more to the world than what I personally face, more than the face of the other, a world of many others, near and far, a world that goes on after my death. Morality is at the basis but it is not the entirety of ethics. It must be supplemented by justice, indeed rectified by justice, since to give all to one person does not by itself take account of what is needed by others, by those who do not face me but who face the other, say, or who face others who are not facing me or the other. Society is made up of more than two persons. One must consider obligations in relation to those whom Levinas names "the third." Beyond morality justice is also always required, whereby each person, singular, unique, unequal to any other, must be treated fairly, also be accorded the protection of law and hence treated as the equal to all others. This is in no way to disparage the ultimate sacrifice, not at all. It remains ultimate. Nevertheless, morality demands justice, and justice—to make for equality, to provide equal protections, equal opportunity, equal support and succor—demands knowledge, demands the resources of science, technology, the arts, courts, communications, police, schools, housing, employment, hospitals, parks, farms, and everything else that is required to concretely ensure both justice and morality.

Morality must thus be supplemented by justice, by a care for all others, a care that cannot be accomplished solely in the love and compassion one person can have for another. Stable institutions and laws are also required, as is their real enforcement and efficacy, to postpone violence and to secure a world in which the imperatives of morality can be fulfilled without fear or harm or arbitrary retribution. All this is another way of saying that not only should one give priority to the mortality of the other, but one should live for a time beyond one's own death—honoring and preserving the progressive heritage of past generations, to protect and care for the future of future generations. Near the end of *Totality and Infinity* Levinas will call this concern, this responsibility for the future, for a time not one's own, beyond my mortal being but for the sake of the mortality of those yet to come, the "infinity of time" (281).

"Signification," Levinas writes almost two decades after *Totality and Infinity* in "Diachrony and Representation," "comes from an authority that is significant *after and despite my death*, signifying to the finite ego, to the ego doomed to death, a meaningful order significant beyond this death. This is not, to be sure, some promise of resurrection, but an obligation that death does not absolve" (TO, 114). To serve an authority—the authority of justice—beyond one's own life, "*after and despite my death*"—a completely anti-Spinozist and anti-Heideggerian imperative—is not as strange as it may first sound. It is actually an everyday occurrence. It is paying taxes for schools, parks, bridges, public railroads and buses; it is to plant a tree for one's grandchildren or neighborhood children, or to donate to charity, and all the many things one does or can do to ensure a healthy, happy, moral, and just future for generations one may not live to see or for people far away. *Après moi . . . dautres, notre avenir.*

The futurity of justice, then, lies beyond the futurity of the one who faces. The world is large, its sufferings many and long, and it does not disappear with one's own death. The mortality of the other and all others obligates me beyond my own grave. Levinas:

> There is in the Other a meaning and an obligation that oblige me beyond my death! The futuration of the future does not reach me as a to-come, as the horizon of my anticipations or pro-tensions. Must one not, in this *imperative* signification of the future that concerns me as a non-in-difference to the other person, as my responsibility for the stranger—must one not, in this rupture of the natural order of being, understand what is—improperly—called super-natural? (TO, "Diachrony and Representation," 114)

Levinas invokes the much-abused religious term "super-natural" not at all in a superstitious, otherworldly sense, and not only because morality and justice move counter to our natural selfishness and clannishness, counter to *conatus* and being, but also because an adult meaning of religion, as Kant already understood, lies in its contribution to morality and justice, to living for a better time above and beyond one's own mortal time. "The futuration of the future," Levinas has written, "is not a 'proof of God's existence,' but 'the fall of God into meaning'" (TO, 115).

The meaning of death as morality and finally as justice is precisely and nothing less than the "difficult freedom" of a "biblical humanism." It is the compassion of one for-the-other and the call of one for all others, the "infinity of time," aiming at and working for a future of justice. Not "God or Nature," as Spinoza thought, sacrificing mortality itself to an indifferent Nature, or "Temporality and Historicity," were we to create a parallel formula for Heidegger, for whom a mortal and moral humanity was to be sacrificed to epochal being, but "God or Justice," to extend this parallelism to Levinas, who would have us respect transcendence as the *nobility*—the preciousness, the height, the moral exigency—of the quest for justice, the unfinished personal and communal adventure of social redemption.

Conclusion

Spinoza continues an ancient Greek and perhaps an even more ancient Indian and Egyptian philosophical inheritance, of death in life, of dying to this world, the world of the senses and desires, the flux of becoming, non-being, and mortality, for the sake of the true world conceived as a world of unalterable eternity. Heidegger too in his own way prolongs this heritage, perhaps under the influence of the Cross, not by escaping time, history, and mortality so far, but by embracing death too close. He would convert living into constant dying, being-toward-death, to faithfully play the role of mortal, rising in rare moments to lend voice to the larger historical drama of "ontological difference," the "question of being."

In such a world, Levinas's is a counter philosophy of life, responsible and caring for the life and well-being of the other more than anything else. For-the-other's life all the way to a possible "dying for . . ." to safeguard that other, even for others far away or not yet born. Driven not by truth to the exclusion of all else, nor by care for being before all else, but by the demands of goodness, the obligations of kindness, and the difficult work of justice. To protect one and all from the violence of murder and injustice. Mortality lived as responsibility.

Chapter Eight

Spinoza's Spleen

"Babies, Fools, and Madmen"

To be able to not exist is weakness.

—Spinoza, *Ethics*, I, Prop. 11, Third Proof

I do not know how to reckon a man who hangs himself, or how one should reckon babies, fools, and madmen.

—Spinoza, *Ethics*, II, Prop. 49, Scholium

Let a man but observe who are of greatest authority in cities, and who best do their own business; we shall find that they are commonly men of the least parts; women, children and madmen have had the fortune to govern great kingdoms equally well with the wisest princes.

—Michel de Montaigne, "Of the Art of Conference," *The Essays of Michel de Montaigne, Complete*

Will and Intellect (Commentary on Spinoza's Scholium to the Proof of the Corollary of the Proof of Proposition 49 of Part II, *Ethics*)

All readers of Spinoza know that it is in what he named "scholia" that Spinoza lets his hair down. Freeing himself as the occasion arises from the rigidity, indeed the artificiality, of the "geometric manner" that girds and guards the main body of the *Ethics*.[1] In them we are often treated to the clearest, most accessible, and revealing expositions by Spinoza of his own thought.

Such occurs in the concluding scholium of part II of the *Ethics*. Spinoza defends one of the main pillars of his entire philosophy: the equation of intellect and will. The thesis of their equation had been stated in the corollary of the proof of proposition 49: "Will and intellect are one and the same thing." Spinoza feels the need to defend this thesis against Descartes, who had earlier, in the fourth of his *Meditations on First Philosophy*, affirmed that human will is capable of exceeding intellect, and as such is responsible for errors, but in any event it is not the same thing, is not equivalent to intellect. Many important consequences follow from their differing positions. The issue Spinoza and Descartes grapple with explicitly, and about which Spinoza explicitly challenges Descartes, is the determination of the nature and origin of illusion (erroneous perceptions) and falsehood (false propositions). Let us look at falsehood first and see how it is related to illusion.

The true and the false are bound to one another by disjunction: what is true cannot also be false; what is false cannot also be true. Furthermore, what is true, a true proposition, dissipates, dispels, and otherwise eliminates the false, the alleged reference of a false proposition. What is false, a false proposition, perverts, obscures, and otherwise mistakes the true, what could make up the true reference of a true proposition. The true, however, has a certain priority over the false. True and false are not symmetrical, not simple opposites. This is because the true proposition and it alone indicates reality rather than illusion. When a proposition is true it means that's the way things are, that's how reality is. Not so the false proposition. The question therefore arises regarding the ontological and epistemic status of the false, or rather the ontological status of whatever it is that a false proposition refers to. The issue of falsehood, then, is directly related to that of illusion, because of this question, the question of the ontological status

---

1. There has been a long-standing debate in Spinoza studies regarding the necessity or contingency of the "geometric manner" of the *Ethics*. However one stands regarding the outcome of such a debate, that Spinoza thought it was right to utilize such a form, that a Euclidean garb seemed the best way to present his ultimate thoughts, this is evident from the manuscript he left for publication.

of whatever it is, if it is anything at all, to which a false proposition refers. This same question can also be approached from the direction not of the proposition, true or false, but of the illusory or the real. What is it about the illusory that it gives rise to false propositions, that it fools the mind's judgment? Or, alternatively, what is it about reality, in contrast to the unreal, that it gives rise to true propositions, that the mind gets it right? All these questions are bound to one another and in a certain sense are one question, the question of the relation of will and intellect, and to this question, as to all of them, Descartes and Spinoza give two basically different answers.

Descartes argues that the source of false judgment lies in the *freedom of the will*. The will that is free is not strictly or automatically ruled by, and is certainly therefore not equivalent to intellect. Indeed, for Descartes the human freedom of the will is the closest approximation on earth of God's own infinite or absolute freedom, the "image and likeness of God," as the Bible puts it. The difference between the human will and the divine does not lie in the nature of the will, its freedom, which is infinite or absolute for both, but rather in the range of what the will can will. That range is absolute and infinite for God, for God is omnipotent, but it is only relative and finite for humans. More precisely, the infinite mind of God, His omniscience, and the infinite will of God, His omnipotence, are one and the same. So what God thinks is realized by virtue of His thought alone; His intellection is thus creative or intuitive, will and thought at once. Now human freedom is no less free, in a formal sense, that is, unrestricted in its ability to choose, even if it is not free substantially in the absolute sense in which God's freedom is free, because it does not have or entertain the absolute range of options that God always entertains. "It is free-will alone or liberty of choice," Descartes writes of human will, "which I find to be so great in me that I can conceive no other idea to be more great; it is indeed the case that it is for the most part this will that causes me to know that in some manner I bear the image and similitude of God" (175).

Free will is thus a great gift for Descartes, but it is also the source of error. Because it is infinite, human free will enables humans who are not sufficiently careful, not sufficiently cautious, not sufficiently resolute and firm willed, to affirm what is not "clear and distinct" and hence what is, in fact, illusory or unreal. Truth thus requires a firm and resolute and cautious and careful will. Only such a will by sticking to the clear and distinct and reserving judgment before the unclear and indistinct can avoid making false judgments, affirming propositions that do not refer to the real. Truth requires strength of will.

Spinoza is far from sharing Descartes's view or his enthusiasm for either human will or Divine will. It is a matter of what is absolute: freedom or necessity. For Spinoza, as we have seen, what is absolute about God (or Nature really) is not that he/it can will or think anything at all, but that he/it always and only wills and thinks necessity. Because it is the eternal, immutable, necessary order of the universe that intellect knows as truth, as intelligibility *tout court*, it follows that God's intellect, God's truth, God's necessity, and, why not, God's "freedom," are one and the same. "God's intellect, will and power are one and the same" (E, I, Prop. 17, Scholium, 45). This absolutization of necessity, in any event, is what Spinoza argues for in his first book, the only one to appear in his lifetime under his own name, which was an exposition and critical correction of Cartesian philosophy, as it is what he affirms and elaborates throughout the *Ethics*, as it is also what underwrites the whole of the *Theological-Political Treatise*. Put in its simplest terms: for Spinoza there is no free will, not for God, not for humans. True freedom is cognition of the necessary lawfulness of Nature. True freedom, in a word, is nothing other than the necessity of Nature, which is its true intelligibility. Such a view, equating will and intellect, is a pillar, perhaps the main pillar of Spinoza's entire philosophy. It is what makes Spinoza more strictly Cartesian than Descartes who, for his part, kept one foot, as it were, in the medieval world. We shall shortly turn to the epistemological consequences of Spinoza's exclusive allegiance to necessity.

Our concern and what is at issue for both philosophers is the point where epistemology and ontology meet. A philosophy such as Spinoza's that defends the perfection of being as the necessary intellectual order of the universe, that is, as the truth of the universe, must still explain falsehood and illusion, for falsehood and illusion there is. But there exactly is the rub. What "is" illusion? What twists human judgment to falsity? It cannot be being, cannot be true being. But what is it? What's going on in a false judgment?

Descartes's explanation for error, falsity, and illusion, as we have seen, is that the will, infinite in its freedom, which regarding making judgments means infinite in its ability to affirm or deny, can and does affirm propositions that are not perfectly "clear and distinct" to the intellect. On the practical plane, in contrast to theory, by the way, the same freedom of the will accounts for the human ability to perform and to judge actions good and evil. When in his fourth *Meditation* Descartes asks, "Whence then come my errors?," he answers in a way relevant to both the practical and the theoretical plane, which in a certain sense, that is, precisely insofar as will is involved, function similarly: "They come from the sole fact that since the will is much wider in its range and compass than the understanding, I do not restrain it within the same bounds, but extend it also to things which I do not understand: and as the will is of itself indifferent to these, it easily falls into error and sin, and chooses the evil for the good, or the false for the true" (175–176). The will can be at fault in both theory and practice precisely because it is free, or more exactly because it abuses its freedom. In the case of theoretical judgment it mistakenly affirms non-being as if it were being because it does not restrict, discipline, or confine itself to affirming only what is "clear and distinct." To be sure, this also means that the solution to the problem of falsehood (and sin) also lies with the will. Very simply, it needs to be disciplined. And thus Descartes's famous defense of *method*, his *rules* for the *regulation* of the mind. By binding will to *method*, which is to say, by binding it to intellect, to "clear and distinct" ideas only, the will can affirm truth rather than falsehood, just as by means of practical discipline—moral discipline—it can will good rather than evil. Thus truth and goodness depend on disciplining the free will. As we know, Spinoza rejects such a view entirely, to the point that instead of discipline, restraint, pedagogy, or for that matter therapy of any kind, his philosophy knows only necessity. Everything is always already perfect, no room for improvement.

Descartes is not suggesting that the will is evil. Rather the will is free because by itself it is "indifferent." It cannot be forced one way or another, cannot be compelled. Freedom is the opposite of necessity: it is the ability to choose, to decide, to select. To be a scientist, a knower, a philosopher, is to deliberately constrain the will when it chooses between propositions according to method, limiting the will to true propositions, that is, propositions in accord with "clear and distinct" ideas. Likewise, to be a good person, a morally good person, is to constrain the will's choice of actions to good ones. Both are cases of self-discipline, one for the true and the other for the good. What Descartes demands of the will, then, is a doubling back, reflexivity: it must will upon itself, will to will only "clear and distinct" ideas, or on the practical plane will to will only good actions. Prior to and as a propaedeutic to science and philosophy, then, the will must be educated, trained in self-control, molded, formed, and otherwise disciplined to select the true rather than the false. Such pedagogy is required because the will, with its infinite capacity to choose whatever it likes, is not philosophical by nature. Humans are not born philosophers and philosophy is not native to the human condition. Rather, one can become a philosopher if one so chooses, if one undergoes the proper discipline, and if one has sufficient intellect for it. Philosophy is thus a discipline, an ascesis, requiring a will guided by intellect, a rational will. Unlike God, who presumably always and without exception adheres to truth, is always rational, humans must struggle—helped, to be sure and thanks to Descartes, by adherence to Method—to stay with the truth. Unlike God, too, even the best of humans can deviate, can relapse into childishness, superstition, and myth, say, in what must be a constant struggle for truth. Illusion and falsity can be guarded against but can never be finally eradicated. To be rational is to be ever vigilant, just as to be good is to be ever vigilant. Both are a matter of strength of will: will restricting itself to clear and distinct ideas, on the side of knowledge and intellect, and to the good, on the side of action and desire.

Spinoza has an entirely different account. Despite therapeutic readings of parts III to V of the *Ethics*, despite the efforts that led him to write the unfinished *Treatise on the Emendation of the Intellect*, and perhaps even because of realizations attained while working on the latter manuscript, Spinoza's interest does not lie, nor does his philosophy depend, on disciplining the will. There is no free will in the first place. Can a perfect universe—and the true world is perfect: "By reality and perfection I mean the same thing" (E, II, Definitions, Explication, 63)—contain an imperfect will, let alone many of them? From a scholium, Spinoza speaks his mind:

> Men are deceived in thinking themselves free, a belief that consists only in this, that they are conscious of their actions and ignorant of the causes by which they are determined. Therefore the idea of their freedom is simply the ignorance of the cause of their actions. As to their saying that human actions depend on the will, these are mere words without any corresponding idea. (E, II, Prop. 35, Scholium, 86)

Accordingly, Spinoza's proof for proposition 49 begins with an attack on Descartes: "There is in the mind no absolute faculty of willing and non-willing, but only particular volitions, namely, this or that affirmation, and this or that negation." In other words, there is no such thing, entity, or reality as an independent will, no faculty of willing, and certainly therefore no free will, but only particular judgments, affirmative or negative, which are nowise products of free choice, or even of disciplined choice. Descartes is guilty—as Nietzsche will later also hold him guilty—of reifying what are in fact always only particular affirmative or negative propositions. First of all, then, for Spinoza willing is not a matter of desire but of judgment: affirmation or negation, nothing more, nothing supplementary, nothing *sui generis*. And a true judgment, whether affirmative or negative in form, what Spinoza calls an "adequate idea," is always, unerringly, an endorsement of truth, of reality. In a word, truth compels the will. "[A] true idea involves absolute certainty" (E, II, Prop. 43, Scholium, 91). Choice does not enter into making a judgment. Truth and the affirmation of truth are one and the same. The adequate idea *occurs* as true judgment. This all follows from and is indeed an explication of what Spinoza means in asserting that "Will and intellect are one and the same thing." For the finite human mind, *forced assent* is the accompanying mark or signal of truth, the mark or signal that the human mind is in its judgment coincident with the divine mind. Such is the scientist knowing the true and the philosopher's "intellectual love of God"—beatitude.

From this perspective we can understand too why Spinoza's philosophy, as expounded in the *Ethics*, begins not with doubt, as did Descartes's, but with certitude. Indeed it begins with the most certain of all certitude: the all-embracing unity, necessity, universality, indeed totality of One Substance. For Spinoza it is compellingly true, absolutely true, indeed nothing can be truer, than that all of reality or being is One Substance. Not even by proof, but by definition! The totality of reality, unlike any particular reality within the totality, can depend on nothing outside itself because nothing is or can be outside of the totality of reality, and thus reality also can only be conceived in and of itself. This is also why in the fourth part of the *Ethics* Spinoza is able to enunciate his famous equivalence: "*Deus, sive Natura.*" We can speculate that this is also why Spinoza calls his philosophy *Ethics:* the true is all, the all is true, and hence if good means anything, the all and the true are good also (nothing else could be in any event). Thus Spinoza transforms Socrates's "To know the good is to do the good," from a knowing and a being separate from one another, a knowing striving for being, to an equivalence, a knowing and being that are one and the same, the real realizing itself, the intellect ideating itself, *Natura naturans* and *Natura naturata* (See E, I, Prop. 29, Proof, and Scholium).

So how with such a vision does Spinoza answer to the question of illusion and falsity? Since we know in advance that they are non-being, unreal, "inadequate" ideas, besides wondering "what" they are at all, we must also wonder "how" they arise at all. One hint that will guide us in tracing Spinoza's answers to these questions appears in the *Ethics*: "To be able to not exist is a weakness" (E, I, Prop. 11, Third Proof, 37). God or Nature, which is perfect—omniscient and omnipotent, that is, eternal, immutable, and necessary intelligibility—has no such weakness. Where does such weakness come from?

"Falsity," Spinoza writes in the scholium that concludes part II of the *Ethics* (the same scholium to the corollary that equates will and intellect), "consists only in the privation that fragmentary and confused ideas involve" (97). Here it is not a matter of the fault, unrestraint, or hubris of the subject's infinite will that oversteps intellect, the will's lack of discipline vis-à-vis ideas, as in Descartes. Rather the "fault," if one may use this term, lies in the object of the will or intellect: in "ideas" that are "fragmentary and confused" rather than unitary and clear.[2]

---

2. Let us note that Kant's contemporary, fellow genius, and not too distant neighbor, the celebrated Rabbi Elijah ben Solomon Zalman (1720–1797)—known popularly as the "Vilna Gaon," spiritual leader of traditional Eastern European Judaism—apparently follows Spinoza (whether he knew his writings or not) to "explain" erroneous judgment. Such in any event is how in his Torah commentary, *Kol Eliyahu* (Pietrokov, 1904; reprinted, Brooklyn: Lyon Press), Rabbi Elijah accounts for the High Priest Eli's mistaken rebuke of Hannah for being drunk when in fact she was praying silently while moving her lips (I Samuel 1:13). According to the Vilna Gaon, having consulted the *Urim v'Tumin*, which revealed four Hebrew letters (*shin, chav, resh* and *hay*) Eli read them in the wrong order to form the misleading word "drunken woman" (*shikorah*), when in their proper order they would have correctly formed the word for "worthy woman" (*ksherah*).

In truth, however, neither rationalization or apologia—whether to blame undisciplined will or to blame fragmentary or garbled evidence—succeeds in effacing, legitimizing or even making sense of the contradiction (or "sin") of imperfection in a perfect universe.

Falsity arises owing to a will-intellect tricked to judgment by a partial idea, an idea taken independently of its systematic unity with all other ideas, affirmation of "fragmentary and confused ideas." The partial, the detached, the unmoored, is taken for a whole rather than the part of the whole, the moment in a system that altogether is perfect and real. "Therefore," Spinoza writes in the next sentence, "a false idea, in so far as it is false, does not involve certainty" (97). Certainty, then, which is what compels true judgment, remains the necessary volitional-mental correlate of a true idea. It both compels and is the very signal of a true idea. Thus Spinoza adds for good measure: "For by certainty we mean something positive, not privation of doubt. But by privation of certainty we mean falsity" (97). Falsity arises from uncertain judgment, mistaking fragments for wholes.

Nevertheless Spinoza's answer, thus stated, remains unsatisfactory, at the very least because it is still not sufficiently differentiated from Descartes's answer. A question remains: If the will-intellect in affirming falsity is tricked by a part or a partial claim, a partial "idea," somehow masquerading presumably as an adequate idea, does this not still mean that the will in Spinoza, as in Descartes, exceeds in power the intellect? Is not Spinoza's "privation of certainty" another way of saying that the will can willy-nilly affirm what it wants, whether or not that which it affirms is the sort of proposition that is somehow—but obviously not in a way that is acknowledged by or compelling for the will—accompanied by the sign of uncertainty that should have compelled the will-intellect to deny it? Put more simply: why doesn't the will-intellect recognize a fragment as a fragment? Why would the will-intellect mistake a fragment for a whole, or a legitimate part of a larger whole? Does this not necessarily mean that will and intellect are separate, as in Descartes, tumbling down the central pillar of Spinoza's entire philosophy? In the face of such questions, what does Spinoza mean by placing the "fault" with the idea-object, its partialness, rather than with the will in its undisciplined freedom? Of course we know Spinoza wants to and must eliminate free will as inconsistent with universal necessity, but has he succeeded? Isn't he caught up in all the usual conundrums of philosophies and theologies that claim to eliminate free will, caught up precisely in the *aporia* Kant will later make explicit in the Third Antinomy? In any event Spinoza certainly senses the trouble he is in. Aware that his own formulations, as cited previously, may not be sufficiently clear, or defensible (which from his philosophical outlook must amount to the same thing), Spinoza immediately proceeds to clarify and explain it, and then, no doubt still sensing a problem, he responds to four possible objections.

To solve this matter is of great importance, and not only for the sake of the consistency of Spinoza's thought. It is a matter of overcoming the seemingly insuperable difficulty, which would be fatal to Spinoza's entire outlook, of giving an account of illusion and falsity *without* recourse to the usual ways out, usual for theology, for Descartes, for common sense, and for ethics, and regardless of its own difficulties, namely, acknowledgment of the freedom of the will—freedom not as necessity but as choice, that is to say, the efficacy of practical as well as theoretical freedom. To grasp precisely Spinoza's handling of this fundamental issue—admitting falsehood and illusion, but denying free will—will not only answer to our current perplexity, and thereby go to the heart of Spinoza's entire project, but it will also, as we shall see, help explain the peculiarly unrestrained and ubiquitous contempt with which Spinoza holds "babies, fools, and madmen," to cite the terms of contempt that appear in this same scholium. By recognizing a link between his handling of the aforementioned problem and his contempt for such persons, it is fair to suspect—and we shall shortly argue this thesis—that Spinoza was quite unable to solve this crucial problem and, by his hurling blame elsewhere, was also to some extent aware of his failure, despite constant protests to the contrary. But first Spinoza must be given his full day in court. We return to the scholium to proposition 49, which concludes part II of the *Ethics*, to Spinoza's explanation of his argument and to his refutations of four possible objections.

The explanation is a clarification of what Spinoza means by "ideas." It involves paying greater attention to two related distinctions: between *ideas* and *images* and between *ideas* and *words*. Spinoza writes: "I urge my readers to make a careful distinction between an idea—i.e., a conception of the mind—and the images of things that we imagine. Again, it is essential to distinguish between ideas and the words we use to signify things." To confuse ideas with images and/or words is to misapprehend the nature of adequate or true ideas. Ideas that compel assent do not depend on images or words; their truth-value is independent of imagination, language, or corporeality more generally. They are nondiscursive and should not be misconceived otherwise. "Now one can easily dispel these misconceptions if one attends to the nature of thought, which is quite removed from the concept of extension. Then one will clearly understand that an idea, being a mode of thinking, consists neither in the image of a thing nor in words. For the essence of words and images is constituted solely by corporeal motions, far removed from the concept of thought." Despite his allegiance to modern science, here lies the continued influence of an ancient Parmenidean or Platonic heritage, dismissing anything but pure logic as non-being. Now the "logic" is mathematical or geometrical. Unlike Kant, whose critical philosophy depends on distinguishing mathematical ideation from philosophical reasoning, the former essentially involving construction and the latter not, Spinoza equates mathematical and philosophical thinking such that both are, which is to say, such that all true thinking is independent of constructions or images. As the idea of a mathematical line or a geometric triangle is distinct from any construction or image of a line or triangle, so for Spinoza are all ideas distinct from their corporeal wrappings. This explanation or clarification, however, instead of answering our questions, gives rise to even greater perplexities, ancient ones at that. What is the relation of image and word to ideas? Can ideas "exist" without image or word? Or must ideas somehow be conceived independent of image and word, even if they *cannot actually exist in such independence*? Or is this nonexistence merely a human limitation, one that God transcends? These are indeed old questions. Nevertheless, reminding ourselves of them should make us aware also that Spinoza's "clarification" has not particularly moved his argument along or made it more convincing, let alone clinching it. The question stands: if will and intellect are one, how is it that "fragmentary ideas" trick the will-intellect into affirming that about which it has no certainty?

Spinoza proceeds to raise four possible objections, each of them posing Descartes's alternative position, that is, free will, against his own. His intends, of course, to refute them all. What are these objections? First is the "claim that the will extends more widely than the intellect, and therefore is different from it" because human will is infinite even while human intellect is not. Second, there is the appeal to experience, since "experience appears to tell us most indisputably that we are able to suspend judgment so as not to assent to things that we perceive." Third, a claim to the equivalence of all affirmations, whether true or false, because "we do not seem to need greater power in order to affirm that what is true is true than to affirm that what is false is true." And finally, "Fourthly, it may be objected that if man does not act from freedom of will, what would happen if he should be in a state of equilibrium like Buridan's ass? Will he perish of hunger and thirst?"

Regarding the fourth objection, invoking the quandary of equipoise, the reader must recall Jean Buridan's famous example of the hungry ass that stands exactly in the middle between two exactly equal haystacks—how will it choose one over the other, or will it, as logic suggests, be stuck in the middle and starve to death?[3] Spinoza's invocation of "hunger and thirst" recalls Aristotle's earlier example in *De Caelo* (*On the Heavens*, 295b34) "of a man who, though exceedingly hungry and thirsty, and both equally, yet being equidistant from food and drink, is therefore bound to stay where he is" (433). The fourth objection, unlike the others, instead of offering an alternative to Spinoza's theory of the will-intellect, points to a problem with it: if the will is compelled by truth, as Spinoza argues, then in such instances—where evidence, as it were, truth, adequate ideas, lies divided exactly equally between two alternatives—then the will-intellect cannot affirm or deny, or rather it must affirm-cognize both at once and hence affirm neither. Is such a situation, then, the real source of falsity and illusion: an unresolvable competition, an exact equilibrium, the same evidential weight of two exactly equal but opposed "truths"? Let us review Spinoza's replies to each of his four objections in turn.

To the first objection Spinoza replies "that, if by intellect is meant clear and distinct ideas only, I grant that the will extends more widely than the intellect, but I deny that the will extends more widely than perceptions, that is, the faculty of conceiving." Obscure, yes, but let's try to sort it out. The will in this sense is nothing more or less than the affirmation of what presents itself to perception/conception, an affirmation that for Spinoza necessarily accompanies such presentations. In this sense, too, "the will is a universal entity, or the idea whereby we explicate all particular volitions; that is, that which is common to all particular volitions." As such it is not a "faculty" as Descartes portrays it but rather

---

3. It is apt that Spinoza refers to Jean Buridan (1300–1358) inasmuch as the latter maintained against Aristotle that entities continue in motion because they are internally driven by *impetus*, a notion later important to Galileo's accounts of inertia and momentum, which greatly influenced Spinoza's central notion of *conatus*, perseverance in being.

more like a necessarily accompanying stamp of approval, the inescapable "there is . . ." regarding whatever presents itself to perception/conception. While its capacity is then broader than compelled approval of clear and distinct ideas exclusively (though it must approve these), it is not broader and cannot be broader than the range of perceptions/conceptions presented to it. Still obscure, but it seems Spinoza is granting a very limited sense in which will is not equal to intellect but exceeds it. In this exceeding, of course, it will be tricked by just those perceptions—"fragmentary ideas"—that have not yet been fully conceived in their truth. The problem with this solution, however, is that despite its subtlety or nuance, it is actually a *criticism* of Spinoza's equation of will and intellect, more precisely a criticism of his dismissal of free will.

To the second objection Spinoza simply denies it, "denying that we have free power to suspend judgment. For when we say that someone suspends judgment, we are saying only that he sees that he is not adequately perceiving the thing. So suspension of judgment is really a perception, not a free will." Spinoza gives the example of "a boy imaging a winged horse and having no other perception." Because will always accompanies perception/conception, the boy would necessarily affirm the (imagined) existence of the horse, though he would remain uncertain of its *actual* existence beyond imagination. Spinoza points out that it is the same in dreams, where we necessarily affirm the dream images, even though upon wakening we realize they were but images without substantial reality. In making such a proposal, to this extent Spinoza is surprisingly enough a phenomenologist, taking phenomena as phenomena independent of *doxic* judgment. He goes so far as to "grant that nobody is deceived in so far as he has a perception; that is, I grant that the imaginings of the mind, considered in themselves, involve no error." So images are images, words are words, perceptions are perceptions. To the extent that they have not been fully cognized in their conceptual reality, they lack being. Quite to the contrary of a modern phenomenologist, however, who is satisfied to show how phenomena are manifest in various regions of meaning (imagination, sensing, feeling, perceiving, etc.) without reducing one region to another, or all to "primary qualities," Spinoza insists on judging the adequateness of what is perceived/conceived exclusively by an axiomatic rationalist standard, *in ordine geometrico demonstrate*, according to which truth, as we have seen, is so evident that it compels the will's affirmation, and all the rest is trickery. Again, Spinoza has solved nothing; he has merely attempted to integrate problematic residues—perceptions—back into his will-intellect theory of truth.

His second answer also answers the third objection. While the will affirms all ideas, in the minimalist sense of acknowledging that "there is . . . such and such," in the face of adequate ideas only is it compelled by its own attendant certitude to affirm them as true. Thus with regard to truth, contrary to the objection, the will is equal to and cannot exceed the intellect. What is true is; what is false is not. Spinoza is obviously not a phenomenologist. His rationalism is radically opposed to any phenomenology.

With these three objections and their answers and our skeptical comments in mind, it is Spinoza's answer to the fourth objection that interests us most. It is relatively short but also so remarkable that I reproduce it in its entirety as follows:

> As to the fourth objection, I readily grant that a man placed in such a state of equilibrium (namely, where he feels nothing else but hunger and thirst and perceives nothing but such-and-such food and drink at equal distances from him) will die of hunger and thirst. If they ask me whether such a man is not to be reckoned an ass rather than a man, I reply that I do not know, just as I do not know how one should reckon a man who hangs himself, or how one should reckon babies, fools, and madmen. (E, 98)

Humans reckoned as asses! It is meant as wit (reference to Buridan), as an insult. Stumped by suicides, babies, fools, madmen . . . these figures are certainly also attacked. Let us recall that the fourth objection is but a "thought experiment," a mere hypothetical—only two desires, hunger and thirst, the two desires exactly equal to one another in urgency, and then the equidistance and equality of their objects of satisfaction—surely it is improbable and not likely to have much real-world correspondence. In such cases, the will-intellect *compelled* by no prevailing certainty to choose one or the other, the hungry thirsty person ends up dead, even though the hungry thirsty person stands in easy reach of both food and drink. Like a Freudian slip, or a purloined letter, a current has surely short-circuited in the wiring of Spinoza's rationality. Spinoza's answer reveals more than Spinoza intends. *Suicides, babies, fools, madmen, and the like* . . . they must be denounced as asses rather than humans. Spinoza does "not know how one should reckon" them. What is going on here? What has stymied the master rationalist and raised his ire?

Spinoza's Nightmare: Suicides, Babies, Fools, Madmen, and Women

It turns out that besides the vast hordes, the "multitudes," the "masses," the "people" whom Spinoza regularly abuses for their ignorance and unruliness, there are all sorts of additional and more particular unsavory characters who disturb and haunt the probity of the scientific-philosophic intellectual perfection of Spinoza's well-organized universe. The qualification that unites them is their irrationality. They do not fit neatly into his thought. Spinoza cannot "reckon" them. Instead he attacks them, mocks, castigates, insults, rebukes, scolds, scorns, humiliates, and otherwise casts them into conceptual purgatory.

It appears then that Spinoza has a temper, and quite a temper it is, or rather distemper. Spleen is the older term. Spinoza's spleen has usually gone unnoticed, however, under the more familiar and popular image we have of the gentle withdrawn man of reason, the tranquil and solitary thinker calmly grinding lenses, deliberately modest of means, concentrating on his books, his writing, his correspondence, his ideas, discussing them with select and distinguished friends, secluded and retiring, the sage of Holland. Quiet man of reason, votary of "intellectual love of God," ever sober in his "God intoxication," the divine Spinoza. Indeed, parts III to V of the *Ethics* seem nothing less than a therapeutic manual of intellectual probity in the face of a world mad with clerical and mob fanaticism. Chapters 16 through 20 of the *Theological-Political Treatise*, as we have seen, are devoted to an elaboration of a notion of sovereignty designed above all to ensure peace, tranquility, security, to keep the hordes in check, just as chapters 7 through 15, and indeed chapters 1 through 6 as well, would keep ministers and rabbis from their ravings. Spinoza's first biographer highlights "the tranquility of his soul, which he preferred to all things imaginable" (Lucas, 69). But is this fact or hagiography?

Can this be the same Spinoza who—so the story goes—had to be locked into his apartment to prevent him from rushing into the streets of The Hague to post a placard—"ultimi barbarorum" ("You utter barbarians!")—protesting the mob lynching and mutilation of his friends and Holland's leaders Johan and Cornelius de Witt in late summer 1672?[4] And what about the "evil opinions and acts" and the "monstrous deeds" with which Spinoza was charged and for which he was excommunicated at the age of twenty-three on July 27, 1656, by the rabbinical court of the Amsterdam synagogue? No doubt such accusations—even if they are in fact harsher than the usual Amsterdam Jewish bans—can be dismissed as linguistic formalities rather than specific and actual references.[5] No doubt, too, in the former case, one outburst does not define a man, and what happened to the de Witt brothers was indeed barbaric.

Still, can one so easily deny or excuse—or even fully explain—the harshness, indeed the venom of Spinoza's many abusive verbal attacks, for instance, the censorious invective with which he demeans the greatest of medieval Jewish scholars, Moses Maimonides, as we have seen in chapter 7 of the *Theological-Political Treatise*? There, not content to show the failings of Maimonides's alternative but still philosophical manner of biblical interpretation, Spinoza describes it as "license . . . excessive and rash," concluding: "Therefore we can dismiss Maimonides' view as harmful, unprofitable and absurd" (102). To be sure Maimonides's works were attacked no less viciously, and Maimonides was also excommunicated, during the hundred years of the "Maimonidean controversy" that his writings sparked in Spain and France following his lifetime. But that controversy had long since settled down prior to Spinoza; Maimonides had long since entered the pantheon of great Jewish thinkers; and there is no evidence Spinoza was even aware that it had transpired. No doubt, too, this bit of rhetoric is of a piece with Spinoza's usual and broader denigration of all rabbinic interpretations (Christian ministers are only charged with egoism and superstition, the case is far worse with rabbis). In chapter 9 of the *Theological-Political Treatise*, for instance, Spinoza says of their commentaries: "The Rabbis run quite wild . . ." (121) (and in the same chapter, there are the "Cabbalistic triflers whose madness passes the bounds of my understanding" (122)—but this latter remark is closer to Spinoza's scorn for

---

4. Nadler, *Spinoza: A Life*, 306. The details of this tale are reported by Leibniz, and are perhaps suspect for that reason. But on the face of it the story is questionable, or at least comical, I think, to imagine Spinoza rushing into the streets to admonish the mobs with a sign written in Latin.

5. For a detailed historical account of Spinoza's excommunication, see Nadler, *Spinoza*, 116–154.

"babies, fools, and madmen," to which we shall shortly return), and in chapter 10 Spinoza bemoans "the audacity of the Rabbis" (129). These are just samples, but what they make clear is that when he wishes the calm Spinoza is quite capable of graphic and sharp vituperation.

He is also capable of a subtler denigrating rhetoric. I have already mentioned that he constantly calls the Talmudic rabbis "Pharisees," certainly a negative New Testament appellation, knowing that these same rabbis saved Judaism from Roman ruination and are the same rabbis honored, studied and taught by the rabbis of the Jewish community which excommunicated Spinoza himself. At the same time Spinoza is always sure to call Jesus by the name "Christ," when normal Jewish rhetorical practice would be to call him "Jesus," because "Christ" is the Greek term (and "Christus" the Church Latin transcription) for the Hebrew *Mashiach*, whose English translation is "Messiah," a name that from a strictly Jewish point of view is an incorrect—and therefore from Spinoza's mouth a deliberately provocative—appellation for Jesus. We have discussed Spinoza's kowtowing to anti-Jewish Christian theology in the contents of his arguments against Judaism in the *Theological-Political Treatise*. Here we have tweaks and flourishes of the same misreading. Which is not to say that we can overlook or excuse the many false and cruel attacks on the ancient Israelites in the *Theological-Political Treatise*. Again and again, like a broken record, Spinoza attacks the ancient Israelites—check the text—for their "immaturity," "childishness," "ignorance," "instability," "fickleness," and so on.[6] They are "stiff-necked"

---

6. I am amazed at the Spinoza scholars—and even more amazed at *Jewish* Spinoza scholars—who argue that Spinoza is somehow sympathetic to Jews and Judaism. Where is the evidence? Is it because he is often characterized as a "Jewish philosopher" in the textbooks? Or is it because he usually figures in college courses on Jewish thinkers? Is it because he was born Jewish? Or is it because he writes about Jews and the Bible? But what about what he actually says in those books?! There is nothing in the *Theological-Political Treatise* or in the *Ethics* to indicate any special preferment or even the remotest sympathy toward or with Jews or Judaism—indeed, all to the contrary. Levinas's charge, as we saw in an earlier chapter, is even more severe: Spinoza misunderstood and misrepresented Judaism; he was not sufficiently competent as a scholar to speak with authority about the Judaism he so clearly opposes. Another consideration: Are we supposed to think that the rabbis of Amsterdam were fools? That they actually were as Spinoza would depict them? For the persecuted minority religious community of Amsterdam Jewry, excommunication was quite a serious matter.

rabble. Why all this spleen? Even putting aside his anti-Jewish animus as part of his philosophically based rejection of old-fashioned religion and superstition in the name of science, what drives Spinoza so mad about babies, children, women, suicides, mad persons?

We have seen that it is upon the backdrop of his failure to convincingly answer Cartesian objections, objections defending the notion of free will against his own equation of will and intellect, that Spinoza's distemper against suicides, babies, fools, and madmen was aroused. We will be turning to four more specific instances of Spinoza's spleen, to recognize it first of all, but also to understand its causes, and in so doing to better appreciate the insuperable difficulties of the dehumanization that tears Spinoza's philosophy apart from within. Spinoza's vitriol and its significance are usually overlooked and hence ignored in the secondary literature, with the notable exception of Gilles Deleuze.[7] Before turning to the four cases, I want to make a brief excursus to

---

7. Deleuze, in *Spinoza: Practical Philosophy*, unlike most commentators, does recognize and distinguish a cool and a hot Spinoza. Of the *Ethics* Deleuze has this to say: "The *Ethics* is a book written twice simultaneously: once in the continuous stream of definitions, propositions, demonstrations, and corollaries, which develop the great speculative themes with all the rigors of the mind; another time in the broken chain of scholia, a discontinuous volcanic line, a second version underneath the first, expressing all the angers of the heart and setting forth the practical theses of denunciation and liberation" (29). According to Deleuze, "this was a common procedure that consisted in concealing the boldest or least orthodox arguments in appendices or notes (Bayle's dictionary is a later example)" (29). It seems to me, however, that Spinoza is equally bold in both "streams" of the *Ethics*, that is to say, in the "speculative" and the "practical" portions. It is in the freer talk of the latter, to be sure, the stream Deleuze describes as the "volcanic line," that Spinoza undermines the cool "geometrical" framing that he has constructed for the former. An additional thought: In contrast to the view that Spinoza did not publish the *Ethics* in his lifetime for fear of reactionary religious and political reprisal, and considering its main principles are not only transparent (contra Strauss's oversubtle hermeneutics, which Levinas somewhat humorously refers to as "detective" work) but are precisely put to theological and political use in the *Theological-Political Treatise*, which he did publish, it is perhaps time to consider that Spinoza withheld publication of the *Ethics* in his lifetime because he was all too aware of his philosophy's intellectual shortcomings, indeed its failure and irrationality. I suggest also in the present chapter that to some extent Spinoza's spleen might in truth be evidence of his otherwise unadmitted intellectual disappointment and frustration. To be sure, these are just speculations.

consider an alternative interpretation of Spinoza's spleen, one which I do not accept. I will give my reasons for rejecting it after presenting it.

Brief Excursus: Another Possible Angle on Spinoza's Rhetorical Spleen

To say Spinoza is *upset* that most humans are *human, all too human*, that is, fallible and weak, is to put the matter delicately. In fact he is *angry* about it and angry with most humans, the many. At the same time he wants to encourage the few, those he believes are capable—intelligent enough—for science and philosophy. Spinoza thus encourages the segregation of humanity between the few and the many that Nietzsche will again advocate centuries later in the *Genealogy of Morals*. Unlike Nietzsche, however, who would segregate the healthy and strong from the sick and weak, in Spinoza's case it is a segregation of knowers, intellectuals, scientists, philosophers, from the ignorant, the stupid, the emotional, the yahoos. As we have seen, from a strictly philosophical view, putting aside whatever animus might derive from Christian and Jewish considerations, Spinoza is particularly peeved at the ancient Israelites, at their prophets, and then at the later rabbis of the Talmud—no scientists there. The masses, driven by their bodily desires and emotions, always and everywhere prove their incapacity for science, rationality, and active intellect.

In his defense, one might say that Spinoza's derisive tone, even his anger and spleen directed toward the rabbis, the masses, and all the other ignoramuses he attacks, is in accord with what he asserts in proposition 7 of part IV of the *Ethics*, namely: "*An emotion cannot be checked or destroyed except by a contrary emotion which is stronger than the emotion which is to be checked*" (158). A couple of pages earlier, in the scholium to proposition 1 of part IV, Spinoza had also explained: "So imaginings do not disappear at the presence of what is true in so far as it is true, but because other imaginings that are stronger supervene to exclude the present existence of the things we imagine" (156). So Spinoza could be excused for fighting fire with fire. Because the ignorant masses are in thrall to their emotions, Spinoza can only properly upbraid them, harangue them, countering their passion with greater passion. In contrast to the Enlightenment rational critique of religion, say, as found in Kant, which according to Spinoza can only be ineffective with those who need it most, here, in Spinoza's harangue, we have something angrier but similar to Voltaire's and Nietzsche's mockery. This would be another way, only slightly more generous than my own approach but equally upsetting to the popular image of the serene and sage Spinoza, to interpret and justify Spinoza's all-too-present spleen.

I do not find it convincing for the reasons I have just indicated: philosophically it ignores what Spinoza means by the perfection of Nature; from a theoretical and a practical point of view it misunderstands the nature and status of Spinoza's division of the few and the many, mistakes Spinoza's attitude toward the capacities of the many, and hence it mistakes the proper audience of the *Theological-Political Treatise*. For all his venom, for all his anger and violent rhetoric, Spinoza surely does not want *deliberately* to be shouting at his adversaries. Spinoza's proper world is the world of "freedom" (= necessity), not the world of obedience. It is the world of truth not rhetoric, of ideas not images and words. We turn to the four cases.

Spinoza's Unwanted Babies

Certainly all philosophers and philosophies demand more than childishness in their visions of the truly human life. Philosophy, with its commitment to reason, is a proud discipline, basing itself in evidence, in argumentation, demanding nothing less than a fully adult intelligence at full speed. Therefore it is not particularly surprising that few philosophers have said anything of note about childhood at all, about life's stages prior to the full development of intelligence and reasoning. No doubt one finds some pedagogical advice, such as in Rousseau's *Emile* or Plato's *Republic*, and almost everywhere much encouragement to become reasonable, to embrace knowledge, truth, and the like, and in Levinas's case, in the fourth section of *Totality and Infinity* there is a full-scale phenomenological-ethical account of the essential status of fecundity, parenting, raising children, and the like, but this is an exception.

Spinoza does not ignore childhood, does not ignore children and babies. He positively attacks them. For Spinoza the very fact of having been a baby and child is already a failing in and of itself. We take our four examples from the *Ethics*, where Spinoza speaks as a philosopher to philosophers. In part III, after Spinoza has already laid out the basic axioms and principles that constitute his philosophy in parts I and II of *Ethics* and is about to turn to a more detailed account of modes, that is to say, of mind and body and their relation to one another, in the scholium to proposition 59, he makes the following observation regarding an exclusion that is of particular relevance to our present interest. "I have passed by those external affections of the body," he writes, "which can be observed in the case of emotion, such as trembling, pallor, sobbing, laughter, and so on, because they are related to the body without any relation to the mind" (141). "Trembling, pallor, sobbing, laughter, and so on," are these not precisely what one might expect of babies, women, fools, and the mad? Are these all then to be considered as mere bodies, mindless carnality, reflexes of flesh, of sensuality, nearest to animals, "body without any relation to the mind"? Let us finally turn to the four examples.

Not the Ill Spanish Poet Again

Let us recall briefly from the previous chapter of the present volume what Spinoza said about death. Having defined individual entities as ratios or proportions of motion and rest, proposition 39 of part IV declares that whatever conduces to preserve the constituent parts of the human body's proportions of motion and rest to one another is good and whatever changes that proportion is bad. In the proof Spinoza explains: "The human body needs many other bodies for its preservation. But that which constitutes the form [*forma*] of the human body consists in this, that its parts communicate their motions to one another in a certain fixed proportion" (176). So to reinforce that fixed proportion is good and to upset it is bad. The issue at hand, as we saw, has to do with identity and death. "I understand a body to die," Spinoza writes in the scholium to the same proposition 39, "when its parts are so disposed as to maintain a different proportion of motion-and-rest to one another" (177). So, he continues, a body need not turn into a corpse to die but rather needs only to change its proportion of rest-and-motion sufficiently to die, as it were, to be another body.

The real issue is identity, as is made explicit in the rest of the scholium, which I cite in full. Here again is the sick Spanish poet, but here we are concerned less with him than with what Spinoza says about babies.

> It sometimes happens that a man undergoes such changes that I would not be prepared to say that he is the same person. I have heard tell of a certain Spanish poet who was seized with sickness, and although he recovered, he remained so unconscious of this past life that he did not believe that the stories and tragedies he had written were his own. Indeed, he might have been taken for a child in adult form if he had also forgotten his native tongue. And if this seems incredible, what are we to say about babies? A man of advanced years believes their nature to be so different from his own that he could not be persuaded that he had ever been a baby if he did not draw a parallel from other cases. But I prefer to leave these matters unresolved, so as not to afford material for the superstitious to raise new problems. (177)

We have already discussed the Spaniard in the previous chapter; let us now turn to Spinoza's remarks about babies. While not everyone is struck with an illness such as the Spanish poet's, with its extreme loss of memory, everyone without exception begins life as a baby. The "man of advanced years," Spinoza would have it, believes that his older self has no continuity with his infantile self. Presumably this means, on one level, that the ratio of motion and rest of his infantile body and the ratio of motion and rest of his adult body are discontinuous. This is to say, the baby has "died" and is no longer, and a completely new identity has arisen, namely, the adult, the man of advanced years. The only "reason" anyone binds adult identity to baby identity, then, is by erroneously drawing "a parallel from other cases." The truth, however (Sigmund Freud and mothers' memories to the contrary), is that there is no internal identity between babies and adults. They are two different entities entirely, the one having "died" before the other comes into existence. It is an odd theory, to be sure, but Spinoza dutifully follows the logic of his ideas—as is the wont of an idealist—regardless of common sense, which does not know the true causes of things in any event.

What are we to make of Spinoza's logic? While it is in one sense true, insofar as adults clearly do have capacities and experiences unavailable to babies, in another sense it is patently false and even ridiculous, since adults all do in some real way come directly and continuously from babies, growing up from being a baby to becoming a child, a youth, teenager, and then becoming an adult human being. Even adults are still growing culturally and intellectually. No doubt some humans, owing to pathogenic conditions, never make it all the way from youth to adulthood. Furthermore, there has been little doubt for the past hundred years—one wonders what scientists thought in Spinoza's day—that events in the life of an infant or young child make serious differences in the personalities, capacities, and experiences of an adult, and hence that there must in fact be significant unbroken continuity between child and adult.

It seems that Spinoza is also obliquely aware of the difficulties in his own theory, as we noted in the previous chapter. To delve into such difficulties, however, would do no more than "afford material for the superstitious to raise new problems," he says, and drops the matter. The matter, however, like the repressed generally, is not so easily dropped. In any event, the difficulties do not go away.

Born Free

Proposition 68 of part IV of the *Ethics* states: "*If men were born free, they would form no conception of good and evil so long as they were free*" (192). The proof follows: "I have said that a free man is he who is guided solely by reason. Therefore he who is born free and remains free has only adequate ideas and thus has no conception of evil (Cor. 64, IV), and consequently no conception of good (for good and evil are correlative)" (192). Logical as it may be on Spinoza's premises, it is quite an odd thing to say in fact even hypothetically, referring to an impossible conjunction: being "born" and having "only adequate ideas." Would an intelligence with only adequate ideas from the get-go be born? Manufactured perhaps, launched, constructed, produced, but *born*? What Spinoza seems not to want to say explicitly but must say logically is that to be free, to be completely and entirely free, that is, to have only adequate ideas, to be guided "solely by reason," would be to not have a finite human body at all. God alone, He who is Himself uncreated, always has, has had, and will have, or more precisely eternally has such freedom. Remember, falsity for Spinoza does not come, as it did for Descartes, from a will hesitating before several ideas of which it then chooses the wrong one, but rather, as we have seen earlier, from misjudging a fragment as if it were a whole, hence an only apparent lack of coincidence between will and intellect, a merely apparent lack of the simultaneity of affirmation and truth, since will and intellect are *in truth* one and the same. In other words, however much Spinoza tried to skirt the issue or blow smoke upon it, falsity comes from a separation of will and intellect. And such separation comes, as Spinoza himself says, from the influence of body, from the interference of the body. So if, per impossible, one were "born free," born, that is to say, always affirming truth, one either would therefore not have a body at all, or—and this does not makes sense—one would have a body that never interfered with truth/affirmation, that is, a body that is really not a body but intellect.

In the scholium to proposition 68 Spinoza gives an exegesis of a part of the biblical Adam story. Everything was fine with Adam, and fine with Adam's relation to Eve, "who agreed entirely with his own nature," until "he came to believe that the beasts were like himself," for at that point "he straightaway began to imitate their emotions and to lose his freedom" (192). Interesting hypothesis; is it Spinoza's interpretation of the change in Adam after "eating the fruit"? But Eve ate the fruit first. Do we not once again catch Spinoza off guard, as it were, without an explanation but creating a smokescreen? He has no explanation for the body as body, the body separated from adequate ideas. It must therefore be a beastly body, a body comparable only to animals. Maimonides at least maintained a certain ambiguity between conceiving the body along Greek lines as an original matter (*materia prima*) prior to form-giving creation and conceiving it along Jewish lines as something created ex nihilo. Spinoza is simply stumped, without explanation. The body as body doesn't fit his system; it plays the role within it of a hindrance and distraction, capable—with its fragments, its fragmentation, its parts out of joint with the whole—of eclipsing truth, but one really knows not how. It is clear, between the lines as it were, that Spinoza would rather it simply went away. Unable to explain body as body, disturbed by what body does, this "difficulty," this incongruity, this wrench in his system, all this translates into Spinoza's horror of babies, those gushy, mushy, moaning, crying, giggling, dribbling, excreting, urinating, fleshy little beasts. He must degrade them, better banish them, or best of all take them for "dead," completely alien creatures, completely out of the way, disposed of, gone.

"You shun the things I call wicked because they are opposed to your particular nature," writes Willem van Blyenbergh to Spinoza on February 19, 1665, "not because they contain vice in themselves. You avoid them just as we avoid food that we find disgusting. Surely he who avoids evil things just because they are repugnant to his nature can take little pride in his virtue" (letter no. 23, Letters, 166). In a return letter of March 13, 1665, Spinoza replies that "evil, error and villainy does not consist in anything that expresses essence, and therefore it cannot be said that God is its cause" (letter no. 22, Letters, 161). Essence . . . pure freedom, again there is no body at all—how could such nonentities bother, let alone disgust Spinoza? But they do. And Spinoza's bother bothers us.

So Hang Yourself

In the same return letter of March 13, 1665, regarding the same issue of "essence," Spinoza finds himself compelled to discuss suicide or, more accurately and as usual, to evade this issue.

In his letter, Blyenbergh had made the perfectly reasonable argument that Spinoza had not given a good reason but had really only proclaimed by arbitrary fiat—indeed, by stipulation—that essence applies only to what we normally think of as good and not to what we normally think of as wicked. "For the impious and the pious," so Blyenbergh points out for argument's sake in greater conformity with Spinoza's own ideas than Spinoza seems to want to admit, "both receive their essence, and likewise their preservation or continual creation of their essence, from God as God, not as judge, and both fulfill God's will in the same way, that is, in accordance with God's degree" (letter no. 22, Letters, 161). This being so, Blyenbergh raises three difficulties, which in his reply letter Spinoza sums up as the following three questions:

1. Is murder as pleasing to God as almsgiving?

2. Is stealing, in relation to God, as good as righteousness?

3. If there were a mind to whose particular nature the pursuit of pleasure and villainy was not repugnant, but agreeable, could it have any virtuous motive that must move it to do good and avoid evil? (letter no. 23, Letters, 167)

These are indeed three quite penetrating and troubling questions. Spinoza has clearly grasped the nature and the point of Blyenbergh's objection.

To the first question Spinoza begins by claiming not to know what "pleasing to God" (Spinoza's phrase) means. If Blyenbergh is proposing an anthropomorphic notion of God, then Spinoza rejects the question. If, however, Blyenbergh is suggesting that murder and giving alms in the light of Spinoza's system "are equally good and perfect"—and this is surely the critical edge of his objection, and Blyenbergh has surely made it clear that he is not considering an anthropomorphic notion of God—then Spinoza says no, they are not. To the second question Spinoza gives the same answer, rejecting first an anthropomorphic image of God, and then insisting again that stealing and righteousness are not equally perfect, basing himself on the stipulations he had earlier made in the *Ethics* by which he had defined righteousness in terms of essence and stealing as lacking thereof. The thief "lacks the knowledge of God and of himself; that is, he lacks the principal thing that makes us men" (letter no. 23, Letters, 168). For us, neither of these answers by Spinoza is really an answer. Instead they beg the question, merely repeating the stipulations that Blyenbergh's questions are clearly and pointedly designed to challenge. "[T]his is not the place," Spinoza adds, no doubt aware of his own evasion, "to explain the fundamentals of Ethics, or to prove everything I say" (letter no. 23, Letters, 168). *Again evasion*—at precisely the same moment and for precisely the same reason. Spinoza is stumped by the body, stumped by dark pleasures, villainy, and evil. Surely his evasion cannot satisfy us as it could not have satisfied Blyenbergh. These are our questions also, and they are serious and telling and inescapable.

To the third question Spinoza's answer is ultimately no better, but it is far more revealing, far more revealing we suspect than Spinoza would have wanted. It also responds to the first two questions. Here it is in full:

> Finally, as to your third question, it presupposes a contradiction. It is just as if someone were to ask me whether, if it accorded better with a man's nature that he should hang himself, there would be any reason why he should not hang himself. However, suppose it possible that there could be such a nature. Then I say (whether I grant free will or not) that if anyone sees that he can live better on the gallows than at his own table, he would be foolish not to go and hang

himself. And he who saw clearly that he would in fact enjoy a more perfect and better life or essence by engaging in villainy than by pursuing virtue would also be a fool if he did not do just that. For in relation to such a perverted human nature, villainy would be virtue. (letter no. 23, Letters, 168)

What I early named as Spinoza's question begging reappears quite obviously in the final sentence, where the "villain" is said to have a "perverted human nature."

Nevertheless the prior sentences come as a revelation. If one admits hypothetically that by essence a person is a suicide or a villain then that is what they must be, with no gainsaying it. To add a value judgment, such as "perverted," is as superficial as all talk of "good and evil"; it is the empty ignorant talk of the multitudes who do not know the true causes of things, certainly not of the truth of a scientist or philosopher. Indeed, if the scientist or philosopher were to admit such hollow evaluative language, they would have to say that it is "good" for the suicide to kill himself and "good for the villain to steal and murder." Spinoza is thus quite well on his way to de Sade and Nietzsche. Natural-born killers should, naturally, kill.

After such dangerous talk, it is not surprising that Spinoza concludes his letter, referring to further similar questions by Blyenbergh, with the same evasion that we have noted several times already: "since one could ask a hundred such questions an hour without arriving at the conclusion of any one of them, and since you yourself do not press for an answer, I shall leave it unanswered." Though Spinoza is certainly being a good sport to want to support good over evil, righteousness over villainy, life over suicide, unfortunately his philosophy does not have the *philosophical* resources to do so. Blyenbergh has caught him out. It is a devastating criticism if one wants one's Spinoza good and just, a democrat, supporting liberty, opposed to tyranny, and the like. But it is not so, and Spinoza can hardly not know it. Spinoza has no better answer to queries designed to throw off his mask than a thinly veiled moral exhortation, and then a dismissive evasion. Such responses are unworthy of the brilliant Spinoza, yet they do reveal the dark side of his philosophy, reveal, how shall we say it, let us be kind, they reveal at the very least what Levinas in the preface to *Totality and Infinity* has called "hypocrisy" (24).

Before moving to the fourth and final case, let us recall what Spinoza said of suicide in the *Ethics* itself, related to the issue of Buridan's ass (scholium at the conclusion of part II):

> I readily grant that a man placed in such a state of equilibrium (namely, where he feels nothing else but hunger and thirst and perceives nothing but such-and-such food and drink at equal distances from him) will die of hunger and thirst. If they ask me whether such a man is not to be reckoned an ass rather than a man, I reply that I do not know, just as I do not know how one should reckon a man who hangs himself, or how one should reckon babies, fools, and madmen. (100)

We have seen how true it is that Spinoza does "not know how one should reckon" suicides, babies, fools, and madmen, because he prefers to deny them essence, adequate idea, reality—but at the same time, because he rejects as ignorance the moral grounds of such a preference he really cannot justify such a denial. In such a situation the serene philosopher resorts to name-calling: they are asses not men. And the babies, women, mad persons, fools . . . they too are asses, more animal than human, disgusting.

Let us remark too that elsewhere in the *Ethics*, in part IV, his account of suicides is no better or more convincing. When explaining in the scholium to proposition 18 "that each man, as far as in him lies, should endeavor to preserve his own being. . . . that every man should love himself, should seek his own advantage (I mean his real advantage), should aim at whatever really leads a man toward greater perfection" (164), we see Spinoza's question-begging in the use of the emphatic term "really" ("real advantage," "really leads"). So when Spinoza deduces a few sentences later that "it follows that those who commit suicide are of weak spirit and are completely overcome by external causes opposed to their own nature" (164), this is nothing but a preference masquerading as a truth, or it is again question-begging. It only follows, that is to say, if one accepts Spinoza's stipulation that essence, which applies only to self-preserving nature, to *conatus*, means also that such a nature cannot at the same time be self-destroying (the "contradiction" mentioned in his letter to Blyenbergh), ignoring the fact that self-destruction, like a time bomb, might very well be the essence of this or that entity. We are back, in other words, to the *value judgment* contained in what Spinoza would pass off as truth: "To be able to not exist is a weakness" (37).

If death is no more or less than a change in identity, as it is for Spinoza, then a suicidal person and a nonsuicidal person are really no different in essence, even if one dies by his own hand and the other from some other cause. A baby too would be a self-destructive being and would have—whatever Spinoza's disgust—an essence as much as an adult. To be is to have essence. Nothing in Spinoza—outside of what appears at times to be a conventional subjective prejudice—prevents such reasoning. In view of that prejudice the suicidal person is "weak" and "overcome." But from the point of view of essence, that person does what they must do. We hear Spinoza's unjustified and unjustifiable moral optimism regarding selfishness in many places. For instance, it appears in proposition 20 of part IV: "*The more every man endeavors and is able to seek his own advantage, that is, to preserve his own being, the more he is endowed with virtue. On the other hand, in so far as he neglects to preserve what is to his advantage, that is, his own being, to that extent he is weak*" (165). Spinoza is loath to admit that preserving one's own being, *conatus*, might entail destroying one's own being, or, in a word, that the suicide (or the villain, the baby, the madman, the fool, et al.) might have an essence. It is the usual philosopher's prejudice. Only philosophers have essences; only humans who are philosophers are truly human. "Nobody," Spinoza writes in the scholium to this proposition—and his repetition is telling—"I repeat, refuses food or kills himself from the necessity of his own nature, but from the constraint of external causes" (165). Clearly Kafka's hunger artist did not read Spinoza. "No virtue can be conceived as prior to this one, namely, the *conatus* to preserve oneself" (166). To do otherwise is—surprise—to succumb to "inadequate ideas." The circularity of Spinoza's "argument" is patent. But Blyenbergh's questions, which are our questions also, remain, and remain unanswered.

Born Adult

The best I have saved for last. It is found in Spinoza's remarks on babies—he cannot get them off his mind—in the scholium to proposition 6 of part V of the *Ethics*. It is clever and unforgettable. Spinoza is arguing that the more a person sees the necessity in things, that is, the more insight into necessity is applied "to particular things," "the greater is this power of the mind over the emotions" (206). It is Spinoza's version of therapy: knowledge of necessity makes a person tranquil, quiets their emotions. So the "pain over the loss of some good is assuaged as soon as the man who has lost it realizes that good could not have been saved in any way" (206). The rationalist's *amor fati*, whatever happens must happen, should be accepted graciously.

With this in mind, send in the babies:

> Similarly, we see that nobody pities a baby because it cannot talk or walk or reason, and because it spends many years in a kind of ignorance of self. But if most people were born adults and only a few were born babies, then everybody would feel sorry for babies because they would then look on infancy not as a natural and necessary thing but as a fault or flaw in Nature. (206)

Clever indeed! If most people were somehow born fully adult, like Athena or Aphrodite, then we would pity, if we were not completely disgusted by them, those few abominations born wretched helpless stupid babies. The point of Spinoza's claim is clear: it would be better if we were all born adults, and no doubt best of all if we were all born philosophers. Insofar as the human eye reaches near full maturity by the age of three, we could say—and as a metaphor, by which the eye equals the mind, it works nicely—that Spinoza wants us to catch up to our eyes, or more radically that even our eyes should be born fully formed. The point is that except that infancy appears "a natural and necessary thing" Spinoza would eliminate it—"a fault or flaw in Nature"—altogether. Yet, without being sure we are being more or less Spinozist than Spinoza, because they seem real enough, infancy and childhood, "a kind of ignorance of self," must have an essence of some sort, must be part of an eternal, immutable, necessary intelligibility, but God only knows what part. Spinoza's hypothetical suggestion, however, fits his philosophy to a T. Not better we were never born, the wisdom of Silenus, but to be born fully adult, fully finished, complete—in a word not created or born at all but always from the start fully self-conscious modes of absolute intelligibility: to be born a philosopher. And as we have seen, for Spinoza all philosophers, as all scientists, are born to knowing.

We also see that 350 years ago Spinoza, without being a prophet of course, proleptically articulated a yearning for cloning. A yearning, in any event, for the end of infancy, childhood, parenting, schooling, learning, character development, maturation, and anything else not already fully finished. The philosopher's paradise according to Spinoza: a world without disturbances, no sobbing or laughing, no more *wasted* time overcoming ignorance, no crawling, toilet training, no dribbling, no distracting desires, no push and pull of pleasures and pains . . . again, eternal, immutable, necessary, the world of pure ideas, Diotima's paradise as well. The paradise of pure reason, of necessity, of adequate ideas, of truth . . . absolute intelligibility, the serene realm (not even a "kingdom," because without a king) of pure intellect and intellection. Certainly no more beastly babies, or women, or mad persons, or fools . . . surely, Spinoza must be thinking, not too high a price for some peace and quiet, security, not too high a price to pay for philosophy.

Levinas's idea of time, in contrast to Spinoza's immutable eternity, is far richer, meaningful, attuned to what it means for humans to be *living mortal* beings, beings vulnerable in their being, beings subject to suffering, wounds, hurts, pain, aging, and death, but also enjoyment, laughter, joys, a good meal, a beautiful sunset, comradery, love, celebration, and festival. For Levinas, accepting the temporality of time, in contrast to the stasis of eternity, means not only projective temporalizing, for instance Bergson's duration, Husserl's protensions and retentions, or Heidegger's ecstatic temporality, but far more radically, and yet in line with Levinas's fundamental idea that intersubjectivity is the source of all significance and signification, it means the "absolute future," the "infinite time" of fecundity, the time of human generations (Hebrew: *dor v'dor*, "generation to generation"): "Infinite being, that is, ever recommencing being" (TI, 268). Spinoza's disdain for babies, for growth, for pedagogy, is not an accidental quirk, an eccentricity, rather, according to Levinas, it "indicates the vanity of pantheism" (TI, 269). For Levinas, "In fecundity the tedium of this repetition ceases; the I is other and young. . . . Infinite time does not bring an eternal life to an aging subject; it is *better* across the discontinuity of generations, punctuated by the inexhaustible youths of the child" (TI, 268). Radically contesting Spinoza, the escape into eternity, the closed system of pantheism, Levinas affirms, "Youth as a philosophical concept is defined thus" (TI, 268). And he adds, lest anyone question the philosophical status of youth as a concept: "Philosophy itself constitutes a moment of this temporal accomplishment, a discourse always addressed to another. What we are now exposing is addressed to those who shall wish to read it" (269).

Conclusions

What are we to make of all this? Let us admit we cannot neatly or nearly capture in a few concluding sentences all that the present chapter and the present book have accomplished. Speaking to the present chapter: how to sum up what it is that so disturbs the sublime serenity of Spinoza, so irritates him as to drive him to such associations and deprecations—"babies, fools, and madmen" (E, 100), "fools, madmen, or birds" (TPT, 1)—as we have seen? Why does he rant on and on, why punctuate his discourse with nagging insistence that only the scientist and philosopher, exclusively the scientist and philosopher, no one but the scientist and philosopher is free? And everyone else, the vast multitude of humanity, are they really no better than ignorant masses, nothing but rabble, slavish, deluded, more or less avatars, and variants of babies, fools, women, madmen? There remains one more citation from the *Ethics* too tasty for me to resist presenting, from part III, scholium to proposition 2:

> A baby thinks that it freely seeks milk, an angry child that it freely seeks revenge, and a timid man that he freely seeks flight. Again, the drunken man believes that it is from the free decision of the mind that he says what he later, when sober, wishes he had not said. So, too, the delirious man, the gossiping woman, the child, and many more of this sort think that they speak from free mental decision, when in fact they are unable to restrain their torrent of words. (106)

What a sad human condition. We are all more or less delirious men, gossiping women, angry children, drunken in too many ways to enumerate. Since by now we know Spinoza's brave solution and program ad nauseam—yes, yes, only the scientist and philosopher who know truth, necessity, eternity, God's intellect, and so forth, are free—what we want to call attention to in presenting the previous citation, as in the entire preceding section, is not this but rather Spinoza's spleen, his need for diatribe, his need to go on and on denouncing babies, silly children, timid men, drunkards, delirious men, gossiping women, the list goes on and on. No doubt Spinoza wants us all to rise to science, and no doubt it is a fine aspiration, for science is certainly a powerful and liberating form of knowledge. But Spinoza has turned this aspiration into a monomania and this liberation into a fanaticism. He does not simply admire science, as do I, as does Levinas, and as do so many others, and rightfully. He does not simply advocate and promote science, the truths of science, as do I, Levinas, and so many sensible others. He insists on it and on it alone. He turns it into a hammer, indeed a gun. Only in mathematical science is there truth—nowhere else. All the rest be damned—as superstition, madness, ignorance, and danger. Get rid of that mess, clean it up, use solvent, and sweep away any remainder! The human, all too human—execute it. Thus Spinoza in the name of an impossible ideal of truth ends a misanthrope, an antihumanist, an enemy of all that is human, all too human. His is a philosophy of crisis, in Husserl's sense.

Yes, surely the drunkard, the delirious man, the gossiping woman will later regret what they have done and said, or we hope they will, as we hope they will rise to morally higher lives and words in the future, caring more about themselves and their neighbors. But is it really so that "a baby thinks that it freely seeks milk"?! Does a baby think? Does a baby think about freedom? Is this the right way for us to think about babies, as not yet thinking correctly? Babies as not yet scientists? I should think not. Babies, children, become more independent, freer, they grow up, they are nurtured, their characters develop, and gradually they will, if all goes well, learn the truths of science, more or less, as well. And this is because the "all too human" is not defined by ignorance and knowledge alone. The humanity of the human is not just ignorance, weakness, deficiency, lack, failure, but also and more profoundly the opportunity and arena of ethics, of love, compassion, care, nurture, respect, and dignity. Pedagogy too is an end as well as a means; learning, reading, gaining knowledge, this is something humans do as humans, for their own sake. The human is indeed a kingdom, with or without a monarch, a kingdom of vulnerability and growth, a dialogue of development, of going forward and going backward, a realm not merely of change or difference but of orientation and heights. It is a kingdom in which humans are close and far from one another, where all—whether with advanced degrees or not—are able to rise to the nobility, the selfless devotion of goodness, and beyond goodness to the sacrifices required by a social vocation aiming for justice, justice for each and for all.

In chapter 5 of the present volume there is sufficient evidence of Spinoza's spleen against the masses, the multitude, the people, who for Spinoza are but ignorant and unruly, and in chapter 6 sufficient evidence of his animus toward religious figures, ministers, priests, rabbis, and prophets, who for Spinoza are ignorant, selfish, ambitious, and liars. And here in the present chapter we have certainly reviewed sufficient evidence to make clear his venom and disgust toward babies and children above all, but for the same reasons also—ignorance, emotion, helplessness, and unruliness—toward women, mad persons, and fools. Where has that popular image of the benighted saintly Spinoza, the retiring studious intellectual Spinoza, the bachelor spiritual cerebral Spinoza gone? A better question, in the face of what Spinoza has actually written and the attitude he betrays, would be to ask where such an image came from in the first place. No doubt it comes to a certain extent from his circle of Dutch friends, who respected his mind and savored their intellectual discussions. No doubt too such an image well served a non-Jewish world that for many reasons, though probably not the best reasons, preferred to honor a Jew who attacked Judaism, who shows that apparently a Jew must turn away from and rise above Judaism to become a man of reason and to defend universal reason. Perhaps there is some perverse parallel here to be made with the attacks made within the Jewish world itself against the reputation of another philosopher-Jew—Moses Mendelssohn—who a century later vigorously defended Judaism before the non-Jewish world? Spinoza was certainly not entirely wrong about the prejudice, parochialism, blinding intolerance, and *apologia* that too often distort religious perspectives. In any event, it is not for me to explain these sociologies, or the popular image of Spinoza. What is certain, however, as we have seen throughout the present volume, from several points of view, philosophic, religious, political, rhetorical, is that Spinoza was no gentle saint, no all-embracing sage. Quite the reverse, his philosophy and his attitude too stood in a fierce and unrelenting opposition to actual Judaism, to religion, and in the final account to everyone and everything outside of the very limited rationality he considered scientific and philosophic—that is to say, in fierce opposition to real life in its "blooming buzzing confusion," life with its pimples, pains, errors, its joys and preferences, and its moral highs and lows. Spinoza's is in contrast an antiseptic philosophy, too clean and neat, too rational, one for which only the rational is real and all the rest is irrational, illusory, and false. We have criticized his philosophy philosophically, pointing out inconsistencies, incongruities, *aporia*, but we should be no less aware—and beware—of the nasty religious, social, and political forms such an exclusionary philosophizing can support. I have tried to illuminate some of these consequences too.

In the face of the dehumanizing produced by rationality oblivious or indifferent to its own limits, already concretely realized in the mines and factories of the Industrial Revolution, since the early nineteenth century there has developed a literature of opposition, protest, even horror, whose start one might roughly date with the publication of Mary Shelley's *Frankenstein: The Modern Prometheus* in 1818. It is in Edgar Allan Poe, Baudelaire, in all the *poètes maudits*. It is in *Moby-Dick*, a book that destroyed Melville's literary career. It opposes the normal with the abnormal, the regular with the irregular, the continuous with the discontinuous, the complete with the broken, the perfect form with the unfinished and raw, the socially acceptable with the extreme and excessive. It is clear in the Romantics' love of ancient ruins and jagged mountains. It is clear in Rodin's sculptures; compare them to the Greek and Roman! To use Kant's language, it is a shift from the "beautiful" to the "sublime," to the excessive, the overwhelming, the infinite. It is the Underground Man; it is Kafkaesque; it lives in all the figures celebrated by Bohemian avant-gardism now global: outlaws, outcasts, renegades, drifters, rebels, hermits, loners, freaks, wild ones, exiles, pariahs, misfits, fugitives, curmudgeons, outsiders, criminals, vagabonds, gypsies, the forlorn, tricksters, troublemakers, strangers, dropouts, the mad, deserters, suicides, mavericks, and all those who in one way or another, for one "reason" or another, find themselves out of joint and outside the boundaries of the rational.[8]

---

8. For a good example of the celebration of outlaws, outcasts, renegades, and the like, as heterogeneous exceptions that challenge the homogeneity and smooth functioning of "the system," see the following, a citation from Jules Monnerot's book *Les faits sociaux ne sont pas des choses* (Social Facts Are Not Things) (1946), as cited in a book review by Georges Bataille. In his review Bataille describes and distinguishes the "sacred and the profane." He takes Monnerot's broader distinction between the "heterogeneous and homogeneous" as a helpful additional way to grasp this distinction. Thus for Bataille the *sacred* is what is and is able to embrace heterogeneity, difference, the strange, transcendence, in all their multitudinous manifestations, while the *profane*, in contrast, is what imposes homogeneity everywhere and thus must reject, marginalize, and eliminate the heterogeneous, which multiplicity is castigated as sin, heresy, infidel, evil, injustice, satanic, villainous, animal, and so forth. The relevance to Spinoza is obvious. Spinoza and Spinozism are precisely the imposition of total homogeneity, the regime of the true and the rational without possible exit or escape. Like Frankenstein's creature, a rationality meant to save also destroys, whether through administrative and mass media anonymity and conformity, universal commodification and leveling, electronic surveillance, information retrieval, and the like, monsters of dehumanization are impeccably legitimized in the name of security, health, safety, and public welfare. It is precisely because our aim has been to unmask and criticize—with the help of Levinas's ethics—the intellectual totalizing of Spinoza's philosophy, and therefore also to expose all forms of Spinozism, including today's positivism, to the same unmasking and criticism, which gives meaning to the provocation of the title of the present volume, *Out of Control*.

I cite from Bataille's review, therefore, because I believe the distinction between the heterogeneous and the homogenous made in it, valuable enough as it is, when linked to the distinction between the sacred and the profane, provides rich food for thought spiced with the many figures of marginality who are mentioned, whose singularity we have not yet had occasion to invoke, a combination of ideas, distinctions, and persons, which I hope will open our eyes in yet another way to the intellectual danger of Spinozism that the present volume all along has been exposing.

"The heterogeneous," writes Monnerot,

> can be shown to be anything irreducible to assimilation: the madman, the "accursed poet" like Lautréamont or Rimbaud before he fled to Harrar, the unyielding insubordinate, the "intractable criminal on whom the prison door always closes," but also the outsider with no profession (since a profession is a mark of homogeneity) like Marx or Comte, who lived off the subsidies of their friends; Kierkegaard and Nietzsche, who both in their own way refused to comply with the general; Blanqui, who was almost always in prison and, as soon as he was released, always exhorted the people to rise up against the

It is not with surrealism, or the exceptional and strange, the odd and different, however, that Levinas breaks from the closed system of rationality. He does not oppose the System with "the ineffable of the clandestine or the subterranean" (TI, 301), because their resistance is inadequate in the face of rationality, merely "irrational." Rather, in the name of ethics, in view of the transcendence of the other person—"the widow, the orphan, the stranger"—and of the separation and independence of the self, maintained through responsibility, the totality is breached and finds its own source outside itself. More radical, then, than all the fascinating Romantic figures, if less romantic, is the excess, the exception, the transcendence—Levinas uses the term "anarchy" in its etymological sense—of the *responsible person*, responsible to and for the other before oneself. "One is not an irrationalist nor a mystic nor a pragmatist for questioning the identification of power and *logos*" (TI, 302). "The interest of this opposition does not lie in the very protestation of the individual who refuses the system and reason, that is, in his arbitrariness, which the coherent discourse could hence not silence by persuasion—but in the affirmation that makes this opposition live" (TI, 217). Ethical affirmation, affirmation of the surplus of responsibilities surpassing being. Moral responsibility for the other, and for all others, which may never be fully called upon, but which may well rise to its obligations, in unanticipated and unwanted situations, rise with an unshakable courage able to break conventions and bend rules if need be, *to do what is right* to help the threatened, the endangered, the downtrodden, the needy, the outcast, "the widow, the orphan and the stranger," to alleviate the suffering of others . . . a responsibility at risk, exposed, singular, without substitute, regardless of consequences, all the way to the possibility of "dying for . . ." the other. Nothing could be more astonishing, unnatural, unpredictable, or impervious to power, and no one a greater misfit, outcast, even outlaw, or more singular or sovereign, but nothing is better either.

> established order; all those who are "in breach of convention": not merely the kind-hearted prostitute but the prostitute *per se*, the pimp, and everyone who would be part of what the old jurists would have called the "dangerous classes."

In this way, though, through an inevitable slippage, the category of the sacred extends to the realm of our own lives. (Bataille, "The Moral Meaning of Sociology," 107)

Whatever their stature in the world of the spectacle, however hidden they may be from fanfare and public acclaim, unseen perhaps, eventually forgotten, unrecorded, *moral sacrifices* are not reducible to forms of ignorance, nor are they reducible to imaginary compensations. In morality and justice—in being responsible and working for justice—humans rise to the "better than being," where the very *worth* of human existence finds its concrete reality, in a humanity better for its love and goodness, better too for having and advancing the science and technology that can contribute so powerfully to the alleviation of suffering (however much they are also able to create suffering), a suffering and injustice that surely cannot be assuaged with ideas alone, despite Diotima, despite Spinoza, where accordingly, as Levinas has affirmed again and again, to love the neighbor *is* oneself, one's better self, where morality and justice arise in and demand a *difficult freedom* better than pure mind, pure philosophical freedom that is necessity, a difficult freedom above and better than reason's control, and yet also in their height, in the future they open up, the future of justice, such responsibilities are the very intelligibility of our world.

Works Cited

Allison, Henry E. *Benedict de Spinoza: An Introduction (Revised Edition)*. New Haven: Yale University Press, 1987.
Allison, Henry E. "Kant's Critique of Spinoza." In *The Philosophy of Baruch Spinoza*, ed. Richard Kennington, 199–227. Washington, DC: Catholic University of America Press, 1980.
Aristotle. *On the Heavens*, trans. J. L. Stocks. In *The Basic Works of Aristotle*, ed. Richard McKeon, 398–466. New York: Random House, 1968.
Barnes, Jonathan. *The Presocratic Philosophers*. London: Routledge & Kegan Paul, 1982.
Bartuschat, Wolfgang. "The Ontological Status of Spinoza's Theory of Politics." In *Spinoza's Political and Theological Thought*, ed. C. de Deugd, 30–36. Amsterdam: North-Holland, 1984.
Bataille, Georges. "Andre Breton: Ode to Charles Fourier." In Georges Bataille, *The Absence of Myth: Writings on Surrealism*, ed. and trans. Michael Richardson, 155–157. New York: Verso, 2006.
Bataille, Georges. "The Moral Meaning of Sociology." In Georges Bataille, *The Absence of Myth: Writings on Surrealism*, ed. and trans. Michael Richardson, 103–112. New York: Verso, 2006.
Bennett, Jonathan. *A Study of Spinoza's "Ethics."* Indianapolis: Hackett, 1984.
Ben-Shlomo, Yosef. *Lectures on the Philosophy of Spinoza*. Trans. Shmuel Himelstein. Tel Aviv: MOD Books, 1992.
Boyarin, Daniel. *Carnal Israel: Reading Sex in Talmudic Culture*. Berkeley: University of California Press, 1993.
Peter Burke. *Popular Culture in Early Modern Europe*. London: Temple Smith, 1978.
Cohen, Hermann. "Spinoza uber Staat und Religion, Judentum und Christentum." In Hermann Cohen, *Judische Schriften*, vol. 3, ed. Bruno Strauss, 290–372. Berlin: C. A. Schwetschke, 1924.
Cohen, Richard A. "Biblical Humanism and Its Relevance to the Humanities." *Phenomenological Inquiry*, 24 (October 2000), 27–38.

Cohen, Richard A. *Elevations: The Height of the Good in Rosenzweig and Levinas.* Chicago: University of Chicago Press, 1994.
Cohen, Richard A. "Emmanuel Levinas." In *The Routledge Companion to Phenomenology*, ed. Sebastian Luft and Søren Overgaard, 71–81. Oxon: Routledge, 2012.
Cohen, Richard A. *Ethics, Exegesis and Philosophy.* Cambridge: Cambridge University Press, 2001.
Cohen, Richard A. *Levinasian Meditations: Ethics, Philosophy, and Religion.* Pittsburgh: Duquesne University Press, 2010.
Cohen, Richard A. "Miracle of Miracles: More Ancient than Knowledge: Contra Hume." In *Divine Intervention and Miracles in Jewish Theology*, ed. Dan Cohn-Sherbok, 79–98. Lewiston: Edwin Mellen Press, 1996.
Cohen, Richard A. "Responsible Time." *Cahiers d'Etudes Levinassiennes*, 1 (2002), 39–53.
Cohen, Richard A. "What Good Is the Holocaust? Levinas on Suffering and Evil." *Philosophy Today*, special issue edited by Caroline Bayard and Joyce Bellous, 43.2/4 (Summer 1999), 176–183.
Curley, Edwin. "Kissinger, Spinoza, and Genghis Khan." In *The Cambridge Companion to Spinoza*, ed. Don Garrett, 315–342. Cambridge: Cambridge University Press, 1996.
de Sade, Marquis. *Three Complete Novels: Justine, Philosophy in the Bedroom, Eugenie de Franval and Other Writings.* Compiled and translated by Richard Seaver and Austryn Wainhouse. New York: Grove Press, 1966.
DeBrabander, Firmin. *Spinoza and the Stoics: Power, Politics and the Passions.* London: Continuum, 2007.
Deleuze, Gilles. *Expressionism in Philosophy: Spinoza.* Trans. Martin Joughin. New York: Zone Books, 1992.
Deleuze, Gilles. *Spinoza: Practical Philosophy.* Trans. Robert Hurley. San Francisco: City Lights Books, 1988.
Derrida, Jacques. *Adieu to Emmanuel Levinas.* Trans. Pascale-Anne Brault and Michael Naas. Stanford: Stanford University Press, 1997.
Descartes, René. *Descartes: Philosophical Works*, vol. 2. Trans. Elizabeth S. Haldane and G. R. T. Ross. Cambridge: Cambridge University Press, 1934.
Diogenes Laertius. *Lives of Eminent Philosophers*, vol. 2. Trans. R. D. Hicks. Cambridge: Harvard University Press, 2004.
Dunner, Joseph. *Baruch Spinoza and Western Democracy: An Interpretation of His Philosophical, Religious and Political Thought.* New York: Philosophical Library, 1955.
Feuer, Lewis Samuel. *Spinoza and the Rise of Liberalism.* Boston: Beacon Press, 1958.

Frankel, Steven. "Politics and Rhetoric: The Intended Audience of Spinoza's *Tractatus Theologico-Politicus*." *The Review of Metaphysics*, 52 (1999), 897–924.
Frick, David. *Kith, Kin, and Neighbors: Communities and Confessions in Seventeenth-Century Wilno.* Ithaca: Cornell University Press, 2013.
Grossman, Vasily. *Life and Fate.* Trans. Raymond Chandler. New York: Harper & Row, 1985.
Guttmann, Julius. "Mendelssohn's *Jerusalem* and Spinoza's *Theologico-Political Treatise*." In *Studies in Jewish Thought: An Anthology of German Jewish Scholarship*, ed. Alfred Jospe, 361–386. Detroit: Wayne State University Press, 1981.
Halberstal, Moshe. *Maimonides: Life and Thought.* Princeton: Princeton University Press, 2015.
Hallett, Harold F. *Benedict de Spinoza: The Elements of His Philosophy.* Bristol: Thoemmes Antiquarian Books, 1990.
Hansel, Georges. "Le Midrach n'est pas une exegese." In Georges Hansel, *Explorations Talmudiques.* Paris: Odile Jacob, 1989.
Hartman, David. *Maimonides: Torah and Philosophic Quest.* Philadelphia: Jewish Publication Society, 1976.
Harvey, Warren Zev. "Spinoza's Metaphysical Hebraism." In *Jewish Themes in Spinoza's Philosophy*, ed. Heidi M. Ravven and Lenn E. Goodman, 107–114. Albany: State University of New York Press, 2002.
Herodotus. *Histories*, vol. 1. Trans. George Rawlinson, ed. E. H. Blakeney. London: J. M. Dent & Sons, 1964.
Heschel, Susannah. *The Aryan Jesus: Christian Theologians and the Bible in Nazi German.* Princeton: Princeton University Press, 2010.
Husserl, Edmund. *Logical Investigations*, vol. 2. Trans. J. N. Findlay. New York: Humanities Press, 1970.
Hyde, Michael J. *The Call of Conscience: Heidegger and Levinas, Rhetoric and the Euthanasia Debate.* Columbia: University of South Carolina Press, 2000.
Jospe, Raphael. "Faith and Reason: The Controversy over Philosophy." In *Great Schisms in Jewish History*, ed. R. Jospe and S. M. Wagner, 73–117. New York: KTAV, 1981.
Kant, Immanuel. *Foundation of the Metaphysics of Morals.* Trans. L. B. White. Indianapolis: Bobbs-Merrill, 1980.
Kant, Immanuel. *Religion within the Limits of Reason Alone.* Trans. Theodore M. Greene and Hoyt H. Hudson. New York: Harper & Row, 1960.
Karshap, S. Paul. *Spinoza and Moral Freedom.* Albany: State University of New York Press, 1987.
Kaufmann, Walter, ed. and trans. *The Portable Nietzsche.* New York: Viking Press, 1954.

Kearns, Edward John. *Ideas in Seventeenth-Century France*. Manchester: Manchester University Press, 1979.

Keenan, Dennis King. *Death and Responsibility: The "Work" of Levinas*. Albany: State University of New York Press, 1999.

Koyré, Alexandre. *From the Closed World to the Infinite Universe*. Baltimore: Johns Hopkins University Press, 1957.

LaCocque, Andre, and Paul Ricoeur. *Thinking Biblically: Exegetical and Hermeneutic Studies*. Trans. David Pellauer. Chicago: University of Chicago Press, 1998.

Lampel, Rabbi Zvi, trans. *Maimonides' Introduction to the Talmud*. Brooklyn: Judaica Press, 1998.

Levinas, Emmanuel. "L'actualite de Maimonide." *Paix et Droit*, 15.4 (April 1935), 6–7.

Levinas, Emmanuel. "L'appel d'Auschwitz" (The Call of Auschwitz). *Les nouveaux cahiers*, 85 (Summer 1986), 15–17.

Levinas, Emmanuel. "Spinoza, philosophe medieval." *Revue des etudes juives* (January–June 1937), 114–119.

Levy, Ze'ev. *Baruch or Benedict: On Some Jewish Aspects of Spinoza's Philosophy*. New York: Peter Lang, 1989.

Levy, Ze'ev. "The Problem of Normativity in Spinoza's 'Hebrew Grammar.'" In *Studia Spinoza*, vol. 3, issue on "Spinoza and Hobbes," ed. M. Bertman, H. De Dijn, M. Walther, 351–390. (Hannover: Walter & Walter Verlag, 1987.

Loewe, Howard. "Introduction." In *A Rabbinic Anthology*, ed. C. G. Montefiore and Howard Loewe. New York: Schocken, 1974.

Lucas, Jean Maximilien. *The Life of the Late Mr. de Spinosa*, trans. A. Wolf. In *The Oldest Biography of Spinoza*, ed. A. Wolf. London: George Allen and Unwin, 1927.

Maimonides, Moses. *The Guide for the Perplexed*. Trans M. Friedlander. New York: Dover, 1956.

Maimonides, Moses. *The Guide of the Perplexed*, vols. 1 and 2. Trans. Shlomo Pines. Chicago: University of Chicago Press, 1963.

Marcel, Gabriel. *The Philosophy of Existentialism*. Trans. Manya Harari. New York: Citadel Press, 1964.

Marx, Karl. "Theses on Feuerbach." In Karl Marx and Friedrich Engels, *Selected Works in One Volume*. New York: International Publishers, 1968.

McShea, Robert J. *The Political Philosophy of Spinoza*. New York: Columbia University Press, 1986.

Montaigne, Michel de. *The Essays of Michel de Montaigne, Complete*. Ed. William Carew Hazlitt, trans. Charles Cotton. A. L. Burn.

Montefiore, C. G., and Howard Lowe, eds. *A Rabbinic Anthology*. New York: Schocken, 1974.

Nadler, Steven. *A Book Forged in Hell: Spinoza's Scandalous Treatise and the Birth of the Secular Age.* Princeton: Princeton University Press, 2011.
Nadler, Steven. *Spinoza: A Life.* Cambridge: Cambridge University Press, 1999.
Nadler, Steven. *Spinoza's Heresy: Immortality and the Jewish Mind.* Oxford: Clarendon Press, 2001.
Negri, Antonio. *Subversive Spinoza.* Manchester: Manchester University Press, 2004.
Neusner, Jacob. *History and Torah: Essays on Jewish Learning.* New York: Schocken, 1965.
Neusner, Jacob, trans. *The Talmud of Babylonia: An American Translation XXIII: Tractate Sanhedrin, Chapters 1–3.* Chico: Scholars Press, 1984.
Plato. *Alcibiades I.* In *The Dialogues of Plato*, vol. 2, trans. Benjamin Jowett, 733–772. New York: Random House, 1937.
Plato. *The Symposium.* Trans. W. Hamilton. Harmondsworth: Penguin Books, 1967.
Plutarch. *Lives.* Trans. John Langhorne and William Langhorne. Ithaca: Mack, Andrus & Woodruff, 1839.
Polen, Nehemia. *The Holy Fire: The Teaching of Rabbi Kalonymus Kalman Shapira, the Rebbe of the Warsaw Ghetto.* Northvale: Jason Aronson, 1994.
Salome, Lou Andreas. *Nietzsche.* Trans. Siegfried Mandel. Urbana-Champaign: University of Illinois Press, 2001.
Seeskin, Kenneth. *Maimonides: A Guide for Today's Perplexed.* West Orange: Behrman House, 1991.
Simon, Leon, ed. *Ahad Ha-am: Essays, Letters, Memoirs.* Oxford: Phaidon Press, 1946.
Simon, Leon, ed. *Selected Essays of Ahad Ha-am.* Philadelphia: Jewish Publication Society, 1912.
Singer, Isaac Bashevis. "The Spinoza of Market Street." In Isaac Bashevis Singer, *The Spinoza of Market Street*, 7–32. New York: Fawcett Crest, 1980.
Soskice, Janet Martin. *Metaphor and Religious Language.* Oxford: Clarendon Press, 1985.
Smith, Steven B. *Spinoza, Liberalism, and the Question of Jewish Identity.* New Haven: Yale University Press, 1997.
Spinoza, Baruch. *Principles of Cartesian Philosophy.* Trans. Harry E. Wedeck. New York: Philosophical Library, 1961.
Strauss, Leo. "An Introduction to Heideggerian Existentialism." In Leo Strauss, *The Rebirth of Classical Political Rationalism: An Introduction to the Thought of Leo Strauss*, ed. Thomas L. Pangle, 27–48. Chicago: University of Chicago Press, 1989.
Strauss, Leo. "How to Study Spinoza's *Theologico-Political Treatise* (1948)." In Leo Strauss, *Jewish Philosophy and the Crisis of Modernity: Essays and*

Lectures in Modern Jewish Thought, ed. Kenneth Hart Green, 181–234. Albany: State University of New York Press, 1997.

Strauss, Leo. "Preface to Spinoza's Critique of Religion (1965)." In Leo Strauss, *Jewish Philosophy and the Crisis of Modernity: Essays and Lectures in Modern Jewish Thought*, ed. Kenneth Hart Green, 137–178. Albany: State University of New York Press, 1997.

Strauss, Leo. *Spinoza's Critique of Religion*. Trans. E. M. Sinclair. New York: Schocken, 1982.

Thucydides. *The Peloponnesian War*. Trans. Rex Warner. Harmondsworth: Penguin Books, 1964.

Twersky, Isadore. *Introduction to the Code of Maimonides (Mishneh Torah)*. New Haven: Yale University Press, 1980.

Yovel, Yirmiyahu. *Marrano Patterns in Spinoza*. Jerusalem: Jerusalem Spinoza Institute, 1983.

Yovel, Yirmiyahu. *Spinoza and Other Heretics: The Adventures of Immanence*. Princeton: Princeton University Press, 1989.

Wolfson, Harry Austryn. *The Philosophy of Spinoza*, vol. 2. New York: Schocken, 1961.

Index

absoluteness and the absolute, 24, 31, 282
Active Intellect, 86
Adam and Eve, 114, 302
adequate ideas, 84, 287, 306. *See also* clear and distinct ideas
   and the body, 302
   conversion of all objects of consciousness into, 242
   death and, 250, 251
   freedom and having only, 301
   freedom to conform to, 136
   God as, 195n7
   and intellectual love of God, 84–87
   leaving inadequate ideas for, 89
   and the mind, 86
   reason and, 256, 301, 309
   Spinoza on, xiv, 4, 76, 84, 84–86, 89, 125, 158, 181, 195n7, 196, 213, 242, 243, 285, 290, 292, 301, 306, 309
   truth, knowledge, and, xiv, 4, 76, 125, 158, 196, 242, 243, 249–50, 256, 285, 292, 309
   types of, 84–85
   will-intellect and, 290
aesthetic/"romantic" tradition of thought, 20
Ahad Ha'am (Asher Zvi Hirsch Ginsberg), 57, 73n19

Alcibiades, as Spinozist leader, 170–77, 182
Alcibiades I, 175
Alexander the Great, 167, 169, 170
Allison, Henry E., 162n19
Alpakhar, Yehuda, 227–28
Althusser, Louis, 218–19
Amor fati, 50, 308
Amor intellectualis Dei, 7, 44, 46, 84
Amos (prophet), 71n13, 72n14
Amsterdam, 221–22. *See also* Jewish community
Anderson, John, ix
apocalypticism, 65. *See also* eschatology
Aquinas, Thomas, xvi, 201, 251
aristocracy, 120, 123, 146, 150, 153, 178, 187
Aristotle, 167, 170, 170n22, 171, 250, 255n6
   Active Intellect, 86
   four causes, 193, 240
   Maimonides and, 74, 77, 78
   Spinoza and, 86, 125n5, 193, 240, 251, 290, 290n3
art, 20, 22, 49, 141, 155, 156, 166, 257, 275
ascetic priest, 164–66
asceticism, 49, 238
atheism, 8, 9, 135, 136, 224n30
   risk of, 14

Augustine of Hippo, 215
autonomy, 32, 216n23. *See also* independence

"babies, fools, and madmen," 279. *See also* fools; infancy; infants; madmen
  Spinoza's repugnance and contempt for, 18, 120–21, 279, 288, 292–99, 306–10
Bartuschat, Wolfgang, 160n18
Baruch or Benedict: On Some Jewish Aspects of Spinoza's Philosophy (Levy), 208n15, 221n27
Bataille, Georges, 20, 259, 314n8
beatitude, 49–50, 87, 165, 166, 176, 196, 243, 285. *See also* blessedness
being. *See also Dasein*
  "better than being," 10, 16, 25, 27, 39, 71, 260, 261, 316
  against death, 268
  defining, 246
  question of, 20, 37, 241, 252, 257, 260, 264, 277, 280–81
Dasein and the, 37, 241, 252, 257, 260
Being and Time (Heidegger), 11, 36, 37, 251–52, 254–55, 258, 260–61
being-toward-death, 238, 241–42, 252–54, 258, 260, 261, 263, 265, 277
Ben-Gurion, David, 106
Ben-Shlomo, Yosef, 192, 194–98, 215
Benjamin, Walter, 22
Bennett, Jonathan, 133, 181
Bergson, Henri, ix, x, 20, 250–51, 309
"better than being," 10, 16, 25, 27, 39, 71, 260, 261, 316
"beyond good and evil," 44, 50, 51, 131, 196. *See also* good and evil

Bianchi, Angelo, 267n12
Bible. *See also* Hebrew Bible; New Testament; Old Testament
  authority of, 168
biblical criticism, 124, 125n5, 126, 180
  higher, 3
biblical humanism, 27, 100, 276. *See also* humanism
"Biblical Humanism" (Levinas), 70
binary opposition. *See* dichotomies; dualisms
blessedness, 9, 87, 130, 156. *See also* beatitude
  blessed life, 165
  blessed persons, 166
  blessed philosophy, 131
  blessing of life, 171n22
Blyenbergh, William van, 302–7
  Spinoza's letter to, 88–89
body
  defining, 246
  living, 245–47
  mind and, 226n32, 302. *See also* embodiment
  parallelism/equation between, 5
Borgia, Cesare, 170n22
Bossuet, Jacques-Bénigne, 117n9
Boyarin, Daniel, 226n33
Bruno, Giordano, xvii, 138
Buber, Martin, 110
Buddha, xviii
Bultmann, Rudolf, 78
Burckhardt, Jacob, 45
Buridan, Jean, 290n3, 292, 306

Caesar, Julius, 213, 215
Cassirer, Ernst, 198n9, 261
categorical imperative, 65–66
change
  as an illusion, 121, 248
  Spinoza's opposition to, 180
chosenness. *See* election

Christian ministers and theologians, liberal, 137–40
Christian states, 211
Christian Trojan Horse, Spinoza as, 206
Christianity, 138. *See also* Jesus Christ; New Testament
  early history, 199, 201n10
  Kant on, 201n10, 205
  Levinas and, 72n14
  Nietzsche's criticism of, 47, 49
  Old Testament/Hebrew Bible and, 191n1, 221, 224, 233n39
  politics and, 215–16
  rationalism and, 202–4, 206, 207
  Spinoza never converted to, 7, 205
  Spinoza's family's conversion to, 221
Christianized Judaism, 199–208, 215–16
Christina, Queen of Sweden, 170
Church, xvii, 23, 138–40, 179, 208
church and state. *See also* religion and state; religious authority and moral authority
  separation of, 24, 211. *See also* disestablishment of religion
clear and distinct ideas, 249–50, 281–84, 290, 291. *See also* adequate ideas
Cohen, Hermann, 198n9
communication, 41–42
compassion. *See also* suffering
  Levinas on, xviii, 29, 55, 79, 99–102, 217
  morality and, xviii, 55, 79, 99–102, 217, 275, 276
  politics of, 215, 217
  as route to God, 101, 102
  Spinoza and, 102, 215, 217
  universal social, 217
Comte, Auguste, 314n8

conatus (perseverance/persistence in being), 113, 144, 149, 245, 273, 290n3, 306–7
  all things as driven by, 47, 112, 117, 121, 143
  vs. caring, 16
  lack of authority, 125
  moral being, civil society, and, 115
  morality and justice as counter to, 276
  of the state, 148, 149, 152
conatus essendi, 48, 51
conscience
  individual private, 111, 184. *See also under* religion
  nature of, 111
  science and, 232
contemporary continental philosophy, xv, xix
Copernicus, Nicolaus, 138
Croesus, 237–38
Curley, Edwin, 106, 209n18

Daniel (prophet), 75
Darwin, Charles, 45–48
Dasein, 241, 256–57
  death, mortality, and, 241, 252–57, 260, 265, 266
  end of, 266
  Heidegger and, 37, 241, 252–55, 260, 265
  and the question of being, 37, 241, 252, 257, 260
  temporality of, 20
de Sade, Marquis, 25, 45, 184, 305
de Witt, Cornelis, 138–39, 153n14, 294
de Witt, Johan, 138–40, 153n14, 170, 294
death. *See also* Heidegger: death, mortality, and; Levinas: dying for the other; suicide

death *(continued)*
  being-toward-death, 238, 241–42, 252–54, 258, 260, 261, 263, 265, 277
  and change, 247–49
  characteristics, 253–55
  defining, 244–47
  fear of, 242–44, 262–63, 265
  futurity of, 266, 270–72
  as identity change, 247–49, 253, 299, 300, 307
  murder, 268–73, 303–5
  as a mystery, 263–65
  to not think of, 242–51, 253, 262n7
    "Thinking Least about Death—Contra Heidegger" (Cohen), 253, 262n7
  suffering and, 258, 261–63, 265, 266, 270, 272, 273
  transcendence of, 270
Death and Responsibility: The "Work" of Levinas (Keenan), 267n12
DeBrabander, Firmin, 122n3
dehumanization, 23, 27, 236, 243, 296, 313
Deleuze, Gilles, x, 20, 216n23, 296
democracy
  definitions and meanings, 123, 140–54
  purpose, 149–50
  types of, 132, 142, 146–52
    contract democracy, 146–50
    regime democracy, 132, 142, 146–52
Derrida, Jacques, xi, 267n12
Descartes, René, 170, 283, 284
  dualisms and, 88, 109, 111
  free will and, 281–91, 301
  on Nietzsche, 285
  Spinoza and, xiv, 2, 4, 88, 109, 159, 170, 217, 221, 244, 280–82, 285–91, 301

Principles of Cartesian Philosophy and Metaphysical Thoughts (Spinoza), 2, 88, 119
determinism, 122n3, 152, 156, 158, 160, 181, 243. *See also* free will
  law of determinism governing a totality, 269, 272
Deus, sive Natura ("God, or Nature"), 8, 63, 195n7, 285. *See also* "God, or Nature"
Deuteronomy, 70n12, 225n30
diachrony, x, 10, 38, 69
"Diachrony and Representation" (Levinas), 272, 275, 276
dialectic. *See also* dichotomies; dualisms
  of Kant, 26, 80
dialectical interplay between truth and truth seekers, 41
dichotomies, 179, 314n8. *See also* dualisms
Diogenes Laertius, 122
Diotima of Mantinea, 25, 172, 173, 176, 309, 316
disestablishment of religion, 106, 175, 184, 211–13. *See also* church and state: separation of; religion and state
divine humanism, 103, 104. *See also* biblical humanism
divine law, 158–59
doctor, 22, 99
  death and the, 271–72
Dostoyevsky, Fyodor, 98n8, 214
doublespeak, Spinozist, 108, 136, 158, 213
dualisms, 51. *See also* dichotomies
  Descartes and, 88, 109, 111
  unresolved, 109, 122
Dunner, Joseph, 209n17
duration, 5, 20, 84, 250–51, 267. *See also* temporality; time

dying. *See also* death
for the other, 15, 29, 315. *See also under* Levinas, Emmanuel
"Dying for..." (Levinas), 258, 259, 274
"dying for," 274

"ecstatic" theories of temporality, x, 69, 309
election, 29, 33, 72, 125n5, 184, 197
Jewish chosenness, 184
Elevations: The Height of the Good in Rosenzweig and Levinas (Cohen), 267n12
embodiment, 32–33, 255. *See also* self-sensing
  conceptual ramifications, 15
  death and, 37, 266
  embodied self, 38–39
  embodied sociality, 34
  embodied subject, 33, 53, 266
  independence and, 13, 33, 38
  intersubjectivity and, 15
  morality and, 15, 33, 38, 39, 51, 53
  mortality and, 13, 15, 17, 36, 37, 239
  overview and nature of, 13–16, 36–39
  phenomenology and, xv
  sensibility and, 13–14, 33, 36, 263
  sensuous/sensual, 13, 37
  solitude and, 16, 38, 39
  subjectivity and, 36, 37
  suffering and, 13, 15, 17, 36, 53–54
  transcendence and, 38, 39
"Emmanuel Levinas" (Cohen), 11n2
emotions, 243, 296n7. *See also* ignorant masses: emotionality
  passive, 84–87
Enlightenment, 3

Epicurus, v, xvi
epistemology, 12, 14, 18–20, 41, 62, 113, 282
epochal being, 20, 252, 254, 255, 276
eschatology, 65–67
essence, 269–70
eternal, the, 149
  God and, 84, 85, 88, 193
  Spinoza's intellectual devotion to, xiv, 140, 142, 196, 239
  vs. the temporal, 122, 140, 161, 177, 180
eternal futurity of death, 266. *See also* futurity: of death
eternal (and immutable) ideas, truths, and laws, 2, 5, 63, 84, 126, 132, 139, 158–59, 180, 214, 251
eternal realm of intellect and idea, 249–50. *See also* free thought
eternal return/eternal recurrence, 24, 50
eternal soul, 239. *See also* soul
eternity, x, 121, 239, 240, 309, 310
  Heidegger and, 254, 277
  vs. historical consciousness, 45
  Levinas and, 267, 267n12, 309, 310
  Nietzsche and, 45, 49–51
  Pascal and, 251
  possibility and, 254
  unbridgeable gap between duration and, 5
  wanting/willing, 50
ethical exegesis, 225, 270
ethical intersubjectivity, 95–96
ethical metaphysics, 270
ethics, 108, 196. *See also* morality; suffering
  as based on separation, 32
  as "first philosophy," 42–43

ethics *(continued)*
  first question of, 36
  Judaism and, 196. *See also* Judaism
  phenomenology and, 12
  science and, 40
Ethics, Demonstrated in Geometrical Manner (Spinoza), xi, 8, 35, 44, 131, 133, 159, 162, 209, 296n7, 299
  born adult, 120–21, 307–10
  born free, 301–3
  on Cartesian philosophy, 282
  on conatus, 149
  on death, 242, 244. *See also* suicide
  on emotions, 296n7
  on error of final causality, 19
  on freedom, 242, 301–3
  "geometric manner" of, 279–80
  Gilles Deleuze on, 296n7
  on God, 83–86, 159, 293, 304
  on imagination, 62–64
  on intellect, 159, 217, 242, 280
  intended audience, 132, 177, 298
  Jews, Judaism, and, 202, 206, 209, 220, 295n6
  on knowledge and truth, 76, 109, 130–31, 158, 220, 256
  overview, 3, 119, 124–25, 139
  Parmenides's *On Nature* and, 109
  Part II, 95, 217, 279
    Spinoza's scholium to proof of corollary of proof of proposition 49 of, 279–93
  Part III, 112, 244, 298–99
  Part IV, 101, 242, 244, 280, 297, 301, 306
  Part V, 83–86, 120–21, 308. *See also* "babies, fools, and madmen"
  on pity, 101
  on prophecy, 64
  publication, 3, 64, 119, 135, 296n7

  rationalism of, 64, 202, 204, 206, 212
  reductive idealism in, 111
  religion and, 108, 109, 135, 179, 180, 202, 296n7
  root ideas, 4
  science and, 108, 109, 132, 206
  on sensibility, 93–95
  Theological-Political Treatise and, 26, 61–64, 76, 86n1, 102, 108, 109, 111, 113n7, 119, 120, 123, 124, 130–32, 135, 139, 144, 149, 158, 159, 163, 177, 179, 182, 212, 296n7
  on will, 102, 159, 160n18, 217, 280
Euclid, 3
evil. *See also* "beyond good and evil"; good and evil; suffering
  suffering and, 47, 97–99, 101
evolution. *See* Darwin, Charles
exclusivism. *See under* science
excommunication of Spinoza from Jewish community, xiv, 7, 127n6, 189, 190, 202, 205, 223, 251, 294, 295
existence. *See* being; *Dasein*
Existence and Existents (Levinas), 11, 37–38
existential self-transformation, virtue of, 231–32
Exodus, 57–61, 74. *See also* Moses

faith, 8, 22, 28, 49, 76–77, 155, 183, 185–86
false judgment, 281–82. *See also* illusion
Feuer, Lewis Samuel, 106, 153n14, 209n17
Feyerabend, Paul, 228n36
foolishness, 21, 25, 214, 273. *See also* ignorance

fools, 8, 144, 281, 303, 312. *See also* "babies, fools, and madmen"; ignorant masses
for the other, 16, 71. *See also* compassion; dying: for the other
being-for-another, 54
being-for-death, 253
being-for-the-other, 40
body, 53
care, 29, 54, 66, 71
Levinas on, 10, 16, 20, 26, 32n1, 35, 36, 42–43, 53, 66, 72n14, 99, 111, 112, 114, 251. *See also* Levinas: dying for the other; *Otherwise than Being or Beyond Essence*
responsibility for, 10, 15, 20, 22, 26, 32n1, 35, 36, 39, 43, 66, 68, 70, 71, 72n14, 80, 102, 111, 113–15, 242. *See also under* suffering
Frankel, Steven, 182
response to, 166–70
Frederick the Great (Frederick II of Prussia), 170
free speech, 3, 24, 128, 136, 153n14, 154–56
free thought, 3, 24, 125n4, 128, 136, 153n14, 154–56, 242–44. *See also* philosophical freedom
free will, 155, 283, 287, 296. *See also* determinism
Ben Shlomo on Judaism and, 195n7
Descartes and, 281–91, 301
Levinas on, 32, 91, 218n24
Nietzsche on, 49–51, 164, 217
Spinoza's denial/dismissal of, 35, 49, 160n18, 195n7, 196, 217, 282–85, 287, 288, 291
Spinoza's objections to, 289–92

freedom, 24, 116, 158, 282. *See also* political freedom
Ethics on, 242, 301–3
Heidegger and, 21, 39, 255, 265
meanings and types of, 123, 125, 154–57, 283, 288, 316
to philosophize, 125, 129, 136–37, 154. *See also* philosophical freedom
as purpose of the state, 116
Freud, Sigmund, 13, 31
futurity, 270–71, 276
of death, 266, 270–72

Galileo Galilei, xvii, 138
Gandhi, Mahatma, 72, 239
Gaon, Vilna. *See* Vilna Gaon
Garden of Eden, 114, 302
Ginsberg, Asher Zvi Hirsch. *See* Ahad Ha'am
God. *See also* atheism
anthropomorphic image of, 304
compassion as route to, 101, 102
conceptions of, 8
as eternal, 84, 85, 88
Ethics on, 83–86, 159, 293, 304
hating, 86
intellect of, 84, 88, 89, 162, 282, 311
love of, 293
convergence between Levinas and Spinoza regarding, 83–102
intellectual, 84–87
Nature and, 5, 8
nature of, 158, 195n7
obedience to, 137n10, 183
will of, 84, 185, 200, 281, 303
"God, or Nature," 88, 109, 110, 195n7, 213, 276, 282, 286. See also *Deus, sive Natura*

Golden Rule. *See* "love thy neighbor"
good and evil, 40, 97, 105, 173, 305.
    See also "beyond good and evil";
    Ethics: born free; theodicy
    adequate ideas and, 283, 301
    born free and, 301
    Nietzsche on, 44–45, 51, 196
Grossman, Vasily, 26, 79, 214
Guttmann, Julius, 205n13

Ha'am, Ahad. *See* Ahad Ha'am
Hand, Sean, 25
Hebrew Bible, 61, 126, 127n6, 189,
    191n1, 202, 204, 221, 232.
    See also Bible; Isaiah; Judaism;
    Numbers; Old Testament;
    Theological-Political Treatise; Torah
    Christianity and, 191n1, 221, 224,
        233n39
    hermeneutics and, 126–27
Hebrew Grammar (Spinoza), 4
Hebrew nation, chosenness of the,
    184
Hegel, Georg Wilhelm Friedrich,
    xix, 21, 31
    on God, v
    idealism, 90, 218n24
    Judaism and, 205
    Phenomenology of Spirit, v, 11n1, 93,
        121
    on subjectivity as negation, 11
    will and, 90
Heidegger, Martin, xv, 31, 37, 92,
    198n9, 241, 258
    Dasein and, 37, 241, 252–55, 260,
        265
    death, mortality, and, 240, 241,
        241n2, 257–60, 264–66, 268,
        270, 273–77
    my mortal being, 251–57
    "ecstatic" theory of temporality, x,
        69, 309

on epochal being, 20, 252, 254,
    255, 276
ethics and, 270
freedom and, 21, 39, 255, 265
futurity and, 266
and the good, 20
hermeneutics and, 256–58, 261
Husserl and, 11, 69, 254, 257–58,
    261
on Kant, 20
knowledge, ontology, and, 261
Leo Strauss on, 255n6
Levinas's criticism of, 20, 37, 240–
    41, 241n2, 258, 260–61, 265, 275
moods and, 254
on poetic thinking, 256
reason and, 256, 257
shift from phenomenology to
    ontology and *poesis*, 11n2
on subjectivity, 252
temporality and, 20
truth and, 66n9, 257
writings
    Being and Time, 11, 36, 37,
        251–52, 254–55, 258, 260–61
    Kant and the Problem of Metaphysics,
        20
Henri, Michel, 11n2
hermeneutics
    and the Bible, 126–27
    Heidegger and, 256–58, 261
    hermeneutic claims, 41, 168
    hermeneutic ontology, 258, 261
    and the Talmud, 220, 223, 225
Herodotus, 237
Heschel, Susannah, 201n10
heterogenous vs. the homogeneous,
    the, 314n8
Hirsch, Samson Raphael, 212n20
Hobbes, Thomas, 170n22
    democracy and, 148, 149
    justice and, 19, 105, 110, 114, 115

Leviathan, 3, 167, 181
  on natural being, 115
  on politics as an end, 129
  sovereignty and, 61, 64, 127–29, 143, 145
  Spinoza and, 3, 61, 64, 105, 110, 114, 115, 124, 129, 143, 145, 153n14, 157, 163, 181, 187, 211
  and the state, 19, 61, 105, 110, 114, 115, 129, 143, 145, 153n14, 157, 211
Holland, 138. *See also* Amsterdam
Holocaust, 96, 98, 99
Homer, 58
human types/classes of humanity, 130, 164–65. *See also* ignorant masses: vs. the knowing few
humanism, xvi, 41, 55, 100. *See also* biblical humanism
  enlightened, 206
  joining of divinity and, 103, 104
  Judaism and, 206, 236
  vs. natural science, 41, 231
"Humanism, Religion, Myth, Criticism, Exegesis" (Cohen), 226
humanity, xviii
  defining, xviii, 39, 112–13, 226n13, 311
Hume, David, 69n11
Husserl, Edmund, xv, 20, 93, 108, 261, 309
  on crisis, 12, 260, 311
  "ecstatic" theory of temporality, x, 69
  Heidegger and, 11, 69, 254, 257–58, 261
  phenomenology, 11, 12, 26, 36, 254, 257–58, 260, 261
  The Theory of Intuition in Husserl's Phenomenology (Levinas), 11

Hyde, Michael J., 263n9
hypostasis, 10, 92
  of distinct existence, 10
  hypostatic embodiment, 32
  of sensibility, 10

idealism, 37, 90
  ethics and, 90, 218
  Levinas on, 90, 111, 218, 219, 265
  problems and criticisms of, 2, 111, 218, 265
  reason and, 2, 218n24
  science and, 2
  Spinoza's, 2, 42, 51, 90, 111
  will and, 90, 218n24
ideals, 219
ideas. *See also* eternal (and immutable) ideas, truths, and laws
  clear and distinct, 249–50, 281–84, 290, 291. *See also* adequate ideas
  images, words, and, 288–89
  inadequate, 64, 84, 87, 89, 101, 268, 286, 307
  meaning of the term, 288
identity, 65, 269, 299–300
identity change, 247–48
  death as, 247–49, 253, 299, 300, 307
"Ideology and Idealism" (Levinas), 218, 219
ignorance, 4, 45, 88, 122, 130. *See also* foolishness
  death and, 243, 250–52
  free will and, 49
  imagination and, 44, 63, 97
  of Jews and Israelites, 199–200, 202, 206
  knowing as less painful than, 49
  morality and, 19, 44
  Nietzsche and, 44–45
  of one's own ignorance, 88, 194

ignorance *(continued)*
  prophecy and, 63
  religion and, 19, 77, 212
  of self, 159, 284, 308
  Spinoza's, 88
  suffering as reducible to, 97
  transcendence and, 21
ignorant masses ("ignoramuses"), 108, 109, 132. *See also* fools
  controlling and manipulating the, 64, 116
  emotionality, 44, 132, 166, 178, 180, 243, 251, 297
  vs. the knowing few, 8, 49, 109, 130, 133, 136, 165, 166, 178, 180, 297, 305, 310
  "opium" of, 186
  political leaders and, 64, 165, 166, 178
  religion and, 133
  ruling them without being one of them, 176
  Spinoza's disgust and contempt for, 2, 4, 8, 18, 64, 152, 153n14, 199–200, 251, 293, 295–98, 310–12
  susceptibility to superstition, 131, 134
  Theological-Political Treatise and, 132
illusion (and falsehood), 8, 158, 161, 244, 286, 288. *See also* inadequate ideas; truth; *specific illusions*
  absence of, 284. *See also* adequate ideas
  Descartes's explanation for, 282–83
  determination of the nature and origin of, 280
  guarding against, 284
  the illusory, 12, 281
  ontological status of the world of, 89

  relation between falsehood and illusion, 280–81
  science and, 4, 8, 9, 12, 46
  sources of, 290
  images, words, and ideas, 288–89
imagination, 44, 62–63, 254, 291
  ignorance and, 44, 63, 97
  intellect and, 63, 64
  persons with vivid, 62–64, 174
imaginings, 44, 297
  without reality, 256
inadequate ideas, 64, 84, 87, 89, 101, 268, 286, 307
independence, 13, 14. *See also* autonomy; self-sufficiency; sensibility; separation; solitude
  embodiment and, 13, 33, 38
Industrial Revolution, 313
infancy, Spinoza and, 120–21, 246, 300, 301, 308, 309. *See also* "babies, fools, and madmen"
infants, Spinoza's repugnance for, 120–21, 246–47. *See also* "babies, fools, and madmen"
insanity. *See* "babies, fools, and madmen"; madmen
intellect, 101–2, 126. *See also* fools; reason; will and intellect
  Active Intellect, 86
  and the body, 302. *See also* body: mind and
  "born free" and, 302
  definitions and scope of the term, 290
  Ethics on, 159, 217, 242, 280
  free persons of pure, 243, 309
  God's, 84, 88, 89, 162, 282, 311
  ideating itself, 286
  imagination and, 63, 64
  morality and, 80
  overvaluation of, 54
  persons lacking, 79, 297

of philosophers, 284
political leaders and, 174, 187
primacy of, 73
prophecy and, 75, 79
realm of, 250
and the state, 157
Treatise on the Emendation of the Intellect (Spinoza), 3, 120, 121, 133, 284
intellectual love of God, 84–87
intermediate type. *See* ascetic priest
internal relations, 16, 34
intersubjective theory of time, Levinas's, x, 10, 69, 268, 309
intersubjectivity, 15, 18, 32, 69, 95, 309
  morality and, 15, 18, 95–96, 271
  of truth, 40, 41
Intrinsic Inspiration, 226n32
intuition, 108, 256. *See also* knowledge: of the third kind
irrationalism, xvii, 13
is-ought problem, 196
Isaiah, Book of, 69–70
Israel. *See* Hebrew nation

Jesus Christ, 75, 199, 201n10, 203, 207, 208n15, 233n39, 295
Jewish community, Spinoza's excommunication from, xiv, 7, 127n6, 189, 190, 202, 205, 223, 251, 294, 295
Jewish wisdom, central teachings of, 111
Jews. See also under *Ethics*; Judaism
  as the chosen people, 184
  as ignorant, 199–200, 202, 206
Jonas, Hans, 39
Judaism. *See also* Hebrew Bible; Maimonides, Moses; Old Testament; prophets; religion
  characterizations of, 78
  impact of Spinoza's life history on his attitudes toward, xiv, 23–24, 223, 251, 294
  obligation and, 21, 194, 196, 229
  rationalism and, 202–4, 206, 207, 212, 225n30, 226
  Spinoza's misunderstanding of, 189–93. *See also* Levinas: on Spinoza's misunderstanding of Judaism
    a Christianized Judaism, 199–208, 215–16
    Harry Austryn Wolfson and, 193–94, 197
    Yosef Ben-Shlomo and, 194–98
"Judaism and Christianity" (Levinas), 229
judgment, 68
  legitimate, 105–7
  suspension of, 291
just state vs. unjust state, 116–17
justice, 110, 114–15
  beyond death, 274–77
  futurity of, 276
  Hobbes and, 19, 105, 110, 114, 115
  legitimate, 105–7, 112
  Levinas on morality and, 110–18, 213
  origin, 114
  prerequisites for, 19
  religion, the state, and, 103–7

Kafka, Franz, 27, 307, 313
Kant, Immanuel, 17, 20, 24, 28, 41, 170, 196n8, 198n9, 286n2, 287, 313
  categorical imperative, 65–66
  on Christianity, 201n10, 205
  dialectic, 26, 80
  Heidegger and, 20
  hermeneutics and, 257

Kant, Immanuel *(continued)*
  on Judaism, 201n10, 205
  "kingdom of ends," 65
  knowledge and, 260
  Levinas and, xvi, 20, 32n1, 65–67, 110, 185, 198n9, 260
  morality and, xvi, 20, 32n1, 40, 66, 67, 110, 185, 276
  reason, intellect, and, 67n10, 80
  religion and, 67, 110, 182–83, 185, 201n10, 205, 208n16, 276, 297
  Spinoza and, 6, 162n19, 289, 297–98
  writings, 20
    Critique of Pure Reason, 80
    Religion within the Limits of Reason Alone, 182–83, 201n10, 205, 208n16
Karshap, S. Paul, 209n17
Kazantzakis, Nikos, xix
Keenan, Dennis King, 267n12
Kierkegaard, Søren, 25, 314n8
kingdom, 312
"kingdom of ends" (Kant), 65
kingdom of God, 103, 109, 110, 215–17
"kingdom within a kingdom," xvi, 11, 13, 35, 113n7, 158, 217, 244, 248, 253
knowledge, 19, 76–77, 107–10. *See also under* adequate ideas; *Ethics*; ignorance
  vs. faith, 49. *See also* faith
  of the first kind, 256
  importance and significance, 22–23
  knowing as its own reward, 130
  knowing vs. doing, 130
  power and, 108
  of the second kind, 84–85, 108
  of the third kind, 62, 62n5, 84–85, 87, 108, 197n8, 203n12, 256

La Mettrie, Julien Offray de, 45
Lacan, Jacques, 14
LaCocque, Andre, 233n39
law, 176–78
  obedience and the, 163, 165, 176–77
  purpose of, 163
legitimacy, 104–6. *See also* justice: legitimate
Leibniz, Gottfried Wilhelm, 95
Lévi-Strauss, Claude, 218
Leviathan (Hobbes), 3, 167, 181. *See also* Hobbes, Thomas
Levinas, Emmanuel, x. *See also specific topics*
  central thesis, 34
  dying for the other, 257–62
  the doctor, 271–72
  futurity, 266
  the grim reaper, 268–71
  justice beyond death, 274–77
  morality and, 272–74
  mystery, 263–65
  passivity and weakness, 265–66
  postponement, 266–68
  suffering, 262–63. *See also* suffering
  greatest contributions, 19–21
  "It is true that all men are prophets," 64–72
  morality and justice, 110–18
  rejection of Spinozism, 31–36, 92
  on Spinoza's misunderstanding of Judaism, 198–99. *See also* Talmudic wisdom
    a Christianized Judaism, 199–208, 215–16
    rationality without wisdom, 219–24
    statism and, 209–19
  what is special about humans for, 13

Levinasian Meditations: Ethics, Philosophy, and Religion (Cohen), xiii, 253, 262
Levy, Ze'ev, 121n1, 206n14, 208n15, 221n27
liberal Christian ministers and theologians, 137–40
liberal religion, 182–86
liberal state, 209–10
life, true, 249–50
Lingis, Alphonso, x
literalism, 226n32, 227
living body, 245–47
logos, 9, 17, 90, 240, 315. *See also* reason
love. *See also* God: love of
meanings, 86
"love thy neighbor," 15, 20, 29, 39, 81, 100, 137, 183, 214, 316
loyalty, 209
Luzzatto, Samuel David, v

Machiavelli, Niccolò, 73, 116, 163, 167, 170n22, 187
Machiavellian politics, 212, 214, 215, 219
madmen, 314n8
  Spinoza on, 8, 144, 200, 279. *See also* "babies, fools, and madmen"
Maimonides, Moses, 74, 221n27, 229, 231n38, 294
  Aristotle and, 74, 77, 78
  ethics and, 78–79
  on Garden of Eden, 302
  on Judaism, 200–201
  Levinas and, 73–75, 78, 79
  overview, 73, 74
  philosophy and, 74
  reason, rationality, intellect, and, 73–79, 200
  the sage prophets of, 73–81

Spinoza and, 73–78, 86n1, 125n5, 126, 189, 200–201, 294, 302
  key difference separating, 77–78
  Theological-Political Treatise and, 294
Marcel, Gabriel, 264n10
Marx, Karl, 31, 65, 186, 314n8
masses. *See* ignorant masses
materialist reduction, 22, 27
mathematics, 239–40, 259, 260, 289
  equating mathematical and philosophical thinking, 289
  mathematical science, 8, 78, 225, 234, 256, 259, 311
  Spinoza on truth and, 4, 158
McShea, Robert J., 153n14
meaningless
  of separation, 97
  of suffering, 96–99
Mendelssohn, Moses, 205n13, 312
Merleau-Ponty, Maurice, 11n2, 14, 111, 228n36, 263, 273
middle term, religion as a, 182, 185. *See also* liberal religion
mind. *See* body: mind and; intellect
"Miracle of Miracles: More Ancient than Knowledge: Contra Hume" (Cohen), 69n11
monarchy, 61, 120, 121, 123, 142, 146, 150, 151, 187
Monnerot, Jules, 314n8
Montaigne, Michel de, 279
moral exigencies, 12, 16–17, 25, 28, 32, 53, 258, 261, 276–77
moral freedom, 155
moral obligation. *See* obligation(s)
moral transcendence, 67
morality. *See also* conscience; ethics; justice; suffering
  compassion and, xviii, 55, 79, 99–102, 217, 275, 276. *See also* compassion

morality *(continued)*
  denial of the metaphysical underpinnings of, 43–44. *See also* "beyond good and evil"
  embodiment and, 15, 33, 38, 39, 51, 53
  is not good enough, 114
  Kant and, xvi, 20, 32n1, 40, 66, 67, 110, 185, 276
  Levinas on justice and, 110–18
  Nietzsche and, 44, 51, 54, 113, 164–66, 196
  obedience and, 8, 109, 215. *See also* obedience
  orientation of, 17
  singularity and, 34, 36, 51, 53
mortality. *See also* death; Heidegger, Martin; Levinas: dying for the other
  embodiment and, 13, 15, 17, 36–37, 239
  life, death, morality, and, 237–42, 277
Morteira, Saul Levi, 222
Moses, 57–61, 63, 72, 75, 200, 203, 204, 208n15
murder, 268–73, 303–5
  "Thou shalt not murder," 273
mystical reading of Spinoza, 196n8
mysticism, 6
mythology, 100, 112, 213, 284

Nadler, Steven, 138, 139–40, 166–67, 181, 222n28, 294n4
national security. *See* security
nationalism, 186
natural being(s), 113, 115. *See also* conatus
natural law, 159
natural science, 108–9
  vs. humanism, 41, 231

nature, 124–25, 244. *See also* "kingdom within a kingdom"
  state of, 142–44
Nature, 144, 282
  perfection of, 5, 101
Negri, Antonio, 153n14
Netherlands. *See* Holland
Neusner, Jacob, 228
New Testament, 64, 126–27, 202, 224, 233n39, 295. *See also* Bible; Jesus Christ
Nietzsche, Friedrich Wilhelm, 15, 16, 18, 20, 22, 31, 45, 47, 48, 113, 314n8
  on art, 49
  on ascetic priest, 164–66
  Christianity and, 47, 49
  on classes of humanity, 164–65
  on Descartes, 285
  differences from Spinoza, 45
    from mechanism to vitalism, 45–50
  eternity and, 45, 49–51
  on evolution, 45–46
  on free will, 49–51, 164, 217
  on freedom, 50
  Levinas's opposition to, 34–35
  on life, 45–49
  "live dangerously," 42
  morality and, 44, 51, 54, 113, 164–66, 196
  on perspectivalism, 48–49
  on pity, 25, 54, 55, 101n10
  rationalism and, 43, 49, 50, 54
  on relation of the good to the true, 40
  religion and, 58
  and the responsible body, 51–56
  on Spinoza, 44
    criticism, 298

genealogical homage to
  Spinoza, 43–44
praise, 217
Spinoza and, 164–66
Spinoza as precursor of, 43
Spinoza compared with, 101n10,
  165–66, 196, 216n23, 217, 248,
  297, 305. *See also* Spinozism:
  Nietzsche's
Spinoza contrasted with, 297
substance and, 14n3, 48, 52
on suffering, 47, 166
virtue, values, and, 18, 40, 45–51,
  54–56
on weak/slave vs. strong/master
  types, 164
on will to power, 34–35, 47–52,
  165
writings
  Ecce Homo, 15, 50, 52
  The Gay Science, 46–48
  On the Genealogy of Morals,
    164–66, 297
  "On the Use and Abuse of
    History for Life," 45
  "The Philosopher: Reflections
    on the Struggle between Art
    and Knowledge," 49
  Twilight of the Idols, 44–45
Numbers, Book of, 57–58, 58n2,
  60n3, 61, 63, 71–72, 72nn14–15

obedience
  and the Bible, 70, 137n10, 213–14
  freedom and, 76–77, 110, 116,
    124, 126, 132, 155, 158, 170,
    176–78, 180, 183, 298
  to God, 137n10, 183
  of the ignorant masses, 19, 108,
    109, 163
  and the law, 163, 165, 176–77
  morality and, 8, 109, 215
  motives for, 163, 165
  philosophy and, 76–77, 129–30,
    132, 170, 176–78, 180, 182, 183
  politics, the state, and, 77, 110,
    116, 124, 125, 129–30, 152, 155,
    158, 163, 167, 170, 178, 180,
    182, 183, 209, 212, 215, 217
  prior to all representation, 70
  religion and, 70, 77, 109, 110,
    124, 125, 129–30, 158, 167, 170,
    180, 183, 185, 212, 213, 215
objectivism, 14, 234, 260, 263
obligation(s), xviii, 25, 71
  compassion and, 100. *See also*
    compassion
  death, mortality, and, 275–77
  free will and, 194, 196
  God and, 196
  Judaism and, 21, 194, 196, 229
  Levinas and, 12, 15–16, 21, 32,
    33, 35, 40, 69, 100, 102, 112–15,
    219, 229, 257, 269, 271, 275–77
  responsibility(ies) and, xviii, 12,
    15–16, 21, 35, 40, 69, 100, 113,
    114, 219, 271, 277, 315. *See also*
    responsibility
  transcendence and, 15–16, 33, 35,
    68
Old Testament, 57–58, 221, 224,
  232, 233n39. *See also* Bible;
  Hebrew Bible; Isaiah; Judaism;
  Theological-Political Treatise; Torah
  Christianity and, 191n1, 221, 224,
    233n39
Oldenburg, Henry, 119, 133
  Spinoza's letters to, 89, 135–37,
    139, 158, 177
"On Escape" (Levinas), 27, 36, 262n8
One Substance, 6–7, 24, 27, 48, 124,
  285. *See also* substance

ontological difference, 257, 277
ontology, 25, 261
   epistemology and, 280–82
   hermeneutic, 258, 261
Opera Posthuma (Spinoza), 3, 119, 120
Other. *See also* dying: for the other; for the other; self and other; *Time and the Other* (Levinas)
   time to be for the, 268
Otherwise than Being or Beyond Essence (Levinas), 15, 21, 27, 30, 38–40, 53–54, 65, 68–71, 80, 81, 115
"otherwise than being or beyond essence" ethics, 92
"out of control," 27–29
Overbeck, Franz, 43

pain, 84. *See also* suffering
pantheism, 34, 196, 309
   atheism, positivism, scientism, and, 9
   Judaism and, 194, 195, 202
   Levinas on, 309–10
   philosophy and, xiv, 9, 31, 181, 194
   rational, xiv
   temptation of, 197
   transcendence and, 31, 34, 195
pantheist God, 195
Parmenides, 9, 17, 21, 109, 243, 250, 289
Pascal, Blaise, 251
passive emotions, 84–87
passive synthesis, 14
passivity, 87–89, 243, 255
   activity and, 231
   of being-for-another, 54
   of the body, 39
   death, weakness, and, 265–66
   of the self, 42
   suffering and, 262, 266, 270

pathos, 90
patriotism, 186
pedagogy, 120–22, 133, 152, 283–84, 309, 312
   Spinoza's lack of, 152, 283
   Spinoza's problem with, 120–21, 309
Peden, Knox, 17n4
Peloponnesian War, 171, 176
perseverance/persistence in being. *See* conatus
perspectivalism, 48
"Pharisaic Judaism," 224
"Pharisees," 78, 126, 201, 203, 223, 295. *See also* Talmudic rabbis
phenomenology, xv, 12, 257–58, 261, 269–70, 292
   of Husserl, 11, 12, 26, 36, 254, 257–58, 260, 261
   Levinas and, 11, 257, 261
Phenomenology of Spirit (Hegel), v, 11n1, 93, 121
Philip of Macedon, 170
Philo of Alexandria, 77
philosopher-king, 170n22, 177, 187
philosophers, 166. *See also* freedom: to philosophize; ignorant masses: vs. the knowing few
philosopher's paradise, 309
philosophical errors, 1–2
philosophical freedom, 128, 132, 136, 154, 156, 157, 180, 209, 242, 316. *See also* free thought
philosophy. *See also under* theology; *specific topics*
   aim of, 76–77
   blessed, 131
   vs. religion, 175, 182
physicians. *See* doctor
pity, 25, 54, 55, 101
Plato, xvi, 220, 250
   Alcibiades and, 170–77, 182

Heidegger and, 255n6
knowledge and, 16
philosopher-king and, 170n22, 177, 187
Spinoza and, 25, 42, 125n5, 140, 158, 177–78, 187
writings. See also *Alcibiades I*
Phaedo, v, 22
Republic, 298
Symposium, 25, 170–75
pleasure, 84
pluralism, 228
Plutarch, 170n22
poesis, 20, 22
poetic thinking, 22, 37, 256, 261
polarities. See dichotomies; dualisms
Polen, Nehemia, 98n9
political freedom, 125, 126, 128–29, 132, 136, 141, 154–57, 178, 209. See also freedom
political leader(s), 164–66, 177, 186–87
  compared with prophets, 174
  and the ignorant masses, 64, 165, 166, 178
  imagination of, 64, 174
  manuals for, 167
  profile of a Spinozist, 170–78
  tasks of, 175
political sovereignty. See also sovereignty
  holding exclusive authority ("royal right"), 58, 60, 64
Political Treatise (Spinoza), 3, 120, 123, 144n12, 150, 151, 153, 160n17, 161, 187
politics and political thought, 3, 129, 182, 215. See also aristocracy; democracy; monarchy; obedience; state; totalitarianism
  Christianity and, 215–16
  philosophy and, 180–81

Popper, Karl, 209n18
positivism, xv–xvii, 1–2, 7–10, 12, 13
postponement, time of, 267–68
power, 107–10
  democracy and, 147
  knowledge and, 108
  maintenance of, 116
  and the state, 116. See also statecraft
prince (political leaders), 164–66
Prince, The (Machiavelli), 167. See also Machiavelli, Niccolò
Principles of Cartesian Philosophy and Metaphysical Thoughts, 2, 88, 119
properties of things, adequate ideas of the. See adequate ideas
prophecy, 70–71. See also prophets; *Theological-Political Treatise*: Spinoza contra prophecy and prophets
  defined, 64, 65
  Levinas on, 79
prophetic speech, 17, 66. See also *specific topics*
prophets, 61, 203. See also under *Theological-Political Treatise*
  all people of as, 57, 64–72
  defined, 62, 64
  political leaders compared with, 174–75
  the sage prophets of Maimonides, 73–81
  Spinoza contra prophecy and, 58–64
  true vs. false, 74
  vivid imagination, 62–64
Putnam, Hilary, 228n36
Pythagoras, 108

rabbis, 227–28, 235. See also Talmudic rabbis
Rabelais, François, 174n23

Index

Rashi (Shlomo Yitzchaki), 57n1
rational-irrational dialectic, 13
rationalism, xv, 4
  atheism and, 224n30
  and the Bible, 201n11, 202–4
  Christianity and, 202–4, 206, 207
  contemporary thought vs. modern, xviii
  death and, 242, 250
  of *Ethics*, 64, 202, 204, 206, 212
  forms of, 219, 225n30, 243, 250
    modern, xvii, xviii, 225n30, 240
  Heidegger and, 254, 257–58
  vs. humanisms, xvi
  Judaism and, 202–4, 206, 207, 212, 225n30, 226
  Levinas and, 34, 66, 90, 92, 240, 254, 257–58
  Nietzsche and, 43, 49, 50, 54
  phenomenology and, 292
  religious consequences, 62n5, 64
  scientism and, 17–18, 206
  of Spinoza, xiv, xvi, xvii, 6, 11, 14, 17, 34, 35, 43, 49, 50, 62n5, 64, 88, 126, 201n11, 202, 204, 206, 207, 212, 214, 219, 224n30, 226, 239, 240, 242, 243, 250, 254, 257, 258, 291–93, 308
rationalist dualism of Descartes, 88
rationalist intention of Spinoza's philosophy, 6–7
rationalist science, 214
rationality. *See also under* Maimonides, Moses
  without wisdom, 219–24
reason, 19, 309. *See also* intellect; knowledge: of the second kind; logos
  adequate ideas and, 256, 301, 309
  Heidegger and, 256, 257
  idealism and, 2, 218n24
  impersonal, 62n5. *See also* knowledge: of the third kind
  Maimonides vs. Spinoza vs. Levinas on, 77–79
  used without constraint, 216n23
reasoning about the whole, 6–7
reciprocity, ethic of. *See* "love thy neighbor"
reductionism, xvi, 243. *See also* will and intellect: equation of
  materialist, 22, 27
reductive idealism, 111
religion, 74n20, 107. *See also* Church; *Theological-Political Treatise*; theology
  as an affair of individual private conscience, 77, 110–11, 184, 186, 211, 213, 214, 219
  controlled internalized, 215
  Ethics and, 108, 109, 135, 179, 180, 202, 296n7
  ignorance and, 19, 77, 212
  Kant and, 67, 110, 182–83, 185, 201n10, 205, 208n16, 276, 297
  nature of, 67
  obedience and, 70, 77, 109, 110, 124, 125, 129–30, 158, 167, 170, 180, 183, 185, 212, 213, 215
  as opium of the people, 186
  vs. philosophy, 175, 182
  politics and, 125–26, 169–70, 215–16. *See also* church and state; religion and state
  Spinoza's attitudes toward, 26–27
    impact of Spinoza's life history on, 23–24
  terminology, 74n20
  types of, 108, 109, 213, 214. *See also* Christianity; Judaism
religion and state. *See also* church and state; religion: politics and

disestablishment of religion, 106, 175, 184, 211–13. *See also* church and state: separation of
justice, and, 103–7
reasons religion must be marginalized by the state, 212–13
solution to the problem of divided loyalties between, 211–14
Religion within the Limits of Reason Alone (Kant), 183, 201n10, 205, 208n16
religious authority and moral authority, 107–10. *See also* church and state; religion: as an affair of individual private conscience
religious persecution, 23
"Render unto Caesar," 211, 216
responsibility
as condition of the intelligible, 92
obligation and, xviii, 12, 15–16, 21, 35, 40, 69, 100, 113, 114, 219, 271, 277, 315. *See also* obligation(s)
responsible being, 53
responsible body, 51–56
responsible self, 53, 54, 68, 69
"Responsible Time" (Cohen), 69n11
return of the repressed, 13
"Revelation in the Jewish Tradition" (Levinas), 229–30
Ricoeur, Paul, 233n39
Rosenstock-Huessy, Eugen, 110
Rosenzweig, Franz, 69n11, 74n20, 110, 179n25
Rousseau, Jean-Jacques, 20, 298
"royal right" (exclusive sovereignty), 58–60, 64

sacred vs. the profane, the, 314n8

Sartre, Jean-Paul, 11, 37, 39, 263
Schelling, Friedrich Wilhelm Joseph, 20
Schiller, Friedrich, 20
science, xiv, xvi, 7–8, 212
ethics and, 40
Ethics and, 108, 109, 132, 206
as exclusive truth/exclusive way to all things, xvi, 7, 13, 168, 212, 223, 310
faith in, 8
illusion and, 4, 8, 9, 12, 46
modern, xiv, xvii, 1, 6–9, 19, 34, 76, 77, 202
vs. ancient/medieval science, 244
overestimation of, 1–2. *See also* scientism
rationalist, 214
religion and, 108, 136. *See also* scientific religion
science totalized, 13, 259. *See also* scientism
vs. science justified, xviii
scientific religion, 213, 214
scientism, xvi, 7, 20–22, 181, 197n8, 243, 259. *See also* science totalized
death and, 253
defined, 243, 259
irrationalism and, 13
rationalism and, 17–18, 206
science and, xvi, 1, 17–18, 259
Spinoza's atheism and pantheism as rooted in his, 9
scientists, 166. *See also* ignorant masses: vs. the knowing few
securing peace, 149, 156, 157, 178–79, 209
security, 116, 150, 151, 157, 162, 179, 209, 210
self, 69. *See also* identity

self *(continued)*
  substantial, 14n3. *See also* substantial being
  true, 29, 39–40
self and other
  distinction between, 16
  relation between, 34
self-destruction, 306–7. *See also* suicide
self-preservation. *See* conatus
self-sacrifice, 273, 274
self-sensing, 14, 15, 32–34, 36–39, 52, 94
self-sufficiency, 92–98. *See also* independence
sensibility, 17, 32, 38, 91, 92, 96. *See also* Talmudic wisdom
  embodiment and, 13–14, 33, 36, 263
  Ethics on, 93–95
  independence and, 11, 13–15, 33, 93, 95, 96
  intelligibility of, 93–95
  irreducible separation/hypostasis of, 10
  reason and, 94, 95
  self-sufficiency of, 95–97. *See also* self-sufficiency
  and sensitivity, four dimensions of a hermeneutical/exegetical, 225–26
  subjectivity and, 11, 92, 95
  suffering and, 96–98
"sensible people," 135–37, 139, 177
sensuality, 35–37, 92–94, 299. *See also* embodiment
separated being, 31–34, 36, 91, 267, 268. *See also* separation
separation, x, xvii, 10, 13, 14, 21, 36–38, 96, 97, 195n7, 286. *See also* independence; separated being; solitude
  defined, 32
  suffering and, 96, 97

Shakespeare, William, 267
Shapira, Kalonymus Kalman, 98n9
Singer, Isaac Bashevis, 25
singular responsibility, 65–68. *See also* singularity
singularity, 28–30, 34, 36, 51, 53, 65, 71, 233, 314
  morality and, 34, 36, 51, 53. *See also* singular responsibility
skepticism, 14
Smith, Steven B., 138, 166–67
Socrates, v, 171–72, 175, 250, 286
  Alcibiades and, 171–75
  death, 179
  speech, 171–72
  Spinoza and, 64, 88, 108, 172–75, 179
solitude, 7, 14, 16, 37, 93. *See also* independence; separation
  of death, 271. *See also* death
  embodiment and, 16, 38, 39
Solon, 237
Soskice, Janet Martin, 228n36
soul. *See also* eternal soul
  unity of body and, 226n33
sovereign authority, exclusive, 58–60, 64
sovereignty, Hobbes and, 61, 64, 127–29, 143, 145
speech, 17, 41–42, 71. *See also* free speech; prophetic speech
Spinoza, Baruch. *See also* Spinoza's philosophy; Spinozism; *specific topics*
  assessment of, 6
  as the "first modern man"
  life history, xiii–xv, 23, 221, 222
  modern study of, 1
  nightmares, 64. *See also* "babies, fools, and madmen"
  offshoots of, 21–22
  overview, xiv, xv, 1, 6
  reasons for the attraction of, 7

shortcomings, 1–2
temper/distemper. *See* Spinoza's spleen
unwanted babies, 298–310
why he is bad for Judaism. *See* Judaism: Spinoza's misunderstanding of
writings of, 3–4, 119–20. *See also specific writings*
 banning of, 127n6, 235
 ill Spanish poet in the, 246–47, 299–301
 publication of, 120
 yearning for cloning, 309
Spinoza's philosophy. *See also* Spinozism; *specific topics*
 failure of, 6
 intentions, presumptions, and pretensions of, 6–7
 internal failure of, 4–5
 instances of the, 5
Spinoza's spleen, 141, 293, 296, 297–98, 311, 312. *See also* "babies, fools, and madmen"
Spinozism, 181. *See also* Spinoza's philosophy; *specific topics*
 harshness of, 23
 Levinas's rejection of, 31–36, 92
 meaning and scope of the term, 31
 Nietzsche's, 43–45. *See also* Nietzsche: Spinoza compared with
 Levinas contra, 51–56
 root intent of, 7
spiritualism, 203, 227
state. *See also* church and state; justice; political leader(s); totalitarianism
 conatus of the, 148, 149, 152
 criticism of the, 104–6
 Hobbes and the, 19, 61, 105, 110, 114, 115, 129, 143, 145, 153n14, 157, 211
 intellect and the, 157

 legitimacy of the, 104–6
 purposes and functions of the, 115, 116
state security. *See* security
statecraft, 116, 129, 168, 170n22, 171
statism, 105, 106, 109, 210, 217–19. *See also under* Levinas: on Spinoza's misunderstanding of Judaism
Stirner, Max, 91
Strauss, Leo, 18, 125n5, 127n6, 140, 163, 166, 179, 198n9, 224n30, 255n6
 "How to Study Spinoza's *Theological-Political Treatise*," 179
 Spinoza's Critique of Religion, 179
 postscript on, 179–87
sub specie aeternitatus, 2, 89, 196, 226, 250
substance, 14n3. *See also* One Substance
 attributes/modes and, 15, 95, 121, 122, 180
 vs. essence, 269
 Nietzsche and, 14n3, 48, 52, 55
substantial being, 14n3, 50, 51
substantialist assumptions, 14
suffering, 96–97, 262–63. *See also* compassion; pain
 alleviation of, xviii, 9, 15, 17, 25, 29, 30, 38–40, 98–102, 236, 272, 273, 315, 316
 for another's suffering, 54, 99–101
 another's vs. one's own, 99
 blaming the victims of and justifying, 98
 characteristics, 96–99
 death and, 258, 261–63, 265, 266, 270, 272, 273
 embodiment and, 13, 15, 17, 36, 53–54
 ethics and the moral responsibility for another's, 15, 25, 29, 30,

suffering *(continued)*
    37–40, 54, 69, 96, 98–102, 272, 273, 315. *See also under* for the other
  evil, sin, and, 47, 97–99, 101
  freedom and, 263
  giving meaning to, 98–99
  God and, 100, 101
  Heidegger and, 265
  ignorance and, 97
  internalization of another's, 53–54
  Levinas on, xviii, 9, 13, 15, 17, 35–39, 53–54, 69, 96–102
  meaning/meaningfulness/meaningless of, 15, 96–99
  Nietzsche on, 47, 166
  passivity and, 262, 266, 270
  prophecy and, 69
  reason and rationalizing, 98
  sensibility and, 96–98
  separation and, 96, 97
  Spinoza and, 97–102
  of suffering, 96–99
  theodicy and, 96–100
  will and, 263
suicide
  by hanging, 279, 292, 303–6
  Spinoza's distemper against, 292–93, 296, 303, 305–7
supernatural, the, 183, 276
superstition(s)
  criticism of, xvii, 24, 67, 109, 112, 167, 182
  influence on political leaders, 169
  Levinas on, xvii, 24, 67, 78, 112
  of the masses, 131, 134
  philosophy and, 181, 182
  reason and, 185
  religion and, 78, 109, 112, 182, 183, 185
superstitious religion, popular, 213, 215

Symposium (Plato), 25, 170–75

Talmud ("Oral Torah"). *See under* Talmudic wisdom
Talmudic exegesis, four dimensions of, 225–36
Talmudic rabbis ("Pharisees"), 295. *See also* rabbis
  Spinoza's derision toward, 9, 126, 200–203, 294–95, 297
Talmudic wisdom (and Spinoza's misunderstanding of Judaism), 224–26
  authority or the renewal of a living tradition, 232–36
  Oral Torah, 80, 191, 224, 225, 231, 232
  pluralism of persons and readings, 228–30
  productive integrity of spirit and letter, 226–28
  virtue of existential self-transformation, 231–32
telos, 7, 77
temporality, 20, 276. *See also* duration; time
  "ecstatic" theories of, x, 69, 309
Thales of Miletus, 6
theodicy, 96–100
Theological-Political Treatise (Spinoza), xi, 119–23, 177–79. *See also specific topics*
  aim, 76–77, 169
  biblical criticism and, 3
  central thesis, 76–77
  Ethics and, 26, 61–64, 76, 86n1, 102, 108, 109, 111, 113n7, 119, 120, 123, 124, 130–32, 135, 139, 144, 149, 158, 159, 163, 177, 179, 182, 212, 296n7
  Hebrew writers referred to in, 221n27

impact, 3
intended audience, 127n6, 166, 167, 177, 178, 182, 298
  paradox of possible readers, 129–37
  letter no. 30 to Olderburg, 135–37
  liberal Christian ministers and theologians, 137–40
  overview, 167
  postscript on Leo Strauss's reading of, 179–87
  the prince (political leaders), 164–66
  rationalism and, 201–2
  reasons for taking human laws seriously, 157–63
  response to Steven Frankel, 166–70
  Spinoza contra prophecy and prophets, 58–64
  Spinoza shows his hand, 163–64
  Spinoza's reasons for writing, 135–36
  structure of, 123
    preface, 133–35
    three parts, 123–29
  two meanings of "democracy" and "freedom," 140–57
theology. *See also* religion
  philosophy as handmaiden to, 127
  philosophy's alliance with, xiv
  politics and, 125–26, 215–16
  reason as the handmaiden of, 134–35
  separation of philosophy from, 76–77, 126–27, 129, 137, 138. See also *Theological-Political Treatise*
  chief obstacle to the, 138
"thinking least about death," 241, 242, 249–52

"Thinking Least about Death—Contra Heidegger" (Cohen), 253, 262n7
third, the, 114, 275
Thucydides, 176
time, x, 69, 239, 240, 252. *See also* duration; eternal; eternity; temporality
  to be for the Other, 268
  infinite, 309–10
  Levinas's social/intersubjective theory of, x, 10, 69, 268, 309
  of postponement, 267–68
Time and Free Will (Bergson), ix
Time and the Other (Levinas), 10, 11, 37–38, 68, 241, 258, 262–64, 266–68
time-consciousness, 69
Torah, 227–29, 230n37, 231–32, 272. *See also* Deuteronomy; Exodus; Garden of Eden; Hebrew Bible; Numbers; Old Testament
  Oral. *See* Talmudic wisdom
totalitarianism, 24, 64, 105, 106, 141, 146, 209, 210
totality. *See* One Substance
Totality and Infinity (Levinas), xvii, 298
  preface to, 305
totalizating systems of thought, 19
totalization, 27, 91. *See also* science totalized; scientism
transascendence, 39
transcendence, 15, 21, 68, 270, 315
  denial and rejection of, 31–32
  embodiment and, 38, 39
  moral, 67
  obligation and, 15–16, 33, 35, 68
  pantheism and, 31, 34, 195
  of the responsible person, 315
transcendental dialectic. *See* dialectic: of Kant

Treatise on the Emendation of the Intellect (Spinoza), 3, 120, 121, 133, 284
true and the good, the, 39–43
true self, 29, 39–40
truth, 19, 76–77, 311. *See also under* adequate ideas; eternal (and immutable) ideas, truths, and laws; *Ethics*
  dialectic of, 41
  ethics as the source of, 42–43
  and falsehood, 161, 280–82, 284–87, 290. *See also* illusion
  value of, 18
truth claims, 40–41
truth seekers, 40, 41, 130, 179, 180
truth seeking, 12, 131, 154
tyrannical governments, 148–51, 211

"unified field theory," 7

values, 79–81, 219. *See also under* Nietzsche, Friedrich Wilhelm
  revaluation of all, 54–56
van der Tak, Willem Gerard, 221–22
Vaz Dias, A. M., 221–22, 222n28
Vilna Gaon (Elijah ben Shlomo Zalman), 229, 286n2
virtue. *See* values
Voltaire, François Marie Arouet de, 298
vulnerability, 10, 13, 15, 16, 26, 33, 35, 37, 39, 51, 54, 69, 92–95, 218, 231, 241, 261, 271–73, 309, 312

Wahl, Jean, 241n, 264
whole, thinking about the, 6–7
Wiesel, Elie, 1
will, 263, 281, 283–85. *See also* free will
  Ethics on, 102, 159, 160n18, 217, 280
  of God, 84, 185, 200, 281, 303
  reason and, 91–92, 218n24. *See also* will and intellect
will and intellect, 286
  Descartes on, 159, 280–83, 287
  differences between and separation of, 90, 159, 280–83, 286, 287, 289, 291, 301–2
  equation of, 35, 84, 88–90, 102, 159, 160n8, 193, 217, 280–87, 289, 291, 292, 296, 302
will-intellect, 287, 289, 290, 292
will-intellect theory of truth, 292
will to power, 113
  Nietzsche on, 34–35, 47–52, 165
wisdom
  of love and love of wisdom, xviii
  rationality without, 219–24
Wolfson, Harry Austryn, xi, 11, 77, 108–9, 191–94, 197, 217
women, Spinoza's repugnance for, 120–21, 286n2, 296, 299, 306, 309–12
words, images, and ideas, 288–89
Wyschogrod, Edith, 270

Yovel, Yirmiyahu, 106, 206n14, 221

Zeno, x

www.ingramcontent.com/pod-product-compliance
Lightning Source LLC
Chambersburg PA
CBHW030126240426
43672CB00005B/42